Merrill Morse

Kosuke Koyama
A Model for
Intercultural Theology

PETER LANG
Frankfurt am Main · Bern · New York · Paris

Die Deutsche Bibliothek - CIP-Einheitsaufnahme

Morse, Merrill:

Kosuke Koyama : a model for intercultural theology / Merrill
Morse. - Frankfurt am Main ; Bern ; New York ; Paris : Lang,
1991
  (Studien zur interkulturellen Geschichte des Christentums ;
  Bd. 71)
  ISBN 3-631-43962-8

NE: GT

ISSN 0170-9240
ISBN 3-631-43962-8

© Verlag Peter Lang GmbH, Frankfurt am Main 1991
All rights reserved.

Printed in Germany 1   3 4 5 6 7

Kosuke Koyama

STUDIEN ZUR INTERKULTURELLEN GESCHICHTE DES CHRISTENTUMS
ETUDES D´HISTOIRE INTERCULTURELLE DU CHRISTIANISME
STUDIES IN THE INTERCULTURAL HISTORY OF CHRISTIANITY

begründet von/fondé par/founded by
Hans Jochen Margull†, Hamburg

herausgegeben von/édité par/edited by

Richard Friedli
Université de Fribourg

Walter J. Hollenweger
University of Birmingham

Theo Sundermeier
Universität Heidelberg

Jan A. B. Jongeneel
Rijksuniversiteit Utrecht

Band 71

PETER LANG
Frankfurt am Main · Bern · New York · Paris

To

The Right Reverend Lesslie Newbigin

A Christian Model

For Any Culture

ACKNOWLEDGEMENTS

A variety of people deserve grateful mention for their part in making this study possible. Great thanks must go to the Lutheran World Federation Department of Studies for providing the scholarship assistance for three years of study at the University of Birmingham and the Selly Oak Colleges. Their generous support was indispensable and much appreciated.

Professor Walter J. Hollenweger deserves special thanks not only for his expert assistance and guidance in this particular study but also for enabling the kind of exploratory approach to theology reflected in his own work and among his students as a whole.

Further individual thanks must go to such people as the Right Reverend Lesslie Newbigin, the inspiring faculty of the Selly Oak Colleges, such able and cordial staff members as Mrs. Joan Pearce, and not least of all, fellow students from around the globe who personally incarnated the kind of issues this study seeks to address.

Kosuke Koyama's generous personal cooperation deserves special note. He not only responded freely with interviews, but also made available, unsolicited, various private papers. Others who provided interviews also deserve special thanks.

Finally, very special thanks must also go to parents and many friends without whose strong support this project might never have been either begun or completed.

CONTENTS

PART II—KOYAMA'S THEOLOGY—KEY THEMES

PART III—KOYAMA'S STYLISTIC CONTRIBUTION

PREFACE

The study which follows was originally part of a larger Ph.D. study done through the University of Birmingham in Birmingham, England. In preparing this study for publication substantial reductions were made in certain areas. While the reductions do not affect the main thrusts of the study, it may be instructive to identify the kind of material omitted.

The bulk of it had to do with various approaches to other religions. The basic questions involved and some examples of contemporary attempts to formulate various theologies of other religions were explored. Kosuke Koyama's particular views and an evaluation of them do remain part of this study.

Other omitted material includes brief topical presentations on Koyama's view of technology, Buddhism, and missionary theology. These subjects, while of interest in their own right, are not essential to this presentation of Koyama's theology. Furthermore, Koyama's work on Buddhism remains very much in flux, as do some other areas of his theology.

Two omissions which merit attention were a detailed analysis of Koyama's writing and an examination of his exegetical approach. The literary analysis revealed a strong dependency in Koyama's writing on grammatical structures inherited from his Japanese linguistic background. The brief exegetical study, in turn, illustrated that while Koyama is remarkably creative at utilizing Scripture as part of his theological presentations, and while his usage of Scripture reflects insight and methods rooted in an Asian context, he is nevertheless very familiar with and highly skilled at traditional Western academic methodology when it comes to biblical exegesis.

Any other omissions were minor or had to do either with general methodological concerns or with questions about Koyama's theology and style that are adequately raised in the remaining material.

Several further practical notes need mentioning. Part I includes the names of several Japanese theologians. Normally, in the Japanese language a person's surname is given first in writing or speaking. However, when Japanese names are put into English contexts, the surname commonly follows the given name. It is the English style which is utilized here. Vowel lengths in the Japanese names are not generally noted.

Given the variables in the English language itself, however, another notation is required. Spelling differences between British and American English will surface in the study. Consistency has been sought in this area, but where variables are noticed it usually has to do with the source material being utilized. The spelling used by Koyama and other quoted authors is preserved as in the original as much as possible.

Also, it should perhaps be noted that biblical quotations which occur in the study are taken from the Revised Standard Version, unless designated otherwise. Koyama's biblical quotes also sometimes include free translations or adaptations of his own. Biblical references have used the consistent form of a semicolon between chapter and verse numbers, whereas Koyama occasionally uses simply a period.

INTRODUCTION

Prolegomenal Perspectives

The three little words "Thy kingdom come" in the Lord's Prayer constitute both a petition and a statement of fact. On the one hand, these words voice the aspiration of many Christians that human history be consummated by the coming of God's kingdom in its universal totality. Simultaneously, these words contain a recognition that God's kingdom has not yet come in its anticipated fullness. There is a commonly expressed tension between the "now," i.e., the belief that God's kingdom has in fact already been inaugurated in human history, and the "not yet," i.e., acute awareness that human life is very far from the perfection, peace, or bliss envisioned as characteristic of God's kingdom.

There is, in other words, a dynamic tension built into Christian faith, a tension which expresses itself in the relationship between belief and experience. On the one hand, Christians believe in God's kingdom as present reality and universal destiny. On the other hand, their daily experience yields abundant evidence of the absence or incompleteness of this kingdom.

Ultimately, it is with the tension between belief and experience that the following study is concerned. The Lord's Prayer petition about the kingdom of God is only one means of introducing the tension between belief and experience. One might also speak of the tension in terms of faith and unbelief, in terms of the universal intention of the Christian message vis-a-vis its limited embodiment in the Christian church, or even in terms of the tensions between the Christian worldview and the "scientific" world-view as they collide with each other in the minds and lives of many Christians today.

The way in which this study addresses this tension is by exploring the contemporary intercultural context in which Christianity finds itself. Confronted by a multitude of powerful and viable alternatives in the highly pluralistic world of today, Christianity is reconsidering the meaning of the "now" and the "not yet" of the kingdom of God. For example, is God's kingdom present in other religions and world-views as they are experienced by Christians today, and if so, how? Or do these other religions and world-views merely intensify the "not yet" of God's kingdom? This study looks at "encounter," that is, the contemporary meeting between Christian faith and other faiths, as one primary arena for examining the tension between Christian belief and Christian experience.

Motivation for such an undertaking derives from personal experience. Some years ago I had occasion to leave small-town, rural America for a brief sojourn in the cosmopolitan, wartime culture of Bangkok, Thailand. I stepped from a world shaped by Scandinavian Christianity into a society steeped in Theravada Buddhism. My faith, morality, way of thinking, and culture were all called into question by the existence of radically different ways of interpreting and conducting human life.

Such challenges are, of course, natural and inevitable in human life. For, as all human beings are limited in capacity and experience, their beliefs accordingly derive from and are expressed within limited situations and frameworks. The beliefs expressed by any individual or group of people necessarily reflect the finite capacity and situation of the person(s) involved. These beliefs are adequate and comfortable insofar as they are applied within the limited context to which they belong. But when that context is altered, tensions arise between belief and changing experience. Insofar as human contexts are always in flux, human beliefs are thus always changing and tensions are ever present.

This may be said to hold true for Christian theology, as well, which, as the expression of Christian belief and experience, develops in particular contexts in response to the needs and tensions experienced there. Today, for example, as inherited Christian beliefs and attitudes toward other human faiths are increasingly felt to be in tension with contemporary Christian experiences of those faiths, Christian theology is seeking to provide responses appropriate to contemporary Christian experience. This is a natural process in that all Christian theology essentially derives from experience. While experience molds beliefs, and beliefs in turn direct and interpret experience, the recorded theological reflections on Christian encounters with other faiths are basically formulations of belief in response to questions and tensions produced initially by experience. From this point of view experience is, then, the framework for all theology.

Therefore it may be said that theology is inevitably existential. It is dynamic, not static. Authentic theology, if it derives from, describes, and changes with human experience, cannot be frozen or absolute. In a sense theology is actually biography. It tells a story about human life, both in its individual and in its corporate expressions. Accordingly, as encounter with other faiths or between faith and unbelief is a constitutive element in this story, all theology is to some degree theology of encounter.

While the ideas presented so far may themselves be debated and will be more fully examined later, they nevertheless delineate the main assumptions or prolegomenal perspectives underlying this endeavor. As pointed out, this study derives from experience. Its intention is to address an experience being expressed by many Christians today as an authentic challenge for Christian theology, namely, the experience of encounter.

To inform this experience, the study focuses on the theology of encounter developed by a specific contemporary theologian, one who self-consciously seeks to derive his theology from and taper it to experience. The intent here is to offer that man's theology as a model for Christian thinking in the contemporary situation of encounter, addressing not only the reality of other religions, but of global inter-cultural developments in general. At most, his theology of encounter may make some contribution towards diminishing the contemporary tension between belief and experience. At least, it illustrates some main features of both contemporary Christian belief and contemporary Christian experience.

Some further delineation of the modern situation of encounter, which serves as the context against which a theological model is presented, can illustrate the nature of the task at hand. While there are various ways to depict this context, the following sketch will at least outline some of its more salient characteristics.

The Modern Situation of Encounter

In these latter decades of the twentieth-century, Christianity influences the lives and values of as many as one out of every four people on this planet. That in itself is not remarkable. Other value systems have been equally or more influential in just this century, including, for example, Maoism in China, Islam, or contemporary Western materialism. That *only* one in four people subscribe to Christianity indeed underscores the fact that Christianity today stands over against major alternative beliefs and value systems. In itself that is nothing new. Today, however, in a world of unprecedented awareness of other cultures and people, we may more clearly perceive and delineate the implications for Christianity of alternative faith and value systems.

Historically, both the awareness of and the experience of encounter have been crucial factors in shaping Christianity's self-understanding and self-expression. Christian missionary activity, for example, inherently implies encounter with faith and value systems that are different from Christianity. Christian mission is always an activity on the frontier between the Christian world-view and other world-views. As such it therefore is a key point of definition for Christian faith itself. For, it is through encounter with other values and perspectives that Christian faith is challenged to define and express itself. Thus, encounter is in fact not only central to but also necessary for Christian self-understanding.

This has been true since the beginnings of Christianity. Its scriptures, doctrine, ecclesiology, and historical developments are all products of encounter in one sense or another. Naturally, Christianity's attempts to interpret itself to the world and to understand the world in relation to itself have always been shaped according to the cultural and historical situation of the times. For, Christian faith never exists apart from particular cultural and historical contexts. In that sense, the history of Christianity's formation and development is largely the history of various encounters in particular contexts and times. That whole history of encounter is too broad and complicated for presentation here. But key episodes of Christian encounter are worth mentioning.

The mother of Christian faith was, of course, Jewish faith and culture; its cradle, the Greco-Roman world. From its inception therefore, Christianity was one faith and value system among others. It never existed as an originally pure entity apart from encounter. Its formative language and concepts were adopted from Judaism and from Greek culture. As it spread across the Mediterranean world, Christianity was confronted with alternative sets of belief and practice, some of which became instrumental in forcing the young Christian Church to clarify its beliefs through credal statements. Later, when wedded with Roman civilization, it absorbed imperial practices into its language, organization, and worship.

But after these initial centuries of extensive encounter and corresponding rapid expansion came a period of general isolation and very limited encounter. For, with the rise of Islam, Christianity was virtually sealed off within Europe and within isolated pockets of Asia. Encounter ground to a halt except in the remaining corners of Europe and Russia where Christianity penetrated new tribes and folk religions, and in East Asia where Marco Polo, along with many others, initiated new but largely futile contacts with cultures in which Christianity had already been planted but had suffocated.

Thus began a long period of consolidation wherein the main stream of Christianity, allied to state government, had a monopolistic influence over the lives and beliefs of a large, particular group of people mainly confined to the Western peninsula of the Eurasian continent. Cut off from other major faith and value systems, except for pockets of powerless Judaism and some folk religions within Europe, threatened by and at war with Islam on its borders, and allied to nearly the whole of social organization and government, European Christianity underwent a transformation that significantly affected its outlook and its ability for encounter in subsequent centuries.

Thus when Europeans burst out of their confinement by Islam on the one hand and by the Atlantic ocean on the other, it was by and large an inflexible, aggressive, judgmental and non-compromising Christianity that they carried with them. Encounter with other faith and value systems was characterized more by coercive domination than by exchange and adaptation, as had often been the case previously.

This rigid, one-way pattern of encounter lasted for most of the next five centuries. However, with critical changes in beliefs and values within Europe itself, with an eventual decline in the dominance of the West, and with the corresponding resurgence of other value systems, the scene was set for the current stage of the encounter of different values, wherein Christianity finds itself once again in a situation similar to its early centuries of encounter.

Once again Christianity is aware of itself as a struggling, minority religion in a world of powerful competing claims for people's loyalty. It has lost much of the power and confidence that shaped its encounter with other faiths and values during the period of Western colonialism. It has moved from the security of a relatively monocultural identity to a situation wherein the global Christian community itself includes members from various and often very different cultures. Today, unlike in the European Middle Ages when Christians had little or no concept of a way of living and believing other than that incorporated into the fabric of their own society, Christians are increasingly aware of the existence of a wide range of alternative religions, ideologies and world-views. Thus, although the experiences and dynamics of encounter with other value systems may be similar to those of Christianity's early history, it is also clear that the scale and effects today are quite unique.

Theology for Encounter — Selecting a Model

One important effect of the current situation is its impact on Christian theology itself. With the demise of Christendom, or, that portion of the world upon which Christianity had such a powerful impact and in which most of Christian theology for the last fifteen hundred years has been formulated, the very framework for Christian theology has profoundly altered. Theology in a world of encounter must be more self-consciously theology of encounter. In the contemporary global village Christian theology cannot be grounded in the assumptions and experiences of any particular group of people or any single cultural heritage in any given area of the world. Christian theology must find its base in a more universal framework, if such a framework can be found.

Put another way, all theology today must be missionary theology. For, in a situation reminiscent of the early Church, a situation of unprecedented encounter, it is the missionary experience of the Church that again offers the primary stimulation and the freshest resources for a theology which can address the questions and concerns of people living in the current era.

Until recently Christian theology as it has been shaped in Western culture has been spread into other cultures without sufficient modification to suit their character. After a thousand years of incubation in Western Europe Christianity was generally exported to other cultures in a strong, nearly monocultural, that is, European, form (though Christianity has never been completely monocultural even in Europe). Its rigidity was compounded by power that knew little or no compromise and an entrenched mentality unaware of the possibilities and significance of encounter (even within Christianity's own previous history).

Today a different situation faces Christianity. In the modern situation of nearly unlimited and thoroughly multi-cultural encounter, the type of theology cultivated in Europe and exported via European colonialism is being seen as inadequate for expressing Christian self-understanding in a global context. Ironically, the theologies and Church developments which spawned the global expansion of Christianity have been superseded by the very fruit which they bore. They are themselves no longer adequate to the situation they have helped to create; indeed, they are severely criticized for both their previous and their residual influence.

While in fact the value of Western theology and Church forms may not have altogether expired, and while European Christianity may indeed have made greater contributions to Christianity as a whole than is yet recognized by many newer, Third World churches during this transitional period, it is nevertheless clear that new times and new situations, as always in Christian history, call for new theology. Christianity, now at home in a multitude of cultures, seeks to express itself in fresh ways with theology that is new both in content and in style.

The need for such "new" theology is of particular importance in relation to the other faith and value systems which Christianity encounters. The extent and depth of the present-day encounter calls Christianity to deeper thinking than it has perhaps ever done in regard to the validity and value of these other systems, and in regard to what Christianity's attitudes toward them and relationship with them should be.

Christian theology today, therefore, needs to be original, intercultural, and imaginative in order to respond to the challenges put to Christianity in the modern encounter of different human societies and values. But the questions arise, "How does such theology come about?" and, "Where does it come from?"

It would seem that a theology for encounter would find very fruitful development in situations where the encounter is most intense. Today that could in fact include Western Europe, where Christians are again a small minority, struggling with the various ideologies and world-views that challenge the Christian understanding of existence. Indeed, fresh attempts are constantly being made to re-ground Christianity in Western, secular culture. However, the intensity of Christianity's encounter with other religions and world-views is perhaps more sharply defined in so-called Third World areas, where Christianity is more intensely confronted by a wide range of alternatives.

Third World Christians who have wrestled not only with the alternative faith and value systems of their own situation, but also with the cultural conflicts inherent in their own faith (such as European forms of Christianity) may have a special contribution to make to Christian theology in a situation of encounter. By pursuing different interests and applying different methodologies than those incorporated into European theology, they may find new ways to help Christianity express its experience and beliefs in an intercultural context.

Asia, as the area of the world with the highest proportion of people who do not subscribe to the Christian view of reality, would seem to be fertile ground for pursuing the questions of Christian encounter with other faiths and value systems. In Asia radical shifts in Christianity's status and development have been most obvious: for example, a shift from a position of power and authority to a state of being weak, fragmented and rejected; a shift from being relatively secure in a strong monocultural environment to being highly exposed in a multi-cultural environment of equal or greater sophistication; and a shift from being a majority religion to being a rather insignificant minority religion.

To turn to an Asian theologian as a possible source of "new theology" for the contemporary situation, is, therefore, to turn to one who has first-hand experience in facing the many questions that arise from the radical cross-cultural exchanges in the modern situation of encounter. Such a theologian is Kosuke Koyama. He has experienced the ebb and flow of Christianity in Asia, the struggles of Asia in the modern world, and the meaning of holding a minority faith in various cultural contexts. His Christianity has been "baptized" by penetrating encounters with other religions and value systems. Most importantly, he has been able to give profound theological expression to his experiences in such a way as to challenge Christian proclamation and to stimulate Christian thinking not only in Asia, but also in the wider Christian community.

Altogether, Koyama is one of those Christians aware of and responding to the theological challenges of the new framework for Christian theology. Like so many missionaries before him, he has lived on the frontier of Christianity's missionary presence in the world and from it seeks to respond with a theology that speaks to the challenges of the times. Kosuke Koyama can therefore serve as a model in developing a theology for encounter in the modern context.

His value as a model stems both from the nature of his experience and from the concerns to which he addresses himself. While more information about these experiences and concerns will be provided at length in the body of this study, some general comments at this point can summarize Koyama's potential as a model for intercultural theology today.

First of all, he is a model by experience as an "intercultural person." Having been born in Asia, having been partially educated in the West, having married an American, and having worked in several different Asian and Western countries and cultures, Koyama has extensive exposure to the dynamics of intercultural encounter. Through his work and travel all over Asia he has witnessed the radical transitions brought on by the meeting of Western and Asian cultures. He is, for example, acutely aware of the impact of technology on Asian life. Likewise, the insensitivity of Western culture, and particularly of Western Christianity in its approach to Asian culture, deeply distresses him.

As a non-Westerner, who is nevertheless very familiar with Western culture, he can offer critical reflections on the history of the meeting of Asian and Western cultures. Because he is trained in Western cultural perspectives and methodologies, he can present an Asian perspective in terms fairly understandable to Westerners. In this sense, he can be very much a bridge person between these various cultures. This indeed he sees to be part of his task.[1]

Koyama himself is convinced that Christian theology, when the Christian church in the world is increasingly intercultural, must itself be intercultural.[2] This necessity relates not only to the content of Christian theology, but also to its style. The style and content that suited a Christianity secure in the comparatively mono-cultural womb of Europe is no longer sufficient for expressing the diversity of Christian faith and experience in the modern multi-cultural context. Thus, Koyama, as he communicates various Asian experiences and questions arising from the modern situation of encounter, does so with a style that itself challenges the traditions of Western theology and simultaneously opens the door for alternative Asian expressions of Christian theology. In doing so he offers a stylistic model for intercultural theology.

But it is not only personal experience and style that make Koyama a model for a modern theology of encounter. It is the fact, too, that he directly addresses some of the most outstanding issues of encounter. As an Asian Christian, he wrestles with such diverse Christian concerns as the Christian encounter with other religions, the effects of technology and the scientific world-view on human spirituality, issues of justice and human dignity, Christianity and culture, and so on. His selection of concerns reveals both first-hand experience of encounter and keen awareness of the essential challenges for Christian witness in the modern era. Koyama does not offer definitive solutions to these challenges, but, by setting them in a framework growing out of his Asian experience and Christian faith, offers useful guidance for approaching them while at the same time setting out some possible directions for a Christian response.

It must be noted that Koyama is a missionary, both in person and in print. He is committed to the self-understanding and self-expression of Christian faith in a world that is predominantly not Christian. This missionary commitment is fundamental to his own theology and essential for a theology of encounter. For, encounter is essentially a missionary event.

Likewise, encounter is an existential event, one in which Koyama as a living missionary is still involved. In a self-conscious way, Kosuke Koyama is a man struggling with his own experience in a continuously changing, highly pluralistic world. His theology is unfinished, and many questions will need to be asked about it. But as a model for Christian theology in an intensely intercultural environment Koyama stands out as a potential guide into a theology for encounter in the modern age.

Structure and Presentation

How to present Koyama in a manner that can enable a theology for encounter to emerge is something of a challenge. Because Koyama is a living, still-developing theologian, his theology is not available as a finished set of ideas that can be systematically ordered and packaged for presentation (a fact probably gratifying to Koyama).

Compounding this initial challenge is the fact that Koyama himself does not write in the systematic mode to which Western theology is accustomed and to which this study must conform. He is neither by background nor intention systematic according to Western standards.[3]

Indeed, one of the issues that needs addressing in surveying Koyama's work is the matter of systems. As will be argued in Part III of this study, Koyama's reluctance to write theology in a traditional systematic manner and his modeling of an alternative theological style may well be one of his main contributions as a model for intercultural theology.

At the same time it is fair to say that as all human thinking has a significant degree of systematization—intrinsic to the structure and use of language itself—so is Koyama's thinking systematic. The question is: what kind of system is in operation? Is it a logical, categorical, chain-thinking type of system, an amorphous, holistic system that comfortably includes contradictions, or some kind of poetic system that incorporates imagery and symbolism in a way that creates self-transcendence within itself? Such various "systems" are possible. In fact, more than one may simultaneously be operating in Koyama, who as a product of Asian society and systems, lives and writes in the Western world.

One possible method for presenting Koyama is that of constructing a topical ordering of his main theological publications to date. By distilling a number of key themes or topics from his wide array of essays, lectures, sermons, and books, it would be possible to identify the main concerns and directions of his theology. That there are indeed persistent themes in Koyama's work deserves note. To systematize them in a topical manner would create focal points or tools by which to examine Koyama.

Precisely because of the imaginative, non-systematic nature of Koyama's theology, there is the temptation for many of his readers, it seems, to dismiss or overlook his theology as lacking in substance or depth, which is to seriously misunderstand it. A rough systematization of Koyama's theology in topical categories might open the door for perceiving its deeper dimensions.

However, there are also disadvantages to making a topical presentation of Koyama's theology. For one thing, important pieces of Koyama's theology will not fit into generalized structural categories. Moreover, the categories themselves might need to be altered in time as further stages are reached in Koyama's theological development. Indeed, complete reversals of his previous positions are a possibility.

Another danger in a topical ordering of Koyama's theology is that such a presentation might give too much of a dogmatic structure to Koyama's theology. "Systematizing" Koyama in this manner not only goes somewhat against the grain of his style and intention; it also tends to obstruct the dynamic character of his lively and colorful style.

Accordingly, a middle course has been chosen for presenting and evaluating Koyama's theology. After reviewing Koyama's own background and the overall context of his work in Part I, selected portions of Koyama's theology will be presented in Part II in topical form. These will provide an entrance point into Koyama's overall theology, while at the same time enabling some critical reflection on key issues to be developed.

It should be pointed out that in order to preserve some of the unique flavor of Koyama's thinking, the topics chosen for presentation will include an abundance of direct quotations from Koyama's writings.

The presentation and evaluation of this Asian theologian, who deals with a wide variety of subjects derived from a wide range of experiences and presented in an original, unusual manner, is unquestionably formidable. These problems are compounded by the incompleteness and variety of available data, as well as by the fact that few others have so far attempted such a comprehensive assessment of Koyama. Which information to select, how to present and evaluate it—these are questions with a variety of possible responses. It is hoped that the structure and method applied in this study will not only elucidate Koyama's theology but will also suggest how he can serve as a useful model for others in intercultural theology.

Qualifications

Naturally, various questions need to be raised about some of the assumptions underlying the study as a whole. These have to do with the ideas presented earlier about experience and belief and with the implications of pursuing a theology of encounter.

Implicit to the concept of intercultural and inter-faith encounter is acceptance of a situation of plurality—that there are component parts, distinct from each other, involved in the experience of encounter. [Admittedly, the concept of plurality depends on categorical definitions of existence. But that plurality (or diversity) has a perceptual reality even in religions which then proceed to describe plurality as an illusion, testifies to its functional validity at some level of human descriptions of reality.]

Such a concept of plurality carries the implication that Christianity, too, is one component among others. It is one religion among many religions, one human faith in the midst of various human faiths. Such an implication is immediately objectionable to many Christians. Fortified by a branch of Christian tradition that insists upon the unquestionable primacy and uniqueness of Christianity or of the Christian revelation, many Christians would argue that thinking of Christianity as merely one faith among others, even as a working hypothesis, misunderstands and compromises Christianity.

To start with the tensions experienced in encounter and to work from there towards a theology of encounter could be seen as a prioritization of experience over belief in such a way as to possibly diminish or betray the belief itself. In fact, this study does propose the experience of encounter as the primal grounds for dealing with tensions between belief and experience. But this does not necessarily mean that experience supersedes belief. Rather, experience is used as a critique of belief within a perspective that envisages a dynamic, mutually influential relationship between the two. In fact, the endeavor to explore a theology of encounter presupposes a belief structure or view of reality (for example, the Christian idea of God's kingdom) that seeks to embrace all human experience. Universal truth-claims by definition assume applicability to all human situations.

The issue at hand is not to set experience over against belief or even to exaggerate a polarity or dichotomy between the two, since they belong in fact to one reality (human existence). Rather, the point is to explore the tension between them as experienced by Christians in the modern context of encounter and to pursue a theology of encounter that contributes to some resolution of these tensions. By presenting a dynamic, relational picture of experience and belief, this study at the same time advocates what could be called a "middle way" between on the one hand a belief in the truth of the Christian revelation that rigidly resists Christianity's being questioned by human experience, and, on the other hand, the view that so endeavors to define Christianity by human experience that its basic truth claims are diluted to complete relativity.

The test of these initial perspectives and intentions of course rests at least partially in the study itself. Does the model chosen reflect or speak to tensions of belief and experience in the modern situation of encounter? Does he offer a significant and unique contribution towards diminishing these tensions? These and other questions must be taken up later. At this point some further attention needs to be given to the concept of encounter and its implications.

Returning to the implications of plurality, it becomes clear that awareness of plurality necessarily means that any component of encounter (i.e., Christianity) must inevitably formulate some concepts and attitudes for defining its relationship with other components in that situation of encounter. In a direct, practical way this also means that Christianity, like any other faith system, must come to terms with its own limits. At the same time that Christianity makes universal claims, it formulates ways of understanding its own particularity. Various formulas for such self-understanding have arisen in Christian theology.

Inevitably, coming to terms with the particular limits of one's own universal belief is a tension-producing experience, more so because it involves at least an implied threat to one's own identity. John V. Taylor, writing on interfaith dialogue, points out the natural human tendency to seek resolution to contradictions or to antithetical beliefs. People would rather pretend that antitheses to their way of believing are unreal or invalid. At worst, people will even seek to destroy that which threatens their beliefs.[4]

This human tendency to resist or oppose contradictory beliefs grows out of the human tendency to universalize one's own belief and experience. Tension is inevitable when the beliefs associated with one set of experiences are challenged by beliefs associated with different sets of experiences or by similar experiences interpreted in a different way. This is exactly the kind of challenge that comes in the modern experience of encounter.

There are a wide variety of reactions or responses to encounter current on the theological scene today. One tends to choose that response which is most in harmony with one's own experience and perspectives. That Koyama, however, offers a particularly constructive theology for encounter, one which offers a useful sense of direction for the church as a whole in the future, will hopefully become clear in the course of this study.

PART I

KOYAMA IN CONTEXT

CHAPTER ONE

BIOGRAPHICAL AND CULTURAL CONTEXT

A theologian, as anyone else, has a particular personal history which has shaped him or her and influenced the work produced. A biographical survey of Koyama's life not only helps to place his theology in a context, but also reveals much about why and how he addresses the issues he does. The following sections provide such a survey, along with a review of cultural and theological factors that have contributed to Koyama's overall development.

Personal History

Being born into a Japanese Christian family in 1929 meant a unique life for Koyama in two distinct ways. On the one hand, it placed him in a context where Christians were a tiny minority within their own society, a minority which during Koyama's early years was increasingly distrusted by the Japanese government. Secondly, living in Japan during the 1930's and 40's meant that Koyama experienced the preparations and devastations of war during some of his most formative years. The significance of this latter fact will be delineated later. First, several important aspects of the Christian environment in which Koyama was raised will be mentioned.

Koyama himself appreciates the visionary impact of a missionary whose influence upon his grandfather Koyama remembers. This missionary was, in Koyama's mind, a man who knew the difference between Christianity and culture, i.e., he did not insist that Japanese people conform to European cultural molds when they became Christians. At a time when the West exercised a high degree of influence and often an attitude of superiority over the Japanese—who were still emerging from feudal culture—this missionary's perspicacity was remarkable.[1]

The very fact that Koyama's grandparents were already Christian had a similarly important impact on Koyama's Christian environment. Whereas first generation converts to Christianity tend to relinquish much of their own culture in favor of that represented to them by the missionary who affects their conversion, third generation Christians have, as Koyama puts it, "more elbow room" vis-a-vis their own local culture. They are more able to distinguish in it that which does not necessarily contradict their faith, but which can be seen and used positively.[2]

The fact that Koyama grew up in a Christian home meant, too, that he was exposed to other interpretations and descriptions of life than those predominant in his own culture. Reading a translation of *Pilgrim's Progress* when he was twelve years old, for example, made a lasting impression on Koyama. Through it he was exposed to a symbolic description of Christian life and to symbolic language in Christian literature.[3] Such symbolic use of language echoed that of indigenous Japanese language and literature and thus opened the way for Koyama to express his own Christian faith in familiar cultural terms.

This development was reinforced by Koyama's exposure to Kanzo Uchimura, who Koyama describes as one of the single greatest influences on his theology. Uchimura's "exciting exegesis and beautiful" style make him, as far as Koyama is concerned, one of Japan's outstanding indigenous theologians.[4] Such influences as Uchimura, plus the link between Japanese language in general and Koyama's profuse use of imagery in his theological writing, will receive further attention later when considering his unique style.

Next, it is necessary to record the events that most motivated Koyama to pursue theology in the first place, namely, World War Two. In several segments of Koyama's writing he recalls an experience that deeply affected his perspective on life and directly inaugurated a long theological quest in which he is still intensely involved. He writes,

> It was 25 May 1945. All night Tokyo was bombed by the American B29s. Our tiny wooden house was reduced to ashes together with the whole of Tokyo. The morning came as though nothing had happened. I knew the morning came because I saw the sun rising over the devastated wilderness that had been Tokyo. I saw the sun. . . . but it was a sun I did not know. The sun I knew did not come up "that" morning. It was a different, strange sun that came up over the wilderness. Overnight Tokyo was changed. I felt homeless. I felt misplaced and lost. I felt an intolerable loneliness encircling me. Tokyo was a forsaken city and I a forsaken person. I was orphaned. I felt as though I had been deserted by time . . . as though submerged into lifeless timelessness.[5]

For Koyama this was the beginning of a process that is still going on. "Something started within me,"[6] he says, involving him in a continuing process of interpreting that experience of devastation. As he reflects upon his own theological development, Koyama considers it to be an "interpreting of who I am, dealing with my existence, with what has shaken my ground of being."[7]

Thus, Koyama's war experience, in conjunction with his Christian upbringing, turned Koyama towards theology as an avenue for interpreting his own experience and that of the world around him. Initially he intended to become not a missionary, but a minister within Japan. But in seminary Koyama began to question the Christian education he was receiving as to its relevance for his own culture. Its heavy Western orientation disturbed him. The fact that at the time of the Allied trials of Japanese war crimes very little mention was made of those trials in the seminary struck him as incongruous. He had himself interpreted Japan's defeat in war as the judgment of God on Japanese wickedness. That the seminary should not even discuss this unsettled Koyama.[8]

In the end, instead of taking up local ministry, Koyama decided to pursue his studies further and went to the U.S.A. to do so. It is understandable that he went there, for, Germany, the predominant source of much of the theology taught in Japanese seminaries at the time of World War Two, also lay in defeat and ruin. America, the victorious, occupying force and dominant influence in post-war Japan, was the most natural venue for post-graduate theological study.

It is difficult to assess the effect on Koyama of his years in the United States. Koyama has not written about his U.S. experience as he has about his experiences in other countries. Certainly this was a period of significant cross-cultural exposure (Koyama's first, in fact) and study. Koyama earned a B.D. degree at Drew University, Madison, New Jersey in 1954 and then a Ph.D. degree from Princeton Theological Seminary in 1959, where his study examined Martin Luther's exegesis of penitential psalms. However, one of the most important results of Koyama's sojourn in the U.S. was undoubtedly his marriage to an American woman, Lois Rozendaal, also a student at Princeton.

Together, after the completion of Koyama's studies, they returned to Japan, and were subsequently assigned to be missionaries to Thailand by the United Church of Christ in Japan (*Kyodan*). This assignment inaugurated Koyama's missionary and teaching career, and out of it came his first published works. The particular effects of this period of Koyama's life in terms of his encounter with Buddhism in Thailand and the effect of that encounter on his theology are taken up elsewhere. Suffice it to say here, first of all, that it was this experience that persuaded Koyama that theology must be done in relationship to the experience of the people it addresses and serves—much as his own theology had been motivated by his own wartime experience. Secondly, it was Koyama's encounter with Buddhism and particularly with Buddhist people in Thailand that contributed to his theology of self-denial which could be used both to critically examine the impact of Western Christianity on Asia and to formulate a theology of other religions.

After eight years of teaching in a Thai seminary, Koyama moved to Singapore as Dean of the South East Asia Graduate School of Theology, Executive Director of the Association of Theological Schools in South East Asia and Editor of the South East Asia Journal of Theology. Six years there brought extensive exposure to the various struggles of Christianity in the midst of the great Asian cultures during a period of immense social change.

His essays of this period explored the impact of radical social change, especially through technology, upon the lives of Asia's people. At this time, too, Koyama contemplated the relationship of Christian values and views and the values of contemporary Asian society, particularly in urban situations. By this time Koyama's concept of a style for Christian mission had solidified, based on his theology of self-denial and his concern for experience-orientated theology, both related to his critical evaluation of Western missions in the Asian world.

In 1974 Koyama moved again, this time to become senior lecturer in phenomenology of religion at the University of Otago in Dunedin, New Zealand. While there his seminal book on Christianity's relationship with other religions was published, including further comments on the destructive aspects of Western Christianity's impact on Asia, and further development of the idea of self-denial, or the "crucified mind." This period too, saw Koyama becoming more concerned with Christianity and social issues, and more involved with international church affairs.

By the end of his time in New Zealand Koyama had begun to return to some of his original theological questions as well, but in a new way because of the information accumulated through his years of intercultural life and learning. These questions, having to do particularly with the encounter between the Judaeo-Christian tradition and the experience of ultimate reality as "cosmological" by people in Asia or in other parts of the world, are questions Koyama is presently pursuing in his post as Professor of Ecumenics and World Christianity at Union Theological Seminary, New York, where he located in 1980. By this time Koyama had been internationally acclaimed as a highly creative theologian and contributor to international church conferences. Popular as a lecturer and preacher, particularly in Asia and the U.S., Koyama had also become a key resource person for the World Council of Churches, actively involved in its commissions and their studies on Faith and Order, Inter-Faith dialogue, Humanum Studies, Church and Society, Technology and Faith, and Mission and Evangelism. At the World Council of Churches 1980 Assembly in Melbourne, Koyama was a keynote speaker.

Today one finds Koyama's name and ideas widely and ever more frequently quoted, e.g., in World Council of Churches documents, inter-faith dialogue, reviews of Asian theology, and even in such unlikely fields as linguistics and anthropology.[9] Usually, however, such references are to limited (and sometimes misunderstood) aspects of Koyama's theology. No comprehensive assessment and presentation of his theology exists. This is due not only to Koyama's "youth" as a published theologian, but also to the wide diversity of his theological subject matter, the unique, non-traditional style of his writing, not to mention lack of comparable experience by many of his readers. Reviewing his personal background thus contributes to a fuller understanding of Koyama's theology. Also necessary is a look at the cultural and theological influences that affected his development. These are the subjects of the next sections.

Formative Culture

Irreversibly, Koyama is a man of several cultures. However, by considering his original, most formative culture it may be possible to find certain clues or reference points which can contribute to a broader understanding of Koyama's overall theological outlook. Because of the complications of considering a person in relationship to an altogether different and highly complex culture, conclusions about the relationship of that person to his culture must be rather tentative. Nevertheless, a variety of observations in regard to generally recognized features of Japanese culture, particularly in the light of some of Koyama's own reflections on his relationship to his home culture, may yield further useful insights into the formation of Koyama himself.

Koyama's own sense of belonging to Japanese culture surfaces at various points in his writing. One of his most thought-provoking reflections is that on "The Moon and Irresponsibility" in which he considers Japanese spirituality, curiously linking it with an account of the suicide of Admiral Takijiro Onishi, creator of the Japanese kamikaze corps in World War Two.[10] There Koyama reveals a sympathetic appreciation for Japanese spirituality as something which on the one hand transcends all human ethical concerns, yet on the other hand carries within itself the capacity for sacrificial commitment to others. It is a uniquely Japanese perspective.

Of a more humorous nature, but also demonstrating Koyama's appreciation of his own heritage, is Koyama's comment on the Japanese-ness of his own tongue, stomach, and values:

I realized one day than [sic] an almost insignificant thing about me has a complicated historical background. Why do I have a miserable English pronunciation? It is because my father, my grandfather, my great-grandfather and all the way back to my first known ancestor who was a mountain bandit some two hundred years ago, spoke the Japanese language. My difficulty in distinguishing the short "a" from the short "u" sound ("please flash the toilet") does not derive from my private shortcomings but from the historical chain of Japanese ears and tongues. I could make the same point about my preference for eating raw tuna, trout and squid, though I do not enjoy raw oyster. It is because the community from which I derive my sense of taste did not appreciate raw oyster. Why do I have this or that particular mysterious type of emotion, psychological reaction or sense of value? What is it that attracts me to the idea of nothingness or absolute detachment? Why am I always suspicious of activism? Where did I get my appreciative understanding of *hara-kiri*? Why is there pantheistic emotion within me even though I reject it theologically?[11]

The answers to Koyama's queries lie, as he realizes, in his Japanese heritage. Koyama goes on not only to turn this personal recognition into a universal theological reflection; he also turns it into a unique Christian doxology:

One aspect after another of my life came under scrutiny until emotionally, at one point—and this may sound irrational and perhaps ridiculous—I felt the love of God in the fact that my tongue fails to say "flush toilet" and my stomach accepts rice naturally and accepts hamburger unnaturally![12]

Still another story that reveals Koyama's Japanese heart and personality is that of the pine tree he used to touch every day on his way to the university in New Zealand.

I have a special feeling about the pine tree. What is it that moves mysteriously within my soul when I see this tree? What is it that my inner ear hears when the wind rumbles through the branches? What do these pine cones speak to me when I pick them up? Why is it that I feel I want to touch the pine tree? Am I trying to receive its "supernatural power" (*mana*). Do I have this strange sensation about the pine tree because I am Japanese? One spot of the trunk I touch every morning as I pass. There are commuters in Tokyo who do this. On the way to the railway stations, they touch. . . it may be a roadside postbox, a telephone pole, the edge of a table of a vegetable stall. If they fail to do so they do not feel well that day. I touched this morning the same post of the great tree and I feel assured.[13]

While Koyama uses such stories to make various theological observations as a Christian, he at the same time simply affirms his own cultural heritage. In it he finds keys for his own self-understanding and for understanding and proclaiming Christian faith.

In a more general sense it may be possible to discern a variety of themes within Japanese culture that have particular relevance for Koyama's Christianity. Naturally, some sympathetic correspondence between the values expressed in these themes and Koyama's own values is to be expected. What is especially worth noting, however, are apparent contrasts between traditional Japanese perspectives and the views Koyama has come to as an intercultural Christian.

One important area of correspondence between indigenous Japanese values and Koyama's theology is that of suffering and self-denial. The importance of suffering and self-denial, not only to Koyama, but in the experience and theology of other Japanese Christians as well, cannot but reflect the influence of indigenous cultural attitudes stemming from Japanese history, Buddhism, and, in particular, Bushido.

Bushido, as the code of honor for Japan's samurai, or warrior class, during Japan's feudal centuries, penetrated and shaped the whole of Japanese society even into the modern era.[14] It cultivated almost unlimited self-denial, whatever physical or other suffering that entailed, as a means to personal perfection and to corporate well-being. Though not necessarily pursued for their own sake, suffering and self-denial were viewed as necessary, acceptable, and instructive for human character development and for social cohesion.[15] Not surprisingly, in the feudal, agrarian economy which prevailed in Japan for many centuries, the self-imposed suffering of the samurai was paralleled by both the natural and enforced suffering of the majority of the population, i.e., the peasants.

Buddhism, a religion directly concerned with the origin and meaning of suffering, influenced the Japanese attitude towards suffering as well. Although, as

Koyama himself points out, "the Buddhist doctrine that 'life is suffering' (*dukkha*).
.. was too pessimistic for the Japanese Soul,"[16] it nevertheless found some expression in the strict self-discipline of Zen Buddhism which could utilize personal deprivation or pain as a stepping-stone to the discovery of ultimate reality.[17] (It should not be overlooked here that Christianity, too, has an abundant history of religious devotion based on suffering and strict self-discipline.)

Intimately related to self-denial in the Japanese social code was unlimited fealty to those of superior social standing in one's own hierarchical community. The concept of duty to one's superiors and to one's social grouping became intensely and uniquely refined in Japanese culture.[18] It is not surprising therefore to find that for many of the disinherited samurai who became Christian in Japan (especially after the Meiji restoration of 1867 and the concurrent opening of Japan to the West), their conversion was to some degree essentially a transfer of loyalty from one ruling lord to another, often for merely utilitarian purposes.[19]

While a precise link between Koyama's theology of self-denial and his Japanese heritage cannot be demonstrated, especially given the fact that Koyama himself refers more to Thai Buddhist self-denial than to Japanese tradition as an impetus for his own theology of self-denial, it is nevertheless not inconceivable that Japanese cultural roots undergird some of his appreciation for self-denial as well. To be sure, Koyama was not the first Japanese theologian to speak of self-denial and the "pouring out" of one's self in following Christ. The same idea was developed and utilized by various other Christian movements and theologians in Japan before Koyama. What is instructive is that Koyama does not convey this concern for self-denial in the "duty" and obedience terms that would have been so predominant in the Japan of his childhood. Instead, his Christian roots, his understanding of a loving, non-coercive relationship between God and humanity, and his deep respect for the integrity of individuals mean that he sees Christian self-denial as an act of freedom and love rather than of mere obedience.

In this connection it may be worth noting a realization Koyama has of his own compound personality. In a meditation entitled "Stories Within Me"[20] Koyama recognizes a tension between the authoritarian influence of pre-World War Two Japanese society and the democratic experience of post-World War Two Japan. Within himself he finds an "authoritarian self" and a "democratic self." Having two such contrasting selfs in one person is, Koyama says, "a troublesome arrangement." It creates a feeling of ambiguity and tension, more so because it is not merely the experience of one individual but because it signifies the dramatic redirection of history for a whole people. Yet out of this experience comes both the stimulation and resources for formulating a theology that in the long run clearly transcends any static cultural situation.

Another key theme of Japanese culture, as in Asian civilization as a whole, is that of harmony. A fundamental assumption of Shinto, Japan's most ancient, indigenous "religion," is that there is an inner harmony to all life, a universal order and unity.[21] There is in Shinto no dualistic separation of the natural and the supernatural; nor can life be "departmentalized."[22] Contradictions are absorbed; paradoxes can be accepted. Key differences and apparent conflicts can be ignored or subsumed into the inner harmony of reality.

Alien though such a perspective may be to the Western mind, it is nevertheless a persuasive and powerful perspective in Asia. It gives Japanese culture the ability to absorb widely divergent strains of human thought and experience. Such has been the case in Japan's exposure to such diverse influences as Chinese philosophy, religion, and social organization over several centuries, Portuguese and Dutch trade, science, and religion in the fifteenth to seventeenth-centuries, and more recently, Western religion, science, government and ways of life, especially as channeled through the U.S.A. in the nineteenth and twentieth-centuries. This history has led one Japan scholar to remark that "Japanese culture is essentially a conglomerate affair."[23]

Yet Japan has at the same time been able to balance tolerance and absorption with a strong indigenous culture and relatively cohesive social development. On the one hand seen to be excessively absorptive, even in Japanese eyes,[24] Japanese culture has also maintained an exclusivity that included, as Koyama himself notes, the belief that the Japanese people, as superior to all others, were destined to rule the world.[25] While Shinto espoused a fundamental universal harmony and unity to life, it served, at the same time, the state doctrine of particularity and exclusivity.[26] Even Japanese Buddhism as represented by Nichiren, founder of the influential Buddhist sect by that name, exuded exclusivity. In contrast to the international spirit of Buddhism, Nichiren portrayed Japan as the center of the universe and considered Japanese Buddhism to be the only true Buddhism.[27] Thus Japan freely absorbed the influences of other cultures while always tempering them with an exclusivism and utilitarianism based on what was seen as serving the good of Japan.[28]

Of course, Japanese culture and government was hardly so cohesive over two thousand years that what served the good of Japan could always be clearly distinguished. Inevitably the diverse influences of Confucianism, Buddhism and Western values which deeply penetrated Japanese culture produced a kind of relativism, especially in the selection of ultimate values.

The utter demolition of nationalistic Shintoism after World War Two increased this sense of relativism in modern Japan, undermining Japanese confidence even in her own religious heritage. [29] This relativism, combined with the notion of an ultimate harmony to all life embracing all apparent divergences, blunted the edges of particular religious truths and reinforced the inclination toward utilitarian, selective absorption.[30] However, it is important to note that Shintoism, even in defeat, offers a sense of security and familiarity, a sense of history and identity that speaks to the Japanese longing for harmony, unity, and community in the modern day as in past ages.[31] Other religions that can speak to the same longing and provide similar security can expect to find a considerable following in Japanese culture still.

Koyama, naturally, sees Christianity to be capable of offering a sense of security, history and identity to modern-day Asians. More than that, Koyama discovers in Christianity an ultimate, universal, all-embracing context for human life, one which in fact incorporates contradiction and diversity into its very center. The Cross of Jesus is, as it were, God's self-contradiction. In Jesus God takes on the discord and pain of the world and embraces it with love.

Contradiction and ambiguity are not as uncomfortable for Koyama as for those from cultures where precise distinctions are sought when making assertions about the nature of reality. For Koyama, reality may be more meaningfully expressed in an indirect or even contra-positive manner, as Koyama does in saying, for example, that Christ demonstrated his lordship by crucifixion; his glory, by humiliation.[32]

In fact Koyama sees this style of affirmation to be very attractive to Asians and especially to Japanese culture. He points to the example of Japanese room decor. Unlike the Western world where a room is decorated with a plethora of color, paintings, furniture and other objects, a Japanese room may be decorated by placing a single flower in one corner of an austere room. For a Japanese this flower then charges the whole space with vibrancy. It perhaps corresponds to the idea that what is *not* said can be more important than what *is* said.

Koyama, accordingly, finds God's contradictory methodology to be "intuitively meaningful," as he puts it. In fact Koyama can rather passionately proclaim, "It's only stupid to say that the strength of God is strongness,"[33] by which he refers to St. Paul's enigmatic affirmation that God's very weakness is strength and his foolishness wisdom.

However, returning to the issue of harmony to which Japanese Shintoism and Asia in general are so predisposed, Koyama's resistance to a benign, contradiction-absorbing harmony in the world must be noticed. Particularly in his contrasting the biblical picture of history with the Thai Buddhist view of history, and the biblical picture of the wrath of God with the Thai Buddhist dedication to tranquility,[34] Koyama the missionary seeks to rattle the complacency that often resists the

Christian message. Nor does Koyama hesitate to display the scandal of Jesus Christ crucified as a disturbing challenge to Christians and non-Christians alike. The cross is not an obtuse, unfortunate event to be absorbed into the tranquilizing harmony of the universe. It is a piercing reality with which humanity must contend.

Yet, in the end, Koyama testifies that God embraces even the cross of Jesus just as the cross of Jesus embraces the brokenness and disharmony of humanity. The harmony of love prevails. But, it is a different sort of harmony than that envisaged in usual human perspective. It is not a harmony which absorbs God and God's salvation, but a harmony established by God in the turmoil of the cross.

In relation to the issue of harmony as a key theme in Asian and Japanese culture, one which Koyama in his theology responds to, the notion of divine immanence and how human beings respond to it deserves passing attention as well. In indigenous Japanese perspective, human beings as part of the harmonious unity of life recognize and participate in that harmony through their relationship with *kami*, the gods, spirits or life-forces present in all the natural world.[35] Paying tribute to or giving due reverence to *kami* is the human reaction to the mystery of life.[36] This is all the more important given the immanence, the closeness, the presence and effect of the *kami* on everyday life.

What impact, if any, the ancient Japanese reverence for *kami* had on Japanese Christianity has not been fully explored. But one might suspect that the ancient Japanese sense of the immanence of the divine is somehow meaningful or influential even in contemporary Japanese Christianity. Whether related or not, the immanence of God and God's kingdom, for example, was a strong theme in the Student Christian Movement as well as in other Japanese social theologies in the decades prior to World War Two.[37]

Likewise, Barthian theology, with its emphasis on the transcendence of God originally found a large following in Japan, but lost much of that in the turmoil of World War Two partially because people were then again preoccupied with the crisis of their immediate situation and sought a theology that spoke to that situation and to their particular history.[38]

Koyama, interestingly, does not refer much to Japanese *kami*, while he does refer to the spirits (*adats*) worshipped in Indonesia[39] as an important area of study for missionary Christianity in Asia. (Although in a more recent essay, [*Mount Fuji and Mount Sinai*, pp. 145–150], Koyama does use the Japanese understanding of *kami* as the prelude to a missiology for Japan.) But the idea of "spirit" is important to Koyama. The "spirit of man," the "spirit of technology," "curved spirituality," "linear spirituality" are all terms or concepts which Koyama finds very useful for expressing personal experience and theological insight. Koyama surely does not equate the "spirit of technology" or other spiritualities with the *kami* of Japanese culture-faith. But the concept of spirituality as a descriptive tool for dealing with human experience is at least one which is familiar to Koyama.

Again in relation to the Japanese predilection towards harmony and divine immanence, a key contrast of Koyama's must be observed. Nowhere does Koyama focus on purely personal religious devotion or mystical union with God. Always, Koyama's concern is for Christian participation in kenotic witness to God's love. But this participation in Christ's self-denial is not self-orientated; it intends the communication of a story and a reality to other people. Koyama's understanding of being is intensely relational. The priority is not personal absorption into the god-head or some similar self-purification. Thus, Koyama's commitment stands in marked contrast to the view common in Zen or other forms of Japanese Buddhism and even in much Christianity in Japan at the turn of this century.[40]

Another ingredient of Japanese culture, corresponding to the appreciation of harmony, is a fundamental optimism about life and a belief in the goodness of humanity. Various Buddhist and nationalistic leaders in Japanese history have maintained, for example, that human nature in Japan is naturally good and to be trusted.[41]

Koyama, too, describes this attitude in essays about *kichi* and *kyo*, the Japanese concepts of good and evil.[42] The Japanese view, he notes, is that history is the process of alteration between these two forces. But in the end, it is the positive force, the harmony and optimism which prevails.[43] As Koyama puts it, "the Japanese people are *kichi*-optimists. Even Hiroshima was unable to change this Japanese metaphysics. . . All Japanese, young and old, share in this philosophy of life."[44]

The persuasiveness of this optimism was reflected in much of Japanese theology, especially in the first quarter of this century. Toyohiko Kagawa, among others, reflected a strong optimism about human nature which undergirded his faith in the ethical possibilities of human beings in society.[45] Danjo Ebina, too, a leading Japanese Christian raised in an environment of Confucian ethics, carried from that environment into his Christianity a firm belief in the natural ability and goodness of human beings.[46] Confidence that human beings could bring about the kingdom of God on earth by their own efforts was apparent not only in the Marxist Student Christian Movement but also in the "social Gospel" liberalism that held sway in Japan for much of the early part of this century.[47]

World Wars One and Two significantly dampened this optimism, especially that which was inherited from Western Christendom where World War One in particular demolished optimistic visions of human evolution. However, optimism and naturalism, that is, the Japanese intimate awareness of humanity's place in the ultimately harmonious order of the world, could not be expunged from the Japanese character.

Even Koyama exhibits a fundamentally positive picture of human worth and potential: "I have unresolved difficulty with Augustine's doctrine of 'man of perdition' even today!"[48] His deep respect for human dignity is intrinsic to his missionary theology of appreciating the richness in other faiths and cultures. It underlies his penetrating criticism of Western missionary approaches to Asia—for they did not exhibit a self-denying, appreciative valuation of people from different cultures and faiths.

Two stories from Koyama's own experience illustrate his affirmation of human love and dignity on its own terms. Koyama relates how he presented the story of Jesus' encounter with the Canaanite woman (Matt. 15:21–28) to his Thai students in the light of Luther's *Anfechtung* interpretation of this passage.[49] The disastrous result led Koyama to reconsider the story in terms of Jesus' implicit affirmation of the natural human love which the woman had for her daughter. The basically positive character and devotion of this human love was, for Koyama, the key to an Asian understanding of the text.

In a second story Koyama relates his failure as a missionary to communicate Christian faith to a hospitalized Thai woman precisely because he did not respond to her on her own terms. This experience sparked the development of Koyama's "neighbourological" theology, a theology built on the affirmation of the intrinsic positive value of human life and culture in all its diversity. While this perspective belongs independently to the Christian theology of creation as well, it is not unlikely that Koyama inherited some sympathy for this affirmative view of humanity from his own Japanese culture.

However, lest too easy an association be made at this point between Koyama's affirmation of the human character and Japanese optimism about life, Koyama's war experience needs to be recalled, for it marks a clear divergence between Koyama's Christian understanding of life and the attitude of Japanese society. To Koyama the devastation of his homeland was none other than the judgment of God upon the wickedness of Japan.[50] The destruction of Tokyo was not merely the product of "the fierce anger of Americans"; it resulted from "the fierce anger of the Lord."[51]

"When I moved from 'the fierce anger of Americans' to 'the fierce anger of the Lord,' I made a decisive theological move," says Koyama.[52] It was a move that heralded for him a new sense of time and history. It changed Koyama's understanding of the continuity of life as represented by Japanese culture, leading Koyama to in fact challenge the Japanese concept of harmonious continuity by a new concept of continuity based on the discontinuity of the crucified Jesus.[53] Koyama now founds his affirmation of human value and his affirmation of the harmony of the universe not on human concepts and criteria. Rather, he grounds it in the value and harmony God gives to creation by establishing, in the crucified Jesus, a free, loving relationship with God's own handiwork.

Theological Discontinuity

The presentation of just such a message in Japanese culture, however, is partially hindered by the fact that concepts and terms which are basic to traditional Christian theology lack precisely corresponding terms and expressions in Japanese culture; they are sometimes lacking altogether. The Christian term "sin" offers one example of a case where Japanese concepts and concepts of Christianity, particularly as embodied in the Western form in which Christianity was introduced to Japan, lack precise correspondence. Danjo Ebina, again, illustrates this point. His conversion to Christianity was not based on a recognition of sin with consequent repentance and faith, but on the transfer of personal loyalty from one lord to another.[54] To Ebina sin was not an eternal reality but a functional tool of human reason which served to explain failure and to educate one towards personal growth. Such a concept reveals the direct impact of Confucian philosophy on Japanese Christian thought.[55]

Liberal and Marxist Christianity in Japan reflected another sort of attitude towards the Christian idea of sin. Their emphasis on social justice and development pictured sin as social selfishness in general, not as a permanent or personal human state.[56] While this view has not been uncommon to Christianity in other places and times, it may in this case also reflect some of the evolutionary optimism inherent in the Japanese outlook on life.

Still today there is concern that the idea of sin in Japanese Christianity does not have the same meaning or function as in Western theology,[57] where certain ideas about sin have been considered crucial for Christian faith. Guilt, as a closely related term which has altogether different connotations in Japan than in Europe,[58] further points out important conceptual divergences between Christianity in the cultures of the West and Christianity in the culture of Japan.

Such divergences necessarily mean that theology done by Asian Christians, unless it is mere parroting of theology done elsewhere in the world, will develop in different directions or with different emphases than theology elsewhere. Already this is apparent in the emphasis in various Asian theologies not on personal sin and redemption but, for example, on the meaning of suffering, or on the particularity of Christ in a context where suffering is an ancient, overwhelming problem and where Jesus comes as but one more unfamiliar saviour amidst the diversity of Asian faiths.

Thus Koyama in formulating his theology does not use the standard doctrinal terms of European Christianity to organize his thinking. Rather than using such terms as sin, grace, and atonement as the formative questions of his theology, Koyama speaks of history, continuity, self-denial and the like. These concepts he sees to be more effective in communicating the fundamental message of the Gospel to people of Asia, particularly the people of Thailand and Japan.

The concept of history functions as an especially useful tool for Koyama's purposes. He challenges both the Thai people and the Japanese people to consider the meaning of history as represented in the Judaeo-Christian tradition, which declares a purpose to history in a way quite in contrast to that of Buddhism.[59]

What is perhaps ironic is that Koyama most probably derives some of his appreciation of history from the intense historical awareness of his own Japanese culture. Through various written records over thirteen centuries, in the recurrent emphasis on lineage of the emperor and various ruling families over many generations, by oral transmission of myths and historical events, and through various other artistic, literary and cultural devices, the Japanese people have cultivated an impressive sense of their own history, such that it acts as a cohesive, guiding force in shaping their society and identity.

Of course, Koyama realizes the depth of this history-consciousness in his own culture and therefore can apply the historical meaning of Jesus, as he understands it, all the more effectively. This is exactly what he does in contrasting the "continuity philosophy" of Japan with the scandalous continuity of Christ crucified.[60] Koyama's ability to use relevant theological ideas for the interpretation of Christianity in an Asian context stems, naturally, from his own roots in Asian culture.

Ethics

However, tracing the correspondence between Koyama's conceptualization and application of various themes indigenous to Japanese culture can produce ambivalent results, too. Ethics, for example, as one key area of concern for both Christianity and Japanese culture, exhibits as many contrasts as links between Japanese instincts and Koyama's interests.

For a society built on the combination of Confucian ethics and the high ideals embodied in the whole code of Bushido, ethics is an issue of paramount importance. The Puritan Christianity that came to Japan in the late nineteenth century, with its strong ethical emphasis, found a ready response from those who were seeking a new moral basis for their society. Indeed, a main motive for conversion to Christianity was the search for a new morality to serve Japan's emergence from feudalism to being a modern industrial state.[61] Christianity seemed a useful religion to adopt, for it both espoused familiar strains of strict moral discipline and served as a vehicle for the importation of other desirable elements of Western culture.

While this manner of religious borrowing led to many genuine conversions, it also produced situations of ambiguously Christian character. In a sense, the adoption of Christianity as an ethical system without grasping its historical substance and make-up was similar to Japan's adoption of parliamentary democracy without the concepts of equality and social organization—developed in the West over centuries in the context of a totally different culture—that lie behind it.[62] While the system may somehow work, it cannot be true to its original character, at least not without extensive adjustment and familiarization with the historical experience and values behind the system. For example, the very idea of Jesus had to be modified to suit Japanese and Confucian presuppositions.[63] In no way, it seemed, could Jesus be divine, particularly in a religious environment where divinity was thought of very differently from in the Judeo-Christian tradition. Jesus could, however, be accepted as a great moral teacher.[64]

Another complication of the meeting of Japanese and Western Christian ethics was the nature of ethical action itself. While ethics in the West generally imply action and a causal link between concept and action, ethics in Japan are open to other alternatives.

For example, Yoshiro Ishida, a contemporary of Koyama's, points out that to the Japanese mind, nothingness, or doing nothing, can be considered as the "most doing." Japanese civilization, he notes, has different standards of action, different ethical criteria and methods than other cultures.[65]

These different standards and attitudes can be seen, for example, in Zen Buddhism which teaches that ethics are not after all a matter of the essence of life. Rather, the religious truth discovered in Zen is beyond the realm of distinguishing between good and evil. Ethics merely function as a tool for testing and cultivating one's spirit.[66] The important thing is to be in harmony with the flow of life. Spontaneity and natural action may be more valued than premeditated norms in achieving this harmony. In any case, life will flow on without deliberate human action.[67] Indeed, reflective withdrawal or "doing nothing" may be seen as a very valuable contribution to world order.[68]

Koyama also expresses this perspective when he remarks,

> The sentiment of aesthetic nothingness is deeply embedded in
> the soul of each Japanese even in today's highly industrialized
> society. It is different from the West's concept of
> "nothingness."[69]

This observation comes in the context of Koyama's meditation on the Japanese appreciation of the moon, which he then uses as a clue to the Japanese sense of responsibility. For the Japanese, even the moon can have ethical implications:

> What the moon represents to the Japanese soul is an instant
> experience of transcendence. It is instant in the sense that it is
> basically aesthetic and not ethical. The ethical automatically
> becomes silent. It is quite out of tune to discuss, or even medi-
> tate on ethical issues (social justice, political organization, prob-
> lems of modernization, ecology, pollution, international power
> struggles, nuclear balances of terror) while you are looking at
> the moon. You meditate on the transitoriness of your life and
> forget all modern headaches.[70]

This particular passage of Koyama's illustrates not only the distinctive character of Japanese ethical thinking, but also the Japanese inclination towards introspection. Such introspection tends to prioritize changing one's attitude about a situation over changing the situation itself.[71] Emphasis is placed on mental attitude,
which is itself action (perhaps transcending the situation, perhaps affecting it), or
from which action flows. This intuitive inwardness in the Japanese religious heritage tends ultimately to effectuate a divorce between religion and morality.[72]

This concern for attitude seems to be particularly relevant for understanding the
fact that Koyama concerns himself primarily with Christian attitudes and spends
very little time formulating a system of Christian ethics, at least in traditional
terms. Unlike many other Japanese theologians who gave specific attention to
Christian ethics (e.g., Kumano, Kagawa, Japanese Christian social and dialectical
theology and so forth), Koyama seeks to place ethics in a relative relationship to
history and eschatology, which in turn are discussed on a highly conceptual rather
than an existential or action-orientated level.[73]

This is not to say that Koyama ignores practical ethics. On the contrary, his concern for social well-being surfaces in his frequent drawing of attention to destruc-

tive situations and to particular instances of human degradation.[74] Also, in more recent writings he begins to develop an approach to ethics based on the concept of human greed as a fundamental reference point for making ethical determinations.[75] On the whole, however, it would seem that his attention is focused more on the attitudes that guide Christian behavior than on systematic exposition of specific Christian ethics. That this reflects an inherited Japanese posture as well as an awareness of ethical relativity as understood through cross-cultural living seems not unlikely.

One Japanese ethical perspective, however, to which Koyama certainly objects, is the Shinto view that Japan, as the land of the gods, had no need to formulate moral teachings, because the people's hearts retain their divine purity.[76] Koyama's own experience of the devastating breakdown and defeat of Japan's "pure," "superior" civilization was evidence enough for him of the sinfulness of which Japanese people were capable. The view that the Japanese character has an inner purity which needs only polishing to shine forth, belief in the moral superiority of the Japanese which transcends even the contraposition of good and evil[77]—such ideas receive no countenance in Koyama. While he does not present a systematic theology of human sinfulness, it is clear that his understanding of the redemptive love of God includes a critical awareness of human imperfection—in Japan as elsewhere—manifested in idolatry, greed, the dehumanization and exploitation of others, and so forth.

The preceding observations on the distinctive character of Japanese ethical perspectives do not contradict the Japanese concern for social ethics. They do, however, illustrate the fact that Japanese concepts and criteria of ethics may not coincide with the concepts and criteria utilized by others, e.g., Western Christians.

That ethical concerns are in fact of critical importance in Japanese society is evidenced not only by the heritage of Confucian and indigenous ethics but also by the fact that as Japan has undergone the radical changes of the last century, even Western ethics were explored as a possible means for achieving stability and progress in post-feudal Japan. As already mentioned, many Japanese leaders in the latter part of the nineteenth-century turned to Christianity as a possible source of ethical direction for Japanese society. Christianity had unusual appeal in its unique combination of ethics and religion in a society where religion traditionally only touched on the realm of morality.[78]

Under the influence of early liberalism and later American social-Gospel theology, Christianity in Japan played a large role in affecting major social changes in Japanese society, e.g., in elevating the status of women, in spreading prison reform, and in altering images of marriage and family life.

In the decades prior to World War Two Christian social ethics were the concern of activist students and liberal theologians alike, and the church was much involved in social action.[79] The economic depression of the 1930's, the turmoil of militarization and war, and the aftermath of destruction intensified the concern for a sound ethical basis to society. With the initial disillusionment in Shinto-based society following World War Two, Christianity experienced resurgent popularity. The sheer misery of post-war Japan drew the church, as a surviving institution with links in the West, into extensive relief action and social work.[80] At the same time, however, critical questions about Christian ethics were being raised, particularly in regard to imported Western theologies that had advocated uncritical obedience to the state,[81] or, had become too far removed from biblical, doctrinal rooting.[82]

Indeed, both these tendencies reflected not only developments in Western theology, but also the problem of Christianity being too closely and superficially amalgamated into Japanese society. Already in the early days, liberal Protestantism in Japan had succumbed to pressure to conform to nationalistic cultural patterns, thereby losing much of its capacity to provide a prophetic critique of social developments.[83] By mid-twentieth century this liberalism was criticized as trafficking in cheap spiritualism and optimistic evolution theory rather than ethics based on Scripture and established Christian doctrine.[84]

Given the powerful influence of Christianity on Japanese social ethics during the last one hundred years, and given the wide attention accorded to ethics by the Christian church in Japan, it is somewhat surprising that ethics do not play a more dominant role in Koyama's theology. Certainly, Koyama is keenly aware of the complex, profound heritage of Japanese ethics, the unique characteristics of Japanese ethical thinking, and the ethical impact of Christianity on Japanese society. However, so far, Koyama seems not to take up the debate on Christian ethics in Japanese society per se. Instead Koyama concerns himself with what he sees to be a more basic issue—the meaning of Jesus' cross experience—for it is from there that information is derived to direct Christian activity or ethics in human society. Clearly, as Koyama understands Christ, Jesus is not merely a great moral teacher. More than that, Jesus is not just a pattern or concept to be accommodated to Japanese society to suit its own ethical interests. Above all it may be concluded that, for Koyama, any sense of Christian ethics that is divorced from the scandal of Jesus' cross, bound up as it is in the whole saving history of God, implicitly misses the point. Christian ethics find their origin, function and form in the light of God's self-sacrificing love in Jesus.

Individualism

One further example of an area where divergent cultural concepts affect the context of Christian theology in Japan, an area inevitably affecting Koyama as well, is that of individualism and the relevance of personal experience for religious faith. Traditionally, Japanese society is community-orientated; individual concerns are subordinated to those of the family, village, clan, nation, and so forth. Community organization, law and social mores are the priorities of society as a whole. Individualism was in fact seen to be a threat to the hierarchical ordering of Japanese society and was therefore strongly discouraged, especially during World War Two.[85]

The Protestant Christianity that came to Japan in the late nineteenth century, in contrast, emphasized the importance of the individual and of personal religious experience. The individualism of Western culture as it was being absorbed into Japan had a significant impact on Japanese ideas of the self in society. Indeed Christianity and Western influence effected noticeable changes in the Japanese concepts of the individual and human personality.[86]

At the same time, this Christian emphasis on the individual proved also to be a hindrance to the spread of Christianity in Japan. In pre-war Japan, Christianity was still seen to be "highly individualistic and strongly city-centered"[87] which meant that it still met heavy resistance in a group-orientated society, especially in rural areas (which were not only more community-orientated but where there was also a long history of anti-Christian propaganda and persecution of Christians). Largely because of its emphasis on individualism in a family-orientated society, Christianity was and still is considered by many Japanese to be an alien religion.[88]

With the renewed onslaught of American culture immediately after World War Two, there was again an emphasis on the individual. Even the new religions which sprang up in Japan in the post-war decades concerned themselves with the meaning and role of the individual in modern society,[89] while at the same time providing a community in which the individual could belong and find identity as in the past.

Christianity grew after the war as people accepted its individualism, ethics, and world-view during a period when traditional perspectives seemed to have broken down. Japan's western-orientated education system (established in the last decades of the nineteenth century and reinforced after World War Two) gradually changed the understanding of the individual in Japanese society. Interestingly enough, however, there was also within Japanese Christianity a reaction against the sort of Protestantism that had produced an uncritical individualism and obedience to the state during the war.[90]

The corresponding importance of personal experience in religious faith was perhaps not as alien to Japanese culture as the Western emphasis on individualism. Zen Buddhism in particular focused on the immediate personal experience of its followers as the purpose of religious exercise. Deliberately counter to faith and reason, Zen promulgated the discovery of religious truth by direct personal experience. The content of the discovered religious truth, however, was intrinsically non-individualistic, but rather an experience of transcending individuality and entering the basic harmony and unity of the universe.[91]

Around the turn of the century emerging strains of individualism in Japan did combine with a fervor for personal religious experience. This period produced not only public suicides by spiritually anguished individuals but also a surge of emphasis in personal religious experience which invigorated both the Buddhism and the Christianity of the day. The mood of this period of stormy spiritualistic individualism was in no insignificant way influenced by the popularity in Japan at the time of various European philosophers and poets such as Tolstoi, Nietzsche, Kierkegaard, Ibsen, Byron and Heine.[92]

In Koyama's writings there is no preoccupation with either individualism or personal religious experience for its own sake. He does not set out a personal-salvation theory in line with the classical European theology that was generally echoed in Japan.[93] Overwhelmingly, Koyama is concerned with the relational meaning of human existence. Repeatedly, Koyama discusses Christian life in terms of how it motivates persons to love, to serve, and to "pour themselves out" for others, just as Jesus himself did. In this he parallels other Japanese Christians (e.g., Kagawa and the SCM in Japan[94]) and perhaps ever-so-slightly echoes the self-denying heritage of Japanese culture.

At any rate, relationship, or neighbourology, is near the heart of Koyama's theology. While that accords with the relational emphasis of Japanese society, it must be remembered that Koyama's understanding of relationship is based not only upon traditional Japanese categories of relationship, but upon religious insights informed by the variety of cultures in which he has lived.

Koyama's personal experience and his exposure to Western culture in fact set him in a context between that of Japan and the West, one where he can perceive, utilize, and appreciate both the Japanese and the Western understandings of the individual. Individualism which is self-serving he can pointedly criticize.[95] Individuality as an expression of human uniqueness and as a mark of God's redemption he can doxologically affirm. [96]

Summary

The fact that Koyama is a person of intercultural identity and not merely the product of Japanese society reveals the limits of locating a single individual in relation to an old, highly complex culture. The associations so far made between aspects of Koyama's theology and various themes of Japanese culture are at best only indications of the links that may exist between the two. Inescapably such connections do exist. Those offered so far deal with general characteristics of Japanese culture which may contribute to an understanding of Koyama in relation to his original cultural background. The next chapter will take up more specific theological influences as well as general patterns of Japanese Protestantism that may yield further clues to the formation and background of Koyama's own theology.

CHAPTER TWO

KOYAMA AND JAPANESE THEOLOGY

In the previous chapter the Japanese cultural context was surveyed in relation to its impact on Koyama and his theology. It is also instructive to examine more specifically the Christian milieu out of which Koyama emerged. This will be done in two successive chapters. First, a brief survey of Protestant Christianity in Japan will describe the shaping forces of the Church out of which Koyama comes. Secondly, mention of several key Japanese theologians of the past century will provide points of connection and comparison with Koyama's theology.

Overview

Japan, despite the fact that it is not generally associated with great Christian persecutions and martyrdoms, was nevertheless the scene of one of the most intense and effective persecutions of Christianity in history. As many as forty thousand Japanese Christians were martyred for their faith early in the seventeenth-century, some by betrayal and fiendish torture, most in a pitched military battle against government forces intent on totally eliminating Christianity from Japan.[1]

Consequently, the thriving Christian community founded by Portuguese and Spanish missionaries was virtually wiped out. So successful was the government campaign against Christianity that with the exception of a few "crypto-Christians" who retained fragments of the faith over the next three centuries[2] Christianity virtually died in Japan. It remained a strictly banned religion until well after the opening of Japan to the West in the mid-nineteenth century. At that time missionaries were allowed to return to Japan, and Christianity in both its Catholic and Protestant forms was introduced once more.

The Protestant form of Christianity soon came to the fore in Japan in terms of adherents, theology and social impact. To this branch of Japanese Christianity Koyama belongs. Generally, the development of this Protestant Christianity in Japan can best be considered in three distinct but overlapping phases. The first and most complicated of these is that of Christianity during the Meiji period, or, roughly, from the mid-1800's to the turn of this century.

Early Protestant Christianity in Japan

Samurai Influence

The dominant feature in the rebirth of Christianity in Japan was the fact that Christianity was initially received as an ethical system which could be utilized for social reform in the turbulent decades of Japan's encounter with the West. For, the arrival of American military forces and traders in the 1850's had precipitated a major change in the Japanese government itself as well as in the entire structure of Japan's social and economic system.[3] The social upheaval and anxieties created by these changes caused many in Japan to examine Christianity as a tool for adjusting to the demands of the modern era into which Japan was so suddenly flung.

Some of the first and most significant converts to Christianity came from Japan's samurai or educated warrior class, who lived in the urban areas to which Christian missionaries first came.[4] Many of these samurai were young, middle-class and jobless, and had been economically and politically disenfranchised by the return to imperial government in what was termed the Meiji Restoration of 1867.[5]

Out of concern for their own position and in earnest zeal to make a contribution to Japan's new society, individual samurai embraced Christianity as a means of continued involvement in Japan's changing social situation.[6] Having been impressed by Christianity's use of modern science, and believing that Christian beliefs and morality were the keys to Western success, the samurai converts sought to establish Christianity in Japan as the first step towards bringing Western civilization to Japan.[7] For them Christianity was commonly seen as a means for national reform.[8]

Typical of such men was Jo Niishima, who journeyed to the U.S.A. to learn the "secret" of Western civilization, became a Christian, and returned to Japan convinced that Christianity was one of the keys for Japan's future. This conviction led him to found Doshisha University, one of Japan's first universities and a lasting, leading center of Christian education.[9]

The reception of Christianity in Japan, therefore, was closely tied with the socio-economic conditions precipitated by Japan's encounter with the West and by the aspirations and concerns of specific groups within Japanese society at the time.

The Puritan character of the Christianity presented in Japan (predominantly by American missionaries in whose own culture Puritan Christianity was strong),[10] with its emphasis on industriousness, sincerity, honesty, abstinence and other such ethical traits[11] appealed to the sensibilities of Japan's highly disciplined warrior class in this time of social upheaval and changing values. There were, to be sure, genuine faith conversions in this period as well,[12] but the fact remains that many of the conversions to Christianity were distinguished by an ethical comprehension of Christianity that coincided with the concern of many in Japan for a new moral basis for the society in general and indeed for the new state in particular.[13]

That Christianity was first appropriated mainly by Japan's samurai had specific impact on the character of Christianity at the time. For example, it meant that Christianity was often understood and expressed in relation to the heritage of Bushido, the warrior's code. The influence of Bushido, with its emphasis on being willing to die in loyalty to one's sworn lord, is evident, for example, in the faith statements of the first Christian church in Yokohama, a church composed largely of young samurai who had experienced persecution for their sworn obedience to Jesus Christ.[14]

It was in fact to a large degree the discipline of Bushido that enabled Christianity to spread so quickly and effectively among the samurai.[15] Swearing allegiance to a lord, especially for the good of one's community, was a familiar, esteemed cultural pattern. Moreover, the loyalty required in doing so included accepting self-sacrifice, external demands, and differences from one's previous patterns of living, to the extent even of accepting the many aspects of Christianity that were quite alien to Japanese culture.[16]

There was, however, resistance even among Christian samurai to a wholesale appropriation of Western Christianity. Inazo Nitobe, samurai-Christian, writer, statesman, and one-time under-secretary general of the League of Nations[17] upheld the idea that Christianity was good for Japan—but without its Anglo-Saxon "freaks and fancies."[18] Nitobe himself illustrates the inner tensions of those who sought to integrate Christianity into Japanese life while retaining an intense respect for their own pre-Christian tradition. In contrast to others, Nitobe argued that Christian missions did little to mold the character of the new Japan. "No, it was Bushido, pure and simple, that urged us on for weal or woe."[19] For Nitobe, Bushido was the highest human code of honor, and it was with regret that he lamented its passing, prophesying, "Christianity and materialism. . . will divide the world between them."[20]

That numerous samurai constituted the early Protestant church in Japan also influenced the nature of that church. Because the samurai were individual converts, middle-class, urban, and intensely concerned with both personal and social ethics, so was the church largely individualistic, middle-class, urban and ethics-orientated. One of the positive results of this latter orientation was that the samurai social concern led the church to active and effective social involvement during the latter decades of the nineteenth-century and well into the twentieth-century.

One further, predictable complication of samurai conversions to Christianity was the inevitable divergence between the concepts and values of their previous background and those of their Christian faith. Several of the most significant of these concepts—sin, guilt, individualism, and understanding of Jesus—were mentioned in the preceding chapter. While such conceptual problems mirror the deep differences of whole cultures and not merely the perspectives of one small group within a society (such as Japan's samurai) it is also clear that the ideas of Japan's early church leaders—who were largely samurai steeped in the combined traditions of Confucianism, Buddhism, and Shinto—should have a major impact on the subsequent theological formulations of the Japanese church. While this becomes apparent in the case of Danjo Ebina and his Confucianist idea of sin (see preceding chapter, p. 28), it may also be apparent in the fact that the early Japanese church, composed of men whose regimen of Bushido emphasized simplicity and practical concerns over abstruse philosophy,[21] did not direct itself towards a systematic or philosophical presentation of its faith. Theology and church organization, despite pressures from the West, retained a certain pragmatic flexibility.

On the other hand, the pragmatic flexibility of the church itself was at the same time circumscribed by the very fact that the church was samurai dominated. For this meant that the church readily assumed the hierarchical character of Japanese society as a whole. Moreover, the church to some degree took on the nature of a restricted community or club.[22] But such a development was understandable in a society with a rigid social order and a strong emphasis on group-consciousness. Altogether, the fact that the bulk of the leadership and much of the membership of the early church came from samurai origins was a determining factor in the character and structure of Protestant Christianity in Japan remains significant for understanding even the modern Japanese church.[23]

Wider Impact

While the history of Protestant Christianity in Japan must be told with special attention to the role played in it by the samurai, it must also be recognized that early Christianity in Japan had many other dimensions. These included such factors as Christianity's relationship to the Japanese government, Christianity's impact on Japanese society, and the impact of Japanese society on Christianity, to name a few.

The period during which the imperial government was restored to power was one of rapid and radical social change. Almost overnight Japan moved from the feudal ages into the twentieth-century. In a mere three decades, for example, Japan was able to switch from education for the elite only to universal education for both sexes. Her becoming the first fully literate Asian nation largely accounted for Japan's domination of Asia for most of the next century.[24] Likewise, her armed forces went from swords and primitive muskets to battleships and modern armaments. By 1905 she had become the first Asian nation to defeat a European colonial power in modern warfare,[25] having already crushed Chinese forces in an invasion of Korea. Such revolutionary developments reflected the remarkable adaptability of Japanese society and her unusual capacity for absorbing new methods and values to utilize for her own benefit.

The whole social environment of these days was one of adaptation and liberalism, as the old society was breaking down, new values were being explored, and a new society was taking shape.[26] Christianity benefited from this environment, and made significant contributions to Japan's social development. Christian schools contributed to the education of the populace and set the foundations for much of Japan's subsequent system of higher education. The ethical interests and social concerns of Japan's samurai church leaders, among others, contributed to the Christian drive behind many social reforms, such as the elevation of the status of women, prison reform, changed attitudes on marriage and family,[27] and the education of women.[28] Many Christians advocated parliamentary democracy, monogamous marriage, and abstinence from alcohol, and opposed concubinage and prostitution.[29] So profound was the influence of Christianity in opening up the whole field of social work in Japan and in affecting social consciousness that for the subsequent century social work in Japan continued to be a key area of Christian involvement and witness. But this activity influenced Japanese society in a wider way, too, as evident in the view that even "the socialist movement in Japan. . . owes its beginnings to Christianity."[30]

In the modernization process as a whole Christianity was seen as a positive, utilitarian means to Westernization.[31] Not only Christians saw Christianity this way. Despite the fact that Christian journals of the time were openly critical of the Japanese government, it was generally considered that Christianity could serve as "a progressive ideology which would provide the spiritual foundation for a modern civil state."[32] The degree to which Christianity was viewed in this way is evident in the fact that the Japanese government actually went so far as to debate adopting Christianity as the national religion.[33] It is clear, though, that besides the concern for an ideology to undergird the state, there was also consideration of what benefits Christianity could bring to Japan in terms of international trade and relationships. Underlying such a perspective, obviously, was the idea of accepting Christianity only in form, while keeping the inner Japanese spirit and culture uncontaminated.[34]

The reception of Christianity in Japan was not entirely or consistently positive, however. Memories of the previous ban and subjugation of Christianity lingered, and where Christianity was perceived as an alien religion, representing Western dangers and undermining traditional Japanese culture, it met stiff resistance. With a rise in nationalistic fervor in the 1880's anti-Christian sentiments grew strong. Opposition came from renascent Buddhist and Shinto religious groups as well as from political parties that criticized Christianity as a foreign religion. As the government developed the educational system pioneered by the churches, schools became centers for nationalism, with an increasing emphasis on imperial authority associated with Shinto values.[35] According to one prominent Christian leader of the time, the ill will towards Christianity in the late 1880's was "difficult to exaggerate."[36]

Christians, in turn, even those non-liberals who were part of the nationalistic fervor of the era, themselves devoted to Japan, felt it necessary to resist the growing anti-Christian pressures around them.[37] Tensions came to an historical head with the issue of the Imperial Rescript on Education in 1890, which promulgated emperor exaltation[38] and thus laid the foundation for emperor divinization and the Shinto national cult that eventually justified Japan's initiation of the Pacific war.

In an incident that became known throughout Japan, a young Christian teacher named Kanzo Uchimura refused on the grounds of his Christian convictions to bow to the imperial Rescript as required by law.[39] His singular resistance to the government became a rallying point for many in the church and brought to public awareness the fact that Christianity was now established as a religion of Japanese people, too, and, moreover, of Japanese people who were like Uchimura, ardent nationalists. At any rate, by the turn of the century, resistance to Christianity had somewhat receded, and Christianity had even begun to enter a successful dialogue with Buddhism, previously a source of opposition.[40]

In regard to Christianity's overall relationship to Buddhism and to other religions in Japan in this early period, several observations may be made. First of all, it is to be remembered that Confucianism and Buddhism, two of the dominant religions, were themselves imports to Japan. Both had, as Christianity, at one time been foreign religions in Japan, but had been indigenized over many centuries. Both were altered in the process; both had affected Japanese society; and both had offered foundations on which Christianity could successfully build when it arrived.

Although Buddhism was received in a selective, piecemeal fashion in Japan,[41] and in a way that did not upset the existing order,[42] it nevertheless introduced significant new elements into the Japanese way of thinking. Whereas in the traditional Japanese perspective, there was no sense of ultimacy, no radical break between the sacred and the secular,[43] Buddhism presented the notion of an ultimate truth. Such an idea presented at least a precedent for the later coming of Christianity's truth claims.[44] Similarly, because various schools of Buddhism in Japan had also established concepts of salvation and a reality beyond this world, Christianity was first conveyed in Buddhist salvation terms.[45]

Likewise, Confucianism provided starting points for Christian faith and proclamation. It was a concern for ethics, grounded in Confucianism and nurtured through Bushido, that many samurai saw reflected in Puritan Christianity. Correspondingly, it was the sense of loyalty fostered by Confucianism and Bushido which these samurai transferred to Christ in their conversions that grounded and sustained their faith, especially as a minority group in turbulent times.[46]

Part of the reason that Christian ethics and faith attracted people at this time was that the Confucianism of the day had itself become legalistic and lifeless.[47] As Confucian ethics waned, Christian ethics gained.[48] Various converts to Christianity themselves described Confucianism as thus preparing the way for Christianity.[49]

Naturally, the first Japanese converts to Christianity brought with them the perspectives of their previous faiths. Confucian converts saw Christianity as a means of implementing Confucian patterns. Shinto converts, who had little concept of a personal god or individual soul, struggled with such Christian notions. Buddhist converts saw Christianity as a fulfillment of Buddhism or at least in harmony with it.[50]

At any rate, Christianity attracted followers from each of Japan's major religions. Although this created some tensions, the general relationship between Christianity, Buddhism and Confucianism was good. Each of them was tolerated by the government; each prospered.[51] But as Japan moved into the twentieth century, Shinto, which under government favor had been on the rise all through the latter half of the nineteenth century,[52] eventually came to dominate the religious scene in Japan and to cause major difficulties for Christianity.

General Features

Having examined the samurai influence on early Protestant Christianity in Japan and having surveyed Christianity's wider impact and relationships in society, it remains to add a few further comments on other general features of early Japanese Protestant Christianity.

As noted already, it was a strongly ethical brand of Christianity. But the Christianity which the missionaries brought to Japan was also very evangelical and emotional.[53] While the ethical aspects found a response in the zeal of the samurai,

Japanese stoicism[54] and the lack of emphasis on the individual in Japanese society meant that the missionaries' efforts to evangelize along emotional, individualistic lines were seriously hampered. However, the impact of Western education and values contributed to an increased awareness of the individual in society, which in turn fostered more individual spiritual struggles.[55] This, in conjunction with the radical social changes, contributed to a religious revival in the 1880's that drew some important converts into the Christian faith and at the same time helped redirect Protestant Christianity from its ethical emphasis to a concern for deep personal experience.[56] Although this revivalism resulted subsequently in faith that was too subjective and individualistic,[57] it was a helpful step in further rooting Christianity at the time.

Being ethical, evangelical and emotional in emphasis, this early Protestant Christianity, as fostered and influenced primarily by American missionaries,[58] was not highly theological. Unsystematic in its theology, it could not be characterized either as liberal or non-liberal.[59] But beginning in the late 1880's and continuing for several decades, German theological liberalism became increasingly popular in Japan, along with utilitarianism and other European philosophical and scientific trends of thought.[60] In some sectors of the Japanese Christian community theological liberalism, utilitarian interests, and lack of a solid, systematic base in Christian Scripture, tradition, and creeds led to an over-accommodation with Japanese culture. Such liberalism, having lost its prophetic potential, generally succumbed to the pressures of nationalism that were directed against the church in this period.[61]

However, there were those in the church who resisted both the pressures from within Japan and those from without. For, very early in Japan, there was an interest in indigenizing Christianity.[62] Japanese Christians, who themselves feared the encroachment of the West on Japan, or who wanted to demonstrate the independence of Japanese Christianity from the domination of Western churches[63] endeavored to "Japanize" Christianity, even to produce a type of Christianity that transcended that of the West.[64]

Chief among proponents of this sort of Japanese Christianity was Kanzo Uchimura and his followers in what later came to be known as the "Non-Church Movement" of Japan. Seeing a radical simplification of Christianity as the means for its indigenization in Japan,[65] and believing that Christian freedom allowed Japanese Christian spirituality to develop its own forms, quite different from those in the West,[66] the Non-Church movement became an independent Japanese church, without the type of buildings, clergy, liturgy and doctrine that typified most of Japanese Christianity. As such, it was recognized as an "authentic" Japanese church.

Yet, other groups of Japanese Christians were also seriously concerned with establishing themselves as authentic Japanese churches, independent of the West.

Thus there was, for instance, a strong movement to achieve financial independence at an early stage.[67] Also, as part of its endeavor to demonstrate its independence and authenticity, the wider church in Japan sought to exhibit an ecumenical unity, to transcend the denominational differences introduced by the Western missionaries.[68] These endeavors bore fruit not only then, but also decades later in the formation of a union of Protestant churches in Japan called the *Kyodan* or United Church of Christ in Japan (Koyama's church), which is today the largest of Japan's Protestant churches. However, the movements toward unity and independence did not stem from blanket animosity towards Western Christianity and culture. As mentioned earlier, many Japanese Christians looked to Christianity and the West as the source of renewal for Japanese society. Moreover, one of the salient features of early Japanese Christianity was the exceptional closeness between converts and missionaries, their good relationships and strong unity of spirit.[69]

Summary

All in all, the early decades of Protestant Christianity in Japan were critical in establishing patterns and structures that continued to influence the church in the century to come. Koyama was a product of that church, and while specific correspondence between Koyama's theology and church developments of this period are indirect, this period nevertheless produced some of the figures and concerns which were later to have an effect on Koyama.

Finally, it may be noted in passing that it was towards the end of this period that Koyama's grandfather was introduced to Christianity. The fact that Koyama's grandfather, who was not a samurai, became a Christian as the result of meeting a lay British missionary who came to Japan on his own rather than with a missionary society, Koyama sees as a positive factor in the formation of his own theology. For, Herbert Brand, the Cambridge-educated British missionary who introduced Koyama's grandfather to Christianity, was someone who exhibited a respect for Japanese culture as he found it, and did not insist on a conversion to Western patterns of faith and culture. Likewise, because Brand came on his own cognizance rather than as agent of a mission society, his message was perhaps seen as less colored by institutional interests.[70]

Thus it can be seen that Koyama's own theological heritage had unusual elements in it, deriving from his own family experience. However, the fact that Koyama grew up and was educated in the Protestant church of Japan meant that his faith and theology was also influenced by that environment. He did not, like many

Japanese Christians, remain outside the main Protestant church in one of the numerous small splinter groups of Christian fellowship.

Koyama's own direct theological heritage was that of twentieth-century events and figures. These are presented briefly in the following sections.

Early Twentieth Century and War Years

Theological Developments

By the turn of the century the Protestant church in Japan had moved into a new stage in its development. Proselytizing tapered off considerably by 1910;[71] numerous stable churches had been established. Christians had already met with considerable success in founding schools and hospitals and in leading social reforms. They enjoyed a reasonably wide degree of public acceptance. The first decades of this century were, then, a period of consolidation and some growth, characterized especially by continued active involvement of Christians in social work. No one epitomized this social involvement more than Toyohiko Kagawa, whose extraordinary efforts in such areas as slum clearance, worker's cooperatives, agricultural development and disaster relief won him international acclaim.[72]

During this period, too, the viability of indigenized Japanese Christianity emerged in the form of the Non-Church movement, which combined a fervor for the Japanese national heritage with a dedication to Jesus Christ. Its leaders, who came primarily from the intelligentsia,[73] dispensed with traditional Western church patterns, believing that the essence of the Gospel was not related to and did not require ecclesiastical forms.[74] While this group naturally engendered controversy, it nevertheless later attracted the attention of various European theologians, Emil Brunner among them,[75] who deemed it a unique and legitimate type of indigenized Christianity in Japan.

From the 1890's until the 1930's German philosophy and liberal theology in particular came to the fore in the Japanese Protestant church.[76] This may have been facilitated in part by the compatibility of liberal theology with Japanese social concerns. Conservative evangelical theology, which dwelt on individual sinfulness and the need for individual conversion, continued to arouse tensions in the non-individualistic, community orientated culture of Japan.

German liberal theology, along with the Social Gospel movement in the U.S.A., fed into the Student Christian Movement in Japan, which sought to address the need for social changes and justice in the turbulent years preceding World War

Two. Believing that theology was to be derived from personal experience and social crises, and believing that salvation consisted of selflessly building the kingdom of God through overcoming the "sins" of social injustice and selfishness, the SCM sought a total integration of society and Christianity. Initially opposed to Marxism, the SCM soon became a radically Marxist organization itself.[77] Opposition from the mainline Protestant church, government pressure and internal dissension soon led to the demise of the Japanese SCM[78] which in turn reflected the death of liberal theology in Japan as a whole and the loss of a prophetic voice in the Japanese social context.[79]

For, by the late 1930's, liberalism in Japanese theology was on the way out. The post-World War One optimism with which it was associated had faded. Political and economic strife was again increasing; pessimism predominated.[80] Liberal theology had been strong in Japan through its creative concern for the relationship between faith and culture, church and society.[81] Most of the extensive social work that had been done in Japan was carried out by liberals.[82] However, liberal theology proved weak in its diluted understanding of human sinfulness, in its propensity towards compromise, and its connection of faith and social issues in inappropriate ways.[83]

Thus, the 1930's saw the return of conservative Reformation theology,[84] especially in its dialectical, Barthian forms.[85] It was a theology directed both against purely individualistic, subjective faith and against liberalism. Emphasizing God as subject and humanity as object, this theology called into question the grounding of truth in religious experience.[86] Likewise, it attacked the kind of social Christianity in Japan which some believed had "forgotten the basic problem of Christianity. . . to traffic in a cheap spiritualism and optimistic evolution."[87]

Dialectical theology in Japan also addressed itself to the question of ethics, which continued to have special significance in Japan. It provided a more biblical, dogmatic base for Christian ethics, emphasizing ethical behavior as a matter of obedient love, a faith response to the experience of forgiveness. This theology also re-introduced the idea of eschatological tension between the future kingdom of God and present human society—in distinct contrast to the then current views of Biblical liberal theology.[88]

There were some alternatives to these dialectical views in remnants of socialist Christianity and in groups which emphasized the Holy Spirit and personal experience.[89] But dialectical theology prevailed during the late 1930's and the 1940's, and Barthian theology in particular became the preoccupation of numerous Japanese theologians.

By this time, too, Japanese theology had assumed the structures of Western theology. Japan's main theologians, at least those recognized as such, were those who adopted the doctrinal concerns and dogmatic forms of Western theology. Thus various Japanese theologians addressed themselves to traditional doctrines regarding the church, ethics, personal salvation, and so on.[90]

But there were a few Japanese Christians who envisioned a more original type of Japanese theology. One of those was Kanzo Uchimura who envisioned a pure form of Christianity coming out of Japan to rejuvenate all Christianity.[91] (Uchimura's theology will be taken up in more detail later.)

The War Year

Throughout the early decades of this century, Japanese society continued to undergo major changes as a result of its exposure to the West. Japan's incursions into Korea and Mongolia reflected her growing power and changing political vision. Naturally, social and political changes brought economic pressures that were compounded by the depression of the 1930's. In this milieu Japanese nationalism flourished. Focused on the person of the emperor and fortified by the increasingly pervasive doctrines of state Shinto, aggressive nationalism became the dominant ideology of the day.

As in other periods of resurgent nationalism (e.g., in the seventeenth-century and again in the 1880's) this meant intensified pressure on the Christian church, and in some cases outright persecution. All through the 1930's there was active legal and religious resistance to Christianity.[92] Inevitably, the church, as a fragmented, minority institution, was forced to make choices in response to government pressures and policies.

A key response came in 1941 when the government, for purposes of control and indeed to foster inter-church dissension, required the various denominational bodies to consolidate into one representative Christian organization.[93] To its credit, this government-instituted church, taking the name *Kyodan*, or United Church of Christ in Japan, succeeded in establishing an ecumenical institution that eventually emerged from the war as Japan's leading Protestant church. However, during the war, it generally succumbed to the pressures of the government.

Overall, there were three sorts of responses to government pressure.[94] Christians of the liberal theological school in Japan tended towards a syncretism of faith that accommodated itself to the aims and actions of the government. Those of a more Barthian persuasion opted for a dualism that distinguished between matters of temporal government and matters of divine revelation and eternal salvation. Conservatives, however, those belonging to the school of Biblical orthodoxy, opted for resistance to the government.

The *Kyodan* consisted predominantly of Christians in the liberal and Barthian schools of thought, and thus ended up supporting, or at least not actively resisting, government policies. One such Christian theologian in this latter category was Kazoh Kitamori, who, though not a Barthian, counselled that a theology of resistance was neither necessary nor appropriate to the Japanese situation. Kitamori, schooled in a Lutheran dual kingdom understanding of church and society, maintained that to preach the Word alone was sufficient (though by the end of the war Kitamori was saying that the church must preach theology of the pain of God over against the theology of the Word).[95] Moreover, he argued, and with good reason, the situation of Christians in Japan was significantly different from the position of Christians in Germany at the time. Japanese society, for example, lacked the Christian heritage upon which any appeals to Christian values could be based.[96] At any rate, as a tiny and recently converted minority in a radically different cultural context, Japanese Christians had neither the distance from their own cultural indoctrination nor the acceptance of their surrounding culture to make a prophetic impact.

The lack of a prophetic voice stood in contrast to the active and critical role played by Christians in the arena of social reform before dialectic theology and government pressure subdued social Christianity and such movements as the SCM.[97] But it also reflected the growing institutional self-interest of the church. Concerned for self-preservation, the church tended increasingly toward complicity with social or governmental interests. This tendency was compounded by the leadership of the church which, consistent with the cultural patterns of Japan's hierarchical society, was motivated more by its paternal responsibility, e.g., for protecting the community, than by the critical demands of the Gospel.[98]

The end result of such factors as these was *Kyodan* support and approval for the government actions of World War Two. The *Kyodan*, for example, sent clergy to assist in the administration and thus domination of Korea. In 1944 the *Koyodan* even went so far as to publish a statement of government propaganda calling Western churches the enemy of Asia and proclaiming Japanese Christianity to have been perfected in that it resisted individualism, socialism and communism.[99] This complicity in the war efforts of Japan was an issue which naturally led to painful memories later, and finally issued in a controversial statement of confession by the *Kyodan* in 1967.[100]

However, there were Protestant Christians in Japan during the war who chose a different path of witness, that of resistance. Most of those Christians who resisted were from smaller, less institutionalized churches, groups often considered heretical by other churches.[101] Included were Christians whose strong eschatological convictions relativized all earthly powers, which meant that they could not accept the absolute or divine status of the emperor.[102] Other Christians opposed the government on the basis of pacifism or opposition to Shinto.[103] Leaders of Holiness churches and of Korean churches in particular resisted the government and suffered for it.[104] In the latter case, Korean Christians suffered not only for their theological convictions but also for their ethnic and political resistance to Japanese domination.

In the end the war years represented a time of challenge to Japanese Christianity, challenge which produced a combination of success and failure, a testimony of both complicity and heroism. For Koyama, these were definitive years. For it was his experience of war that triggered his theology. Although Koyama was not a participant in the theological and institutional events of the church during this period, his teachers were. Moreover, it was this legacy that he inherited as a theology student and later as a clergyman of the *Kyodan*.

Koyama has had to deal with some of the main issues that came out of this period. Not only has a deep concern for the dynamics of emperor worship emerged as a dominant theme of his entire theology, but also, Koyama has felt it necessary to comment on such issues as the failure of the Japanese church to deal with the burning issues of the war years, the courage of those who resisted, and the role of the church in Japanese society as brought into question in recent years.

Koyama's concern that the Japanese church failed to deal with the burning issues of the war years stems from personal experience. He recalls in particular the fact that his seminary education did not deal very much with the war trials that were going on then in Japan. So far had the Japanese theological education system bought into Western theological interests that it was failing to address the crucial, immediate issues of Japan. Koyama, who as a student was then reading Brunner's writings on Christian ethics, realized that such study was irrelevant to the Japanese situation. "I was," he says, "a victim" of a theological education that dealt with a totally different language and framework than that of his culture.[105] While this situation reflected the dominance of Western culture, and the inadequacy of Western theological education, it also illustrated the acquiescence of the Japanese church and its problem in finding an authentic, definitive theology for its own cultural situation.

Koyama's intense concern for the dangers of emperor worship—or, in broader terms, the absolutization of any ideology—is poignantly expressed in Koyama's account of some of those Christians who courageously resisted and criticized their government. In his writing Koyama remembers one protester, a follower of Kanzo Uchimura, who was throughout the war harassed by the government, and one Holiness church pastor whose critical testimony against the government brought him imprisonment and death.[106]

That Koyama continues to be interested in church issues in Japan and that he feels responsible to respond to them, surfaces in such places as his meditation, "Japan Expo '70."[107] There he touches on an intense controversy that rocked the *Kyodan* throughout the 1970's. While Koyama's comment on this issue is very brief, it gives evidence of a continuing relationship to and concern for the church from which he came. This relationship is renewed through Koyama's trips to Japan, which include theological discussions to which Koyama contributes as both a speaker and a writer.

Post-War Years

Initial Developments

An entirely new situation prevailed in Japan at the close of World War Two. Never before had Japan been defeated in war with a foreign power. Not in two thousand years had she been occupied by an alien army. Now her economy was shattered; her people, exhausted and dazed. The national myths that had justified and sustained the war and which had inspired people to great personal sacrifice, especially the myth of the emperor's divinity, had now been suddenly and summarily debunked. Inescapably, Japan stood at a crossroads of her history in which nearly all her values and social structures were being called into question.

Naturally the church was dramatically affected by the new situation. Almost immediately, for a variety of reasons, it gained a new prestige. Many people associated Shinto with defeat and turned to the religion of their conquerors as an apparently superior religion. In a time of great spiritual vacuum, many sought in Christianity a new source of spiritual fulfillment and guidance.[108] Others simply turned to Christianity as a vehicle for deriving Western material or social benefits, as numerous Japanese had done nearly a century earlier. Thus, the decade after World War Two was one of accelerated numerical growth for the Christian church in Japan.

On a national level, the church gained a new significance in Japan in relation to the American occupation itself and the introduction of a multitude of Western ideas, values and social structures. Above all, the Occupation meant the introduction of a democratic constitution and laws to a society that had never before experienced such a form of social organization. The church, as an agency that had firm, established ties with Western culture, became a conduit for the transfer of democratic values to the new society. Moreover, it became a public forum for discussion of the issues of defeat and occupation.[109] The church even became involved in the restructuring of Japan's post-war labor order and business hierarchy.[110]

As a result of the sheer misery that prevailed at the end of the war, the church, again as a channel of funds and concern from Western churches, became the predominant social welfare agency in the country, being drawn into relief and reconstruction work on a grand scale.[111] While this produced major strains within the church itself, it nevertheless enhanced the church's position in the society.

In the new situation of the post-war years, obviously, the church's relationship with the government changed considerably. Because the government leaders of the war years were so closely allied with the state Shinto that had led to defeat, it was not so surprising that a Japan occupied by American forces elected a Christian prime minister in a government that included a notable number of Christians in the cabinet and in parliament.[112] This development established a precedent in that Christians have continued to take an active part in national government even into the present day.[113]

Theological Shifts

Japan's military defeat and the radical social changes that ensued precipitated changes in the theological climate as well. The uncritical complicity of the larger Protestant churches in Japan during the war led to a re-evaluation of predominant war-time theological currents. Above all, Japanese Barthian theology came under strong attack as having produced uncritical individualism and obedience to the State.[114] Barthian theology was hotly criticized as pietistic, non-functional in the Japanese situation, and as affirming a corrupt status quo. In more general terms, dialectic theology was criticized for giving insufficient attention to personal religious experience and for being much too intellectual to be effective in communication with and evangelization of the masses.[115]

Theological attention was thus turned in other directions in the post-war years, especially as newer theological currents flowed into Japan through her renewed contacts with America and Europe. In a church reacting to its past and struggling with the complexities of restructuring a society, a church itself extensively involved in social endeavors, the theology of people like Reinhold Niebuhr, Paul Tillich and Emil Brunner had fresh appeal. These theologians, in turn, personally responded to the Japanese Protestant church through study, correspondence and even visits to Japan.[116] Thus, the Japanese theological spectrum broadened, and in its subsequent encounter with other theological perspectives continued a pattern of diversification.

One aspect of Japan's post-war theological development was, naturally, an intensified search for a theology indigenous to the Japanese situation, i.e., a theology that both grew out of and spoke to the Japanese experience. Such a theology emerged at the very end of the war from the hand of Kazoh Kitamori. His painful wrestling with the Japanese experience of war and defeat led him to formulate what he called a "theology of the pain of God."[117] This theology related the intense Japanese experience of tragedy with the experience of God in Israel's history and with the experience of Jesus at the cross. It took up a theme that had been carried by Christians in different ways before the war, e.g. by Toyohiko Kagawa and by the SCM,[118] namely, the theme of pouring one's self out for others as a witness to God's love or as a means of heralding God's kingdom.

Kitamori and others, such as the Christian novelist, Shusaku Endo, believed that the sense and experience of tragedy that permeated the Japanese consciousness could enable Japanese Christians to identify in a unique way with the experience of the cross. Japanese Christians could therefore make a unique contribution to Christian theology in terms of their understanding of God and God's way of working in the world.[119] This theology, which was received by the West as some of the first original theology from Asia also served to help Christianity seem less alien to Japan.[120]

Recent Japanese Theology

Under the influence of imported Western theology for more than a century, Japanese theology naturally reflected the characteristics and concerns of that theology. Those Japanese theologians who garnered attention were often those like Seiichi Hatano[121] or Yoshitaka Kumano—called by some the "giant of Japanese theology"[122]—who dealt with predominant themes in Western systematic theology such as salvation, eschatology, church history, Christology and ecclesiology. Even in the last few decades the theological debate in Japan has followed that of the West, particularly in regard to philosophy of religion and the perspectives of Karl Barth and Emil Brunner.[123]

However, more recently, shifts have begun to occur in both the content and understanding of theology in Japan. Beginning with Kanzo Uchimura, there were Japanese theologians who envisioned a unique form of Christian theology—indeed a pure form of Christianity[124]—coming out of Japan. Uchimura believed that as the

West was losing its Christian foundations, the Christians of Japan should revitalize Christianity for the sake of the world.[125]

Kazoh Kitamori, although he felt that Uchimura's view of Japanese Christianity was inspired much more by nationalism than by the Gospel,[126] shared Uchimura's global vision, believing that what the Japanese people had to offer to Christianity as a whole—particularly in terms of their understanding of the pain of God—would be comparable in effect to the Reformation.[127] Kitamori saw Japanese theology as a theology liberated from the drawbacks of Greek and German ideological traditions and therefore able to offer fresh insights to Christianity.[128] Just as Europe had produced various theologies, so Kitamori considered it natural and necessary that in response to the world's expectations Christians in Japan should produce a theology of their own.[129]

At the other end of the spectrum there are those who maintain that Japan has as yet little theology of her own, and that that is in fact good, given the Japanese tendency towards insularity.[130] Others decry the "Germanic captivity" of Japanese theology—the tendency to be so preoccupied with German theology that many Japanese theologians will not even read each other's writings.[131]

Modern Japanese theologians recognize that they can no longer take their cue from the West. The world of "corpus Christianium" in which missionaries from Christian countries in the West evangelized people from such non-Christian lands as Japan, is gone, if indeed it ever existed.[132] Today, Christian witness in Japan must be in independent, indigenous terms, relevant and prophetic to the Japanese situation. Even some Western theologians recognize today that they have communicated too much Western theology as if it were faith itself, thus preventing theology from becoming relevant to or a reflection of the faith of Japanese Christians.[133]

As a result of the various shifts in Japanese Christian theology, that theology is now more confident and independent. Building on a basis of Biblical orthodoxy, it is developing a strong mission emphasis based on belief in what humanity with God's grace can do as opposed to what humanity without grace cannot do.[134] Western observers note that Japanese theology, having naturally and necessarily borrowed for a time from the West, now seems to be standing on its own two feet. The time has indeed come for the West to look to Japan to see what is may glean from their experience.[135]

Koyama is an obvious example of what Japan has to offer to Christianity on a global scale. Of course Koyama's theology is shaped nearly as much by his experiences outside Japan as by his experiences there. But he remains, to a striking degree, given his broad exposure, an offspring of his mother culture and church. Koyama thus has the unusual advantage of having deep roots in a particular cultural and religious heritage while at the same time having been able to branch out into an exceptionally wide field of human experience and theological exposure.

Koyama's relationship to the post-World War II period of Japanese church experience demonstrates both his connection with it and his detachment from it. Already referred to was the enormous impact that Koyama's experience of war had on his theological "birth." Also mentioned was the centrality of the theme of emperor worship and its related issues in Koyama's theology. Recently, these and other themes have been emerging more and more in Koyama's theology with particular reference to the Japanese scene of his youth. The experiences of that time he sees as crucially relevant to the present.

At the same time, in assessing Koyama's relationship to the post-war period in Japanese church history, it must be remembered that Koyama was not a first-hand participant in the church during these times. In 1952 he left Japan, almost penniless but with a one-way ticket paid for by collections from the American military chaplaincy,[136] to study theology at Drew University in New Jersey. After spending ten years in the United States, supporting himself with various jobs, including work in a mental hospital and acting as an interpreter for government-sponsored Japanese visitors to America,[137] Koyama finished a Ph.D. in theology and accepted a call to become one of the *Kyodan's* first overseas missionaries, going to Thailand in 1960. This meant that for over thirty years—more than half of his life—Koyama did not live in Japan. Thus, his later theological development was largely independent from the currents of theology predominant in Japan over the last three decades.

Nevertheless, the foundations for Koyama's theology were clearly laid in Japan. His inheritance from particular Japanese theologians is explored in more detail below. In the meantime, some general connections between Koyama's theology and modern Japanese theology may be briefly noted.

The drift away from Western dominance which has typified Japan's theology in recent years was an element in Koyama's world-view, too. Implicit in Koyama's experience of seminary education in Japan—with its Western bias being irrelevant to the critical issues of Japanese society—was a disillusionment not only with his own church and society, but also with Western theology. Later, having had considerable first-hand exposure to the West, having experienced its benefits and having even married an American, Koyama nevertheless began to develop a sharp critique of the Western impact on Asia—a critique much in tune with the perspective of other Asian and Japanese theologians. Koyama's critique of Western dominance expressed itself even in the form of his theology. Its narrative style signaled a sharp, deliberate break with Western theological methodology.

Like other Japanese theologians, Koyama laments the complicity of the Japanese church with the government in World War Two.[138] Like other Japanese theologians, he senses and explores the impact of traditional Japanese values and contemporary experiences on theology.[139] Also, like many others in Japan, he considers Christianity's relationship to Japan's other religions and the contributions they have made to Japanese ethics and spirituality.[140]

Furthermore, Koyama, as a product of an Asian culture in which Christians are a tiny minority, is keenly aware of the complex challenges facing Christianity in the non-Western world. Although he does not address himself to the particularity of the Japanese situation, many of the issues Koyama discusses relate to Japan as well as to other parts of Asia. At the same time, because Koyama knows what it is to belong to a minority group counter to the mainstream of the surrounding culture, he can also be more critical of Christianity. He knows first-hand the strength and worth of other religions and world-views.

Thus, while Koyama is not a Japanese theologian in the sense that he deals exclusively with Japanese concerns, he is a Japanese theologian in a broader sense, having derived many of his main themes from the Japanese scene, utilizing the language and culture of Japan to inform his theology, and sharing the insights of his Japanese background with a global audience. In this latter way, Koyama continues the task of people like Uchimura and Kitamori who sought to formulate an indigenous Japanese theology which contributes to Christianity worldwide.

In a still broader sense, Koyama may be seen as a product of the whole century-long development of Japanese theology. Initially focused on practical and ethical concerns, Japanese Protestant Christianity went through a subsequent stage of subjectivism when faith became personal and internalized. In reaction liberalism developed with a strong emphasis on social reform. Dialectical theology moved Japanese Christianity to the abstract level from the preceding practical, emotional and social levels. As the aridity of abstract theology stultified Christianity, Koyama and others developed an existential kind of theology that could do justice to the multiple levels of Christian life and faith. Koyama thus consciously or unconsciously draws together various pieces of the Christian tradition that he has inherited from both East and West.

That Koyama ends up at a point that is particularly relevant to the current Japanese scene is apparent from the reflection of another outstanding Japanese theologian, Masatoshi Doi. In the widespread contemporary search for meaning in Japan, the church is inescapably led to a deeper theology of mission. Its need is to focus not on systematic theology and church dogma but on the contemporary history and experience of Japanese people.[141] Masatoshi Doi, as an existential evangelist in the current Japanese milieu, believes that it is the missionary task of the church to find the meaning structures that will communicate to people the ultimate meaning of

Jesus' Cross and Resurrection. Appropriate language, in other words, is the key to Christian proclamation, and it is the contribution of theology to find that language.[142]

Here, Koyama comes in as one who has worked diligently at creating a new theological language, not only for the Japanese scene, but also for Christianity in general. His theology, built on human experience and informed by critical scholarship—as opposed to theology which is built on church dogma and then abstractly related to human experience—offers a language to which people can more readily respond. In this sense, Koyama addresses the Japanese scene, the more so because he uses so many Japanese events as reference points.

Living outside of Japan and being absorbed with theology on a more global scale, Koyama will inevitably be out of touch with the exigencies of modern Japanese theology and society. He himself tells of spending an initial day or two watching television when he returns to Japan for visits, just in order to keep up with changes in the language, not to mention catching up with topical trends.[143] Nevertheless, because of the background, content, and nature of Koyama's theology, Koyama can legitimately be considered an authentic Japanese theologian.

CHAPTER THREE

SPECIFIC INFLUENCES

A consideration of Koyama's Japanese theological background would be incomplete without taking brief note of a few Japanese theologians who have made a special impact on Koyama or who have stood out as key figures on the Japanese Christian scene in Koyama's time.

Toyohiko Kagawa 1888–1960

Into the latter category fits Toyohiko Kagawa, the great social reformer of Japan. A man of many laurels, Kagawa has been called "one of the greatest Christians of the twentieth-century,"[1] "the creative, dynamic initiator and promoter of almost every movement for constructive social reform in Japan for more than forty years,"[2] a man whose work and witness continues to affect the ethical ideas and social awareness of even the current generation of Japanese.[3]

An intense, idealistic, highly motivated man, Kagawa both physically and spiritually poured himself out in service to Japan's poor and downtrodden in the decades before and immediately following World War Two. He was a man of exceptional literary talents, for which he was recognized throughout Japan. Adept at many fields of study, more meditative than systematic, he brought to his theology such diverse perspectives that as a theologian he is said to have lacked "ultimate internal unity."[4] For Kagawa, theology was secondary to evangelism and social action.

In some of these ways similarities between Koyama and Kagawa are already apparent. Like Kagawa, Koyama is an intense, highly motivated theologian, one with exceptional literary abilities and with a curiosity that carries him into fields beyond the common scope of theology. Like Kagawa, Koyama is more concerned with evangelism, with communication and application of the Christian message than with abstract reflections and formulations of it. However, unlike Kagawa, Koyama has not channeled his faith into the arena of social reform. Instead, he seeks to address the main ideological issues that shape the modern global scene, e.g., militarism, the encounter between different cultures, and the encounter between religions.

Koyama and Kagawa share further basic tenets in their understanding of God and his work in the world. Kenosis was for Kagawa, as it is for Koyama, an important concept. Kagawa's chief image of God was of a God who continues to suffer in the reconciliation between God and humanity.[5] The cross was for Kagawa the center of God-consciousness for the believer, and the center of redemptive love. As people are redeemed, so must they act with the kind of redemptive love that suffers for others.[6]

The parallels between this perspective and Koyama's are strong. He, too, prescribes a life of self-denying love that patterns itself on the cross. For, participation in God's self-denial as exhibited at the cross is the key to faithful Christian discipleship.

Where Kagawa and Koyama diverge in their thinking is perhaps in the area of eschatology. Kagawa's social labors reflected his extreme optimism about human nature, his belief that human beings can realize the kingdom of God by their own cooperative efforts. Koyama, with his experience of the destruction humanity is capable of wreaking, does not pursue this line, though he is not, on the other hand, comfortable with a pessimistic picture of sinful humanity, lost, hopeless and unable to change their situation.[7]

At any rate, Koyama does not speak in terms of establishing the kingdom of God on earth, as did Kagawa and others of his time. Neither does he altogether relegate the kingdom to a future moment. Rather, for Koyama this is not in itself a primary topic of discussion.

In the end, Koyama and Kagawa share a peculiar public image. For just as Kagawa was seen as a confusing blend of East and West, not readily understood by either,[8] so is Koyama often perceived.

Kanzo Uchimura 1861–1930

Some attention has already been given to one of Japan's most famous Christians, Kanzo Uchimura. Founder of the Non-Church Movement, champion of the independence of Japanese Christianity from the West, Uchimura is also the figure whom Koyama considers most influential in his own theological formation.[9]

Uchimura gained prominence in 1891 when as a young teacher he publicly refused to "bow in worship" to a government decree. Two years later his first book, which became a Japanese Christian classic, was published,[10] establishing him as a Christian leader. Not long after that Uchimura became a pacifist, opposing Japan's war against Russia. Because the church in general supported the war,

Uchimura drew heavy criticism from the church and lost the support of one of his main defenders, Masahisa Uemura.[11]

Uchimura, for his pacifism and criticism of the government was nonetheless an ardent nationalist. His passion for Christianity combined with a passion for his Japanese heritage led him to describe his faith as an ellipse with two centers—Christ and Japan—each of which strengthened and clarified the other.[12] Uchimura's pride in Japan fed a zeal for the independence of Japanese Christianity from Western forms, as exhibited in the Non-Church Movement. To Uchimura, "When a Japanese truly and independently believes in Christ, he is a Japanese Christian, and his Christianity is Japanese Christianity."[13] Uchimura, as mentioned earlier, even envisioned a pure form of Christianity emerging from Japan to rejuvenate Christianity worldwide.[14] For his gravestone Uchimura summarized his view in this way:

> I for Japan
> Japan for the World
> The World for Christ
> And all for God.[15]

It is in some ways surprising that Koyama feels particularly influenced by Uchimura. While they share on the basis of their Christian faith a great resistance to the divinization or absolutization of any human being or institution, and consequently are willing to take critical and sometimes controversial positions in regard to government policies, they on the other hand have very different approaches to issues of nationalism.

Uchimura belonged to the class of samurai disinherited from power and status earlier in the nineteenth-century. That class, believing that the policies of the new government and the encroachments of the West were a danger to Japanese traditions had a natural interest in criticizing the government and in working for the independence of Japanese institutions, including the adopted faith of Christianity.

Koyama, on the other hand, himself a product of an era when Japan's nationalism was at its peak, had an altogether different experience of nationalism, one that convinced him for decades to come of the destructive potential of Japanese nationalism.

Also as a samurai, Uchimura was intensely anti-clerical, and pursued theological studies only with the condition (in a pledge to God) that he not be required to become a clergyman. "It were better for me to die than what I should become a salaried minister."[16] Koyama, on the other hand, became a clergyman and a representative on the traditional church, though his ministry, too, was at the academic rather than the congregational level.

Both Uchimura and Koyama studied in the United States. For Uchimura, despite many inspiring personal contacts, this period shattered his idealistic illusion of Christianity in the West and fed an antipathy that caused him later even to turn down a prestigious teaching position in Japan because it was supported by Western funds.[17] For Koyama, although he has remarkably little to say about these ten years of his life spent in the U.S.A. and although there are occasional traces of actual antipathy to the West in Koyama, by and large Koyama's experience in the U.S. was not as influential as Uchimura's was on his theological attitudes. However, Koyama had the opportunity to spend many years outside Japan in various locales, years which convinced him of the relative nature of Japanese society and Japanese Christianity. Thus, Koyama entertains no visions such as Uchimura had that Japan will demonstrate a superior morality or pure Christianity to the rest of the world. Koyama's awareness of the complicity of the Japanese church with the government in World War Two tempers any such vision.

One further point of distinction between Koyama and Uchimura rests in their following. Uchimura stayed in Japan, attracting a cadre of like-minded samurai followers and others whose personal loyalty to Uchimura kept the Non-Church Movement alive.[18] Koyama, on the other hand, left Japan, and as a consequence has surprisingly little recognition there in comparison to his widespread popularity elsewhere. (Indeed, for the past twenty years there has been no major mention of Koyama in as well-known a theological journal as the *Japan Christian Quarterly*.)

Given the many differences in cultural viewpoints, in historic experience, and in church practice, and lacking an obvious correspondence of theological ideas such as is apparent with other theologians, it is curious that Koyama finds Uchimura so influential. The reason, according to Koyama, is Uchimura's theological style. To Koyama, Uchimura writes in a practical but poetic way that makes theology come alive in personal experience. Uchimura is passionate, personal and idiosyncratic in his writing. He deals with the Bible extensively and practically, exploring what it has to say to contemporary, concrete situations. It is this style which Koyama finds so appealing. Together with Uchimura's bold independence and his passion for indigenous theology, for theology that respects the people it addresses, Uchimura's style continues to inspire Koyama, who is himself a passionate, independent theologian who seeks to make theology alive, personal and relevant to concrete situations today.

Kazoh Kitamori 1916–

No Japanese theologian has drawn more attention and acclaim perhaps than Kazoh Kitamori. His assessment of Christianity and Japanese culture, his general theological brilliance, and the scope of his work make him known as one of the most original of Japan's theologians, "the Tillich of Japan."[19] While seen as an indigenous Japanese theologian, he has nevertheless been well-received in the West. Some critics have argued that his theology is in fact more Western than Asian.[20] But most observers recognize him as one whose sensitivity, literary artistry, and familiarity with his own culture mark him as very much a Japanese theologian of cardinal significance.[21]

Kitamori was one of Koyama's teachers at seminary. The impact he had on Koyama is evident in Koyama's use of ideas and images received from Kitamori, as well as in Koyama's own references to personal encounters with Kitamori.[22] Koyama seems to treat Kitamori dispassionately in his writing and in conversation magnifies Kanzo Uchimura as perhaps the greatest theological influence in his life. However, a survey of key ideas and attitudes would seem to indicate that Kitamori is in fact the overwhelming influence on Koyama's theology.

Similarities between Koyama and Kitamori become immediately apparent in the relationship between theology and experience in each one's case, and indeed, in Koyama's and Kitamori's common experience of World War Two. Kitamori's primary theological motif, that of the pain of God, was born in the agonizing years of World War Two. While Kitamori's appreciation of pain and its theological significance was rooted in the depths of Buddhist tradition[23] and understood in the context of the Japanese sense of tragedy, it was World War Two that crystallized Kitamori's understanding of how pain, both human and divine, was central to an understanding of God and God's redemptive work. It was in an age of pain that the redemptive pain of God could best be perceived and proclaimed.[24] During Japan's wartime suffering and in her ultimate defeat pain leapt out of every page of Scripture.[25] This external experience was compounded by Kitamori's internal struggle with tuberculosis.[26] Under such conditions it was understandable and indeed necessary that Kitamori's theology should reflect the impact of personal experience.

For Koyama, too, first-hand experience was critical in the shaping of his theology. The hunger and destruction he knew during and immediately after the war inevitably produced many of the basic questions of his theology. Later his missionary efforts in Thailand crystallized his conviction that theology must be a matter of experience.

It was Kitamori's view that theology must grow out of the immediate, concrete circumstances of human existence. It should likewise be formulated and articulated in language appropriate to particular situations.[27] For Koyama, the same view holds. Neither Kitamori nor Koyama, however, made any one situation absolute in relation to the whole of Christian tradition. Both recognized the relativity of each situation and the corresponding possibility of different situations to produce different insights into Christian faith.

Both Koyama and Kitamori were thus highly concerned with contextual or indigenized theology. Part of the originality and appeal of Kitamori's theology is its well-informed usage of material related to the Japanese context, and in particular Kitamori's references to *kabuki*, a type of Japanese drama. Using terms and ideas meaningful in the cultural heritage of Japan, Kitamori sought to indigenize and to explain God's redemptive love in terms familiar to his hearers.

Koyama, in an essay on indigenization, or what he prefers to call "theological re-rooting," offers Kitamori as an example of a theologian who finds practical and conceptual keys to interpret the Gospel message in a particular cultural context.[28] In a similar way Koyama himself pursues tools for interpreting the Gospel in the various cultural contexts in which he has found himself. This is true not only in his explorations of the suitability of some Buddhist terms for Christian proclamation in Thailand, for example, but also in his general efforts to address the intercultural context of global nuclear confrontation by appealing to both biblical images and contemporary phrases which have currency with his audience.[29]

Koyama and Kitamori of course share the same cultural background. Both have known Christianity as a minority religion in the context of other, much more dominant religions. Both, in seeking to understand that context have delved deeply into Buddhism, though, in Koyama's case this study was instigated by encounter with a different Buddhism than that in Japan. Kitamori considered Buddhism to be part of his own tradition and spent time studying Zen and other Buddhist philosophies.[30] Though schooled more in the Theravada Buddhism of Thailand, Koyama has an intuitive grasp of Zen and sees in Buddhist spirituality both a testing point and a meeting point for Christian faith. For example, he sees the antitheses typical of Christianity—e.g., God incarnated, God in the cross, strength in weakness, wisdom in foolishness—as communicating something very close to that which is communicated by Japanese Zen.[31] Both Kitamori and Koyama find in Buddhism key insights which correspond with Christianity, along with constructive challenges to Christian values.

One further reflection of the contextual interests of Kitamori's and Koyama's theology is their similar concern that Asian theology achieve independence from Western domination. As recently as 1967 Kitamori described Christianity in Asia as a telegraph pole stuck in the ground of Asia rather than as a tree planted with natural roots in Asian soil.[32] To Kitamori Western theology was too often an imported package that remained artificial and irrelevant in the Japanese context. Creeds and systems inherited from the Greco-European cultural milieu need to be related to the experience of Asian Christians to be meaningful.[33]

Koyama wholeheartedly concurs with Kitamori. Besides developing the whole concept that the West has crusaded in Asia in such a way as to crucify Christianity, Koyama simply states that while Western theology is appreciated in Asia, it is not necessarily useful there. As Koyama puts it, Westerners write nice books and send them air-mail to Asia, but the fact is, they simply fail to address the Asian situation.[34] Thus, both Kitamori and Koyama are dedicated to resisting a simple acceptance of imported Western theology and to promoting theology rooted in the Asian context.

Where Koyama and Kitamori may disagree is on the significance of Kitamori's theology itself. Kitamori, as mentioned earlier, saw Japanese Christianity as having unique insights for Christianity as a whole. The Japanese understanding of suffering and tragedy, he believed, offered an element in the understanding of God which Greek, German and other theological environments had hitherto not perceived. Thus, in Kitamori's view the Japanese as a suffering people had a unique role to play in Christian history comparable to that of the Christians of the Reformation.[35]

Koyama does not speak in such terms of Kitamori's theology or of Japanese theology in general. He does credit Kitamori with perceptively relating God's suffering love to the Japanese context through the Japanese concept of suffering. But Koyama realizes that the Japanese understanding of suffering is culturally unique and thus could not be a tool for all other cultures to understand the pain of God.

On the other hand, Koyama asks whether or not Kitamori's ideas about human suffering may indeed carry some universal Christological insight. His answer is yes. Koyama, too, concludes that "human pain must be seen Christologically."[36] He sees this perspective as a principle that may have universal value in the indigenization or "theological re-rooting" of the Gospel.[37]

On a wider scale, Koyama adopts Kitamori's key notion that God embraces the pain of a broken world. Both human acceptance of God and human negation of God are embraced by God's love.[38] In essence this is the sum of Kitamori's pain of God theology.

Its broadest implications become apparent in Kitamori's attitude towards those who are not Christian. For Kitamori, they, too, stand in the saving light of God's embrace.

When the believer who has felt the pain of God in his heart loves his unbelieving neighbor as intensely as himself, the unbeliever is borne on the body of the believer into God's pain.[39]

God's pain, as Kitamori conceives it, is that which saves humanity.

While Koyama does not directly follow Kitamori's line, his sympathetic attitude towards people of other faiths is clear. Like Kitamori, he occasionally inserts the image of God's salvation taking place "outside" human expectations, particularly in the religious tradition of Israel, to symbolize God's relationship to people of other faiths and indeed to Christians.[40]

More obvious is Koyama's taking up Kitamori's theme of God's embracing love in some of Koyama's more recent work, albeit in somewhat different terms. Koyama, in wrestling with the discontinuity, the brokenness of human existence, also describes God's saving grace as an embrace, a continuity which contains the discontinuity of a broken world. In doing so, Koyama utilizes the rich imagery of his Japanese heritage, just as did Kitamori.[41]

Koyama acknowledges the value of Kitamori's understanding of the pain of God, the pain which united God's love and wrath in a redemptive manner.[42] Koyama says that Kitamori "contributed the penetrating insight that the love of God is distorted and made superficial when it is divorced from the wrath of God."[43] Koyama recognizes that Kitamori received this insight from Luther, who "restored the critical reality of the wrath of God to Christian life and theology"[44] in a way that shook the Aristotelian, scholastic foundations of medieval theology.[45] In his own missionary situation in Thailand, Koyama found the wrath of God to be a valuable theological tool, both for dialogue with Buddhism and for challenging the *Theologia Gloriae* of the Thai church.[46]

Despite the close connections between the theology of Kitamori and Koyama's theology, Koyama does not simply parrot Kitamori. Koyama discerns various limits to Kitamori's view, e.g., in regard to the universal significance and applicability of theology framed in the Japanese context. Moreover, Koyama shows a different passion from that which absorbed Kitamori in his explication of the pain of God. Whereas Kitamori became almost mystic, proclaiming, "I am dissolved in the pain of God and become one with him in pain,"[47] Koyama exhibits more reserve. Though Koyama too is passionate and though he, too, values the mystical, transrational dimensions of life and faith, his theology generally exhibits a simplicity that is directed more towards comprehensibility by others than towards pure self-expression. Then, too, Koyama's broad cross-cultural experience has taught him of the relativity of all human points of view.

While Koyama certainly and perhaps to some degree unconsciously builds on Kitamori's foundations, he also takes up where Kitamori left off and develops further his lines of thinking. His concept of the "crucified mind" is one such example. For both Koyama and Kitamori Christian discipleship means participation in the crucified life (Koyama), the pain of God (Kitamori).[48] But it is Koyama who develops this thought, giving it a wider foundation in the history of Israel and the lives of Jesus and Paul, and applying it more concretely in the area of Christian evangelism, encounter with other faiths, and encounter between East and West.

Likewise Koyama extends Kitamori's emphasis on human relationships as the locus of God's salvation. Kitamori's understanding of God's pain was informed mainly by the Japanese sense of tragedy in personal relationships rather than by suffering in material events such as war.[49] Koyama took this a step further in his "neighbourology" where he states that one's very Christian existence depends not on doctrines or systems but on one's relationship to one's neighbor in social as well as personal circumstances.

This relationship takes place within the context of God's having embraced the pain of an estranged world, as, to use Kitamori's image and one which Koyama often refers to, a fine silk cloth is wrapped around sharp augers.[50] This means that the life of discipleship and even such things as indigenization take place within the context of God already embracing any given situation.[51]

Underlying both Kitamori's and Koyama's understanding of the pain of God is a common thread of influence. Both were strongly influenced by Luther. Kitamori converted to Christianity at a Lutheran worship service and was educated in the first generation of students at the Lutheran Seminary in Tokyo.[52] For him, Luther was a guide in both faith and ethics.[53] Kitamori's pain of God theology was to some degree a form of Luther's *theologia crucis*, understood in a Japanese context. Indeed, Kitamori's book, *The Pain of God*, in its German translation was entitled "Theology of the Cross".[54]

So, too, Koyama adapted and developed a theology of the cross, not only because of Kitamori's influence but also because Koyama undertook extensive study of Luther in his doctoral work. Frequently in Koyama's writings his Lutheran influence emerges, not only in theological concepts, but also in particular references to Luther. Even today, Koyama feels that one of those closest to him in his understanding of the cross is Jürgen Moltmann.[55]

But this very influence of Lutheran theology causes at least one critic to label Kitamori and Koyama both as Western rather than Asian theologians. Choan Seng Song writes, "Kitamori is essentially in the tradition of Western theology, which turns salvation into an intense struggle of God against God within God himself."[56]

Such a theology, Song maintains, stops at the cross; it misses the love of God[57] which triumphed in Jesus' resurrection. "It cannot in fact accommodate resurrection; it does not have room for it."[58]

But precisely where Song sees a limited theology, Koyama finds a key to understanding God and redemption. For it is exactly in the cross that Koyama and Kitamori see the heart of God, the love which embraces all the pain of human existence.[59] In their eyes the content of the resurrection is that embrace.

Moreover, in complete contrast to Song, it is in Luther's idea of faith in the God of the cross that Koyama sees the very meeting point between Asian and Western spirituality. Luther spoke of faith fleeing to the cross against the cross. Koyama points out that faith merely fleeing to God from adversity is too easy; it is shallow spirituality. But a faith which flees to God against God, when God does not appear to be there or when God is crucified and apparently powerless, faith that meets the contradiction of love and suffering that is present in the cross—this is true spirituality. This kind of spirituality, in Koyama's eyes, corresponds with the spirituality of Zen Buddhism at its zenith,[60] in the sense that truth is met in contradiction.

Kitamori, too, maintains that the resurrection is, as it were, included in the crucifixion. As "Father begets Son" is secondary to "Father causes Son to die,"[61] so is the resurrection dependent on the cross. For it is in the cross that the love of God embraces God's wrath and human reconciliation with God is secured.

Thus, theology of the cross, as Kitamori has developed it and as Koyama has understood and applied it in terms of the crucified mind, becomes a profoundly Asian theology, the more so as it is amplified by the many and various Asian experiences of suffering. In that sense, it may even be suggested that Kitamori's vision of Japan contributing a dynamic Asian insight to Christian theology may prove true.

At any rate, the intimate relationship between the theology of Kazoh Kitamori and that of Kosuke Koyama seems apparent. If Koyama derives inspiration from the temperament and style of Kanzo Uchimura, it is from Kazoh Kitamori that he has absorbed some of his most fundamental theological perspectives. Inheriting the mantle of these two great forerunners, and filling it out with his own theological creativity, Koyama not only enhances the legacy of Japanese theology, but carries that theology to important new, intercultural frontiers.

CHAPTER FOUR

THE ASIAN CONTEXT

Koyama, despite his individual distinctions, is but one actor in a drama of immense proportions now unfolding on the stage of both Christian and world history. In its widest ramifications this drama is the emergence of what Hendrik Kraemer, one of this century's foremost missiologists, has called "a single planetary world."[1] It is a world of intricate, recognized links between the peoples of earth's different countries and cultures, drawing them inextricably closer together.

But Kraemer concentrated on another drama within the planetary drama as a whole that is of particular significance in human history. That is the encounter between East and West, between Asia and Europe (along with North America). This encounter, Kraemer believed, is one of the most radically different in history.[2] For never have two such fundamentally different civilizations met face to face on such a grand scale.

Of course, East and West have had many intriguing brushes with each other over the last two millennia. The Roman Empire, for example, is said to have imported so much Chinese silk that her economy was hurt by the drain on her gold and silver reserves.[3] In northwest India imagery of the Buddha was strongly influenced by exposure to Greek art.[4] The Buddha himself for a while became a Christian saint.[5] During the late thirteenth and early fourteenth century a host of Christian monks and merchants, the most famous being Marco Polo, traversed Asia in a lively religious and cultural exchange between Europe and the Far East. As a consequence, Christian choirs came to sing in Peking; the Peking government sought French, British and Papal aid against Islam; and the superior technology of China was introduced to the West, via gunpowder, paper money, printing, porcelain, textiles, and various medical discoveries.[6] Much of this was made possible by the fact that Mongol armies, in creating perhaps the greatest geographical empire in history, controlled nearly the whole of Asia and the Middle East along with parts of Europe, having refrained from invading Western Europe itself only by chance.[7]

But these encounters between East and West were on a superficial level at best. While sporadic contacts between East and West continued throughout the fifteenth, sixteenth and seventeenth centuries, as European missionaries and traders pressed eastward, it was not until the eighteenth century that European colonial expansion inaugurated a full-scale encounter between East and West. The West prevailed, achieving overall domination of Asia throughout the nineteenth and well into the twentieth centuries. Western values, material goods, political and economic structures, and other aspects of Western culture overwhelmed the civilizations of Asia, triggering enormous and irreversible changes.

But now the pattern seems to be changing again; the drama, taking a different turn. Already in the 1930's Kraemer saw Western hegemony as a thing of the past. The East was becoming the equal of the West.[8] In this century numerous Asian nations have shaken off at least the direct political yokes of Western colonialism. Japan and Vietnam have warred vigorously and with surprising success against Western powers. Both China and Burma were able to seal their borders against all manner of coercive Western influence at a period when nations such as Russia and the United States of America were supposedly at their zenith. India, too, increasingly competes with the West on her own technological terms, e.g. in medical research and nuclear weapons capability.

In this century, as Kraemer sees it, the tables have turned. Whereas the West shaped the world's destiny for the last five centuries, now comes the dawn of Asia.[9] What great consequences this might have for the human future is unknown. But the drama of the encounter between East and West in a single planetary world—if it is as real and important as Kraemer suggests—surely merits reflection.

Koyama, as noted earlier, is a player in this drama. His importance as a theologian relates directly to how he both personifies and responds to the encounter between East and West. To examine his contribution to Christian theology in this historical context, attention will thus be given to three broad areas, namely, a) the Asian scene in general, b) the nature of Christian theology in Asia, and c) some specific features of recent Asian Christian theology.

The Asian Scene

Approximately fifty-six per cent of the world's people today are Asian. By the end of this century that figure could increase to sixty-two per cent.[10] Sheer numbers make Asia impossible to ignore in terms of her significance in a single planetary world. At the same time, Asia covers a vast geographical area, containing some of the world's greatest diversity of languages, cultures, religions and social structures. Her civilizations are as ancient and sophisticated—and in some cases much more so—than those of the West. While far from uniform or cohesive among themselves, these civilizations nevertheless have a character that sets them apart from the civilizations of the West. Embodied in their cultures are values and social patterns that represent fundamental alternatives to Western perspectives.[11]

Although having bowed for a short period in world history to the domination of Western power, Asia is today resurgent as a dynamic area of human civilization in her own right. But Asia's resurgence is inextricably linked to her encounter with the West. Today East and West are intensely interdependent, linked by myriad economic, political and cultural ties.

For Christianity this encounter means both challenge and opportunity. Less than five per cent of all Asians are Christian and in some areas the percentage is as low as 0.01%.[12] Historically, Christianity—itself an Eastern religion in origin—has intermittently had toe-holds in central and east Asia. There were probably Christians in India from the first century A.D. onwards.[13] Nestorian Christians were found in China already in the seventh and again in the thirteenth centuries.[14] Catholic missionaries established significant churches in Japan, China and the Philippines in the sixteenth century; various Protestant missions grew in India throughout the seventeenth and eighteenth centuries. The nineteenth century, the great century of Christian missionary activity, saw churches planted nearly everywhere in Asia.

Yet, everywhere except in the Philippines, Christianity attracted only a tiny proportion of Asia's population. Thus, Christianity today finds itself both at home in Asia and alien to it. In fact, Christianity has a long, if spotty, history in Asia. But its form and content, especially insofar as that form and content are Western in character, have not been widely accepted by Asia's people.

Now in a planetary world the scene is changing. The Christian church, whether Eastern or Western, has unprecedented access to Asia's peoples and cultures. Concurrently, the doors are open for the history and values of Asia to penetrate Christianity. Among the peoples and cultures of Asia, Christianity is challenged to define and to express itself in unique and unprecedented ways. Increasingly freed from its Western cultural shackles and confronted by the richness and diversity of Asia, Christianity may thereby gain some of its freshest insights for Christian faith and proclamation. Altogether, Asia, as neither Western nor Christian, as the home of powerful, proud and ancient civilizations with great religious traditions, is perhaps the greatest testing ground Christianity has encountered at least since the Mediterranean world of the first century.

To further understand some of the key dynamics of this world, four aspects of Asia's current situation need to be briefly examined, after which Koyama's role will be considered.

Contemporary Asian Ferment

One of the key dynamics of the Asian world is that Asian societies today are caught up in an "historical revolutionary ferment."[15] Far-reaching technological developments have come hand in hand with secular and humanist influences, creating a new environment of both changing circumstances and changing attitudes.

There is, for instance, a "revolution of rising expectations" in the areas of poverty, justice, and material wealth.[16] This includes a desire to demolish traditional structures in the creation of what are intended to be more just, prosperous, and egalitarian societies. Most often, political change is seen as the primary avenue for accomplishing these social changes.[17]

Nationalism has taken precedence over parochialism and the traditional group loyalties of Asian society. New political and authority structures are developing. The Asian masses are more interested in politics, more aware of their own poverty. Social equality and dignity have become common ideals. In general, secular world views have found increasing acceptance at the expense of traditional perspectives.[18]

Moreover, while these or similar changes occurred in the West over a period of four centuries, they have jolted through Asia in a matter of four decades.[19] The ground was prepared gradually in Europe; in Asia the changes were often sudden and rootless.[20] The result is often radical and sudden discontinuity with Asian traditions. For, rapid social change tends to disrupt and destroy tradition. Surviving traditions persist in a tense dialectic with modernization.[21]

Modernization, however, has also been viewed as positive by many Asians, not only in terms of its material benefits, but also in its acting as a potent force for the de-sacralization of the world. Its emphasis on the value of matter, its ability to develop knowledge for controlling and humanizing the environment and its stress on the openness of history and nature clears the world of demons, spirits, and gods, "delivering it from the control of magic and religion, and turning it over to man for him to humanize."[22]

Altogether, modernization has brought about dramatic changes in every sphere of Asian life, from politics to family life, from religion to fashion, from education and communication to warfare, and so on. By many in Asia and by some outside, too, "the Asian revolution" is seen as the most dynamic factor in the history of the twentieth century.[23]

Asia's Suffering

Another key factor in the Asian world is Asia's poverty. Bishop Julio Xavier Labazan of the Philippines has described the unique nature of Asian suffering in four ways.[24] One, it is different in sheer magnitude. More people in Asia are hungry, homeless, unemployed, and illiterate than in all the rest of the world put together. Secondly, Asian suffering is centuries old; it is ancient and endemic to Asian history. Third, Asian suffering is unique in that it has inspired great religions. Whereas other religions answer such questions as "Which gods protect the empire?", "How do we control the floods?", and "How did we get out of Egypt?", Asian religions centered around pain and suffering, asking, "How can we explain and escape suffering?".

Fourth, Asian suffering is non-Christian. For Christian mission this must be a problem, for how can Christianity claim God's presence in suffering to those who have never known the Christian God?

> Such is Asian suffering. It is vast, ancient, spiritualized and non-Christian. In a way Asia and suffering are one. It doesn't seem a likely place to find Christ. To talk of Christ's Lordship in Asia where 95% of the people are non-Christian, to say that Christ is Lord of all this even though the people don't know him, is a provocative statement.[25]

Of course, suffering anywhere in the world does not take place in a vacuum. It is largely social suffering created by human beings. For many young Asians today the creators of Asian suffering are considered to be the nations of the West. The tale of Asia is often told as the tale of a people under Pharaoh (Western colonialism) for the last five hundred years.[26] Christianity, which is often seen as an extension of Western colonial power, is rejected as a religion which cannot speak to Asian suffering because it is not rooted in Asian soil.[27] Insofar as the signs of redemption for Asia's suffering are few and primarily secular, some feel that "Asia's suffering and hope are equally non-Christian."[28]

In such a setting, Christianity faces the extremely difficult challenge of addressing Asia's deep suffering in a meaningful way while being neither acknowledged nor accepted as a relevant voice by many of those who experience the suffering.

Asia's Religiosity

"The Asian context can be described as a blend of a profound *religiosity* (which is perhaps Asia's greatest wealth) and an overwhelming *poverty*."[29] Along with Asia's suffering, Asia's religiosity must be recognized as a crucial element on the scene of modern Asia. This religiosity is no longer confined to the traditional structures of Asia's religions.

> We must recognize that we live and work in a vortex of an unremitting religious, even spiritual, interaction between cultures, religions, and ideologies.[30]

In this vortex, technology and the values that go with it also comprise a faith system which enters the circle of other human faith systems in the world, challenging them as they challenge each other.[31] Likewise, political systems such as Marxism, by which some Asian societies seek to accomplish radical social changes, are channels for Asia's religiosity.

The challenge to Christian mission is therefore first of all to discern the technological, religious, or political forces which act as expressions of Asian spirituality and as responses to Asian problems. Such a task is not easy.

> We are, in general, not prepared to recognize the religious elements in our environment. Consequently we are ill-equipped to teach people how to deal with the religious pressures which bear down upon them at every turn of their daily lives.[32]

In the early Christian era, it was the religions of the Jews and Greeks, the ideologies of a colonial power and its opponents, and the technology of Roman civilization that challenged Christianity's substance and self-expression. Today Christianity interacts in Asia with Buddhism, Hinduism, and Taoism, with the politics of communism, totalitarianism and democracy, and with the technology of the computer age.[33]

> There is, however, one very important and decisive common denominator for all of the Asian churches. Asia holds since ages past within its boundaries rich treasures of deep philosophy and devoted religiosity . . . (Asia is) one of the most important sources of the spiritual inheritance of mankind. . . . We find

therefore in Asia a growing recognition of what unites the
churches there, namely their common obligation to give witness
to Asian spiritual and cultural values transformed in them
through their Christian faith and to carry this witness to the rest
of the world, so much impoverished by superfluous secularism
and materialism.[34]

The Church in Asia

Modernization, the struggles concerning suffering, poverty and justice, a profound religious heritage, and the general impact of secularization—these are all
key dynamics in Asia's revolutionary emergence onto the stage of a planetary
world. All of them affect the church in Asia.

As Asia itself faces powerful religious and secular forces, so does Asian Christianity. Christianity now more frequently encounters Asia's other religions, search-
ing for a more harmonious relationship with them and a more indigenous Asian
form of expression for it own spirituality. At the same time, Christianity, seen as a
western, colonial religion, is confronted by Asian nationalism with its anti-Western
biases[35] and by Asian Marxism—both more products of the West than Christianity
itself.[36] In short, Asian Christianity finds itself in a complicated situation.

Because Asia is 95% non-Christian, and because its religious and philosophical
frameworks are so different from those of the West, Christianity finds itself with
no ready base from which to communicate, no accepted language for Christian discourse. Christianity has yet to widely baptize and utilize for itself the terms and
ideas of Asian spirituality, as it used, for example, terms and ideas from the Greco-
Roman world.

The type of difficulty Christianity in Asia faces can be illustrated by Paul Tillich's observation that the issue is not that of Asia's highly developed religious
sensitivities rejecting Christ. Rather, as Tillich puts it, their basic nature is such
that they do not ask the questions to which the gospel provides a response.[37]

Besides having communication difficulties, Christianity in Asia must wrestle
with various problems in regard to the church itself. As such a tiny fellowship in
the vastness of Asia it is not altogether surprising that a sort of "ghetto mentality"
can be found in Asian Christianity, a preoccupation with the church's own existence and organization which inhibits a prophetic stance and fuller involvement in
Asia's rapid and radical social changes.[38]

In like manner Christianity has often been seen as a "potted plant," to use D. T. Niles' frequently quoted expression. That is, Christianity is seen as having been transported into Asia without having been transplanted into Asian cultural soil.[39]

The very remoteness of Asian churches from churches in the West has given rise to some problems. Having had different histories and experiences, it is difficult for Asian and Western churches to identify with each other. Not only have Asian churches long been dependent upon Western assistance which they cannot reciprocate (an injury to Asian pride), they have also had a long history of suffering, persecution and minority status quite unlike the prosperous, influential, and accepted churches of the West.[40]

As to be expected, there have always been sharp divisions within the Asian Christian community on matters of church doctrine and practice. In the midst of Asia's social and political upheaval and in the face of vast human suffering in Asia, there exists a strong polarization between Christians who urge the church to play an active social role and Christians who believe in a more circumscribed role for the church. Universal, timeless, and inevitable as such a polarization may be, it is an important issue for Christianity in the Asian environment where such people as Mahatma Gandhi stand out in part for their very symbiosis of structural reform and personal spirituality.[41]

In a similar way, denominationalism has plagued Christian witness in Asia. While on the one hand, denominationalism is a healthy expression of natural differences, and while competition between denominations may actually advance Christianity, there are many in Asia who feel that denominationalism has brought unnecessary and sometimes destructive disunity to Asian Christianity. With the diminishing influence of Western parent churches Asian Christians have thus increasingly followed an ecumenical direction.

Changing relationships between Asia's newer Christian churches and churches of the West are themselves reflections of the changing relationship between East and West as a whole. As Western influence in Asia has receded since colonial times, so has the Christian church lost some influence. Thus, Asian churches have much greater autonomy, but, lacking in resources and experience, they find themselves still in a pioneering stage of mission in their own environment with somewhat limited patterns to follow.[42] However, the increased autonomy of Asia's churches better girds them for witness in their own situation.

Unfortunately, Asian theological education often does not match Asian church needs. While skilled in Western church dogma, Asian seminarians may be ignorant of Asian spiritual doctrines.

Most graduates of Asian Theological colleges will be able to give you a fairly accurate explanation of terms such as Stoicism, Gnosticism, Docetism, Sabellianism, Arianism, Traducianism, Pelagianism, Kenosis, Hypostatic Union, and Perichoresis to mention some of our favorite examination topics. But how many of them could give you anything like an accurate explanation of *visishtadvaita, pradurbhava, paramapurusha, Asuddhaniscaya, Nirmanakaya, pancakkhanda, paticcasamuppada, tauhid, khadlan,* and *kalam*? We shall not produce a form of Christianity which is recognizably Asian unless and until we acknowledge that there are Asian concepts and thought forms which may well unlock doors which have too long remained barred. I am not asking that we join in the adoration of *Saraswati,* I am simply asking for the recognition that what she represents is as noble, and as relevant, and as real as that signified by the name of Aristotle.[43]

In like manner, Western Christians are abysmally ignorant of Asia's religious heritage and therefore severely limited in their ability to identify with the Asian church and Asian mission. Lacking in sufficient study of anthropology, other cultures, other religions, and the like, as well as usually embodying in their very structure the methods and perspectives of Western culture, church seminaries often become built-in stabilizers of the static and outdated structures and ministries of the church, often buttressing all that is desirable to change.[44]

Asian churches, then, face considerable challenges in addressing the Asian context. In an overwhelmingly non—Christian environment where the disturbances of modernization, added to traditional struggles, are stirring people to important decisions about what values will serve them best in the future, Christianity is trying to establish solid moorings. To find authenticity in this environment, as recently noted, Christianity will have to accomplish three tasks.[45] It will have to relate to ancient traditions, respond to Asia's socio-economic realities, and deal with the past and present relationships between Asia and the West, and Christianity and the West. The ultimate fate of Christianity in Asia is yet to be determined. However, that fate is "one of the most fascinating of the questions which only the future can answer."[46]

Koyama's Contribution

At this point part of Koyama's contribution to Asian Christianity can be brought out, for Koyama is a theologian who is familiar with Asia as a whole and with the challenges to Christianity in the Asian world.[47] Koyama has experienced and observed the effects of modernization on Asian life, commenting in numerous essays on the encounter between East and West, on the "spirit" of technology, on the need for contextual theology in Asia and so forth. Koyama's awareness of Asia's religiosity surfaces both in personal essays and in books on the subject (such as *No Handle on the Cross* and *Mt. Fuji and Mt. Sinai*). Concern for the political and social struggles of ordinary people caught in the crush of militaristic, economic and political struggles is voiced less stridently than is the concern of some other Asian theologians, but it is authentic and persistent (e.g. Koyama, *Waterbuffalo Theology*, Chapter 1 and Koyama, *Three Mile an Hour God*, Chapter 4).

In general, Koyama does not address abstract issues as such. That is, he does not systematically discuss Asian modernization or justice politics in purely theoretical terms. He does not deal with Marxism at all. Instead, Koyama sets out to explore the theological questions raised by these issues. In the process he tries to personalize those issues for his audience, helping them to relate issues to Scripture and challenging his audience to respond to such issues in terms of a "crucified mind."

Yet in two areas Koyama has made specific contributions toward helping Asian Christianity speak to the modern situation. In a context where there is no common language for Christian discourse Koyama has sought to create one. On the one hand, he has passionately advocated "contextualized theology," setting an example himself by endeavoring to communicate the Christian message in the cultural terms of Thailand. There he sought to frame Christian faith both in the ordinary terms of a peasant's life and in the more sophisticated language of Thai Buddhism. Koyama has even explored the use of Buddhist terms and concepts as vehicles for Christian expression (e.g., *Waterbuffalo Theology*, Chapter 13; *Mt. Fuji and Mt. Sinai*, Chapter 13).

That Koyama's efforts were recognized as valuable on a wider scale is apparent in the view expressed by another Asian theologian, T. K. Thomas, who notes with gratitude that Koyama has succeeded in opening a new communication concept in Asia. "Indigenization," says Thomas, is basically, "a refinement of communication."[48] In a situation where most Christian theology is urban, abstract and out of touch with ordinary life, Thomas believes Koyama has enhanced Christianity's indigenization in Asia by moving Christian theology from abstract to concrete images. As another commentator puts it, Koyama is able to "spot the essential" in a situation and dares to express it in a fresh idiom that "makes the theoretical concrete."[49] Thus one of Koyama's recognized contributions to Asian Christianity is his development of a theological language appropriate to the Asian scene.

Of course, many other Asian Christians operate with this sort of language, too. That Koyama has achieved international recognition with his theology is not to say that his theology is without precedent or peer. Rather, his success serves the recognition and acceptance of a whole stream of Asian theology, encouraging others to pursue this line.

A second way in which Koyama has contributed practically to Asian Christianity as a whole is in his work as an educator and as Dean of the South East Asian Graduate School of Theology. While the impact of this sort of work is more difficult to assess, it is clear that Koyama's leadership affected the education of many Asian theological students.

One example of Koyama's interest as an educator was his emphasis on exposing theological students in one area of Asia to events and ideas in other Asian settings. Koyama was concerned that Asian theological students receive a clearly ecumenical and contextual education.[50]

Likewise, Koyama along with other educators sought to encourage the teaching of theology written by Asians as well as theology written by Westerners. Thus as Executive Director of the Association of Theological Schools in South East Asia he joined others in a project to put together source books, or theological "area handbooks" to be used alongside "standard" i.e., Western, textbooks.[51]

As a well-known theologian and educator Koyama has naturally also developed a wide sphere of personal influence. This influence is enhanced by a personal charisma. One Australian theologian recalls attending an Asian Christian conference at which Koyama appeared to speak. He remembers Koyama's presence as "electrifying" and recalls that Koyama sparked the liveliest discussions of the conference.[52]

In short, Koyama's personality along with his administrative and literary accomplishments enhance his role as a contributor to modern Asian Christianity.

CHAPTER FIVE

ASIAN THEOLOGY

The Nature of Asian Theology

To speak of Koyama's contribution to Asian theology requires further delineation of Asian theology itself. The very term "Asian theology" is problematic. It has been said that "pure Asian theology is a Western concept."[1] Given the vastness and diversity of Asia, it must be understood that in theology as in other areas, "Asia is not one, but many."[2]

> Asia's cultural diversity should keep us from expecting to find an easily identifiable "Asian Christian theology," as we have grown to expect of European, Latin American and North American theologies, or even as we might anticipate from Africa. What is actually emerging in the Asian church is a variety of Asian approaches to Christian theology, ranging from Indian and Indonesian in the south to Japanese and Korean in the north.[3]

Yet, while Asia exhibits wide diversity in culture, political ideologies and social structures there are, as M. M. Thomas put it, common features in the Asian experience and in the Asian contribution to Christianity as a whole that justify use of such a term as Asian theology in the singular.[4]

There are some Asian theologians, such as C. S. Song, who see in the modern international context the emergence of specialized Third World theologies as necessary challenges to the dominant "monolithic" European theology of the past.[5] At the same time, others point out that the purpose of developing Asian theology is not so much to create an Asian versus a European theology as to enrich theology as a whole with Asian resources.[6]

After suggesting some of the possible advantages to be derived from Eastern, including Orthodox theology, Arend Van Leeuwen concludes that arguments in favor of a distinctive "Eastern" theology in its own right are insufficient. Rather, Van Leeuwen suggests,

It would seem on the whole wiser to let go the idea of a specifically "Eastern" theology. As ecumenical discussion grows amid this planetary world, what we need rather is a broad variety of cross-fertilization.[7]

Van Leeuwen views the idea of Eastern or Asian theology in a wider context, recognizing the limits of Western theology but seeking to avoid a mere switch to some other theological provincialism.

It is time the missionary encounter were set firmly at the center of our theological concern. That—and not some independent kind of "Eastern" theology—offers the real way of escape from the narrow limitations of a one-sided "Western" theological tradition. A shift of that sort, which for the theology of the twentieth century will be tantamount to another Reformation, is urgently needed and will require a concerted ecumenical effort.[8]

A missionary encounter such as Van Leeuwen refers to is surely what is happening on a vast scale with Christianity in Asia. While an independent Asian theology may prove no panacea to Christian theology as a whole, it is more than probable that the already very ecumenical theology of Asia will have a major contribution to make to world Christianity. Thus it is worth giving further attention to Asian theology in terms of its formation, its character, its significance, and some of its dominant features.

The Formation of Asian Theology

Some Asian scholars, Douglas Elwood among them, maintain that Asian theology has developed primarily during the last two decades or so.[9] To illustrate the prior state of theology in Asia, Elwood quotes from an Indian Christian who exclaimed that in the Christian movement in India not long ago there was "no theology, not even an indigenous heresy."[10] The reason for the late blooming of Asian theology, according to Elwood, is that Asian theology has been hampered by syncretism, suspicion about indigenization, the very youthfulness of most Asian churches, and the lack of theologians among missionaries.[11]

But by far the overwhelming factor inhibiting the development of Asian theology is the near total domination of Asian Christianity by Western theological influences. It is widely recognized that

> the Asian. . . churches have been theologically educated so far by a more or less straightforward transference of Western theological ways of thought.[12]

Asian theology has consisted primarily of a parroting or rewriting of Western theology.[13] Its models, mood, and method have all been Western.[14]

Today, the changed relationship of East and West and the maturity of Asian churches have made Asians aware of the need to grow away from their Western, often conservative roots.[15] This awareness is evident in remarks like that of C. S. Song:

> In recent years, however, it has become increasingly obvious to many thinking people, both in the East and in the West, that the theology constructed on the marriage between Christianity and Western civilization cannot serve the spirituality that grows, develops, and creates outside the framework of Constantinian Christianity.[16]

A Korean theologian, Yong Bock Kim, asserts that because theological thinking in Asia remains predominantly Western, Christian churches in Asia remain to some degree isolated islands in a non-Christian sea, more continuous with the West than the East.[17] "However," Yong notes, "there has been a progressive approximation of theology to the historical conditions of the Asian peoples."[18] Yong, in contrast to Elwood, credits Western missionaries with having taken the first step in "historicizing" Christianity in Asia, that is, in relating Asian history to Christian faith. However, these missionaries naturally studied Asian history for their own purposes, generally holding a negative view of Asian civilization, and of discontinuity between Asian history and the Gospel. One result was a lasting gap between theology and the local situation.[19]

Today, as Koyama points out, "There is a quiet determination among Asian Christians that their commitment to Jesus Christ and their word about Jesus Christ must be responsible to the life they live in Asia today."[20] Relating Asian theology to the story of the good Samaritan, Koyama explains that Asia needs a living theology, one which actively addresses its own situation, not one which "passes by on the other side" as much Western theology has done.[21] For some Asians such authentic Asian theology has been developing in the struggles of Asian nationalism and more recently through "people's liberation movements."[22] At any rate, there is at least a growing sense of Asia's need to discard her "Western dress"[23] and fashion her own theological clothes.

Accordingly, there is now a remarkably rich and diverse body of theology emerging on the Asian scene. It is clothed in a variety of forms, including songs, poems, diaries, reports and art.[24] It comes from conferences, consultations and other gatherings of Asian Christians as well as from individuals. But the cooperative, multiform nature of Asian Christian theology does not signify any theological incompetence on the part of Asian Christians. For, as one authority points out, it would in the first place be an illusion to picture indigenized Asian theology merely in terms of its being a counterpart or mirror image to Western theology, i.e., organized into systematic tomes and innumerable volumes on church history, ecclesiology, and the like.[25] Instead, Asian theology will have its own character and form.

H. Dan Beeby, in discussing the indigenization of theology in reference to the Asian context, makes several noteworthy observations. Indigenized theology, he remarks, "is done first and foremost in fragments."[26] It begins with biblically grounded statements in special circumstances, often as ad hoc responses to crises in church life.[27] Such an observation is very appropriate to the Asian situation where so many recent individual and group theological statements have directly addressed specific Asian issues in a milieu of radical change.

Koyama himself fits neatly into this pattern in that many of his essays are deeply biblical reflections on specific contemporary issues. What perhaps distinguishes Koyama somewhat in this regard is that his training and experience mean that he could operate in other theological patterns. In other words, to a large degree, Koyama has deliberately chosen to apply this "fragmentary" Asian methodology.

Beeby also stresses the situational, modest character of Asian theology, noting that such theology exists in abundance in Asia, albeit in pieces. Beeby further observes that the Gospels themselves, like Asian theology, were very much indigenized theology, addressing the needs of particular situations where decisions were being made for the life of the church. Finally, Beeby emphasizes the importance of a sound biblical basis for Asia's Christian theology, especially because the great philosophical base of Asia would otherwise be so tempting to lean on, as was the philosophical base of the West for European Christianity.[28]

That Asian Christianity's struggle to forge her own theological perspective is compounded by outside forces is apparent in the dilemma presented by Christian theologies elsewhere in the world. As one theologian sees it, "the Asian church, for the moment, is caught between two 'theologies,' both of which are. . . Western."[29] The first of these theologies is classical European theology; the second, the liberation theology of Latin America. Between them exists a tension resulting from diametrically opposed methodologies.[30] While European theology concerns itself with philosophical analysis, Latin American theology directs itself toward theopraxis, including the changing of situations of social injustice.[31]

In its praxis-orientation and its interest in radical change, Latin American liberation theology has a certain appeal to the Asian situation. However, Latin American theology is in the end no more rooted in Asia than is European theology. Its theoretical foundations and operational techniques can be just as alien to the Asian mind and to Asian needs as the classic European theology to which Latin American theology seemingly presents itself as an alternative. Asian Christians are therefore left to discover the theological perspectives most appropriate to their own situation. Increasingly, they are succeeding in doing so.

Some of the themes of Asian theology, such as contextual theology, and a theology of religious pluralism, and some of the forms of Asian theology will be new to Western theologians, but these themes and forms have already had much consideration in Asia.[32] From its encounter with Asian change and Asian secularism and from dialogue with Asia's other great religions, Asian theology will inevitably produce insights beyond those developed by Western Christianity. Oddly, because of the uniquely open, ecumenical nature of the Asian context, many of the key contributors to Asian theology may in fact speak from outside Asia. This applies both to Asians who live outside Asia, e.g., C. S. Song, Koyama, Y. K. Lee, and Shoki Coe, and also to some Westerners who have become students and partners in Asian theology such as Douglas Elwood, John England, Gerald Anderson, and several others.

The pioneering position of Asian theology naturally opens it to various dangers as well as to many creative possibilities. Arend Van Leeuwen has pointed out the danger that because Christians constitute such a tiny minority in Asia, because they generally come from rural backgrounds, and because they are not significantly involved in the dramatic political and economic changes of their situations, Asian Christianity could be left on the sidelines in relation to the torrent of Asia's rapid and radical changes.[33]

In a situation where "the really strategic points for the church in the discharge of her apostolic obligation lie in the processes of 'rapid social change' in the non-Christian world,"[34] the Asian church could opt out, retreating into the type of ghetto mentality referred to earlier. However, the past influences of Christianity in

Japanese social changes and the more recent political statements and involvements of Christians in such areas as Taiwan and the Philippines serve as indications that many Christians will seek to play an active role in Asia's social changes.

At the opposite end of the spectrum there is a second danger to Asian Christian theology, namely, "the curse of ideologies."[35] In seeking to address Asia's changing society some Asian theologians have used the Gospel as a Marxist ideological tool. In that the Gospel is not entirely compatible with any human ideology[36] Christian theology must beware of becoming but an instrument for a particular ideology, be that Marxist or Capitalist, Eastern or Western. Asian theology, while sensitive to Asia's needs and attuned to the dynamics of change, must also preserve its own integrity as a word that transcends its own time and context. As Elwood points out, these and other risks facing Asian theology must be taken;[37] they are part of Asian theology's formation. So far, that theology is proving dynamic in form, content, and as will be considered next, character.

The Character of Asian Theology

Asian theology is clearly being born, at least in character.[38] One necessary and obvious aspect of that character is the diversity of Asian theology. Even a Roman Catholic commentator asserts that in Asia pluriformity is both inevitable and indispensable. To emphasize unilateral orthodoxy could even be harmful for the Asian church. Rather, Asian theology needs flexibility and an openness to cooperation with other perspectives.[39]

Another necessary aspect of Asian theology is that it must emerge from experience, just as did the Christian scriptures.[40] In other words, Asian theology will not come from formulating Western theological principles "in an Asian way"; rather, it must come from the ground up,[41] from Asians coming to understand and interpret Christian faith in terms of their own experience. This is a conviction broadly shared by Asia's theologians who sense a significant gap between the theology they have inherited from the West and the Christian life they are called to lead in Asia. Koyama exemplifies those who explore avenues for developing such an experience-based Asian theology.

In regard to Asians formulating theology in the same manner as the Christian scriptures were formulated, it is interesting to consider the view of J. A. Veitch. He proposes that the world-view of Asia is intrinsically closer to that of the Bible than is the world-view of the West. Consequently, he argues, the historical-critical tools so important to Western theology are not so significant for Asian theology. The direction of Christian understanding, as it were, is not from the Bible to Asia via Western critical theology. Rather, it is direct from the Bible to Asia. A more existential apprehension of Christian faith is what better suits Asia.[42]

This view accords with the perspective of many who feel that the Asian view of life is more intuitive than that of the West. C. S. Song emphasizes the contrast between what he calls the conceptual, rational approach to faith in the West and the perceptual, intuitive approach of Asians, who he too feels are more in tune with Scripture.[43] Song in fact constructs a major portion of his theology on the conviction that what is needed in theology in general and in Asian theology in particular is to recover the "lost heart" which is so crucial to theology.[44] For, as Song sees it, the heart is the prime mover of theology.[45] Because Asians are skilled at perceptions of the heart, Song believes that Asian theology can serve as a resource for Christian theology as a whole.[46]

An outgrowth of the intuitive dimension of Asian theology is its stylistic expression in theology. Cecil Hargreaves explains that "Asian thinking seems to take its shape from the symbols and parables which it uses rather than from any very systematic structure of propositions."[47] Hargreaves points out a preference in Asia for symbols over concepts, synthesis over analysis. In such a setting parables are as convincing as logical arguments.[48]

To illustrate this point Hargreaves uses the image of a tree. Trees and plants have often been used as symbols for conveying Asian religious understanding. Hargreaves traces the use of tree imagery through various Asian cultures in both Christian and non-Christian traditions, finally suggesting that "Asia's tree-shaped thinking" is noticeably amenable to the tree-related story of Calvary, or what he calls the tree-shaped thinking of the cross.[49]

One aspect of this tree perspective, or of the Asian mind in general, is a sense of relatedness, or harmony in life. This Asian concern for harmony, Hargreaves adds, is one of the useful contributions Asian theology can make to the rest of Christianity.

Luis Gutheinz, a Jesuit concerned with Asian theology, likewise highlights the deep yearning in the Asian mind for harmony and integration. He terms it one of the key hermeneutical characteristics of Asian theology.[50] To this Gutheinz adds three more key characteristics: 1) a high awareness in Asia of the interpenetration of history and praxis; 2) an emphasis on community in Asia such that whereas in the West a prevailing dictum is Descarte's "Cogito, ergo sum" (I think, therefore I am), in Asia the fundamental perspective is "I belong, therefore I am"; and 3) a recognition that Christianity bears two "crosses" in presenting itself to Asia, one the paradox between Jesus' particularity and his universality and the other the paradox between God's immanence and God's transcendence.[51] These paradoxes are not altogether new to Asia, but the particular Christian blend of them, for example, claiming exclusivity for Jesus and transcendence for an incarnated God, have been at worst offensive and at best perplexing to many Asians.

As far as the interpenetration of history and praxis is concerned, that might best be explained by C. S. Song's observation that "What is historical is political."[52] In the midst of Asia's dramatic changes it is essential that the relationship between Christianity and the social sphere be recognized. As Christ and Christian faith are historical, so must they have historical and therefore political effects, at least in the lives of Christians who are themselves part of Asian social change.[53] While Song and some other theologians may go too far in maintaining that therefore salvation is primarily a political process, it is nevertheless important to Asian theology that it addresses the relationship between Christian praxis and the dramatic social changes of modern Asia.

Given this important challenge to Asian theology, it is somewhat surprising that Koyama does not give more attention to a theology of politics. For, while Koyama recognizes the political turmoil of Asia and relates considerable portions of his theology to particular political situations, he does not directly expound upon a Christian political perspective. It could be that Koyama prefers to avoid political categories and language altogether. Or, he may oppose theological sanction of any political viewpoint as inevitably a step towards idolatry. Rather, there is a sense in Koyama's writing that he is more concerned with a comprehensive approach to human problems than a categorical approach. Political concerns being always culturally conditioned and imperfect in implementation must always be subjected to evaluation by the crucified mind. No political or social principle stands absolute or inviolable by itself.

One final aspect of the character of Asian theology which deserves special note is its ecumenicity. Asian theology is ecumenical both in composition and in application. Douglas Elwood notes that no reader of Asian theology ought to search only for exotic or esoteric themes which may never have been studied by Christians before. For, Asian theology addresses issues common to the whole church.[54] This is

> due to the global nature of the issues that affect people living in the Third World, and partly also to the impact of the Asian church upon the ecumenical movement, as well as to the positive influence of that movement in the Asian church.[55]

The special significance of the ecumenical character of Asian theology, as well as the significance of Asian theology as a whole are taken up in the next section.

The Significance of Asian Theology

Asian theology naturally adds color to the worldwide theological spectrum. Its idiom will be fresh; its response to Asian challenges, informative. But the value of Asian theology reaches far beyond its novelty. For, its confrontations with the great religions of Asia, its response to the dramatic encounter between Asia and the West, and its approach to contemporary, global issues should yield major new insights for Christianity as a whole.

For one thing, Asian theology exposes the parochial character of Western theology, which has so long confused cultural dominance with spiritual universality. Today it is increasingly apparent that "Western Christian thought is now only one contribution to the whole, alongside Asian, African, and Latin American contributions."[56] Or, as Koyama puts it, "The theology of the West is as culturally conditioned as the theology of the East."[57] As Asian theology wrestles with Christian responses to a cultural milieu significantly different from that of the West, it inevitably reveals the relativity of the theology formulated in the Western cultural milieu. Recognizing this, Charles West asks,

> What then does the Westerner have to learn from all this? First of all, repentance for the narrowness of his own vision of Christian faith and life, steeped as it is in at least a thousand years of Christianized culture and at least two hundred years of capitalist technology. Second, new and liberating insights into the way of Christ with culture and society also in our own countries.[58]

Difficult though it may be for Westerners to comprehend the relativity of their own theological perspectives, it is nevertheless necessary and may even prove beneficial. Paul Tillich records an experience from his own life that illustrates the problem of parochialism in an intercultural world.

> When, soon after the victory of the Nazis in Germany and after my removal from the chair of philosophy at the University of Frankfort, I decided to accept an invitation from Union

Theological Seminary in New York, I wrote to a friend who had already left Germany: "There is everywhere in the world, sky, air, and ocean." This was my consolation in one of the most tragic moments of my life. I did not write: "I can continue everywhere my theological and philosophical work," because unconsciously I doubted whether one could do this anywhere except in Germany. This is what I mean by the term "provincialism" . . . After having lived for a few years in the United States and having worked with theological and philosophical students and colleagues, I became aware of this formerly unconscious provincialism; and after having learned and taught several more years, the provincial outlook began to recede.[59]

As the United States "saved"[60] Tillich from theological parochialism, so Asia can save the West. In a planetary world such salvation is indispensable. Theological parochialism must everywhere recede.[61]

Douglas Elwood notes that indeed some theologians in the West do recognize the maturity of Asian Christian thinking and welcome its contribution to Christianity as a whole. However, the urgency of the West's learning from the experience of the Asian church, as felt by many Asian Christians, is something usually missed by Westerners.[62]

Elwood illustrates his point by quoting from several prominent Asian theologians who emphasize that a) the credibility of Western Christianity is at a low ebb; b) Christianity in the West is seen as desperately in need of help; and c) that in the view of some, Western Christian theology is bankrupt and doomed to collapse.[63]

A Westerner, Alan Geyer, also picks up this note, stating that in the face of current world needs and contemporary technological and social revolutions, "the poverty of prevailing Western theologies" has been mercilessly exposed through recent inter-church encounter.[64]

The time seems to have come when the superstructure of global Christianity, shaped by the dominance of Western theology, needs to give way to a superstructure shaped by an ecumenical, intercultural theology. In this reconstruction process Asian theology has a leading role to play. For, Asian theology is already exceptionally ecumenical and intercultural.

To study Asian theology is to discover an ecumenical theology in the making, as well as to recognize the ecumenicity of the church of which Asian Christians are already a part. On the one hand, ecumenism motivates the study of Asian theology.[65] It recognizes that Asian theology is not merely an appendage to Western theology. Nor is it a mere adaptation of Western theology to Asian contexts. Rather, "It is an integral part of the theology of the church ecumenical."[66] On the other hand, Asian theology with its Western background, its Asian character, and its wide diversity offers not a "theology for Asian Christians only," but the development in Asia of an ecumenical theology that is the property of no particular nation or region, but belongs to the heritage of the whole church.[67] To global Christianity then, Asian theology provides a pattern of ecumenicity at the same time as its encounter with the Asian world produces new understanding of Christian faith.

Koyama summarizes the significance of studying Asian theology and of dialogue between the theology of Asia and theology of the West as a liberating possibility.

> The study of the theologies of Asia by Westerners and the study of theologies of the West by Asians may led to Christianity's emancipation from its Babylonian captivity.[68]

The contributions Asian theology has to make to Christianity as a whole are further highlighted by two facts. One is simply that Asian theology by definition develops in the context of and addresses the concerns of the growing majority of earth's people. In other words, Asian theology derives some significance simply from being the voice of Christians who share in the majority experience of humanity, even if that experience is no more than a common participation in changes wrought by encounter with the West.

Secondly, Asian theology already operates with an awareness that must increasingly inform all Christian theology, namely, that Christians live and witness only as a minority group in the world's population as a whole. The universal claims of Christianity are tempered by the fact that the great majority of the people in the world do not accept them.

Particularly in Asia, but increasingly in the modern world as a whole, Christianity is once again in an overtly apologetic situation.[69] Christian theology must adjust, both in message and method, to this non-Christian context. This entails developing what one writer has called, a "God's eye view" in theology,[70] i.e., a widely ecumenical theology incorporating, insofar a possible, the perspectives of Christians in all parts of the world as opposed to a theology based primarily on European and American views.

Arend Van Leeuwen also argues for the development of an "ecumenical theology of history" and a planetary approach to Christian theology. Such a theology would be marked in two ways by its encounter with the non-Christian environment. First, it would by intention be highly provisional and relative in nature, as the world and all theology are provisional and relative.[71] Secondly, it would need to insistently relate every aspect of Christian theology to the questions thrown up by the non-Christian world.[72]

> In this planetary world the encounter with non-Christian ways of life and thought belongs at the very heart of Christian theology. . . we simply must. . . bring the *whole* world into *all* our thinking.[73]

Obviously, this would mean including the experiences and theological reflections of Asian Christianity in a planetary theology. But, Hendrik Kraemer points out the still wider dimensions of this attitude. A new Christian world outlook, he asserts, would necessitate the kind of

> self-forgetful disinterestedness and of self-sacrificing other interestedness which was revealed in Jesus Christ as the impelling force in God's decisive handling of the secret sore of man and the world.[74]

This view, which has very close echoes in Koyama's theology of the crucified mind particularly in relation to the Asian situation, is amplified by Kraemer with special reference to Asia. A new world outlook in Christian theology would, as circumstances allowed, imply

> a deep, sincere and devoted interest in all things that are bound up with the spiritual, moral, social and intellectual rebirth of the Eastern peoples.[75]

Asia, despite the massive impact of the West, has retained her inner character and integrity. She has absorbed Western influence while staying Eastern and is now re-emerging as a dynamic force in world history with great insights and goals of her own.[76] Christianity as a whole thus stands to learn both from the insights of Christians within the Asian context and from the profound experiences and values of non-Christian Asia.

This learning of course does not come without tension. There is a history of at least tension and at times outright animosity between Christianity as represented by Western Christians, and the cultures and religions of Asia. As Asian religions have, in the long run, resisted Christianity's onslaught and even begun to penetrate Western culture in turn, tension has grown.[77]

Kraemer points out on the other hand how deeply Asia has come to distrust the "Christian" West, calling it the "white man's burden" now to have to live with that mistrust which inhibits an open exchange between Asia and the West.[78] Koyama, as an Asian, has often addressed this very issue from a theological perspective. The values of Asia, he notes,

> were, in a package, decided to be against the values for which Jesus Christ stood, while in most cases such judgment has been given in terms of the values found in the Western lifestyle for which Jesus Christ does not necessarily stand. That which was unfamiliar to the church was condemned as anti-Christian value.[79]

Koyama concludes this analysis with the observation that "one of the few most critical problems posed to the life of the Christian faith is this lack of appreciation-perspective."[80]

The "appreciation-perspective" to which Koyama refers, i.e., the capacity of Christianity to appreciate the positive aspects of non-Christian religions and cultural values, is something Christianity as a whole might gain through Asian theology in particular. For Asian theology is increasingly a product of Christianity in an apologetic environment. There, Asian theology not only embodies the intrinsic Asian character of Asian Christians, but also finds in the richness of the Asian (non-Christian) heritage meaningful ways to express Christian faith.

Increasingly, it is being recognized that Asian Christianity, or non-Western Christianity in general, has come of age. Karl Barth, for example, saw it coming, and wrote an encouraging, open letter to Asian Christians, stating there was truly no need for Asians to be "Europeans," "Western" or "Barthian" in their theology. Barth encouraged his Asian audience to create a theology appropriate to their own situation, to be themselves neither arrogantly nor faint-heartedly. "In my long life I have spoken many words. . . Now it is your turn."[81] Charles Forman also describes the dramatic change that has been taking place in the shift of Christianity from the West to the East. "Recently there has been a significant change. . . Christianity has been breaking with the idea that it depends on a Western base and has been asserting its Eastern identity."[82] Yet, Forman points out that this shift is not merely one of locales, not, in Tillich's terms, a shift from one provincialism to another. Rather, the shift of Christianity into the non-Western world signifies a new grounding for

Christianity altogether. For, while non-Western Christianity has come of age, it is also evident that this Christianity is involved in "a larger field of relationships."[83]

> From this point on it becomes more difficult to identify a non-Western Christianity, just as it becomes more difficult to identify a non-Western world. The direction is toward one Christianity, as it is toward one world.[84]

Asian theology, however, insofar as it offers a model and a method for Christian theology, is a pointer of key significance in the direction of "one Christianity." Within the context of this Asian theological enterprise Kosuke Koyama, one of its pioneers, finds his significance, too. His voice joins the chorus of other Asian Christians who are attempting to speak to the issues of modern Asia and at the same time to represent Asia to the world in general. Only the future can tell how effective and important these Asian voices will be.

Key Features of Asian Theology

Given the enormous diversity of the cultures and situations in which Asian's Christians live, there are naturally a multitude of issues which Asian theology must address. Four concerns, however, seem to feature in theology across much of Asia. These are liberation theology, contextual theology, Asian Christianity's encounter with other religions, and the implications of Asian modes of theology for traditional Western theology.

Liberation Theology

It has already been stated that one of the key issues for Christianity in Asia today is Asian suffering, particularly in relation to the dramatic social, economic and political changes of the last century. In response to this suffering and in reaction to Western domination as a whole, many Christian leaders in Asia have turned to the kind of liberation theology developed by Latin American theologians as a tool for addressing their own situation.

A recent expression of this kind of theology, with its obvious Marxist bent, is the final statement of a conference of Third World theologians who met in Sri Lanka in 1979 to articulate a theology appropriate to Asian struggles.[85] According to this statement the socio-economic sphere is the primary context for theology.

Within this context only the poor can legitimately formulate a liberating Asian theology. In short, the hermeneutical principle of this theological declaration is class struggle.[86]

Loud and passionate though this perspective has been in some quarters of Asia, it is nevertheless a view of limited acceptance. Some theologians have mixed feelings about it. Others reject it as too narrow and biased. C. S. Song, for example, romantically embraces liberation theology at some stages, but rejects the violence it often implies, and goes on to explore a wider basis upon which to establish Christian theology in Asia, namely, that of spirituality.[87] Aloysius Pieris plainly advocates those aspects of liberation theology which Asians can utilize but does recognize that liberation theology itself is much more Western than Eastern.[88] A more critical reaction to the liberation perspective, specifically as that perspective is expressed by the Sri Lanka statement, is that such a view is one-sided, generalized, loose in its use of terms and ideas, and altogether meager on theology.[89]

The Christian Conference of Asia, the most prominent corporate voice of Christianity in Asia, firmly maintains that the key issue which Asian theology must address is injustice. This injustice, apparent in physical poverty and in unequal social, economic and political structures, involves Christians in the battle for power in the decision-making process of Asian nation-states.[90] However, one of the Christian Conference of Asia's most eminent leaders, M. M. Thomas, cautions that while Christianity must work for the liberation of Asia's people from injustice, Christians must never simply equate these people or this process with messianic fulfillment. The Christian justice struggle, Thomas warns, runs the risk of being corrupted from within by self-righteousness and a false equation of human utopian visions with the kingdom of God.[91]

Liberation theology, in other words, is at best a controversial tool for the making of Asian theology. Koyama reflects this sentiment, too, in his analysis of liberation theology. On the one hand he admires the methodological shift underlying liberation theology, i.e., its starting with the socio-economic needs of people rather than with abstract, doctrinal principles of classical theology. On the other hand, Koyama laments the complicated content that liberation theology has produced.[92]

Koyama recalls a conference of Latin American theologians at which the papers presented were written in French and English rather than in the languages of the people about whom they were concerned. These papers were, Koyama recounts, the most abstract he had ever heard. With some irony, Koyama states,

Now whether any Latin American native people understand that kind of very extremely sophisticated, delicate theological discussion or not, I don't know. I have some background myself in theology, but I couldn't follow quite all the way because it was such a sophisticated discussion.[93]

Koyama in fact believes that few Latin American people can appreciate Latin American theology.[94]

Koyama agrees with liberation theology's appreciation of the liberating God of the Exodus. But the Exodus paradigm, Koyama insists, is not the whole story. In Asia, Koyama states, there is rather a concern for the whole person, for human beings in a wider context than that described by the socio-economic situation. Analysis of socio-economic status must come within the context of God's covenant, not the other way around, as the liberationists would have it. Here Koyama considers himself to be in concert with Preman Niles and various other Asian theologians. He believes that this Asian perspective, in fact, is one of Asia's important contributions to ecumenical theology worldwide.[95]

As a secondary point, Koyama notes that an understanding of the relationship between culture and social justice is very important in effecting any social changes.[96] To accomplish changes in the arena of social justice, careful consideration must be given to the cultural background, patterns and values that are being affected. Also implied in this observation is the recognition that understandings of justice are themselves to some degree culturally conditioned and that application of justice may be subject to cultural conditions.

Koyama himself is sensitive to the urgent need for social justice in Asia. He refers to particular crisis situations in his writing and advocates change (e.g. Koyama, *Three Mile an Hour God*, Chapter IV, entitled "Justice Insisting"). However, Koyama also seeks to place contemporary crises in broader historical perspective, relating them to past crises and emphasizing that the crises of Asia are neither unique nor one-sided. With painful honesty Koyama remarks,

> For a long time it was fashionable in Asia to speak about the white domination which brutalized the Asians. Since 1950 this theme has rapidly become anachronistic. What we see today is that Asians are persecuting and murdering fellow Asians; Indians against Indians. Koreans against Koreans, Filipinos against Filipinos, and Cambodians against Cambodians. . . The reality of Asians victimizing Asians has replaced the image of white exploitation and brutality. What we see today forces us to review our self-identity. History today is demonstrating to the whole world that Asian brutality against fellow Asians can be of extreme intensity. Asians can no longer hold a simplistic

self-image of "innocent victim." Human history is far more complex and treacherous than we were accustomed to think. What is happening in Asia is seen as well in many places in the world.[97]

Ultimately, a liberation theology which does not take into account the total picture of Scripture and human history, as Koyama has illustrated, proves to be an inadequate tool for Asian theology.

Contextual Theology

Massive attention has been given to the issue of contextualization in recent Asian theology. The issue itself is hardly new. The contextualization, or indigenization of Christianity in Asia has been discussed over many decades.[98] But with the increasing independence of Asian churches from the West more attention has been given by Asians themselves to the importance of contextualization and to means for accomplishing it.

Behind contextualization are several concerns, e.g., a maturing self-consciousness on the part of Asian Christians, a concern for more effectively communicating the Gospel in the Asian environment, a keen awareness of the foreign associations of Asian Christianity which inhibit Christian witness in the current era, and simply, a certain amount of undisguised anti-Western sentiment.

The need for contextualization is clear. Effective proclamation of the Gospel always depends upon sensitivity to the people and cultures addressed, in this case the people and cultures of Asia. As one Asian has expressed it, "The universal dimension of Christian faith is only conceivable in its interaction with the particularity of our own reality, here and now."[99] While the Gospel is always presented in some "cultural overcoat," which is indeed of the very nature of the incarnation,[100] it must also find clothes that suit the cultural climate into which it is introduced. Asia today must discover what the Gospel is in her own situation, discerning which are acceptable of the cultural forms in which the Gospel comes, and which must be translated into Asian cultural terms.

The importance of contextualization in Asia has been expressed by many. Yet time has shown that the limits of contextualization must also be kept in mind. Out of an eagerness to indigenize Asian theology in local situations the danger arises that the context alone may become determinative for Asian Christian thinking.[101] This would be to ignore the fact that Christian theology never takes place in a vacuum, cultural, geographical, historical, or otherwise, but is related to what has preceded it as well as to theological developments in other contemporary situations. "Contextual relevance, while necessary, should not be for its own sake but always for the sake of the mission and task of the church in the world and in history."[102]

Because the Christian is called to be *both* culturally appreciative *and* faithful to the gospel, it is also necessary for Asian Christians to be careful that the gospel is not distorted in the process of translation into Asian cultural terms. It is no better muddled with Asian culture than muddled with European or some other culture. Ultimately, the gospel transcends and judges all cultures.[103]

Douglas Elwood argues that to balance itself, all contextual theology must be ecumenically orientated so that the necessary mutual correction and mutual enrichment can take place.[104] He warns,

> While allowing the gospel to speak meaningfully to particular cultures, we must at the same time seek to avoid the kind of captivity to particular cultures or class interests which blunts the church's faithfulness as a messenger of the gospel.[105]

Elwood intends this warning for Asian as well as Western theology. Yet his sympathies incline him to state that "It is especially true today that Western forms of Christianity need to be questioned from the point of view of an Asian Christianity."[106] For, Western theologies have often been locked into their own contextual patterns.

Van Leeuwen discusses the issue of indigenization in somewhat broader terms, referring to it as an "inevitable category of church history."[107] In that the church which proclaims the gospel is an historical entity, its proclamation always takes place within an historically and culturally conditioned environment. Yet its theological inheritance always includes the incarnation of the Gospel in other environments. Even the Western churches, Van Leeuwen points out, were foreign in origin,[108] dependent upon the Gospel's incarnation in previous cultures.

Thus Van Leeuwen warns against indigenization as merely a reaction to "foreign" influence, particularly in a world where no culture remains static.

> There is a real danger that a church beset with too tender a conscience about her foreign origin and character may waste her energies on adapting herself to aspects of an indigenous culture already consigned to the past and doomed to become out of date.[109]

Van Leeuwen also questions indigenization in relation to the models offered by European Christianity. It is precisely the excessive identification of Western churches with Western societies that has given rise to some of the problems experienced by Asian Christians. At worst, the Germanized Christianity of the Nazi's stands as an example of indigenization gone too far.[110] It gives substance to the contention of another writer that "a national Christianity is a contradiction in terms."[111]

Interestingly enough, even Koyama, one of Asia's most ardent advocates and pioneers of contextual theology appeals to Asians to keep contextual theology in a wider perspective. Koyama asserts that there is a "Christian-ness" that transcends all particular contexts. While particular situations provide the building blocks of theology, and while Christians are free to apply various ideologies and interpretations in strategic ways for the mission of the church in specific situations, Koyama maintains that in the end no particular context or theology based on a particular context may be regarded as absolute.[112]

Ultimately, contextual theology, like liberation theology, is an important but limited tool in the hands of Asian Christians seeking to shape the future of Christianity in Asia.

Systematic and Asian Theology

One of the salient features of Asian theology is its form. By and large it is not systematic, i.e., it does not usually take the form of "comprehensive logical systems whose parts stand or fall together."[113] As mentioned already, it may indeed be a mistake to define theology in Western systematic terms, expecting Asian theology to take similar forms.[114] "This may not be the form theology should take in Asian settings."[115] At least, it may not yet be time for Asian theology to adopt systematic structure.[116]

M. M. Thomas argues that it is foolish to underrate Asian theological efforts because they do not produce theological systems.[117] What is of more importance is that Asian theology be alive and growing. "It is a small matter whether it gets systematized or remains unsystematic. The important thing is that it should emerge."[118]

Western theological systems can actually prove detrimental to Asian theology.[119] No one has put this more pointedly than Alan Geyer.

> Systematic theology, by and large, remains in a state of Teutonic captivity. The Aryan bias of Christian doctrine is perhaps

the most serious intellectual obstacle to full ecumenical fellowship with the younger churches, to their own theological creativity and to Christian evangelism in Asia, Africa and Latin America.[120]

The cultural forms in which Christian theology was presented to Asia are dispensable. They are "clay pots" which may be discarded in the creation of theological forms more appropriate to the Asian context. In their place may come the poems, stories and art work already typical of Asian theology. Elwood puts forth the intriguing idea that what remains as systematic theology in the future could in fact be a corporate affair.

> I believe that the ecumenical vision should eventually inspire an entirely new kind of textbook in systematic theology that would be a work of collaboration of scholars from all six continents, incorporating insights from the experience and reflection of Christians in every land.[121]

Such a shift in the nature on Christian theology—both to non-systematic forms and to increasingly ecumenical composition—could be a shift essential to the apologetic task of Christianity in an intensely intercultural world. Insofar as the Asian context stands pre-eminent as an apologetic, intercultural milieu and insofar as Asian theology in that milieu already exhibits alternative modes for Christian theology, Asian theology may provide important leads for Christianity as a whole in undertaking its missionary task in the modern world.

The Significance of Encounter with Other Religions

Asia is the home of some of humanity's greatest religions. Asian religiosity, as mentioned earlier, figures as an important factor in the cultural complexion of Asia as a whole. Thus, Christianity, if it would find a significant place in Asia, must come to terms with Asia's religious heritage.

Asian Christians, those on the front lines of this encounter, are keenly aware of the necessity for this task. From their theological wrestling with the issues emanating from Christianity's encounter with other religions may come some of the most important lessons the church has to learn in the present day.

First of all, Asian Christianity's encounter with other religions triggers a reappraisal of Christianity's previous theologies of other religions. No longer can Christians simply condemn and conquer peoples of different faiths. The "Christendom" experience and the colonial power which fed Christian illusions of superiority and which enabled Christian expansion no longer exist. Asian cultures and religions, at the same time, have demonstrated a resilience that has kept Christian penetration to a bare minimum. Christians are thus challenged to reconsider their relationship to people of other faiths.

Some Asians count this a blessing. To learn from the alternative views of life and reality embodied in Asian religions, and to recognize in them other experiences of the holy is seen as a "great theological step forward."[122] By studying the living faiths of Asia in their home context Christians can perhaps discover a new understanding of religious life altogether.[123] They will at least develop a sense of inter-religious ecumenism in which other religions become neighbors rather than strangers.

Dialogue with other religions, already a lively concern in Asian churches as well as elsewhere, is seen not only as a means of increased understanding of other religions but also as a source of fresh insights for Christian theology.[124] Some Christians see in other religions a treasure-house of wisdom and experience from which Christianity and humanity in general can benefit in the continuing creation of a planetary world.[125]

In a wider sense Christianity's encounter with other religions in Asia exemplifies what all Christian theology must increasingly come to terms with, namely, the apologetic position of Christianity in a dramatically changed world. Christian attitudes toward other religions, so long a peripheral aspect of Christian theology, are now becoming a central concern. Insofar as other faiths—religious or secular— challenge Christian claims,[126] the study of other faiths becomes, as one writer puts it with particular reference to Asia, part of the prolegomenon of theology.[127]

Further, the religions and cultures of Asia stand as a source of judgment on Christianity. "The Asian Theopraxis is born of a submission to. . . non-Christian judgment."[128] That is to say, not only will the appropriateness of Christian witness be measured by how Christianity is received, but Christianity's sense of humility in relation to Asia's religions will be tested. As Aloysius Pieris puts it, the question is whether or not the church will be humble enough to be baptized in the Jordan of Asian religiosity and bold enough to be baptized on the cross of Asian poverty.[129]

In regard specifically to the issue of Christianity's humility in relation to Asia's religions and cultures, Koyama has surveyed traditional Christianity and found it noticeably wanting. Koyama encourages a positive Christian attitude toward Asia and other religions as a natural outgrowth of the crucified mind. Koyama even goes so far as to suggest that other religions can be more in harmony with the crucified mind than Christianity. The test is the fruit they bear. "If humanity is ruined by Christianity, Christianity is wrong; if Buddhism can save humanity, OK."[130]

Koyama does not betray Christianity in saying this, for he remains biblically Christocentric in his understanding of what underlies salvation. But Koyama, as an Asian who has lived closely with people of other faiths, realizes the need for a new Christian understanding of other religions. Along with the relationship between Christianity and culture, and the relationship between Christianity and militarism, Koyama sees the relationship between Christianity and other religions as one of three primary challenges for Christian theology in the decades to come.[131] Increasingly, Koyama believes, the Bible will become a book belonging to all humanity, Marxists and Buddhists for example, included. Then Christianity's relationship with other religions will take place at least in part in the context of a common text.[132]

Of course, Koyama's point of view is that of one Asian Christian among many who are concerned with the relationship between Christianity and other religions. In a context where Christianity remains a tiny religion in the midst of great and ancient faiths, the whole issue is one which will long continue to dominate the formation of Asian theology and the proclamation of the Christian Gospel in Asia.

PART II

KOYAMA'S THEOLOGY—KEY THEMES

CHAPTER SIX

STARTING POINTS

OVERVIEW

Not long after the publication of Koyama's *No Handle on the Cross*, some people asked, "when is he going to write a book?" The implication of this tongue-in-cheek comment was that Koyama's writings lacked the systematic, fully-developed character of a "normal" theological tome. Indeed, to many, Koyama's books have appeared to be simply a collection of unrelated essays.

However, these reactions reflect an all too superficial encounter with the depth of Koyama's thought. Perhaps understandably, the simplicity and imagination of Koyama's style of writing may distract the reader from the substance of his thought. His use of imagery and humor may not conform to the expectations of readers conditioned by traditional European theological writing. But substance there is in Koyama's theology in a consistent manner.

Koyama's theological system may not easily fit into the straightforward, abstract, linear patterns common to European theology (even though the foundations of his system are thoroughly shaped by European-style research and analysis). Rather, Koyama's theology may be better described as imaginative, narrative, and molecular.

That is to say, while Koyama writes with logical consistency, he also makes masterful use of images, contrasts, and stories to convey his ideas. His system resembles a many-faceted sphere or a compound molecule of inter-related concerns more than it does a linear, chain-like progression of independent ideas.

Since a book such as this one must present information in a linear manner, some of the molecular wholeness of Koyama's theology cannot be fitted into it. However, a presentation of some of the major themes in Koyama's theology produced in response to his surrounding context may convey the basic concerns around which Koyama's theology is focused. It can also provide a good "taste" of the overall flavor of Koyama's creative theology.

To this end, Part II is divided into five chapters. The first presents a variety of themes which describe Koyama's general attitudes towards the modern world and his view of Christianity's place in it. The second chapter deals with the hermeneutical core of Koyama's theology, based on his understanding of "neighbourology" and the "crucified mind." The third chapter outlines Koyama's thinking on Christianity's relationship with other religions. Finally, critical evaluations are made of Koyama's crucified mind theology and of his theology of other religions.

This particular ordering of Koyama's theology has a two-fold intention. As a somewhat systematic presentation of Koyama's theology, it deals first of all with the general framework of Koyama's thinking. Then, the flavor of Koyama's theology having been established, detailed attention can be given to the unique aspects which lie at the heart of Koyama's theology.

The components and style of a theology born in and addressed to the challenges to Christianity in the complex world of today will thus be laid out. Supreme among all these elements is the force which binds them all together, namely, Koyama's commitment to a theology of the "crucified mind." This particular Christo-centric commitment, worked out especially in Koyama's concern for Christianity in Asia and for people of other faiths, is the heart of Koyama's theology. It is a commitment which finds its fulfillment in an intense concern for other people. Thus, Koyama seeks in his theology to appreciate people in a variety of situations, and to draw the connections between their story and the Cross of Jesus, the story of God's self-giving love. Naturally, a theology embodying such considerations will be one in which the medium, such as "writing a book," will be subordinate to the message itself. An understanding of that facilitates a topical look at the varied areas of Koyama's theological concerns.

Koyama's World Picture

The world is scattered asunder; The all is not held together; We are pressed between two realities. On the other hand (sic), the reality that "in him all things hold together," and, on the other, the reality that all things are confounded, scattered and sick. The former is a theological eschatological reality (a hidden reality). The latter is a brutally obvious reality to all men. The Christian church confesses her faith when she bodily proclaims that the language which can bind these two realities is the language of the cross . . . The lordship which can relate these two mutually hostile truths is the crucified lordship: Here is the global significance of theology of the cross.[1]

Contained in these words are the most fundamental elements of Koyama's whole theology and world view. On the one hand, he sees the world as broken, scattered and sick. At the same time he believes in another reality or truth in the world which coexists with the obvious reality of the world's brokenness. This other reality is that described by the Christian faith. While these two realities appear to contradict each other, Koyama believes that they are held together in the cross of Jesus Christ, who himself is a testimony to the other reality.

Koyama does not hesitate to admit that the hiddenness of the reality associated with Christ, namely, that in him all things hold together (Col. 1:17), is a "stumbling block," a scandal to normal human understanding of the world. That there is a non-broken reality in the world and that this reality is visible in Jesus Christ is hardly obvious or sensible to normal human perspective:

With sheer good sense the very people for whom Christ came stumbled at him . . . With "sheer good sense" the people who live at proximity to the Buddha stumble at Christ as well. The lordship of Christ in theology of the cross—the crucified lordship!—is universally "sheer nonsense" to man.[2]

But, this "sheer nonsense" is the heart of Christianity. Despite the apparent contradiction of the world's brokenness, the reality that in Christ all things hold together has always been an essential element in the Christian understanding of the world. Puzzling and incomprehensible as it may be, the decision of God that the world should continue in its turbulent brokenness is not a peripheral decision but a fundamental one of the New Testament. As such, it is a mystery.[3]

However, Koyama sees meaning in this mystery. The eschatological tension of the "already-not-yet" of God's Kingdom, that is, the fact that believers in Christ's lordship must struggle with the fact that that lordship is not apparent, actually serves to shape and guide their Christian life in the broken world as it is. There is, therefore, a functional purpose to the coexistence of the "two mutually hostile truths." The tension between them is a dynamic and creative one.

While Koyama's interpretation of the world rests on his prior commitment to a Christian description of it as presented so far, he nevertheless can present his interpretation of the world in more general terms:

There is today a profound sense of spiritual uneasiness among us. We are educated. We are modern. We are scientific. We have had considerable experience in political and economic organization. We are schooled in the histories of nations and are aware of the historical whereabouts of our own nations. Yet, for all our enlightened understanding, we find our sense of identity disintegrating. Our existence is being threatened. Our communication is breaking down. Our sense of value is crippled. We feel ourselves to be living in a time of *spiritual* crisis for mankind. I do not think there is among us anyone who can offer a satisfying explanation of why we are the very source of tragedy to ourselves. We are aware that it takes human spirit to bring forth human tragedy and equally that it takes human spirit to bring forth human glory. Our spirit is confronted by two awesome possibilities: human tragedy and human glory.[4]

Koyama sets this crisis of human spirit in the context of the global influence of Western civilization. "Our everyday experience confirms that this latest civilization is the most forceful and most universal civilization that has ever appeared on the horizon of the history of mankind."[5] But, Western civilization, as Koyama sees it, is itself a strong spiritual movement. This reflects Koyama's belief that:

Man is inescapably spiritual. It is the spirit of man that appreciates spiritual value. It is again the spirit of man that rejects spiritual value. Since it is the spirit of man that does these things, all *human* values carry inevitably the dimension of spiritual value.[6]

However, human spirituality may be subject to perversion. Especially as the world moves through the transitions from long-established patterns and traditions to modern ways of life, Koyama senses that "we are witnessing the work of massive misdirected spirituality."[7]

Greed is the term Koyama most often uses to describe this misdirected spirituality.

Isn't our world caught in the devastating tidal waves of greediness, dishonesty and impurity? Our great civilization of the twentieth century is tottering because of human greediness. Our sense of value is gravely ill because it is in the grip of cancerous greed. How tragically the sense of values in the minds of children is destroyed because of the insidious greedy philosophy that the purpose of education is to enable children to make more money . . . Our society is well-tuned to cater for infinite human greediness. It is, therefore, extremely difficult to live a greed-free life in this greedful world.[8]

But Koyama points to other symptoms of brokenness and misdirected spirituality which are similarly threatening to human well-being. "Why is it," he asks, "that the world, so full of fantastic technological means of communication, can remain so parochial?"[9] In today's world people travel extensively, are informed about events the world over via education and modern communications media. Yet too many people maintain a parochial mentality, a mind which does not go beyond the limits of its own narrow scope in relating to the world. Such an attitude, which is narrowly self-centered, Koyama also calls a "middle-kingdom complex."[10]

Parochial mentality is a spiritual malady. If it were not so, it could be healed easily. It is a spirituality of self-centered search for security, the spirit of self-admiration, prejudice and one-way traffic.[11]

"Parochial truth destroys man."[12] It is a sick, poisonous perspective in Koyama's eyes. "Parochial truth is deceptive."[13] It captures people in their own illusions.

The Bible exposes the futility of parochial illusions (e.g., Jer. 7:4), and emphasizes the universality of God's saving intentions.[14] Unfortunately, as Koyama sees it, Christianity has failed to make people free from parochial mentality.[15]

Koyama sees one of the necessary counters to parochialism to be a redistribution of power in the human community "so that the powerful are checked in their blatant exploitation of the weak."[16] This desire envisions a world in which a redistribution or sharing of power is possible. Although Koyama questions whether or not there is a unity of humankind in which such a redistribution could be worked out, he acknowledges that the world is inter-related. He argues that it is not, however, interdependent in the sense that power and prosperity are equally shared. For, human relatedness allows exploitation for the gain of some at the expense of others, whereas true interdependence would make exploitation self-destructive.[17]

Yet Koyama sees signs of promise in the existing inter-relatedness of the world. His estimation of the world, despite all its brokenness, has a very positive side. To describe it, Koyama turns to the history of Israel, the Promised Land, as a model of the world today. Israel was a "busy, dangerous, intersection-land."[18] Life there was "intersected" life. It was not isolated, unthreatened, or static. In a very similar way, the world today is also busy, dangerous and living an "intersected" life.

> Wherever you are today, you cannot but be "encounter people" and "intersection people." We are all now promised land people.[19]

> It seems to me that the world's history is moving towards an unprecedented and massive meeting of different cultures and peoples. No one is allowed to stand aside and take distance from this historical fact.[20]

This modern, massive encounter of people is no longer an encounter of just the elite members of different groups as in the past, but also of ordinary people. While this encounter increases cultural assimilation between peoples, it also naturally creates problems. Yet, says Koyama,

> In spite of all sorts of serious problems caused by this massive global reorganization, I think this process of transition from the world of many tribes to the world of one humanity is a blessing of God.[21]

To Koyama this massive encounter among the world's peoples is a necessary and positive part of human destiny.

> Human experience is limited. Even if a man goes around the world twenty times, his "world experience" is limited. Man cannot become familiar with all things. To live with that which is unfamiliar is part of human destiny. And this destiny is a blessing . . . [22]

The blessings of the human encounter with the unfamiliar (e.g., with other humans) come, as Koyama sees it, through the conflict and corresponding enrichment that the tensions of encounter produce. Conflict and enrichment come together as a natural part of human growth.

As this process of tension and growth takes place for the people of the world, it also takes place for Christianity. Indeed, Christianity without encounter can be *lonely* in Koyama's experience. Christian truth needs, as it were, "sparring part-ners" to hone its understanding and expression of its truth.[23] This need relates to the reality that human identity, both personal and corporate, is shaped through encounter.

> As long as man lives in a concrete historical world of interac-tions, it is obvious that there is no such thing as a "pure, intact self-identity" . . . Self-identity is a concept of historical interac-tion. It is always "shared identity."[24]

To Koyama, shared identity is, however, not a simple concept. It represents the whole complex meeting of different nations and different human histories as they seek to express their common aspirations and frustrations. As such, shared identity is a "deeply *human* concept 'of great importance' for the modern world since it is possibly another name for peace."[25]

The shared identities of earth's peoples are becoming more obvious in a world of massive intersection between peoples and cultures. For Christianity, which seeks to address the world's peoples and cultures, this is a promising recognition. For, "mission is to relate God's history of shared self-identity with people's history of shared self-identity."[26] The grounds for sharing Christianity's message are being continually enriched as the world becomes more conscious of shared self-identity.

In conclusion, it can be seen that Koyama's picture of the world is a primarily theological one (based on personal faith) which seeks to interpret and understand the world as it is in its inherent brokenness and in its modern developments. To this understanding, finally, Koyama brings his concern for Christian mission as the task of uniting the two realities of a world broken and a world in which all things are held together.

Koyama's View of Asia

Koyama's picture of the world, along with his theology, has been shaped, natu-rally, by the Asian context to which he belongs. It is a context of radical historical change, as Koyama sees it, and it is a context of considerable challenge for modern Christian theology and mission.

Koyama attempts to draw Christianity and the Asian context together by describing the present situation of people in Asia, by critically reflecting on the his-tory of Christianity's coming to Asia, and eventually by advocating a new kind of

Christian encounter with the peoples and cultures of Asia based on theology of the cross.

Describing the contemporary situation of Asia in terms similar to that of many other Asian commentators, Koyama points out that Asia is in a time of crisis.

> We are caught at the crashing point of the relentless historical and spiritual forces that are shaking our life in all its aspects; family, culture, religion, language, race, defence and ideology. The history of colonial rule came to its end. Asian nations emerged new and young with a fresh outlook of self-understanding. The unprecedented impact of modernization (universal education, social welfare programmes, giant business enterprises, democratic political systems, medicine, urbanization, electronics, rapid and massive transportation) brought upon the millions of South-east Asians both hope and despair! Traditional values are radically questioned. Aspiration towards the fulfillment of human freedom and dignity is in a violent upsurge. South-east Asians are experiencing discontinuity. Going through the history of construction and demolition (Jer. 1:10) they live in a crisis of identity. Man's life is profoundly disturbed and complicated.[27]

In a comparison of the situation in South East Asia with that of Australia, Koyama further describes some areas of existing turmoil:

> *Young people*—there is a massive chaos of aspirations and frustrations among the millions of young people in South East Asian countries; *family*—traditional family structures and concepts are going through a gradual yet critical crisis of change in South East Asia against the background of centuries old customs; *racial*, *ethnic*, and *tribal tensions* [bring enrichment and conflict to South East Asia on a large scale]; *poverty* [is] general and critical . . . among the masses of South East Asia.[28]

Religious conflicts, too, in the area have increased the general psychological tension. But the fact that great world religions coexist in South East Asia is not altogether negative. Koyama sees this, indeed, as a "colourful" situation.

In South East Asia, any great tradition of truth is encountered
by another equally great tradition of truth, thus religious truth is
always a truth at the intersection with other truths.[29]

Finally, political changes in the post-World War Two period have greatly
affected Asian life, particularly because "No South East Asian country today is not
in essence under martial law."[30]

These crises of life, while not unique in the world, are, however, particularly
notable in places like South East Asia.

Our traditional experience with time, family, language and education is radically disrupted and confused. At these critical
points we have lost our *shalom*. We feel injured.

Time was traditionally experienced as being as unlimited as a
loving mother's milk is unlimited to her baby. Time was gener-
ously given. It was not sold as pork chops are sold . . . Time
was calm . . . pastoral . . . communal . . . Apart from community
no time existed.

Now, this has been changed without any consultation with us!
Time is now to be understood in terms of business achievement
. . . Time is now violently grasped. It was once public commu-
nity property. It is now private business property. Once it was
shared, now it is monopolized. Time does not heal us now.
Time wounds us.[31]

Similar crisis has come to family life in South East Asia. Belonging to a family
or clan used to be the primary value of life. Family was

the source of security, fellowship, encouragement, happiness,
education and spirituality. Family was sacred. The family has
now been invaded by the foreign value called "money." Cash
relationship is replacing personal relationship in our society
today.[32]

Similar disruption has come to the education process of South East Asian life,
as Koyama sees it.

Traditionally, education was not an accumulation of English letters after our names. Education was personality-formation.

Today education is a tool to get a good job. Good education brings more money.[33]

Theologically, Koyama understands these crises to result from human sinfulness, or, in Koyama's language, from the fact that human beings seek to "handle" history. That is, they seek to manipulate and control history for their own gain. This can only be done, however,

> through deceptions and perpetrations of injury to [one's] neighbors. Perhaps this is the main characteristic of the "outside-the-garden civilization."[34]

The situation is not hopeless in Koyama's eyes because God has entered human history in a redemptive, "non-handling" way. Therefore, the "zig-zag course of the hope and despair" that Asia has experienced for the last four hundred years[35] is one which will find its ultimately positive conclusion in God's historical presence. In the meantime, Koyama turns his attention to the historical roots of Asia's current problems to discover how the Christian message might address Asia's present crises and encourage her hopes.

Without question, most of Asia's contemporary crises were precipitated by her encounter with the West. Koyama's primary interest in the historical encounter of Asia and the West is theological. Nevertheless, he describes the whole process as significant in the broadest terms.

> The West's influence upon Asia for the last four hundred years has been substantial. The massive and penetrating effect of modernization is a process of Westernization. This decisive shaking of the foundations in Asian life by the West's mental and scientific-technological impact is a great event in the history of mankind.[36]

For Koyama, this event is one which raises important theological questions concerning the spiritual source and intentions of the West's power and the spiritual effects of that power in Asia. Although critical about this whole process, Koyama does not believe that the effects of Western power were all bad. Indeed, Koyama can speak of the Western colonial process as an avenue of God's historical, saving approach to Asia.

Through the period of immense suffering under the militarily superior colonial West, the East was brought closer to the revolutionary controversy which the Lord initiated . . . This is, theologically speaking, perhaps the most crucial event to touch the depth of Asian existence and history, introducing the ferment of disturbing theological discontinuity into the continuous ontocratic culture of the East. God's saving presence ("the right hand of God") worked upon Asia through the violent storm of man's exploitation of his neighbors ("the left hand of God").[37]

An image which Koyama develops to portray the dual influence of the West on Asia is that of "gun" and "ointment." "Gun" influences are those which wounded Asia either in socio-economic or theological terms. While the military and political imperialism of the Western colonial powers is more obviously wounding to Asia, the more subtle theological imperialism which came through the use of religion to justify and undergird Western expansionism is also seriously wounding to Asian spirituality—and to Christianity itself.

In her dealing with Asia, the West has often been hardened by commercial avariciousness and by theological self-righteousness. These two "hardening" elements constitute the main ingredients of the gunpowder of the West against Asia.[38]

On the other hand, encounter with the West brought healing to Asia's already existing "wounds." "Concomitant with the process of 'gun' came 'ointment,' also from the West, to Asia."[39] This healing in Koyama's eyes can be summed up in the term "modernization."

Modernization does not simply mean a spread of modern technological information and practices. It is a new orientation in the life of mankind which has been effecting radical transformations in all areas of human life.[40]

The healing effect of modernization is in its creative challenge to the static traditions of Asia. There, the combination of "gun" and "ointment" contained in the West's coming to Asia produces compacted and fertile historical dynamism.

Experiencing this accelerated historical process, the Asians begin to have a new feeling about history. From this feeling came two convictions: first, a growing conviction that Asians can become the main force in the universal history of mankind today and tomorrow, that through their active participation they can *change* history; second, an increasing confidence that history has some definite goal. In the "goal of modernization," they have found a practical goal towards which they can "purposefully" move. An "Asian Drama" has begun. The modernization ointment consists outwardly in the transformation of every day life, in increasing physical and environmental comfort, and inwardly in the sense of active participation in history. Modernization is, in this sense, an "ointment" for a stagnant and traditional Asia.[41]

Koyama is quick to add that modernization is not all ointment per se. It also carries wounding elements. In the possibilities for its abuse, as in technology applied to warfare and human destruction, modernization must be recognized as simultaneously "ointment" and "gun."

Having thus considered the impact of the West upon Asia in a general way, Koyama focuses his concern on the manner in which Christianity in particular was brought to Asia during the Western colonial era. His critiques of the process are generally provocative if not devastating.

He speaks, for example, of the "crusade mentality" that not only typified Christian mission in Asia in the past, but continues to be common there today. Recording a Buddhist monk's consternation at modern Christian crusades in his country, Koyama compares crusade mentality with the mind of self-denial, that is, a mind more in keeping with the stigmatic style of Christ's presence in the world—a mind with which Asians can more readily identify.

In many parts of Asia we come across a "Crusade for Christ." In Hong Kong, Singapore, Taiwan, Thailand and Korea crusades come in waves. Asians know intuitively that the holy man Jesus Christ cannot be the man of religious crusade. Strangely Asia knows Jesus Christ as the self-denier. The holy man is the self-denier. Am I just suggesting that the wording "Crusade for Christ" should be dropped? What I am really aiming at here is to place such campaign psychology of Christians under the light of the New Testament theology of the *stigma* of Jesus Christ. What does the *stigma* of Jesus Christ mean in our evangelism? Every crusade event in Asia accentuates the tragic discrepancy between the "theology of the *stigma* of Christ" and the "theology of the crusade for Christ." In this discrepancy I see an equally serious sign of discrepancy between Asian spirituality and that of the Christian West. In rejecting the "theology of the crusade for Christ" intuitively and emotionally, the Asians are indicating their genuine openness to the alternative, the theology of the *stigma* of Christ. Asians know what self-denial and *stigma* mean through their own history and experience. The biblical salvation history moves with the sign of the *stigma* of Christ, not with the religious campaign.[42]

Another obvious problem which the Western churches brought to Asia was their own confessionalism, or denominationalism. The confessional loyalties of the Western Christians create serious obstacles for younger churches, e.g. in Asia. Not only do Asians find it difficult if not impossible to relate to the historical conditions which produced the varying confessional families of the West, they also are disturbed at the theological questions raised by confessional differences. The theological basis for such divisions, and whether these divisions are still helpful or even experiential any more in the lives of the various confessional families are open to serious questioning.[43] Given the discrepancies they create in the church as a whole today, Koyama is hardly alone among Asian theologians in this apprehension over this contribution of Western Christianity to Asia.

A more subtle difficulty engendered by Western mission in Asia is discovered in the theology frequently apparent in Asian worship. While arguing against "happy-ending religion," wherein human beings seek to domesticate God to serve their own desires, Koyama laments that the Asian churches have received God as one who is a predictable *deus ex machina* manager of life rather than as one who stands against man as the sovereign Lord.

Most of the hymns sung in the Asian churches are dominated by the theology of Jesus Christ, the author of happy-ending religion. I count it to be a great misfortune that this God with the predictable finger was preached far more forcefully and universally in Asia than the God with the unpredictable finger. The God of the predictable finger (the answer-God) in truth looked too cheap to be true to the eyes of the Asians whose hearts are much more receptive to the message of the unpredictable finger of God (the invitation-God).[44]

Altogether, difficulties in style of mission, in the confessionalism of Western Christianity, and in the theology inherent in Western Christianity's expansion distress Koyama. In part, certainly, they must have contributed to his support for the moratorium movement which advocated the suspension of personnel and funds sent to churches in Asia, Africa and Latin America by European and American churches. The systems of relationship which have been built upon over the colonial centuries, for example, between Asian and Western churches, need to be, in Koyama's word, crucified. Or, expressed in more pastoral terms, the churches of Asia need some undisturbed "family time."[45]

The specific problems described so far in the coming of Western Christianity to Asia are almost minor compared to the larger issues in Koyama's concern for Christianity in Asia today. His most intense distress is over Western Christianity's arrogant failure to respect and absorb the history of Asia and to meet the peoples and cultures there in the spirit of the crucified Lord.

Koyama speaks of this problem in terms of the Asian story being addressed by and molded by Western theory. The Asian story—the history, values, and experiences of Asia's peoples—has been dealt with as a theory by typically theory-minded Westerners. The existential reality of the Asian story is thereby lost. "When the story is treated as a theory, it loses it life."[46] At least, "When a foreign theory is imposed upon a story," as is the case of Western theory applied to Asian story, "obviously the story suffers."[47] While there is growth and stimulation in the pain of such an encounter, the cost is high. Christianity paid such a high price, Koyama feels, in that it has made only a superficial impact in Asia. Christianity has been guilty of a theory-minded approach to the Asian story. Or, to use a key Koyama image, Christianity has tried to "handle" the Asian story in a "wise," "strong," and self-centered way rather than according to the self-denying way of the cross. Had Christianity been seriously concerned with history, it would have listened to the stories of the Asian peoples. If it had done so, speculates Koyama, Christianity in Asia today might have become a most interesting and vital faith among the Asian peoples.[48]

Instead of listening to and learning from Asia's story, Christianity has been preoccupied with deaf self-proclamation, which Koyama describes as a "militant teacher-complex."[49] This hardened, efficiency-oriented method of encounter by Western Christianity with Asia "has made Christianity in Asia historically superficial and docetic."[50]

Koyama phrases the issue even more acutely in terms of the necessity for Christianity to a) take history (human stories) seriously and b) reflect the nature of Christ's cross in so doing.

History can be approached in two ways: the way of spitting
upon others and the way of being spat upon by others. History
is touched superficially by the former and profoundly by the latter. Ecclesiology and missiology must be rooted in the latter,
since the first-born of all things and the first-born of the dead
came to us in the latter way. I maintain that to the degree that
the church has spat upon other religious faiths and spiritual tradition in Asia, she has become superficial in her Christological
impact upon the Asian man and history. To the degree that the
church has been spat upon, she has become alive in mission and
healing in the history.[51]

Still, Koyama goes farther in expressing the destructiveness and the difficulty
of Western Christianity's approach to Asia. The "militant teacher-complex," so
common in the history of Western Christian mission with its closed-minded, one-
way orientation to Asia, has actually misrepresented Christ and even become "the
mind against the mind of Christ."[52]

Koyama quotes a poem by an Asian which expresses the ultimate product of
anti-historical, theory-minded, self-centered, non-stigmatic Christianity.

> Cross run away, Run away from me.
> I hate you. Take your ideas
> And your civilization
> And go back
> To where you belong.
>
> -Albert Leomala[53]
> (New Hebrides)

Koyama notices that the poet "sees the symbol of hated Western civilization in
the Cross!"[54] rather than in smokestacks, money, or other visible signs of Western
influence. To Koyama, this tragic perspective raises the question, "Is Jesus Christ
then presented as the crucifying Lord instead of the crucified Lord?"[55] Koyama
believes that "In truth Christians have preached Jesus Christ crucified."[56] Indeed,
Koyama never fails to remember, even in his sharpest attacks on the history of
Christianity's coming to Asia, that there were many Western Christians who did
embody the self-denial and love appropriate to followers of Christ.[57] But, to Koyama, the fact that many Asians have experienced Jesus Christ as "bulldozing"
them, that Christ crucified is seen by many in Asia as Christ crucifying them, is the
most serious missiological problem in Asia today.[58]

In response to this unhappy situation, Christianity today must begin to appreciate the history, the story, of Asia. But beyond that, it must repent of its arrogance and narrowness in the past. *"In repentance,"* notes Koyama, *"we become deeply historical."*[59] Put another way, "The future belongs to those who repent."[60] Thus, as Christianity would be faithful to its proclamation today it must face the past and respond to the present.

In a "give and take" context where Western Christianity repented and took more seriously the story of Asia, Asian Christianity itself could speak and have its contribution to Christianity as a whole heard.

> The Church universal is watching us today to see how our
> "Asian kidneys" [here Koyama is referring to the Hebrew idea
> that the most secret stirring of the soul took place in the kid-
> neys: Ps. 73:21, Jer. 17:10)] respond specifically to the message
> of the word of the cross.[61]

It is indeed time for Asian theology, as Koyama envisions it, to assume her own personality. "It must bear 'the marks of Jesus' (Gal. 6:17) at the depth of our Asian 'hearts' and Asian 'kidneys'."[62] "The marks of Jesus," as Koyama describes them, would certainly include Asia's suffering at the hand of Western Christianity's self-centered theology. Precisely because Asian Christianity has experienced so dramatically the fruits of a theology which is used to support human triumphalism, militarism and cultural imperialism, Koyama says,

> Perhaps, the fundamental contribution of the theology in Asia
> to the church universal is to describe, in her own language, at
> what points theology should stumble.[63]

Such a perspective reflects, of course, Koyama's conviction that "stumbling" must be at the heart of the Christian message because it is part of the nature of the cross of Christ.

Another contribution to universal Christianity which Koyama sees coming out of the Asian context rests precisely in the meeting of Christianity with the other religions of Asia. Koyama discusses this contribution in relation to the doctrine of justification by faith. That doctrine, which is meaningful against the background of Western Christianity, loses its punch in Asia, in Koyama's eyes, unless it is set over against the impartiality of God (as given in Romans 2:9–11).

The significant point is that this awareness of the impartiality of God has emerged within the church as a result of its being caught within the inter-religious situation of Asia. The people of the other living faiths are demanding that the Asian Christians take the impartiality of God seriously. *They* are saying that Christian authenticity must be rooted in the sense of the impartiality of God. I believe they are making a historic contribution to the Christian faith.[64]

Taking the impartiality of God seriously reminds the Christian church that she, too, must stand under the judgment of God. Not only does this have humbling implications for the Church itself; it also tempers Christian triumphalism in regard to other faiths.

So significant is the whole experience of Christianity in Asia to Koyama that he proposes that it is the second great critical encounter in the whole history of Christianity. The first was that which took place in the early centuries of Christianity when it had to find its place in the complex Mediterranean world of Jewish, Greek, North African and Roman cultures.[65] Today, Christianity's encounter with other great spiritual and religious forces in the world is going on in an intensified and universalized manner. But it is capsulized in the complex situation of Asia. Therefore Asia and the West must attentively learn theology from each other,

> in order to make the life of the world church rich, enlightened and more obedient to the mind of Jesus Christ, the promised one who died on the cross.[66]

Koyama's Understanding of Theology

In various places in his writings, Koyama deliberates on theology itself. He reflects upon its origin, source, nature and purpose, and frequently discusses the fundamental relationship between theology and history. For discussion purposes, five dimensions of Koyama's understanding of theology may be distinguished. The first is the responsorial-existential dimension. One of Koyama's essays in his book *Fifty Meditations* introduces it.

> There is a difference between God and theology. This is as obvious as the difference between wife and wife-ology. (If they

were the same it would be much easier to handle!) The famous John 3:16 does not say "for theology so loved the world that he gave his only Son . . . "God can neither be equated with theology nor contained in theology. The New Testament speaks about "The Kingdom of God" and not "kingdom of theology." There is the sovereign God but there cannot be the sovereign theology, no matter how great. All theologies are very humble human attempts to say something about God because God has first spoken to us. God first loved us (I John 4:19). Theology does not walk on the street any more than wife-ology does. Man who engages in theology walks. He becomes a "man of theology" (sociologically called theologian). When God comes to him he finds himself saying what the young Jeremiah said: ("Ah, Lord God; Behold, I do not know how to speak, for I am only a youth"—Jer. 1:6). This is the genuine mark of those who engage in theology. In theology we do not know how to speak![67]

With typical imagination yet succinctness Koyama depicts the limited, responsorial nature of theology. As the human response to God's speaking and coming to humanity, it is simply human participation in a process God has initiated. As it were, "theology is a gift from God."[68]

Put another way,

theology is man's understanding of God on the basis of God's understanding of man. It is as a child understands his mother only by way of his mother's far more intense and profound understanding of the child.[69]

Already it is clear that for Koyama, Christian theology takes place "a priori" in the context of faith in a living God. Theology therefore, is neither abstract nor impersonal. It refers to a continuous encounter between the living God and human beings. But, says Koyama,

This particular character of theology is not self-evident. It is a hidden reality. That God is speaking to us today and that he is ruling the histories of nations and the communities, is not obvious.[70]

It is an insight of faith which theology seeks to express.

Moreover, because faith "is a total personal commitment,"[71] so Christian theology must be "a 'committed thinking' involving spirit, soul and mind."[72] Theology then, cannot be divorced from a person's whole attitude towards life and God. Herein lies the existential dimension of Koyama's understanding of theology.

Koyama relates that during a lecture series presented to farmers in Northern Thailand, he was challenged to define theology. To do so he invented the example of "chicken-ology" to make the point that, while we can observe, dissect and study a chicken, the subject of "chicken-ology," we cannot do thus with God, the intended subject of the word, "theology."[73] God cannot be contained by human categories, e.g. by analysis and description.

Rather, we "understand" God in terms of a dynamic, existential relationship with God.

> The "logy" of theo-logy is a special kind of "logy." It is not a "logy" that comes from "observing" God. It is a "logy" that develops within our heart, soul and mind (Matt. 22:37) when we obey, repent, hope, love, believe, worship God. It is a "logy" of obedience, repentance, creation, hope, judgment, love, faith, worship and eternal life. It is an unusual "logy" indeed![74]

This kind of theology, which is responsorial and existential, might also be called "relationship theology." Relationship theology reflects the whole pattern of God's own presence and participation in the world and our consequent understanding of God.

Koyama turns to Genesis and the words God spoke to Adam and Eve for a primary expression of the relationship between God and humanity. God said, "Where are you?" (Gen. 3:9). "In the perspective of theology and ministry, this simple question consisting of three words summarizes the history of mankind, Israel and the Church."[75]

God's question, "Where are you?", addressed to humanity, reveals God's attitude towards history. It is an attitude of relationship. But, a key aspect of the revelation in God's question "Where are you?", apparent already in the question,[76] is that God does not act mechanically and arbitrarily in history. God does not comprehensively change the world by the flick of a finger, as it were. Indeed a God who would do so would be more like an idol, whom we could domesticate for our own purposes.[77]

For theology, this means two things. As already pointed out, theology as an existential response to God is by nature relationship theology, and as such reflects our perception of God and God's acting in history. But, secondly, this relationship theology, focused on God's will and being, must resist any theology which would seek to prioritize human will and being.

Koyama uses the terms "answer-theology" and "happy-ending religion" to describe two types of non-relationship theology. Answer-theology, among other things, is that attitude (all too common in Christian evangelism in Asia according to Koyama)[78] which presents Jesus simply as "the answer." It is a theology which tends to produce exclusive, mechanistic, and culturally-based pronouncements as to what the Gospel is and what Christian life should be. In contrast, Koyama emphasizes the relational, self-yielding way in which God enters human history. Rather than seizing human history in a manipulative, mechanical way, God penetrates history in the person of Jesus Christ. Says Koyama, "Jesus Christ means a continuous *story*, not a *deus ex machina answer*."[79] One knows what Jesus means when he says, "I am the Way . . ." by walking with him: "Unless one walks on the way, one does not know the way."[80]

To give an image to this idea, Koyama employs the symbol of hands. He contrasts the open, mercy-giving hands of Japanese Buddhist statues with the closed fist of Lenin in his glass coffin in Moscow. Closed hands, in Koyama's eyes, symbolize "ideological rightness and dedication."[81] Christ's crucified hands, however, painfully neither open nor closed, suggest to Koyama that theology must be "neither open nor closed."[82] For, there needs to be a distinction between theology and ideology.

> "Handle" stands for a means of efficient control . . . Theology that puts a handle to the power of God is no longer a theology but a demonic theological ideology. Theology must refuse to "handle" the saving power of God. It tries to speak about it. It tries to sing "Magnificat" about it. It meditates about it. But it does not "handle" it as we handle our car or washing machine.[83]

Answer-theology has more of the flavor of ideology. Relationship theology, on the other hand, is less secure. Relationship theology, in Koyama's view, precludes the closed style of answer theology. Relationship theology, reflecting God's participation in human history, must itself be open and non-manipulative.

Walking the way of Jesus does not necessarily produce happy results, and therein lies a critical distinction between relationship-theology and answer-theology, between Christianity which takes for its focus the Cross, and "happy-ending religion" which seeks the gratification of the person involved.

"The Gospel (good news) is anything but a happy-ending religion."[84] Koyama takes the prophet Jeremiah, Jesus himself, and the apostle Paul as poignant examples of this truth. For Jeremiah there was no answer at all to his agonized cries to God. Jesus, too, felt forsaken by God as he faced death. And Paul, while he lived his Christian faith in missionary service, experienced relentless suffering and trial (e.g., II Cor. 11:23–29).[85]

A religion that involves such pain for the participant and puts upon him such demands, is clearly in contrast to a "happy-ending religion" that seeks to minimize the discomfort of the participant, and maximize his gratification. Yet, warns Koyama, "we are capable of making a superstition out of Christianity."[86] In this sense, "Superstition is a practice which is guided by the spirit which says, 'I am interested in what the gods bring to me!'"[87]

The Biblical faith rejects such a view. It is not a "luck-bringing religion." The Apostle's Creed, Koyama points out, says, "*I believe in God.* It does not say: 'I believe in what God brings to me if I believe in God.'"[88]

Therefore, Christians must avoid answer-theology or happy-ending religion, for they pervert the essential pattern of God's involvement in human life, and betray the relationship of the believer with Jesus Christ, which is a relationship founded always on Christ, not upon the believer's designs.

Koyama initially understands Christian theology as a response in faith to what God has initiated. As God has come to humanity and has spoken in the past, God continues to do so. This coming and speaking is always within and through history. Therein lies the second major dimension of Koyama's perspective on theology itself.

All human beings live in history and themselves make history. Necessarily, this involves them in interpreting the history that they inherit and create. This interpretive activity is, in turn, theological. "Theology is an intelligent and spiritual reflection on history in its fundamental relationship . . . to the Word of God."[89] Because this reflection on history in the light of God's Word is a process which takes place within a relationship, it is a dynamic, not a static process.

> To engage in theology in the historical context does not mean then that the context, whatever it is, is there as something unchangeable and beyond our control. Context is something which must be constantly challenged and forced to change.[90]

This view recognizes that history is neither monolithic nor uniform in its unfolding. History, for example, is local as well as global; the history of China is distinct from that of Egypt though both "histories" are part of universal history. Theology must take the differentiations of history into account as it considers them in relation to God's Word. This means of course an appreciation of the global cultural differentiations of which history is composed. "Theological expressions are relevant and persuasive when they are constructed with the raw materials of the local cultural life."[91]

Putting it even more strongly, in the context of Koyama's experience of Christianity in Asia, he says,

> Theology which is not rooted in the aspiration and frustration of the local people is an a-historical (docetic) theology. It gives people an impression that the Christian faith is neither rooted in, nor concerned about, history.[92]

Christian theology, therefore, must take all human history seriously, as indeed it is the very realm of God's encounter with humanity. Precisely because it is the continuing story of God's encounter with creation, history is not an abstract, speculative category of theology. For, history is people; theology which would appreciate history must concentrate on its participants.

This formulation points to the third dimension of Koyama's theology, namely that theology must be "neighbourological." That is, it must be concerned with the experiences, values and needs of human beings in history. "Theology is talk that takes one's neighbour seriously."[93]

> Theology lives and stays meaningful only by breathing the aspirations and frustration of man in a concrete historical situation. It pays attention to credos and liturgies as a summary expression of human spiritual struggles. It listens to all kinds of comments on man from a variety of disciplines and viewpoints. In listening to them, theology concentrates its attention on man. Man must be always recovered and restored. Man must not be allowed to be lost in the jungle of power, knowledge and events. "Theologically speaking," then, means speaking with sharpened concern for, and critical appreciation of, man in his effort to preserve human value in this world.[94]

Theology which reflects this kind of concern for people patterns itself on God's own relationship with humankind. Because God does not impersonally manipulate human life, neither must theology do so.[95]

The fourth dimension of Koyama's understanding of theology is its Christological orientation. "One cannot speak about theology without speaking about God who was in Christ reconciling the world to himself."[96] However, insofar as theology testifies to God's presence in Christ, it is bound by the nature of that presence. "Theology can only stammer about the person and work of Jesus Christ. It is because the Lord of *agape* crucified is the subject of theology."[97]

This understanding of theology grows out of Koyama's conception of God's presence in history, epitomized by God's self-denial at the Cross. As noted already, theology may not be a mechanistic, absolute, abstract exercise. As a responsorial and existential expression of faith, it must participate in Christ's mode of being in history. This means that as Christ emptied himself through the incarnation and crucifixion, so theology, "a servant of the Lord of history. . . must be a *kenotic* undertaking."[98]

Too often in the past Christian theology, as expressed in the life and expansion of the Church, has demonstrated self-aggrandizement rather than self-denial in its meeting with the world around it. Unfaithful to God's pattern of incarnation, Christian theology has depreciated the history and experience of the people it addresses.

Today, Christian theology must learn to be "apostolic." It needs to reflect Paul's description of his ministry, " . . . We have become, and are now, as the refuse of the world, the off-scouring of all things" (I Cor. 4:13).[99]

To be "apostolic" and kenotic, to respect and serve people as Christ did, theology must be "ready to listen to historical and human complaints, dissatisfaction, frustration, ambiguities, insult and complexities."[100] This is its duty.

Altogether, the Christological dimension in Koyama's understanding of theology has a two-fold emphasis. On the one hand theology in itself must be modeled on the manner of Christ's incarnation and death. It must be kenotic; it must serve others. On the other hand, proclamation of Christ's person and work is the substance of theology. As Koyama sums it up, in reference to the particular situation of Hong Kong, for example, "Theology is a humble finger pointing to the presence of Jesus Christ through the thoughts and acts meaningful to the people of Hong Kong today."[101]

The final dimension of Koyama's understanding of theology is less explicit. It becomes apparent when he says such things as,

> Third World theology (every time I hear this expression "Third World" it makes me think of the "Atlantic middle-kingdom

complex") *begins* by raising issues, and not by digesting Augustine, Barth and Rahner.[102]

What is echoed in this statement is Koyama's concern that theology be praxis-oriented. His intensive concern that theology take history seriously and his insistence that theology must be neighbour-directed (concerned for people and their experiences) demonstrate his fundamental commitment to theology developing in and speaking to practical situations in human life. This concern for the ability of theology to express human experiences and values in the context of God's saving presence in history penetrates nearly all of Koyama's writing.

Perhaps a story Koyama quotes in one of his discussions on Buddhism describes Koyama's own theological orientation as much as it serves to preface his discussion of a particular issue in Buddhism. The story is of a conversation between the Buddha and one of his disciples wherein the disciple seeks answers to theoretical questions which the Buddha has previously not addressed. The Buddha's reply is in a parable which turns the emphasis from theoretical questions to existential reality.

Koyama applauds the genius of this parable which thereby prioritizes the human situation. To him, "Why do you ask 'non-crisis' questions while you are yourself caught in crisis?"[103] is the key question of the parable. For, insofar as human beings are preoccupied with questions "distanced" from the critical conditions of their lives, they may be harmfully misdirected with "useless" questions.[104]

In the preface to *Waterbuffalo Theology* Koyama's commitment to praxis-oriented theology becomes more obvious. There he maintains that theology, as it is applied in a given situation, must begin with the needs of the people in that situation, instead of with the thoughts of people who have developed theology in other situations.

Such contextualized theology will be the theology that best serves Jesus Christ. And this, in Koyama's view, is the kind of theology that must develop in Asia today.

Koyama and Contextualization

By definition, Christian faith is contextual. That is, its existence and expression is always within a particular framework of human values and experiences. Likewise, in its transmission, the Christian message will always be interpreted, presented, received, or rejected in reference to the cultural frameworks of those involved in the transmission process. Koyama draws attention to this reality when he notes, "The church cannot function simply on the level of the flat text of the Bible. She must have interpreted gospel."[105]

This interpretive process, which intends to convey the Gospel in terms meaningful to people in their particular cultural contexts, is the substance of contextualization. Koyama saw the necessity for the contextualization of the Gospel through his own work in Northern Thailand. There he realized that his responsibility to the people of that context was to relate the Christian message to their own particular situation.

> It is not I, but my audience, who determines this approach of "theology from below." The truth of "self-emptying" ("Jesus Christ who . . . *emptied himself*," Phil. 2:5–7) in the God incarnate means, to me, beginning my sermon with "sticky-rice" and "cock-fighting" when preaching to my people, farmers of Northern Thailand.[106]

Here, the paradigm for contextualization, for meeting people with the Gospel in a form which they can relate to from within their own context is none other than the Incarnation of God in Jesus Christ. Christ is the "inculture One"[107]; he is "in-contact" with people, not "intact," apart from them and their cultural milieu.[108] God's self-emptying in Christ was an act of identification with people in a particular situation. Thus, the Gospel, the message of Christ, must be no less in-contact with people, incarnated into their own cultures.

Such contextualization prioritizes the context and the needs of the recipients of the Christian message over the context and needs of the carriers of the message. Koyama illustrates this by examining the import of classical European theology, e.g., that of Thomas Aquinas and Karl Barth, in the light of the basic spiritual needs of Thai farmers. Says Koyama,

> I decided that the greatness of theological works is to be judged by the extent and quality of the service they can render to the farmers to whom I am sent . . . Do I mean to say that I dare to give priority to the farmers over Thomas Aquinas and Karl Barth in my theological thinking? Yes. The reason is simple: God has called me to work here in northern Thailand, not in Italy or Switzerland.[109]

From this, it is clear that the focus of contextualization as Koyama sees it, and as he applies it in his own experience, is people and their needs as shaped by their environment and culture.

Koyama calls this process of incarnating the gospel in various cultures "theological-re-rooting" or "re-rooting theological thought from one cultural zone to another, one period to another period, one history-consciousness to another history-consciousness."[110] It is a process of immense complexity. However, to Koyama, "Each step of re-rooting must be an experience of the new depth and wealth of the Gospel!"[111] Koyama believes that the very process of re-rooting reveals the hidden power of the Gospel.

Contextualization is, nevertheless, replete with problems. The Word of God, as Koyama illustrates it, cannot be put into a convenient form like a telephone directory to provide simple answers to the questions raised by each human situation. Instead, people must wrestle with what the Gospel means within their own particular situation.[112]

Even when a seemingly simple and straightforward statement of the Gospel is made to a person, e.g., "Believe in the Lord Jesus, and you will be saved, you and your household" (Acts 16:31), as Koyama points out,

> All the history and the culture of the community to which he belongs begin to ask questions about the *fundamental structure and meaning* of the Gospel. What does "to believe" mean? Who is this "Lord Jesus"? What does "be saved" signify? Why "you and your household?"[113]

There are broader questions as well involved in the contextualizing process. As Koyama points out in a reflection on two different cultural reactions to the Biblical story of the Canaanite woman (Matt. 15:211–28—as interpreted by sixteenth-century German culture and twentieth-century Thai culture),[114] different cultures may require or may produce quite different interpretations of the Gospel in order to make it meaningful to their own context. What Koyama emphasizes is the critical function each interpretation plays in establishing and expressing Christian faith in culturally meaningful terms.

A corresponding concern is the degree to which different cultures can share the same theological perspective or insight. "How decisive is the role of any given culture, be it Japanese, Samoan, or Burmese, in the re-rooting of theological truth?"[115] Is one culture more or less capable of comprehending a particular theological truth than another culture? Answers to these questions cannot be easily established. But,

Koyama believes, there may be universally shared human experiences, such as pain[116] and love[117] which can serve as reference points in making known the love of God in any particular human situation. Moreover, different cultures will contain their own conceptual and experiential "agents" for identifying and expressing the love of God as described by the Gospel.

The discovery of these agents, by which the Gospel may be contextualized, requires a deep understanding of the cultures involved and of the process of contextualization itself. Koyama describes the complexity of this issue in terms of his own Asian situation.

> Asian Christians have been unduly timid in understanding and tackling the unavoidable challenge of rooting the Gospel in their own cultural milieu. Asian "secular words" (i.e., *Logos*, *mysterion*, *metamorphosis* etc. in the New Testament) are not seriously searched for in the art of communicating the message of the Gospel to their own neighbors.[118]

But Koyama makes clear that contextualization does not consist merely in finding suitable words for indigenizing the Gospel in a local culture.

> Indigenization is not a sophisticated game of adjusting theological terminology . . . It is to introduce one history to another history by causing the intersection of the two histories. Is it not obvious that this implies a tremendous theological homework? We are today required to study as thoroughly and penetratingly as possible the South East Asian world.[119]

Thorough and penetrating study of a culture includes, as Koyama sees it, attentiveness to the voices of sociology, history, politics, religion and the best secular scientific research. For the Gospel meets people in the total complexity of their lives.

In his own work in Thailand and elsewhere, Koyama has explored the complexities of contextualization. He has endeavored to engage in contextualization of the Gospel in Thai Buddhist culture in particular.

First of all, Koyama has sought to find meeting ground between Christianity and Thai culture in the medium of history. By clarifying the respective concepts of history operative in Thai culture and biblical literature, Koyama is able to contrast the two and to draw implications from the one for the other. The concept of God and the love-relationship of God with human beings are also key themes which Koyama seeks to convey.

But Koyama always endeavors to first present the Buddhist perspective on life and human being, and then to build his presentation on the Christian message either in contrast to these perspectives or using the Buddhist terms themselves. This is a different method than that followed in much previous missionary activity. Too often, the Christian message has come in inflexible, alien terms which appealed for validation to the experience and concepts of people in other cultures rather than those of the people in the culture addressed.

One of the tragic side-effects of this presentation of the Gospel is its effect upon the people's subsequent evaluation of their own culture. Because Christianity, presented and accepted in unyielding Western forms, has ignored and depreciated the spiritual and social values of indigenous cultures, it has produced Asian "cultural cripples."

> We Asians ignore our own cultural heritage: arts, literature, painting, poetry, religious and historical experiences. Frequently, the moment of baptism becomes the moment of "becoming a stranger" to one's own cultural and religious values. It is not so much due to one's faith in Jesus Christ, but one's acceptance of another (American, British, German . . . the West's) way of life as the Christian way. What a misunderstanding![120]

The task of Christianity today which seeks to develop roots in Asian cultures, is to appreciate the cultural wealth and beauty already to be found there.

Koyama focuses on Philippians 4:8f as a Biblical text which advocates the appreciation of whatever is true, honorable, excellent and so forth. This fully applies, as he sees it, to the various cultures of the world. The good that is within them ought neither be ignored nor wasted.

> When I become a Christian, should I discard all Japanese "whatever is true, whatever is honorable, whatever is just"? . . . If one rejects "whatever is true, whatever is honorable, whatever is just" . . . of his own culture, how can he—through what medium—appreciate the wonderful deeds of God in Christ for him (Mark 5:19)? A tragedy of immense proportion takes place whenever a community of Christians underestimates, ignores and rejects "whatever is true, whatever is honorable, whatever is just . . . " of their own community.[121]

Accordingly, as Koyama pictures it, the Gospel becomes contextualized when it allows itself to be "seasoned" by the flavors of the culture it enters. This necessitates for example, the "baptizing" of some previously non-Christian words into the Christian vocabulary (as happened in the birth and spread of the early church) with the confidence that such heathen words can "be employed as faithful servants when they are placed in the strong *kerygma* context."[122]

Above all, however, Koyama asserts that in the Christian concept of history lies the most fertile ground for Asian evangelism and contextualization.

> The study of the relationship between God and history provides the theological discernment and freedom needed for the rooting of the Gospel in the acutely changing Asian world of the past one hundred years.[123]

History finds its focus in individuals. That is why Koyama in the end emphasizes the personal aspect of contextualization.

> Authentic contextualization cannot be done outside "If any man should come after me, let him deny himself and take up his cross and follow me" (Matt. 16:24). This "terrible" passage packs the substance of authentic contextualization. It is such a *life* that engages, consciously or unconsciously, in authentic contextualization.[124]

Personal involvement in contextualization means that it is not a static, mechanical process or event. The interpretation of the Gospel, as it involves the persons of the interpreter—both as message bearer and as recipient—will always be a dynamic, human process. And it is there that Koyama sees the real power of the Gospel.

> The Gospel displays its force only in the process of interpretation. Not by an interpreted Gospel, but by the Gospel ever fresh in a process of interpretation against the background of the complexity of history, man is led to see the reign of the exalted Christ. This difficult assignment of interpretation which requires the sharpest perceptivity into historical and human situation has come to us![125]

Koyama's View of History

One of the most important foundations of Koyama's theology is his concept of history. Seen as the account of human experience and as the arena wherein God's salvation is worked out, history is to Koyama the indispensable framework for Christian life and mission. Set over against the predominant Asian understanding of history, Koyama's biblical understanding of history becomes, furthermore, a primary tool for Christian proclamation.

An understanding of Koyama's concept of history requires a survey of what he sees history to be, of how he sees God to be acting in history, and of what that means for Christian obedience and proclamation. The following sub-sections address these issues.

What is History?

Koyama confesses the difficulty of defining history. Instead he seeks to describe its nature.

> What is history? I do not find myself competent to define it. I cannot put history on my table and look at it as a medical researcher can scrutinize experimental rats. History strikes me as different from the wiring inside a television set. I feel that history is living, unpredictable and constantly moving between hope and despair. History is a biographical story. It is fundamentally a story rather than a theory.[126]

History as a story is the story of people. That means that it is infinitely complex and cannot be neatly codified. History is

> not a fairy story like Cinderella or Snow White. It is a true story of the world, a nation, a community and individuals—a story which always involves people. History is personal. It is not mechanical. It is not systematic. It is neither neat nor clean. That is why history is so interesting. A textbook on history is, strictly speaking, impossible. A personal story cannot become a "textbook."[127]

Koyama goes on to note what that means in terms of application of history.

History is a "lived" story, and it is the "living" that brings out meaningful thoughts for our present life experience. History does not just speak of the past but is also concerned about the present.

History is appreciated, quite obviously, by the *present* man, not the *past* man.[128]

The sensibility of history, therefore, rests in its relevance to the people considering it. How they understand and use the past reflects their own experiences, attitudes, and values. That, too, is part of the human story which comprises history.

Thus, as the dynamic story of human existence, history records and reflects human values, attitudes and activities, both past and present. In this sense, "history is much more than a chronology."[129] It is, as Koyama puts it, "a dynamic purposeful movement in which man's participation and commitment . . . to his neighbors" has formative significance.[130] History therefore entails not only human values but also human questions about the meaning or purpose of life. In this regard, Koyama notes that,

"Meaning" in history is somehow sustained not so much by specialist knowledge and judgement of historical realities as by a human judgement which maintains and perpetuates human value against anti-values in the human world.[131]

What human values are in relation to anti-values, Koyama infers from the examples of the human community's condemnation of such occurrences as South African apartheid, the nuclear bombings of Japan, and the Vietnam war.

The human story, however, is a story which like any other, is open to interpretation. It is a story which invites its participants into a search for meaning.

Obviously all of us are living in history. We are not beyond-history human beings. By living so and by consciously doing so we are *making* history . . . History is not there before us as a cup of coffee is there. History is our awareness or interpretation of history. Because man is and lives in history, to be man must engage in the act of *interpretation* of history.[132]

Naturally, there will be differing interpretations of the meaning of human life. The common Asian concept of history as a whole, for example, is cyclical. This contrasts with the Western, biblical concept which sees history as linear. Both concepts have actual consequences for human attitudes and life-styles.

In contrasting the Asian and Western concepts of history, Koyama notes, for example, how the former has produced a *patient* experience of history as opposed to the *impatient* history of the West.[133]

> The strongly linear view of history in the biblical tradition, based on the faith that God is the governor of history, is not indigenous to the life and thought of the peoples of Asia. A linear sense of history, when appropriated by the man of *hybris*, can produce dangerous *impatience* with history.[134]

Impatience with history Koyama connects with colonialism, cultural insensitivity, and the failure of the West, especially Christianity, to respect the history of Asia.

Koyama also contrasts the cyclical view of history with the linear view in terms of "weak history-awareness" and "strong history-awareness."[135] Weak history-awareness centers on human beings and the history they create for themselves exclusively through their own activities (as described by the idea of *karma*). Strong history-awareness, to Koyama, is built around a God who creates history and who has the power to alter and to end it. Human actions, accordingly, are not ultimately determinative of the content of history.

The latter concept of history, wherein human beings do not have autonomous control over their destiny, does not mean, however, that therefore history is meaninglessly mechanical. On the contrary, the biblical view of history, to which Koyama enthusiastically subscribes, actively involves man in the whole meaning and process of history.

Whichever concept of history one subscribes to, it will influence one's approach to history as a whole. Both the circular and the linear concepts value the past for its influence on the present. But, for holders of the linear view, to whom the past is important but upon whom the past has a less-binding effect for the present, past events may be disassociated from the present into an abstract chronological system.

As Koyama describes it, a person may, for example, study history according to the "helicopter technique." In it one is "carried back over the hundreds of years of history-terrain" to be dropped at a particular point, e.g., apostolic times, and left to walk back to the twentieth century.[136] Valuable though this method is, it misses some of history's dynamics. One's assessment of mere chronological data may be impersonal and selective, which Koyama as an Asian resists. To him, history as the human story is too "wild" to be contained in a systematic sequence.[137] One simply cannot absorb it all.

However, Koyama laments that Christian church history has been a primarily Western affair, and in its transmission around the world, the histories of other great faiths and nations have been sorely neglected.[138] It is important to Koyama that more of the human stories be shared. In his writing, Koyama not only emphasizes this concern but himself incorporates history, i.e., the stories of various people and events, into his theology.

In conclusion, history is, as Koyama sees it, the total story of human existence, including the practically infinite number of particular human stories. These stories are in fact expressions of varying human interpretations of life, and the sharing of these stories is to Koyama highly important. Not only can the sharing of human stories facilitate peace in the modern world, it also generates creative tensions which can be very stimulating in the realm of religious encounter.[139]

Humanity in History

Another way of emphasizing the fact that history is human story is to speak of it in terms of its participants and their relationship to each other. In regard to its participants, Koyama writes,

> History is not a ghost concept. It is an anthropological concept in the sense that it realizes itself in man. No man is either a-historical or trans-historical. Man is man and he remains to be man because he lives rooted in history and participates in making history.[140]

Necessarily, humanity's living in and making history is always particularized. People live in particular cultures and areas, with particular languages and histories. While it is true that more and more people now live in one universal, shared history, they always do so as participants of particular histories.

> We should say that mankind today participates in one universal history, which is something deeper than "technological universal history," within which there are many particular *histories*.[141]

What is important is how fully people are aware of the complexities of the history of their own lives and of other peoples' lives, and how they then react to each other's histories. "Inability to meet man produces tragically a superficial grasp and appreciation of history."[142] Healthy human relationships require some appreciation of the complexities of one's own being and that of others.

In a biographical anecdote, Koyama tells how this realization even affects his appreciation of God.

> The realization of the complexity of human existence has concurred with the realization of the complexity of history. A person is as complicated as history. History is as complicated as a person. Appreciation of this correlation became a point of new departure for my missionary thinking. As I began to appreciate the complexity of history, I began to see the hidden values of history. History became, as it were, personal, and my personal life became, as it were, historical. I realized a strange thing: the appreciation of the complexity of man and history had opened my eyes to a more meaningful appreciation of the love of God in history. The greater my appreciation of the complexity of man and history became, the greater became my appreciation of the love of God. One aspect after another of my life came under scrutiny until emotionally, at one point—and this may sound irrational and perhaps ridiculous—I felt the love of God in the fact that my tongue fails to say "flush toilet" and my stomach accepts rice naturally and accepts hamburger unnaturally![143]

History, then, needs to be appreciated in terms of its particularized human complexities as well as in broader terms.

God in History

Having described history as a story, Koyama proceeds to relate this story to the God of the Bible. "I understand that the Bible has to do with story and not theory. The biblical God is a story-God, not a theory-God."[144] This God surveys the story of humankind, in all its complexity, and addresses it personally by becoming involved in it.[145] The biblical God, as it were, personally experiences history.[146]

Koyama uses the idea of God's covenant with Israel as a model of God's historical involvement. In developing this model over against the passivity of Thai

Buddhism's depreciation of history, Koyama emphasizes God's wrath as a vivid sign of historical involvement. A God who was not passionately attached to human history would not be moved to wrath.

> The wrath of God is provoked by the *historical* violation of God's "holiness and love" . . . history is the *locus* of God's perturbation of soul . . . *God can be moved to wrath because he is God in history.*[147]

"God in history"—this is a stupendous theological assertion, as Koyama points out, for it means that God experiences history in all its complexity and particularity, i.e. in the particular histories of Egypt, Assyria, Rome, etc., as much as in the history of Israel.[148] Thus, it is understandable that because God is ruler of all history and is engaged in history through creation and through God's particular covenant with Israel in it, God is committed to redeeming human history and restoring God's people within it.[149]

Of course, God's involvement in history goes still much farther than this. In the incarnation of Jesus Christ God became ultimately involved in the human story, becoming even a participant of it.

> In Christ, man began to see the glory of God, not as the man who aspires to reach beyond history, but as a man who lives in history. The crucifixion took place in history. And precisely there man sees God's covenantal triumph![150]

This was the ultimate "historical and human coming of God."[151] It unequivocally demonstrated God's resolution to save the people and creation of God's own making. God's experience of history meant actual participation in it.

As with all human participation in history this participation necessarily meant particularity. "Jesus Christ, the true *man*, lived in history. That is the meaning of the incarnation of the Son of God."[152]

To those with a circular concept of history, a karmic understanding of reality, or a cosmic, non-particularized picture of God, the involvement of a Creator-Redeemer God in human history will certainly be a scandalous and offensive idea. To them,

> It is an unfamiliar concept that there is a God who is the Creator of all and the Visitor to prisons, who "neither slumbers nor

sleeps," who is moved to burning wrath against man, who yet promises hope "but of you I will make a great nation."[153]

Still more scandalous will be the notion that this almighty God would enter human history as a particular human being. That this human being, having access to almighty power, would through an ugly death somehow become saviour of all humanity is most scandalous of all.

Precisely at this point, maintains Koyama, one begins to perceive the true nature and purpose of God in relation to human history.

> I understand that the unique and enduring spiritual insight which the Judeo-Christian tradition contributes to mankind is that the personal God, the one who creates, preserves and consummates all things, does not "handle" history.[154]

Koyama's interpretation of God not "handling" history has been introduced earlier, but now it becomes crucial to his understanding of God and how God has acted in history. As Koyama sees it, God

> comes to history, to use an awkward expression, with a great respect for history. When he comes, history at its depth experiences the "shaking of the foundation," because history has never been so profoundly and carefully taken up and respected. History has never been so profoundly penetrated and enlightened because of God's respectful approach to history.[155]

God penetrates history; God does not grab it and coerce a response from human beings.[156] God's dealing with history takes place in hidden, deeper ways.

Koyama describes God's acting in history by distinguishing between comprehensive and fundamental change. In Jesus Christ God changes history "fundamentally," not "comprehensively." Comprehensive change would mean a massive, obvious, irresistible act in human history that would deny human freedom and be inconsistent with the love of God.

> If history is changed fundamentally by Jesus Christ, the change should be obvious to everyone. Yet it is not self-evident. If he does change history comprehensively, his work would become obvious to us all. But this is not what he does.[157]

Instead, Jesus "directs himself to the *foundation* of our lives and gives us the *sign* for the reality of the kingly rule of God within our history," namely, his healing power.[158]

Koyama goes on to draw out the implications of such an understanding of God's presence in history for Christian faith and life, particularly in relation to people of other faiths. Ultimately, the crucifixion stands as the foundation upon which God's experience of human history, God's participation in the human story, finally rests. The cross of Jesus emerges as the crucial point from which the historical presence of God and what that means for human life must be understood.

Christianity and History

History, as conceived by Koyama, has been described as a dynamic human story in which God is deeply involved. Itself part of that human story, Christianity seeks to express God's involvement in history through Jesus Christ. As such, it is an intensely historical religion, i.e., having a specific historical event at the origin and center of its message.

> It is the religion of incarnation (into history, into culture, into language, into the religious situation and so on) of the Son of the history-minded God.[159]

This historical basis and message of Christianity contrasts with and is a challenge to other human concepts of history, e.g., Hinduism's and Buddhism's description of history as illusion. Christianity, rather, affirms history and "takes it seriously," as Koyama likes to put it. At least, Christianity ought to do so.

> Strangely, and I am sure it will surprise you to hear it, I am finding that Christianity is not interested in history. When I was a theological student, my textbooks and my teachers bombarded me with the idea that Christianity is an intensely historical religion. It is a history-rooted faith. It is faith in the Exodus God who is concerned with history. Jesus Christ, the historical man, is God incarnate. In Jesus of Nazareth, God's ultimate saving intention has been realized in history. I think my textbooks and my teachers were right. If we take away the historical dimension from the Christian faith, we take the blood out of the living body.

The Christian faith is rooted in history. It is very much so because Jesus Christ was the crucified and spat-upon Lord. Yet the religion called Christianity can behave otherwise. What I see and experience today in Asia impresses me that Christianity is neither concerned about history nor trying to understand what "the faith rooted in history" means. Christianity has touched the history of Asia only superficially. It has not really been spat upon by the Asians as the Christ was spat upon by the Roman soldiers.[160]

Repeatedly, Koyama emphasizes Christianity's responsibility to take human history seriously—to take *all* human stories seriously—by drawing attention to its many failures to do so, especially in Asia. Elsewhere, Koyama's conviction that Christianity's failure to take history (human experience) seriously creates docetic faith or indeed that it prevents Christian faith, has already been noted.

Koyama even goes so far as to suggest that, practically speaking, Hinduism and Buddhism do indeed take history more seriously than does Christianity. Buddhist self-denial and Buddhist efforts to demonstrate spiritual values reflect a direct awareness of the historical situation of the people to whom its message is addressed. In Koyama's eyes,

In Thailand, Burma and Sri Lanka, if the Christians exert as much "historical effort"—for instance, self-denial—as the Buddhists do, Christianity will certainly be able to represent itself as a "historical" faith.[161]

More concretely, Koyama offers the example of Hindus in India who experience history "with tremendous realism through their famished stomachs" while Christian visitors to India "probably experience it through their (Bachelor of Divinity) brain."[162]

This does not actually mean that because Hindus experience hunger, Hinduism is therefore a more historical religion than Christianity. Rather, Koyama's point is that Christianity, as a history-centered religion, has the responsibility to demonstrate its concern for history by responding to specific human experiences, e.g. hunger. Doing so, however, can be a major problem for Christians who are themselves removed from a particular human situation.

A bank account and an abundant diet somehow (I cannot explain it quite satisfactorily) insulate man from coming to feel the primary truth of history.[163]

Christianity, therefore, needs to develop a spirit of repentance in the face of such situations, and a willingness to learn from them. Repentance is a deeply historical act to Koyama. It redirects Christianity into history in the spirit of the crucified Lord who Christianity proclaims.[164] Repentance is one way of demonstrating Christianity's concern for history.

Secondly, Christianity needs a willingness to learn of and to learn from the many stories of humankind. For, without such learning it becomes a less historical religion. "If religion stands outside the educational process, it begins to assume an uncanny a-historical character."[165] Furthermore, such a-historical Christianity, in its failure to appreciate human experience, betrays the very mode of God's own experience in human history, which Christianity seeks to embody and proclaim. Says Koyama,

> I find that God goes "slowly" in his educational process of man. "Forty years in the wilderness" points to his basic educational philosophy. Forty years of national migration through the wilderness, three generations of the united monarchy (Saul, David, Solomon), nineteen kings of Israel (up to 722 B.C.) and twenty kings of Judah (up to 587 B.C.), the hosts of the prophets and priests, the experience of exile and restoration—isn't this rather a slow and costly way for God to let his people know the covenant relationship between God and man?[166]

Accordingly, as Christianity becomes involved with various human histories, its very character will change. Repentance and a willingness to learn should involve Christianity in a pattern personally established by God in relation to Israel.

Christianity, Koyama implies, must be willing to relate God's message in a slow and costly manner. This requires a deep involvement in and acceptance of the different stories of human life, for which repentance and a willingness to learn are essential.

God's own participation in human history culminated in a willingness to be "nailed down 'full-stop'"[167] for the sake of humanity. Christianity which is not willing to go equally as far betrays the nature of the one whom it claims to represent and proclaim.

142

Christian Theology and History

That Koyama describes theology as a "reflection on history in the light of the Word of God"[168] illustrates the intimate connection he makes between history and theology. History is the ground out of which theology springs. Unless theology stems from human experience—including the particular experiences of ordinary people—it is unfaithful to its origins and will be inadequate for the people whom it addresses. Koyama clarifies the necessity of theology's being rooted in history as he considers the effect of the "neglect" of history embodied in Thai Buddhism and oriental deism.[169]

First of all, theology that neglects history ignores the problems relating to revelation and reason. Such theology seeks enlightenment, discovery of truth, without any entanglement in history which is the *locus* of revelation and reason. Superficial, "lazy" faith results.

Secondly, theology which neglects history is, as Koyama puts it,

> scarcely capable of perceiving the deep existential meaning of the "strange work of God" (*opus alienum dei* Isa. 28:31) in Christian life and theology. Christian faith is, in its depth, inevitably confronted by the tormenting question of the strange work of God. The strange work of God is neither superhistorical nor supernatural work, but the work which is experienced *within history*, as the forsaking of Christ by God took place in the historical crucifixion.[170]

Theology which neglects history avoids the existential tension that faith planted in the contradictions of human experience must face.

Finally, theology which neglects history "fails to see the qualitative difference between God and man." For, as Koyama continues,

> How can a man come to know this crucial difference if he is not consciously involved in history, the *locus* of the particular encounter which takes place between "I and Thou"?[171]

In each of these cases theology depends on history for a fundamental framing of the human concept of God. The Christian God cannot be conceived apart from the biblical account of God's presence in human history. The two concepts—that of God and that of history as depicted by Scripture—are interrelated.

Thus, for Koyama, history as presented from a biblical perspective becomes a primary tool for Christian mission. It is a vital means of making the Christian message relevant and sensible to the world today, particularly in Asia. When the biblical idea of history and the biblical account of the God who shapes and participates in that history are set out in terms which are meaningful to people with other concepts of God and history, Koyama believes that Christianity will become more understandable and more acceptable to those people. His own efforts to relate the history of the people of Israel with history as perceived by the people of Thailand are steps taken with this intention.

Koyama's intense concern with the importance of history for Christian theology and life is, in the end, largely undergirded by a missionary concern to make Christianity meaningful to people in their own particular histories.

CHAPTER SEVEN

KOYAMA'S HERMENEUTICAL CORE

Koyama's Concept of the Crucified Mind

The heart of all Koyama's theology is his vision of "the crucified mind." It is the prism through which his perspective on all other issues is filtered. It embodies his fundamental interpretation of the way God acts in human history and of what that means for human life.

The "crucified mind" takes as its source and model Christ's crucifixion. The following sections therefore present Koyama's understanding of the crucifixion, what it calls forth in a human response to it, and how that response takes shape through self-denial and Christian mission.

The Crucified God

The meaning of the crucifixion and its import for human life rests in the limit-less love God demonstrated for humanity through the utter abandonment of Jesus at the cross. Koyama seeks to express the extremity of God's love, as well as the response it calls forth from humanity, in terms of Christ's rejection. Jesus was judged to be a sinner. He was cast out as an affront to the religious authorities and theologians of his day. He was a stumbling block and an offense. Koyama sees this to be part of a crucial pattern within God's plan for history.

From Genesis, through the history of Israel, and culminating in Jesus Christ, Koyama sees God to be personally taking on humanity's rejection of God and turn-ing it into humanity's redemption.[1] Christ's cross, utterly ugly and offensive to human sensibility, is the supreme act of the self-sacrificing God. There, beyond the pale of even the understanding of God by God's own people, Jesus experiences what God had withheld from all humanity, namely, utter abandonment.

> No one is ever so forsaken as Jesus Christ since no one is ever so close to God! The cry upon the cross came from the same man who said: "I am not alone, for the Father is with me" (John 16:32). He was alienated from man and God.[2]

146

Yet this abandonment, this self-denial by God through Jesus, is the key to reconciliation between God and humanity, humanity with each other. "The word of the cross is the word that summarizes the mission of Jesus Christ."[3]

Koyama sees Jesus' subsequent resurrection from death as God's confirmation to humanity that Jesus' death was for our sake. But at this point it is important to add that Koyama does not intend a dichotomy between crucifixion and resurrection. He resists a separation of resurrection and crucifixion into independent categories.

> The word which was in the beginning comes to us as the Word of Incarnation (Christmas), the Word of the Cross (Good Friday) and the Word of Resurrection (Easter). These Words are one Word. The incarnate Lord is the crucified Lord. The crucified Lord is the risen Lord. There is only one Jesus Christ, the Lord. No one can isolate incarnation from crucifixion, crucifixion from resurrection. Crucifixion does not make sense apart from incarnation, the resurrection apart from crucifixion. Crucifixion is the ultimate depth of incarnation (Phil. 2:6–8) and resurrection is the "therefore" of crucifixion (v. 9). We have no compartmentalized theology of incarnation, theology of cross and theology of resurrection. Theology is to do with the living continuous story of Jesus Christ and how in this life God revealed himself to us.[4]

Koyama turns to Scripture for other biblical images of God's self-denial for the sake of humanity as well. Chief among these is simply God's patient presence in the history of Israel. God went with Israel into the wilderness after the Exodus from Egypt and there patiently taught this people of their relationship with God. This God did through one people for the sake of all people. For, "the people of Israel had this experience on behalf of all of us."[5]

Through all of Israel's development, from the sojourn in the wilderness through the period of judges and kings, through the experience of exile and restoration, God was working within the self-imposed bounds of human society, culture, and politics. Finally, in Jesus Christ God met humanity face to face within the limits of human existence itself, and in the end, as Koyama puts it, "walked towards the 'full-stop'. He lost his mobility. He was nailed down."[6] It was only this ultimate self-denial—the abandonment by God at the cross—that could heal and re-create a broken humanity.

The Crucified Response

In order for this ultimate love to become tangible to humanity, God, again working through human beings themselves, empowers those who perceive and experience this reconciliation to communicate it through their own lives to others. This is the essence of living in the knowledge and power of Christ's crucifixion.

For example, Koyama describes how Paul himself, as he stammered his own believing reaction to the revelation of Christ crucified for his sake, *participated* in a life of crucifixion for others. He himself *experienced* the word of the cross.[7] This, holds Koyama, is the key Christian response to God's action. This is what Koyama calls the "apostolic life." It is,

> the life experiencing and communicating the life of Jesus Christ
> who was "made a curse for our sake." The theology of the word
> of the cross must be expressed and communicated "bodily."[8]

When human beings, empowered in love by God's self-sacrifice, open their lives to the risks of rejection, powerlessness and suffering, they are participating in Christ's crucified life.

Koyama also describes this Christian vocation as a calling to "stumble." The Christian is called to stake his or her life on one who is a stumbling block to all human reason. The God who is on the one hand the supreme power behind all existence and who on the other hand abandons God's Son to be nailed in human flesh to a cross is a contradiction that only a stumbling faith can apprehend. "Christian presence, which is the presence of faith must live this crucial tension."[9] But there is comfort in recognizing that this tension, this stumbling, is itself given by God.

> We do not make our presence a stumbling one. God makes us
> so in his Son. It is not artificial but given. Our stumbling pres-
> ence guards us from falling into superficial triumphalism of
> faith . . .[10]

Triumphalism is a constant danger to faith, in that it distracts the believer from the fundamental perception that Christian life is to be a life lived under the cross.

> Triumphalism encourages us, as it has done with stubborn
> tenacity at many critical times in church history, to make a
> quick jump from "stumbling" to "un-stumbling," from Good
> Friday to Easter.[11]

Instead, those who follow Jesus are called to a life which participates in God's costly self-denial. To accept being stumbling, discomforted, and unfree for the sake of others and for the one "in whom all things hold together" is the basic form of Christian calling and presence.[12]

> In this eschatological hour, we are called to share the pathos of God, God's *pathos* towards all scattered things which are held together in the *glory* of the *crucified* Lord.[13]

This is the substance of the crucified life.

The Crucified Attitude

The recurring difficulty in the human response to God's self-sacrifice in Jesus is that human beings constantly seek to rely on their own resources rather than to take the risks of sharing in the life of the Crucified One. Koyama elucidates this tendency towards self-reliance by using the image of a lunch-box.

A lunch-box is a convenient symbol of human resourcefulness. It contains what humanity needs to sustain itself. Because it has a handle by which it can be carried and controlled, it can stand for all the efficient controls or "handles" which human beings seek to build into their lives. A lunch box, or for that matter, the tools of advanced technology, exhibit the human propensity to "handle-mindedness," that is, the desire for control over their environment and life.

In contrast, Koyama describes the crucified life as one without handles. The crucified mind does not seek to rely on human resourcefulness. It seeks rather to reflect the nature of the crucifixion which was the ultimate demonstration of non-handle-mindedness, that is, of giving up efficient, self-centered control over life.

This is in accordance with God's own pattern of involvement in human history. For, God does not deal with humanity in a manipulative, coercive, "handling" way. Instead, God enters it in a "non-efficient," self-sacrificing manner.

Koyama also describes God's manner of involvement in human life with various other images. He speaks of Jesus' posture of "bending down" in the story about the woman caught in adultery. By "bending down" (a foolish and weak posture, as Koyama notes),[14] God enters more sensitively and deeply into human life, exercising freedom in a way which creates a new mind in those God encounters.[15]

Similarly, Koyama describes God's crucified love with the image of a bridge. Normally, bridges carry people over difficulties from one sphere to another. In this sense they provide an image for many human endeavors and religions. However,

149

The central symbolism of the Christian faith, the cross, does not give us an image of bridge. It gives us, instead, the feeling of confrontation, encounter and conflict. It is the point at which people meet. It is an image of intersection. The main emphasis here is not of a safe passage from damnation to salvation or of connecting this world with that world or of bringing the heaven principle (male) together with the earth principle (female). The cross stands for encounter and conflict and painful solution. It points to the place where we must stop. Why stop? Because it is there that *love* is expressed.[16]

God's love is such that it enters totally into human difficulties, taking the risks and paying the cost involved in that encounter. This is the pattern which the crucified mind—the mind of the person who knows and follows the crucified God—is likewise called to embody. It is the mind that grows out of experiencing and appreciating the biblical God as the one who "carries us."

God carries us. Any "god" we can carry is, according to Jeremiah, an idol. "Such idols are like scarecrows in a field of melons; they cannot speak; they have to be carried because they cannot walk" (10:5). That which we can carry is subject to our control. To suggest that something that we can carry is carrying us is to have an upside-down perspective of life. Such a style of life would be confusing and destructive. Idolatry is just such a confusion. Carrying scarecrows, we do not insult them nor hurt ourselves. It is not up-side-down. But in trying to carry the living God of Mount Sinai, the God of Abraham, Isaac and Jacob, we insult him and we destroy ourselves.[17]

The crucified mind then, is one which apprehends and appreciates what God has done for humanity. Moreover, it is the mind which itself participates in God's self-giving love by adopting the style of the crucified life, i.e. a stumbling life, which no longer relies primarily on human resourcefulness.

The Crucified Mind and Self-Denial

Another way of talking about the crucified mind is in terms of self-denial. In an interpretive commentary on a passage from Hosea, Koyama summarizes the fundamental self-denial expressed by God in relationship with God's covenant people (Hos. 11:86–9).

> My heart recoils within me
> (self-denial!)
> my compassion grows warm and tender
> (post self-denial compassion, compassion informed be self-denial)
> I will not execute my fierce anger
> (self-denial)
> I will not again destroy Ephraim,
> (decision rooted in God's self-denial)
> for I am God and not man,
> (is this act of God's self-denial a pointer to the meaning of "I am God and not man?")
> the Holy One in your midst,
> (is this act of God's self-denial a pointer to the meaning of the Holy One? Does this mean that God stands in our midst in self-denial? Is "midst" the place of "self-denial" theologically speaking? "And with him they crucified two robbers, one on his right and one on his left"—Mark 15:27)
> and I will not come to destroy.
> (Salvation and the beginning of new history flow from God's holy self-denial!)[18]

Koyama here sees God's self-denial to be part of the very essence of God as well as the means by which God redeems human history.

Christ's death on the cross, as already observed, is the culmination of this self-denial. "The Word of the cross is the word of unfathomable self-denial."[19] But this is no sickly or morbid self-denial, as some might suggest. It is, rather, a self-denial motivated by love which frees and unites humankind.[20]

Koyama recognizes the temptation to chafe at and reject this kind of self-denial by Jesus. He pictures it as a temptation of the Devil, the kind of temptation put by the Devil to Jesus in his experience in the wilderness.

The devil's theology aims at speedy and sensational results and speedy solutions. Evil-energy is speedy and sensational. Waiting, enduring and hoping do not figure in the Devil's theology. "I believe in God. I, therefore, wait for him. I hope in him. I endure the difficult times believing in him"—such spiritual attitude (faith) means a paralysis of the dignity of the human personality according to the Devil's theology. The Son of God must act speedily and efficiently in his mission of making this world a happy one. Why should the Son of God let the world continue in its miserable situation so long "for no purpose?" Why does he not pull speedy and sensational feats and reduce things to order? Why does he waste time when he knows that he can perform the cosmic feat?[21]

This temptation appeals to human handle-mindedness. It accords with the natural human priorities such as efficiency and control.

Jesus, however, acted on different priorities, namely those of love, such as freedom, relationship, and acting for the benefit of others.

Jesus indeed did demonstrate his Sonship of God by *not* exercising the power of God for his own personal advantage . . . He rejects the speedy and sensational building of his kingdom. He comes to man slowly and not speedily. He comes to man seeking to establish faith-relationship not sensation-relationship with man. His freedom is the opposite of our ordinary concept of freedom. Man gains his freedom by living as his "servant"![22]

The crucified mind, then, is one of servanthood. It finds meaning and purpose in self-denial, rooted in the self-denial of the Crucified One and directed towards the benefit of others.

It is at this point that self-denial takes on meaning in the context of human life as a whole. Koyama emphasizes this by considering self-denial as a universal human activity.

The practice of self-denial is surely one of the fundamental religious experiences of the great historic religions. I am tempted to say that the presence or absence of acts of self-denial must be a fundamental criterion for the life inspired by religious teachings.[23]

Koyama goes on to posit that self-denial, not at all a necessarily negativistic, pessimistic mentality, has been a major part of the explosive spiritual energy at the heart of most of the world's great religions. This is especially true for Christianity. "The whole gospel radiated from the self-denial of Jesus Christ."[24] It is therefore essential that Christians learn to exhibit self-denial in their own lives as followers of Jesus. "The mark of self-denial is the fundamental qualification for being an evangelist. Religious commitment can be communicated only through the sign of *stigma*."[25] For Koyama, the word *stigma* symbolizes the self-sacrifice, including even physical self-sacrifice, that goes with living according to the crucified mind.

The apostle Paul exhibited the *stigma* of following Christ. His many sufferings grew out of and demonstrated the crucified mentality that guided his life. Unfortunately, as Koyama sees it, the crucified mentality demonstrated in Paul's life gave way to self-centeredness in later centuries of Christian encounter with the world. Especially in the context of Western civilization and in the history of Christian mission during the Western colonial expansion, Christianity lost sight of the fundamental necessity of self-denial in Christian faith and life.[26]

Modern Christianity, maintains Koyama, needs to rediscover the crucified or "apostolic" mind, in which there is no room for self-admiration or one-sided triumphalism. Its spirituality will become "beautiful and edifying when it lives with the stigma of Christ's self-denial."[27] Moreover, rediscovery of the crucified life will, Koyama believes, improve Christianity's theology and service.

> The insight that comes from a life of self-denial will create refreshing excitement in our theological and ministerial engagement.[28]

In fact, in a world wherein Christianity is but one religion among others, a life of Christ-like self-denial will be the key to Christian witness.

> There is only one way by which it can be demonstrated that Christianity is a profound religion to the eyes of the adherents of the other faiths; that is by the life style of being "poured out for many!"[29]

These latter considerations of the importance of self-denial lead into the area of Christian mission and proclamation, and how the crucified mind is to function in the world.

153

Mission and Proclamation of the Crucified Mind

> If a religious man invites another to come to embrace his religion, he must establish the truthfulness of his belief and of his self-identity by no less an act than that of self-denial.[30]

Within this overall perspective Koyama emphasizes how it is especially crucial that Christians, who base their faith on the self-denying love of God, proclaim that love through lives consistent with it. In other words, self-denial is intrinsic to proclamation as well as to faith. "The only way to speak about the crucified and risen name is by participating in Christ's crucifixion and resurrection."[31]

Proclamation of the story of Jesus, especially to people of other faiths, needs to be bound up with the life of the proclaimer. This life, accordingly, must be one which reflects a Christological and apostolic character, namely, that of being "poured out" for others.[32] The apostolic life is one which incorporates a willingness to operate without "handles" (power and control), one willing to accept suffering and rejection. "'To be apostolic' means 'to be ready to be spat upon'."[33]

This was the pattern of Jesus and Paul. As Paul himself described this attitude, it was one of willingness to become "the refuse of the world, the off-scouring of all things" (I Cor. 4:13).[34] Koyama believes that it is this attitude above all which can affect history and accomplish Christian mission. "To the degree that the church has been spat upon, she has become alive in mission and healing in history."[35]

Tragically, this has not been the attitude most often displayed in Christian mission, especially in recent centuries. Along with religious colonialism as a whole, denominationalism has been a good example to Koyama of individualistic Christian self-assertion as opposed to self-denial. In Christian mission today, denominations that seriously seek to contribute to the Christian body as a whole must be willing to receive the contributions of others. Only *after* they have sought to understand the contributions of others can they make their contributions as "refuse-related-contributions."[36]

Koyama discusses what apostolic existence means for individual missionaries as well as for the church as a whole. Mission with a crucified mind means an informed love for others, full participation in their particular situation, and a willingness to suffer for them.

> First, the missionary must live *in* the complexity of living man and living history. This call comes from God who loves man. Love approaches man carefully, feeling and knowing him to be

someone who cannot be tamed and controlled. Love is the mind
that appreciates complexity . . .

Second, the missionary's missionary-quality will be nurtured in
his life-participation in the apostolic existence of reviled-bless/
persecuted-endure/slandered-conciliate. God calls man. In his
call is included the call to go through the experience of "letting
someone pull your beard out!"[37]

That is to say, the missionary must be willing to bear in his or her body the
"scars" of love that expresses itself through self-denial. For it is this kind of suffering, self-giving love that communicates the biblical truth of God's love in Jesus
Christ.

This biblical truth is itself a mediated truth; it is truth expressed in human form.
Because human existence includes difficulties and suffering, the biblical truth is
suffering truth. "The biblical truth is not an *intact* truth but a *suffered* truth. The
truth suffers because it is deeply *in contact* with man."[38]

Again, this reflects the handle-less cross, the God who does not arbitrarily and
powerfully manipulate human life, but who instead "bends down," to share in it,
suffer for it, and thereby redeem it.[39]

Characteristics of the
Crucified Mind and the Risen Mind

In various ways and places Koyama expands upon the content of the crucified
mind. Grounded in God's self-denial and expressed in the lives of Christ's followers, the crucified mind ought both to reflect its roots and to yield its resources for
an apostolic life. Basing his concept of the crucified mind on Jesus' words, "If any
man would come after me, let him deny himself and take up his cross and follow
me" (Matt. 16:24) Koyama writes,

I would call the mind portrayed by Matthew 16:24 a "crucified
mind." It is the crucified mind that can meaningfully participate
in authentic contextualization. It is the mind of Christ. It is not a
neurotic mind. It is not a morbid mind. It does not have a persecution complex. It is a positive mind. It is a healthy mind. It is
the mind which is ready to crucify the self (" . . . deny himself,"
"he emptied himself . . .") for the sake of building up the

community. This mind is a theological mind. It is a free mind. And it is the missionary mind in contrast to the "crusading mind." This mind does not live by itself. It lives by constantly creating the life that practices such a mind. It lives with constant frustration and a sense of failure. Yet, it is joyous. It is resourceful. It is accommodational and prophetic. It knows that only by the grace of God can it be, and remain, accommodational and prophetic at all.[40]

It is a mind which overall relies intensely on God, trusting in God's "weakness and foolishness" over human strength and wisdom. "It is a believing mind. It is weak, yet a strong mind. It is foolish, yet a wise mind. It is the mind confessing 'I believe, help my unbelief'!"[41]

Because of its particular character, the crucified mind is a mind which therefore "invites serious misunderstanding."[42]

> There is no way of proving that the apostolic mind is the truthful mind and not a defrauding mind . . . It tries to demonstrate its power (I Cor. 4:20) by believing in the crucified Lord and crucifying "proofs" to show that it is true."[43]

By its own nature the crucified mind rejects measurement by human standards. It is not a "proof-sign-seeking mind. It is not a speculative-wisdom-seeking mind."[44] Rather than resting its claims on human proofs or understanding, the crucified mind seeks to ground itself on the living presence of Jesus Christ who overshadows all human proofs and wisdom. Because it believes in and trusts in a living person, a person whose being and dying are offensive to human reason, the crucified mind will be highly objectionable to many.

Yet Koyama emphasizes the overwhelmingly positive nature and effect of the crucified mind for human freedom and human community.

> "Let him deny himself" means to become part of a new community . . . "Let him deny himself" is an act of freedom. One has the freedom to "deny himself." The community, the community of self-renunciation, as it were, is a community created of human freedom being exercised. Complete freedom since it means readiness to take up the cross (symbol of tortured death)!
>
> The community is also a community of movement. The call does not say "sit with me." It says "follow me." It is a forward

movement of self-denial. Isn't it rather strange that such a radical self-renunciation is expressed in terms of a forward movement? How can self-renunciation, the opposite of self-assertion, be a forward-directed movement? The secret is found in the "me." Who is the "me"? He is the one heading towards death and resurrection, the ultimate self-renunciation and self-affirmation (Phil. 2:6–10).

Thus, in following him we experience the paradox that self-renunciation is self-affirmation, self-affirmation is self-renunciation. This is the experience of salvation.[45]

The crucified mind, then, is the mind which experiences salvation in the self-denying love of Christ. It is the mind which trusts that love. It is not a crusading mind which acts "as though the whole strategy of God's salvation of man is dependent upon man's performance."[46] Rather, the crucified mind trusts "that *all* is in God's hands and that all that is required of us is 'to take up the cross and follow him'."[47]

The crucified mind is not neurotic, stingy, condemning or paternalistic.[48] "It is not a business-transaction-with-God mind. It is a theologically inspired mind."[49] It is an open mind which seeks to build community and serve others.

The crucified mind approaches evangelism not with the style of the crusading mind but with a servant mind. While obedient to Jesus' command to share the good news of his coming with others, the crucified mind shares that news in the Christ-like manner that "in dying I come to you."[50]

People, says Koyama, are receptive to this kind of mind. "They will ask the secret of this crucified mind. That is evangelism."[51] Trusting the one whom they follow to work in his own times and in his own way (self-denial), Christians are not pressed to measure "success" in terms of numbers of converts.[52]

Altogether, the freedom and constructive confidence of the crucified mind may also be described by what Koyama calls the "risen mind." This is the mind that recognizes the new quality of life, of time, and of humanity ushered in by Jesus' resurrection. The risen mind is established not on its own self-generated resourcefulness, but upon the resourcefulness received from Jesus Christ crucified and risen.[53] Furthermore, the risen mind, with its resourcefulness grounded in Christ is an activist, not a quietest mind. It seeks always to be speaking and acting the reconciliation that grows out of self-denial.[54]

Resourcefulness grounded in Christ does not mean the negation of all human resourcefulness. Rather, it is a question of human resourcefulness being placed in the light of Jesus Christ crucified and risen. It is a question of baptizing the crusading mind by the crucified mind "so that human resourcefulness will become resourceful 'in the sight of God'."[55]

Ultimately the crucified/risen mind is a gift from God.[56] "Does not the Crucified One create the crucified mind within us and nurture it?"[57] With it comes also a sense of joy and the confidence to act for and to turn to the God who rules over history.

As examples of those who live with the power of the crucified and risen mind, Koyama points, among others, to Abraham, and Martin Luther King. Martin Luther King was one whose faith and self-sacrifice enabled him to proclaim a new humanity with "healthy confidence and joy."[58] Likewise, with confidence did Abraham negotiate with God for the people of the city of Sodom (Gen. 18:26–33). While recognizing himself to be utter dust and ashes before the sovereign God, Abraham trusted the love and identity God had given him and used it for others. Koyama calls Abraham's "dust and ashes" self-identity before God "theological." Because it is based in God's will and not in any significance of his own, Abraham's identity was healthy and powerful.[59]

By referring to these examples Koyama illustrates that the life of the crucified mind is not quietistic, morbid, negative, or powerless. It is quite the opposite: bold, active, healthy, positive and effective. It is the life of salvation, freedom and human community. It is the mind which should be the mind of all Christians,[60] the guide for Christian life and proclamation. To Koyama, it is the well-spring of all Christian life and mission. "The mission of the church begins with the nurture of the crucified mind, the mind of Christ."[61]

Neighbourology

"Neighbourology" is the term which carries what might be called Koyama's "doctrine of man." The word itself, centered on the term, "neighbor," reflects Koyama's interest not in abstract deliberations on human beings, but, rather, in personal relationships. His concern is more existential than theoretical.

The importance of Koyama's concern for people shows through repeatedly in his theology whether he is considering technology or other religions. Sensitivity to human feelings, experiences and relationships is an essential, formative ingredient for his whole understanding of Christian life and mission.

While Koyama does not develop an image of human being apart from his understanding of God's relationship to humanity, the following sections will nevertheless present Koyama's understanding of human being in three separate categories. The first section will draw together elements of Koyama's general picture of humanity. The second will deal with spirituality, human values, and the human capacity to choose between good and evil. The third section will emphasize the profound relationship between concern for one's neighbor, and Christian life and witness as seen by Koyama. Together, these segments present the substance of Koyama's "neighbourology."

An Image of Human Being

One of the first things that Koyama notes about humanity is that no definition can suffice to express or contain what a human is. Linguistically, Koyama points out that "the English verb 'define' comes form the Latin word *definere* (*de*—from, *finere*—to set a limit to, from *finis*—a boundary)."[62] In one sense it is clear that certain bounds can be affixed to human being, e.g. in terms of human physical limitations and in terms of what a human is not. On the other hand, "the word 'man' indicates some quality which refuses to be completely controlled by any word"[63] (that is, any word that qualifies man). Humans, for example, readily enough accept definitions of other animals, but "as soon as we come across a definition of man, we want to challenge it."[64]

Because we humans have the unique capacity to be self-critical, we will never be satisfied with a single definition of ourselves. We are too "wild" to be contained in a definition.[65] At best, any definitional description of human being will be but an outline of being human. This is because, as Koyama sees it, freedom, the inner quality at the center of the human personality, refuses to be nailed down.[66]

The freedom and "wildness" of being human, the impossibility of capturing the totality of humanity in a definition bears significance for human relationship. It means that human encounter will never be a static affair but will always be dynamic and unpredictable.

> Personal encounter (human community) is pregnant with unpredictable possibilities. The living person who confronts me defies the best possible definition of him. He is far more mysterious and complicated than I can possibly delineate even with the help of Freud, Marx, Dostoievsky and Heidegger.[67]

Koyama illustrates the importance of this recognition in his own life as a missionary. He regrets having failed to appreciate the distinctions between humanity as abstractly conceived and as existentially experienced.

> I am sorry that I have not personally appropriated and experienced in my whole existence this simple distinction and what it means. If I had, it would have contributed greatly to my manner of appreciating other persons when I came to meet them. Is it perhaps possible—what a dreadful thought!—that the study of theology blinded me in this respect? Has not theology inflated my language and thought? Has this inflation kept me from real contact with man? Truly, theology is more manageable than God himself. "Wifeology" is more tranquil than any wife! While I was in Thailand, I studied Buddhism. What a wonderful time I had in the quiet library of the seminary as I went undisturbed through the pages of the Buddhist Canons. Thanks to some knowledge of library-Buddhism, I began to say a few sensible words about Buddhism. But when I realized the difference between library-Buddhism and street-Buddhists, my library-Buddhism was paralyzed. Library-Buddhism and street-Buddhism are, of course, related. In fact, I felt quite often that the street-Buddhists should study more about library-Buddhism. Yet it is the street-Buddhists who are the brothers whom I see, with whom I speak and with whom I live. To love them *as they are* in all their complexity and not just to love anthropological, sociological, theological "formulations" of the brothers is the command of God whom we have not seen (I John 4:20). Only through such love can my theological "inflation" be brought down. I began to examine as carefully as I could the relationship between "the idea of man walking in the idea of history" and "the living person in the concrete historical situation." . . . A person is an unfathomable complexity.[68]

When one starts to appreciate history as the story of humanity in all its complexity, one can begin to see the issues and tensions of the changing world in a different way. For example, the contemporary encounter of traditional local cultures with the universal technological civilization and the tensions it produces become less an abstract confrontation of concepts than an internal human struggle. For, Koyama points out, "the traditional and the revolutionary do not meet directly; they meet only in *man*, who shapes and values them."[69]

The meeting of world religions also takes on a personal dimension when one understands it as a meeting between people rather than between doctrines. "Perhaps we pay undue attention to *ism*, and in contrast, too little attention to *ist*."[70] Koyama explains this in relation to his experience as a Christian missionary in a Buddhist culture.

> We must study Buddh*ism*, of course, if we wish to understand the Buddh*ist*. Our ultimate interest must lie, however, with understanding the Buddh*ist* and not Buddh*ism*. What matters for the Christian gospel is not Buddh*ism*, but the Buddh*ist*.[71]

Koyama develops this point by contrasting the ambiguity and abstractions of religious doctrine with the concrete realities of the human beings who produce and practice doctrines. Buddhism, for example, as a doctrine, does not hunger, sweat, suffer, or want. A Buddhist, as a human being, does. No matter what religion or doctrine a human being subscribes to, that human being will remain essentially a dynamic living creation, sharing emotional, physical, spiritual and intellectual needs not unlike those of others—no matter what religion or doctrine those others subscribe to.

Therefore, Koyama notes, that "even the best of all doctrines is not identical with the living man whom we see everyday everywhere."[72] Even the Christian church must avoid the trap of equating human beings with doctrines about them. For doctrine is only a servant of relationship.

> Now, man is, according to the Bible, the "image of God." This is a great doctrine about man . . . Whenever the church opens her mouth on the issue of the "dignity of man," this doctrine of the "image of God" has been the point of departure. But this doctrine, in short, must not remain simply a doctrine. It must become integrated into our appreciation of man with whom we come in contact everyday . . . It must be actualized in man-to-man relationships if it is to display its dynamic and real power.[73]

Koyama strongly warns against the danger of being bound by doctrines in our understanding of humanity. An excessive preoccupation with *isms* over *ists* brings about, in Koyama's mind, a disastrous tendency to judge other human beings without knowing, understanding or appreciating them. This is especially contrary to the Christian commitment to love others.[74]

Christianity, in fact, at its heart focuses on a person, not a doctrine. As Koyama sees it,

> If one of the doctrines on man had been adequate to explain him to himself, then, to use theological terminology, the "incarnation" would not have been necessary. Instead of the costly incarnation, God becoming man and dwelling amongst us, God might just as well have sent some wonderful doctrine about man. The best of all the good doctrines cannot compete with the one fact of God's incarnation in Jesus Christ.[75]

In summary, it may be said that for Koyama, proper understanding of human being begins with a recognition of human freedom and indefinability. It resists any depersonalization of humanity according to doctrines or abstractions. Finally, it rests on relationship. For, this is the pattern chosen by God for God's own participation in and redemption of human history.

Human Purpose and Potential

"We must ask ourselves, what does 'to be human' mean? 'To be human' means to live in relationship."[76] This is the fundamental perspective from which Koyama considers human being. But the question immediately arises as to what the nature and meaning of relationship is. A partial answer lies in Koyama's contrast of "human" relationships with the "subhuman" and "inhuman" relationships of which humans are also capable.

> Oppression, exploitation, persecution, discrimination—all these are not human relationships but the experience of subhuman and inhuman relationships.[77]

Ultimately, the Christian idea of loving one's neighbor as one's self is, to Koyama, the critical criterion for measuring human relationship. But because loving one's neighbor is not at all easy, this criterion of relationship cannot simply be applied as a general moral guideline. It needs to be grounded directly in the acting of God.

To make this point clear, Koyama uses the example of two people who see in the Ten Commandments a standard for human relationship. One disassociates the commandments from the God who gave them in the belief that they are sufficient as general guidelines for human behavior. The second person, however, finds a fuller understanding of the commandments within the salvation context in which they are set. This enables the second person to come to grips with the reality that people can rarely fulfill the commandments.

> We know what human values are, but they cannot be easily realized in our world. At this point of difficulty, we are forced to interpret human value in a more involved way.[78]

One comes to understand human value, that is, the ability to live in the constructive manner encouraged by the Ten Commandments, and as embodied in the idea of loving one's neighbor, by relating it to God-value.[79] God-value consists in the fact that God values human beings—so highly as to give the Son's life for them. God loves and accepts people despite their inability to live as the commandments command.

Likewise, human ability to accept and love one's neighbor begins with the knowledge of this prior act of God. God's own self-denial for the sake of human beings in all their imperfection and failure therefore becomes the root and model for human relationship. Human relationship "is nourished and healthy, as long as we see the Mind of God behind it."[80]

As Koyama surveys the range of human difficulties today, he is keenly aware of how unhealthy and corrupt human relationships—lacking the perception of the "Mind of God"—can be. The world of modern technology, which thrives on cash-relationship and self-fulfillment by expensive lifestyles, offers one example of where this corruption can occur. In affluent society, as Koyama sees it, human spirituality is easily paralyzed in an expensive search for identity. This search usually ignores the need for responsible human relationship. It creates more alienation than it overcomes.

In contrast, Koyama sees the commandment to love one's neighbor as one's self to be the fundamental meaning of responsibility and the means to fulfill human relationship. However, the "economy" of the meaning and identity that one finds in living by love for one's neighbor, which Koyama also calls "the apostolic tradition" as it carries on Christ's example of relationship, is different from the "economy" of self-enlargement. "The 'apostolic tradition' is inexpensive in terms of hard-cash. It is 'expensive' in terms of love and self-giving."[81] This apostolic economy is the one which is, however, ultimately less costly for the world.[82]

Another example of corrupt human relationship is racism. In Koyama's eyes racism devastates human dignity. It attacks not only the periphery of human social life; it injures humanity at its very center. "It is blasphemy against the deepest level of human identity."[83]

Likewise, the suffering of minorities is a subject which Koyama sees to be not a peripheral issue, but a pervasive reality in the fabric of human society today. It further demonstrates the capacity for human refusal to love one's neighbor. At the same time, it sharpens the definition of what for Koyama it means to be human.

Thinking in terms of the human need to be rooted and secure in a given environment, Koyama describes being human as "living peacefully upon the land."[84] But to this he immediately adds living peacefully with one's neighbor and with God. For to injure others is to destroy our own dignity and to ignore God or to ignore the source of all human dignity.[85]

One further activity of humanity in which the capability of corrupting relationships is revealed is that of naming things.

> Adam—humankind—creates meaning in his environment and lives in the network of meaning and value which he has made. This, he does, as an intelligent person, in the naming of things.[86]

On the one hand, naming things is a constructive, even holy act by which we relate to the created world. But our ability to name things can be abused, especially when it covers up corrupt human relationship.

> Because he can name, he can misname. Outside of "Eden" naming always involves the risk of misnaming. When man names he gives meaning to cosmos. The cosmos is enlivened by him and for him. When man misnames he creates a "mis-cosmos," a chaos . . . human well-being does depend on how we name things.[87]

Koyama offers Japanese imperial interests during World War II, British labor exploitation as it was criticized by Karl Marx in the nineteenth century, and jails in South Vietnam as examples of atrocities which were justified by names intended to make them socially acceptable.[88] For example, to "name" inhuman working conditions as "necessary for the sake of economic development" is, as Koyama sees it, "demonic naming."

In naming ourselves as human, we must reject that which contradicts being human. This is true, as Koyama sees it, no matter what religion or society one belongs to. For all human beings have a fundamental dignity, which resists being insulted or denied.

Even in a world where human beings number in the billions, Koyama asserts that each one has worth and dignity. In a reflection on world evangelization Koyama maintains that human being cannot be grasped in terms of massive numbers. To him two billion people, for example, cannot be conceived in a direct, abstract way. To Koyama, two billion people means,

> Personal freedom two billion times, human dignity two billion times, mystery of the image of God two billion times, personal history two billion times, two billion ways to experience life. There is a sacred dimension in man which defies and rejects being numbered.[89]

Koyama accounts for the "sacred dimension" of humanity by remembering that we are made in the image of God. As God is a mystery, so is humanity. God has given us special abilities and gifts, which, when applied as intended, exhibit God's image. Koyama mentions three of these abilities in particular.[90]

First is the human ability to understand and appreciate stories. By this Koyama means our ability to describe and interpret our own existence. Through stories we understand the world. Through the biblical story we discover God's presence and love. Unfortunately, the human ability to use and understand stories includes the possibility of misunderstanding reality, of false and even self-destructive interpretations of life.

The second great human ability is that "man is specially endowed to live in a relationship with God and man . . . Relationshipless life is both an impossibility and a monstrosity."[91] However, tragedy comes when our relationships are not founded upon love—love for God and love for one's neighbor. *"Because man is able to live with others in sound relationships he can produce broken relationships."*[92]

Humanity's third special ability as the image of God is the ability to criticize itself. We are capable of self-evaluation. We can look at ourselves critically and admit our faults, which in turn entails the possibility of change. However, the tragic side of this critical ability is that it can be devastatingly aimed at others as well. Our ability to criticize ourselves contains the possibility of criticizing others in such a way as to violate love and destroy relationships.

Underlying these special abilities of humanity, making both their positive and negative uses possible, is the primary mark of our being made in the image of God, namely, our freedom. "Freedom is not something man carries or man possesses. It is his very essence. *Without freedom man is not a man.*"[93]

Perhaps nothing else in our being so reflects God's image as our freedom. To Koyama, the fact that God respects human freedom is the greatest testimony to human dignity. God does not compel us to acknowledge or obey him. God does not, as it were, make the whole world Christian.[94]

However, human freedom can be abused. It is by misusing our freedom that we create the tragedies of broken relationships, with all that that means in terms of injury to others and alienation from God.

But by properly exercising human freedom for the sake of love for God and for one's neighbor, humanity both finds fulfillment and points to the God in whose image we are created. "Man's happiness consists of his right use of freedom."[95]

Still, the "right" use of freedom, which leads to human happiness, cannot be determined without some reference point. Human spirituality shows the way to the necessary reference points. Our spirituality functions to put us in touch with that which will make our freedom meaningful and constructive.

Like freedom, spirituality is part of our being in the image of God. It sets us apart from other animals. Our spirituality is apparent even at the most fundamental level, the level of our physical needs.

> Man's life would have been much simpler if he were merely a
> digestive system and nothing more . . . as soon as man becomes
> physically hungry he seeks bread and *something with it.*[96]

For Koyama, even human hunger points to the spiritual needs of humanity. For, while humans must naturally have bread to exist, we cannot live by bread alone. Because we are spiritual, we need spiritual as well as physical fulfillment to survive.

"It takes both bread and the Word of God to make man live in the way God wants him to live."[97] Koyama here uses the word "bread" to refer to a variety of physical human needs, e.g., clothing, shelter, sex, money, brain, work, technology, and religion. All of these, taken out of relationship to human spiritual needs, can injure humanity.

> "Clothing alone" becomes obscene and perverse. "Shelter
> alone" becomes spiritually wasteful "grand-house-prestigeism."
> "Sex alone" becomes paralyzing sex-ism. "Money alone"
> becomes anti-human exploitative egoism. "Brain alone"

becomes dangerous idolatry of human intelligence. "Work alone" becomes a system of self-imposed slavery. "Technology alone" becomes a threat to human life. "Power alone" becomes destructive power which produces a repressive society. "Religion alone" becomes an irrelevant, monkish, self-righteous mentality.[98]

All these aspects of ordinary human life need to be illuminated and judged by the Word of God and be brought into relationship with one another. Unfortunately, it is very difficult for human beings to bring all these aspects into the constraint of the commandments to love God and to love one's neighbor. For, in reality people prefer to love money, power and the other sorts of personal satisfaction. They do not even know how to relate their physical life and the commandment to love others as one's self. But without an encounter between human "bread" and God's Word, Koyama believes that human preoccupation with self-fulfillment will be finally self-destructive. Unless human beings learn to share their "bread" they will become extinct.[99]

This reality reflects the corporate nature of human spirituality.

Man's spiritual life is not an isolated life. It participates in the spiritual value upheld in the community in which he belongs. The spirituality of man is a corporate experience.[100]

Koyama believes that a critical understanding of this fact is urgently needed, particularly in Christian theology.[101]

All in all, in his consideration of both the human ability to live in relationships based on God's love and the human failure to do so, Koyama comes down to describing the human situation as one of choosing, i.e., in choosing between the use or the misuse of human capabilities, gifts, and resources. Of course, "use comes with misuse . . . Use and misuse are tragically inseparable in human life."[102]

But Koyama also pictures these possibilities of use and misuse in broader, theological language. He describes the use of human gifts and resources in ways which ultimately diminish life and destroy relationships as the use of things for Baal. On the other hand, the use of human gifts and resources for relationships which are based on love of others, is the use of things for God. These are humanity's two great possibilities.

The Significance of
Neighbourology for Christian Witness

Our sense of the presence of God will be distorted if we fail to see God's reality in terms of our neighbour's reality. And our sense of our neighbour's reality will be disfigured unless seen in terms of God's reality.[103]

No statement could more vividly demonstrate the significance Koyama attaches to awareness of and love for one's neighbor as being intrinsic to the Christian faith. The fact that in Jesus God, who created humanity, was personally present as a human, is supreme testimony to the importance God attaches to human being. Moreover, Koyama holds, God continues to use humanity as an instrument and communicator of God's presence and purpose.[104]

This has special significance for those involved in the task of transmitting the Christian faith. To relate the Word of God to the lives of the people addressed in Christian mission, Koyama proposes that a missionary must undertake two kinds of exegesis: "exegesis of the Word of God, and exegesis of the life and culture of the people among whom he lives and works."[105]

This places the missionary in what Koyama calls a "sandwiched" position "between Christ's saving reality and his neighbor's 'other-than-myself' reality."[106] One's life and theology then take on meaning through interaction with one's neighbors, no matter what their faith may be.

With realism, Koyama takes note of the fact that, "Our neighbours are not concerned with our Christology, but they show, from time to time, their interest in our 'neighbourology'."[107] Thus, when Christian faith is translated into relationships rather than simply presented as doctrine it is able to meet people in terms which are meaningful to them. Then, they may in turn develop interest in the belief that motivates the relationship.

In emphasizing the importance of appreciating one's neighbor in the context of Christian obedience, Koyama turns to the Scriptural account that "He who does not love his brother whom he has seen cannot love God whom he has not seen" (I John 4:20). The significance of this idea for relationship is the order with which it challenges the believer. The order is "neighbour-God." "It does not read: 'He who does not love God whom he has not seen, cannot love his brother whom he has seen'."[108] For Koyama, this serves as an illustration which reinforces the fundamental necessity of awareness and concern for the situation of one's non-Christian neighbor.

Koyama even goes so far as to say that a person's Christian existence "hangs on the claim his neighbour makes on him."[109] That is, one cannot be Christian apart from one's relation to one's neighbors.

This is because Christ, the center of Christian faith, accepted the reality of his neighbors and their claims upon him. The Incarnation was an act of identification with and for others. Christ suffered because he was involved with others. Likewise, those who follow Christ must undertake the same kind of involvement.

Koyama describes this involvement and the difficulty it means for those who follow Christ as "Christological discomfort."[110] "It is a dialogue," he says, in the sense that Christian discipleship is always an activity involving others rather than a monologue between an individual and God.[111] "The 'Christological' implies immediately 'the neighbourological.' They are inseparable."[112]

Of course, it follows that Christian theology, too, must embody and exhibit a "neighbourological" dimension. It cannot be a private affair; it needs to take its shape in the community life of humankind.[113]

Neighbourological theology will be a humble, limited attempt to take seriously the situations, values and needs of all the different kinds of neighbors. Naturally, this will require a wide flexibility in theological thinking, as various situations will demand various formulations of theology.[114] At least, as Koyama sees it,

The reality of one's neighbours—all that they are and all that they do—must become a motivating force for our theological engagement.[115]

CHAPTER EIGHT

AN EVALUATION OF KOYAMA'S CRUCIFIED MIND THEOLOGY

Having so far presented key themes of Koyama's theology, both his unique style and primary concerns should now be clear. Part III provides a more in-depth analysis of Koyama's style and examines his value as a model for intercultural theology. Before moving on, however, it is expedient to provide an evaluation of Koyama's Crucified Mind theology and general reflections on his theology of other religions.

Since Koyama's theology of the Crucified Mind is arguably the fundamental hermeneutical core of his theology, from which most of his other perspectives develop, it will be considered first. Accordingly, the following chapter examines specific aspects of his theological center-point, setting it in a broader context, raising appropriate questions, and evaluating some of its limitations and advantages. A brief discussion on the role of ethics in Koyama's theology, which is an outgrowth of Crucified Mind theology, will conclude the chapter.

The Crucified Mind

Echoes of Luther

Luther's theology of the Cross, it has been said, represented a new principle of theological epistemology.[1] Over against the deductive, naturalistic theology of the Greek philosophical heritage, Luther's theology of the Cross emphasized knowledge through practice, knowledge through a faith which knew God even in the face of paradox.[2] For his time, Luther provided a new look at faith, one which became the theoretical basis of a Reformation in Christian faith and practice.[3]

Koyama may not be another Luther, but his theology of the Crucified Mind echoes Luther's theology of the Cross in an exciting way during another critical period of Christian history. Like Luther, Koyama brings out the intuitive, experiential dimensions of Christian faith and discipleship. Koyama, like Luther, understands and makes central to his theology the paradoxes of Christian faith, such as God's self-denial at the Cross, God's powerful powerlessness, a world broken yet redeemed, and so on. As Luther recognized God's presence in suffering, so Koyama stresses the centrality of suffering to discipleship. Faith, to both Koyama and Luther, is not wholly subject to reason; it is essentially a matter of relationship. This relationship is based on trust in God and expressed in loving relationship with one's neighbors.

Of course, perspectives such as these are not exclusively Lutheran; nor is Koyama alone in addressing these concerns. Other contemporary theologians, especially in their concern for relating faith to experience and praxis, in their attempts to construct a theology for addressing human suffering, or in their struggle to liberate theology from the bonds of European rationalism are doing much the same as Koyama.

However, Koyama's balanced integration of such concerns into a theology of the Cross (especially in the highly complex, non-Christian world of Asia) provides a unique model for Christian theology—not only in Asia but for Christians elsewhere as well. For his time and context Koyama does in his own small way what Luther did. That is, over against a dominant theological, philosophical, and cultural framework, Koyama sets a Christian spirituality which he sees as faithful to Scripture and understandable to ordinary Christians. In an intensely Christocentric, cross-centered, Scripture-based theology, Koyama sees the resources for Christian life and witness in a world of profound complexity and change. In such ways as these it may be said that Koyama, whose own education and theology have strong Lutheran roots, resembles Luther in the shaping of a theology of the Cross during a critical period of Christian history.

In further consideration of Koyama's theology of the Cross, or, his theology of the Crucified Mind, two general questions emerge. The first concerns the application of the Crucified Mind, especially in relation to the use of power. The second question relates to Koyama's understanding of the Resurrection. Before taking up these questions, however, the question of consistency in Koyama's theology deserves attention.

Koyama and Consistency

The question might be asked—to what extent is Koyama's theology itself and Koyama's own life "crucified"? Does it exhibit the self-denying, crucified character of which he speaks? No simple answer is possible, especially because defining what a "crucified life" for someone else would be is highly presumptuous. However, several points might be mentioned.

Obviously, Koyama's theology does not follow conventional modes. It is "crucified" in style in that it runs counter to the dominant, "handling" mode of systematic, deductive theology. A prime purpose of this style is to make theology understandable and relevant to ordinary people. The "neighbourological," person-centered approach, as opposed to specialized, idea-centered theology, would clearly seem to reflect the values of the Crucified Mind and its relational character.

In his own career Koyama has consistently moved within the elite circles of power and privilege. However, within those circles he has agitated for change and a dispersion of power, not infrequently criticizing the centers of power in the Church and bringing into it a recognizable concern for people outside it, such as students, farmers, and other ordinary people, including those who are not Christian. Koyama recognizes that when people are emphasized, the academic world is criticized.[4]

In his own theology Koyama goes so far as to measure the value of Christianity's greatest theologians by their relevance for illiterate peasants. In his concern for openness to people of other faiths, Koyama is willing to criticize Christianity, willing to respect and learn from people of other faiths, and in favor of dialogue between Christianity and other religions. These attitudes would all seem to reflect the values of the Crucified Mind.

It might be suggested that the Crucified Mind would seem to require more dramatic action, for example, choosing a life of voluntary poverty, disassociating from all positions of power and authority, or something similar. But this is not necessarily the case. Koyama does not suggest this as a necessary consequence of the Crucified Mind. Again, the Crucified Mind refers primarily to one's fundamental orientation, to one's trust in God, and to one's understanding of God's action in history and how that serves as a model or invitation for Christians to follow, whatever their station or position in life.

Specific circumstances or individual commitments may well mean for some that a crucified mentality leads to dramatic changes. But the importance of context in Koyama's theology—as it defines human identity and requires various responses—suggests that the Crucified Mind can be manifested in a variety of circumstances, including positions of wealth or power. Such a pattern would find considerable support in both Scripture and Christian history, though support for alternative patterns could also be found.

Once again, the Crucified Mind must be understood as a fundamental orientation rather than as a legalistic rule. It is to be understood in a dialectic with self-centered, mechanistic thinking. It is intrinsically a flexible attitude which by nature can appreciate and operate in a variety of contexts.

Altogether, the precise degree to which Koyama's theology and lifestyle exhibit a "crucified" or self-denying character cannot be so easily judged. Yet, it seems safe to say that there is in fact a reasonable consistency between the content and the form of Koyama's theology, and credible evidence of a consistency between Koyama's theology and his activity in the career in which he finds himself.

Power and the Crucified Mind

As an abstract idea or a proposition, the Crucified Mind may be hard to comprehend or apply. Koyama himself notes that the Crucified Mind is not provable; it is not a static proposition. The Crucified Mind does not provide legalistic guidelines for Christian practice and proclamation. Rather, it is a modality. It concerns a person's fundamental or ultimate understanding of Christian discipleship. When the Crucified Mind is one's foundational attitude or one's basic hermeneutical principle, specific choices in particular contexts can be made on the basis of how fully they manifest a crucified character.

Inescapably, such a theological perspective involves ambiguity. There will always be questions both as to what actions exhibit a crucified character and as to whether or not such a hermeneutical principle is valid or constructive in all circumstances.

In Christian history many examples can be found of Christian actions which would not seem to be of a crucified character yet which might be considered part of God's plan. At least on the surface, the Old Testament—while pre-Christian and pre-crucifixion, yet, according to Koyama, already exhibiting God's self-denial—is rife with examples of God's people and God personally acting in aggressive, manipulative, and destructive ways to accomplish the divine plan.

The first Christians, of course, had little institutional or political power and could thus easily be "crucified" in character. Yet, Paul—one of Koyama's prime examples of one who led an "apostolic," "crucified" life—was not reluctant to speak and act very forcefully in his dealings with dissension among the missionary churches and in his use of Roman state power to protect himself and his mission.

Later Christian history in Europe is predominantly the history of a Christian community with power which it did not hesitate to use. Positive as well as negative results followed from Christianity's exercise of power—whether measured in terms of the beauty achieved in Christian art and architecture, in the spread of Christianity throughout Europe and abroad, or in terms of the more gentle flowerings of Christian faith and practice upon the foundations laid by the more violent

Christianity of a previous period. It might even be argued that the Christianity associated with European colonialism—which Koyama specifically opposes to the Crucified Mind—was instrumental to God's plan for the world as a whole.

In short, the question of power and how it should be used by Christians is a matter which Koyama's theology of the Crucified Mind leaves, to some degree, unresolved. Can Christians employ force to defend themselves or to protect others? Are there other modes of Christian life and evangelism than that of the Crucified Mind which are acceptable and to be encouraged?

In partial response to such questions it should be reiterated that Koyama emphasizes understanding the Crucified Mind not on its own, but in relation to the Crusading Mind.[5] The Crucified Mind is part of a theological dialectic. In this dialectic the Crusading Mind represents abusive power, un-Christ-like attitudes and actions, and in general, those activities in which humanity places its trust primarily in itself and its own resources.

The Crucified Mind, on the other hand, represents a Christ-like mode of relationship and a fundamental trust in the power of God, knowing that God may act in ways contrary to normal human expectations and standards of effectiveness. Again, one is reminded of Luther's theology of the "hidden God" or God at work "under opposite forms."[6]

As mentioned earlier, the Crucified Mind is not passive or negativistic. As Koyama describes it, it is active, positive, and resourceful. It is not apathetic or opposed to all power, for, to some degree, power is intrinsic to any action. Rather, the Crucified Mind asks what kind of power is being used and how. The Crucified Mind has, as Koyama puts it, its "own kind of energy."[7] Koyama's belief is that the energy of the Crucified Mind—the mind of self-denial and brokenness— ultimately triumphs over the energy of the Crusading Mind, the mind of self-assertion and humanly efficient power.

The Crucified Mind, then, has to do not so much with specific guidelines for particular decisions, but with an ultimate conviction of the way God works and therefore the basis on which human decisions should be made.

If this means ambiguity in decision making, it also means freedom and flexibility. Decisions can be made to suit varying circumstances while remaining consistent with a fundamental hermeneutical principle. This alliance of flexibility and consistency is one of the advantages of the Crucified Mind.

Overall, the Crucified Mind has a variety of advantages as a hermeneutical principle. To an Asia that has been on the receiving end of Christian theology which manifested a self-righteous, power-orientated, crusading mentality, it shows a humbler, more appealing face of Christianity. It allows repentance at a time when repentance is necessary, appropriate, and helpful. It provides a mechanism for dis-associating Christianity somewhat from the West by distinguishing between the "crucified" values of traditional Christianity and the "crusading" patterns of Western culture as experienced by Asia.

The flexible, self-critical, existential character of the Crucified Mind lends itself amenably to certain Asian understandings of the nature of truth. Generally speaking, it may be said that in Asia truth is conceived more in intuitive than in propositional ways. Whether in China or Japan, in Buddhism or Taoism, Truth is often seen more as an existential dynamic than as an empirical principle. It has more to do with human relationships than with abstract doctrines.[8] Japanese logicians of antiquity, for example, were more interested in the human relations of a debate than with abstract ideas about the human situation.[9] In Asia the preservation of harmony in personal and social relations may involve a more important aspect of truth than philosophical or religious assertions. In such a milieu a Christology that emphasizes relationships, and that emphasizes truth as a dynamic event may find a receptive audience.

Another advantage of the Crucified Mind is that in its emphasis on self-denial, it provides both the spirit for and a point of contact with Asia's other religions, particularly Buddhism. Theology of the Cross, which deals directly with suffering, can be readily related to the suffering of Asia. This is especially important for Asian Christianity.

Finally, Crucified Mind theology is by nature self-critical. It allows for all theological statements to be criticized in the light of a Scriptural, yet existential principle. It does not pretend to have the authority of a proposition. It does not depend on a specific set of Western philosophical principles or rational constructs—though it does have a consistent reference point in history as described by Scripture.

By referring to an historical event, an historical pattern, and universal human experiences of love and self-denial, Crucified Mind theology resists being taken as an absolute, abstract principle on its own. It preserves the "event" nature of theology, calling for theology itself to be "poured out," "spat upon," and focused not on itself but on the living person of the crucified Christ. This is an important contribution to establishing a theological hermeneutic for the modern situation of encounter.

What is perhaps ironic in Koyama's adoption and application of Crucified Mind theology is its inherent bridging of different centuries of East and West. Koyama's twentieth-century Asian theology of the Cross stems directly from Luther's sixteenth-century Latin and Germanic theology. In Koyama's theological interpretation of twentieth-century Japanese imperialism and in his development of a theological mode for contemporary Asia, Koyama utilizes theological insights generated in the West several centuries ago. This is not to say that Koyama merely copies Western theology. Indeed, his development of theology of the Cross and his use of Christology goes beyond the same theology in the West. But that there is a unique link or bridge in Koyama's theology between East and West, between past and present, should not be overlooked.

The Crucified Mind and Resurrection

Koyama's emphasis on the Cross and on Christian discipleship's being patterned after the crucifixion raises the question of how Koyama understands the resurrection. An over-emphasis on suffering, and on living a "crucified" life may seem to neglect the Resurrection.[10]

C. S. Song's criticism of Kazoh Kitamori, Koyama's teacher, illustrates the problem. Song claims that Kitamori's theology is essentially Western precisely because of its preoccupation with the event of the Cross as the "struggle of God against God within God himself."[11] Kitamori's theology stops at the Cross, Song asserts. It makes little reference to the resurrection. "It cannot in fact accommodate resurrection; it does not have room for it."[12]

Koyama's theology might also be said to give too little attention to Jesus' Resurrection and its implications. Koyama himself remarks that his theology is primarily a theology of the crucified Christ.[13] The only way he can speak of the risen Christ, he says, is by thinking of the risen Christ as the crucified Christ. Crucifixion remains the primary focus in Koyama's understanding of Christ.

But, Koyama says, his theological orientation is so focused on the crucified Christ because the world today is so much a world of crucifixion. The overwhelming reality of suffering in Asia and in the world as a whole pushes Koyama towards a theology that can address this suffering.

At the same time, Koyama is aware of the danger of neglecting the implications of the Resurrection. "I must know how to speak of the Risen Christ; otherwise I will preach a very cheap Gospel."[14] Christian creeds, Koyama adds, stress the significance of resurrection. They convey the hope of the resurrection. Because of the Resurrection, Koyama says, Christian faith is a "vocation of hope."[15]

Yet Koyama feels torn by the reality of continuing crucifixion in a world that has seen the resurrection. He expresses his tornness poignantly:

> The relationship between the crucified and risen Christ is not
> something I try to explain but something from the other side

that grips me. Maybe someday I will know how to speak about the Risen Christ . . . I am a Christian; I believe in Easter. But I don't know how to express that in the world of today. Yes, I know the literature and some good stories, but . . . [Koyama left this sentence incomplete].[16]

Here again, while his motives stem from a different context, Koyama's attitude towards the crucifixion and his theology of the Cross stand recognizably within the Lutheran tradition. Koyama's emphasis on a crucified theology accords fully with the Lutheran view that "*theologia crucis* is not a single chapter in theology, but the key signature for all Christian theology."[17] In this view all Christian statements stem from the crucified Christ.[18]

Also connected with this view is an understanding of the relationship between crucifixion and resurrection which Koyama basically affirms. That is,

the resurrection of the crucified Christ qualifies his death as for us, and the cross of the risen Christ reveals and makes accessible to those who are dying his resurrection from the dead.[19]

Further, this view suggests that the Cross and the Resurrection are not facts on the same level. Rather, the Cross is history and the Resurrection is eschatology.[20] In a context where Christian eschatology is an alien notion, but where crucifixion of one kind or another is a concrete historical experience, Koyama turns to a this-worldly theology of the Cross as the basis for Christian proclamation.

Intrinsic to this crucifixion theology is a particular understanding of God—of the kind for which Song criticized Kitamori—that sees a triune God as suffering, and as accomplishing the redemption of humanity in a kenotic manner.[21] In this understanding God is found primarily, if not only, in the Cross and in suffering. The meaning of the Cross does not disclose itself in contemplative thought, but rather in suffering experience.[22]

What this Cross-centered theology obviously resists is an unbalanced Christian triumphalism both in concept and in praxis. It opposes "handling," abstract, purely cognitive conceptions of God.

The Cross of Christ makes plain that there is no direct knowledge of God for man . . . Christian thinking must come to a halt before the fact of the Cross . . . The Cross makes demands on Christian thought—demands which must either be acted on or ignored . . . [they] cannot be disposed of in an upper story of the structure of thought.[23]

Theology of the Cross, as Koyama's theology illustrates, is necessarily existential. By nature it opposes Christian action which is disassociated from the Cross. Theologians of the Cross must be not just spectators but participants in the word they proclaim.[24] To use Koyama's terms again, Christian discipleship requires an "apostolic," "poured-out," "crucified" life. With particular reference to Christian life and witness in the modern situation Koyama states, "We have operated with a risen-Christ picture too long; now we need a crucified-Christ picture."[25]

Yet all this emphasis on a theology of the Cross does not ultimately overshadow the meaning of the Resurrection for Koyama. For, the context in which theology of the Cross functions is a context of resurrection. Koyama may not describe this resurrection context in traditional terms. He does speak of the "Risen Mind," the Christian "vocation of hope," and the fact that living a crucified life is ultimately a gift of the risen Christ.[26] But the term which perhaps best expresses Koyama's sense of resurrection is one inherited from Kitamori, namely, "embrace." Koyama's picture of God embracing the world—encompassing the pain of Jesus' crucifixion and through it enfolding the suffering of a broken world in a transforming, healing way—clearly conveys a resurrection perspective.

Nowhere does Koyama question the Resurrection; for him it is a given. Because of the Resurrection, Koyama can believe in the ultimately more effective "energy" of the Crucified Mind. Because of the Resurrection Koyama can speak of the Holy Spirit at work in the world. Belief in the Resurrection gives Koyama's theology both a motive and a vision for Christian efforts toward change in the world.

Altogether, resurrection is a presupposition of Koyama's theology. Some of its possible implications or applications, for example, in relation to the use of power, may not have been fully worked out yet in Koyama's theology. Perhaps they need not be worked out. For, in the time and context with which Koyama is concerned and in relation to the issues which he seeks to address, Koyama's current emphasis on the Crucified Mind is more appropriate and more important.

Christology

To present Koyama's theology of the Crucified Mind is to present Koyama's Christology. However, some further observations may be made about the Crucified Mind in particular reference to Christology.

The most important function of Koyama's Christology is as a principle of critique. That and the way in which this critique makes Koyama's Christology a tool for ecumenical theology will be considered next.

To begin with, it is clear that a variety of experiences have made Koyama critical of ideologies, institutions, and absolutes in general. In war-torn Japan he witnessed the destructive results of Japanese imperialism, or, given the role of Shinto, what might be called an Asian "power-theology." His experience and study of the impact of the West on Asia provided abundant evidence of exploitation for ideological and economic purposes. In particular Koyama criticizes Western Christianity for its ideological and institutional aggression in Asia. But Koyama also acknowledges the complicity of his own Church with the war policies of imperial Japan. Besides that, he himself asserts that Kanzo Uchimura, whose Christianity was deliberately anti-institutional, was a major influence on his thinking. Finally, Koyama's wide exposure to differing cultures and values has made clear to him the cultural relativity of all belief and value systems.

In short, from a variety of sources and experiences Koyama has developed a critical resistance to the absolutization of any ideology, culture, institution, or even religion. Whether expressed in terms of Japanese cultural supremacy, Western political colonialism, or Christianity's judgmental attitudes towards other religions, absolutes are tantamount to idolatry in Koyama's eyes and are inevitably self-centered, exploitative, and dangerous.

Therefore, building upon his inheritance of a theology of the Cross, filtered first through Kitamori and then studied later in Luther, Koyama constructs a Christology that can serve as a critique of all absolutes. In his interpretation of God's non-handling, self-denying activity in human history, culminating in the life and death of Jesus, Koyama finds a tool for criticizing both the events of history and Christianity itself. The crucified Christ becomes a critique of history, culture, and the Church.

In this perspective, Koyama appears close to Paul Tillich, whom Koyama personally admires.[27] Tillich asserted that in its encounter with the world's ideologies, religions, and "quasi-religions," Christianity must look first of all within itself to find the center-point of its identity, of its self-judgment, and hence, to clarify the grounds from which it understands everything else.

> Where does Christianity find its criteria? There is only one point from which the criteria can be derived and only one way to approach this point. The point is the event on which Christianity is based, and the way is the participation in the continuing

spiritual power of this event, which is the appearance and reception of Jesus of Nazareth as the Christ, a symbol which stands for the decisive self-manifestation in human history of the source and aim of all history.[28]

As does Koyama, Tillich emphasizes that active participation in the way of Christ is essential to being Christian. This does not imply abstract, merely cognitive, or formal institutional participation. Rather, personal, existential participation is required.

Participation in an event of the past is only possible if one is grasped by the spiritual power of this event and through it is enabled to evaluate the witnesses, the traditions and the authorities in which the same spiritual power was and is effective.[29]

Koyama describes this critical spiritual power in terms of self-denial and the Crucified Mind; Tillich uses other terms. Yet, Tillich and Koyama may be said to be on parallel paths as, in a situation of radical religious and ideological encounter, they focus first of all on Christianity itself and how Christ acts as a critique on Christian action and belief. Such a posture reveals the thinking of cross theology, of humility and self-denial, rather than arrogance and a judgmental attitude directed towards other faiths.

But Koyama perhaps goes farther than Tillich in appreciating the ways in which Christianity is also criticized from without via its encounter with other faith systems. Tillich was, after all, primarily a product of the West, who only very briefly towards the end of his life began to encounter the East. Koyama, as a recent product of both East and West, has an exceptional understanding of the necessity for Christian theology to be shaped and criticized by both internal dynamics and external circumstances.

Christology as a Tool for Ecumenical Theology

In the predominantly non-Christian world (not only Asia, but everywhere) to which Koyama is conscious of being called as a missionary, it is Koyama's intent to pursue a truly ecumenical theology, that is, one which seeks to involve the perspectives and experiences of a wide range of people, Asians as well as Europeans, non-Christians as well as Christians, and so on.

Consequently, Koyama can point to even Marxism's concern for social justice as a constructive ingredient for Christian ecumenism:

> Whenever Marxism expresses this sentiment (concern for social justice) it is speaking the mind of the invisible ethical God of Israel. In this sense, the authority of the prophetic tradition of the Bible is behind Marxism. Both Marxism and ecumenism are deeply Biblical movements.[30]

Koyama, it should be noted, also criticizes Marxism, particularly in regard to the oppression and inhumanity it has sometimes perpetuated in the name of liberation and justice.

Koyama can also see in other religions the ingredients of a faithful, ecumenical theology. Recalling Jesus' statement that good trees will be known by their fruits, Koyama says,

> If Buddhist societies demonstrate a higher level of domestic peace and social justice we must ask whether it is not producing the fruits which come from a good tree. If animism can teach people to love this planet and Christianity fails to do so, then is not animism a sounder tree than Christianity? This is a bold ecumenical suggestion.[31]

So, too, in the realm of politics Koyama sees the values of an ecumenical theology expressed. Citing the article of Japan's post-war constitution in which Japan renounces war as a sovereign right of the nation or the use of force as a means of settling international disputes, Koyama notes,

> Many Japanese people (though not the government) who are uneducated in the way of the Bible are trying to uphold this peaceful "universal principle of humanity." It is the Christian U.S., not the nature worshipping pagan Japan, which is trying to "revise" this "unrealistic" constitution of Japan. The pagan Japanese know the historical meaning of the words "all who take the sword will perish by the sword" (Matt. 26:52) even without knowing Jesus Christ.[32]

Thus, in universal human experience and thought Koyama sees the resources for shaping a truly ecumenical Christian theology. This does not mean that

Koyama derives Christian theology from "natural revelation." For, the criteria by which Koyama evaluates the contribution of other faiths and experiences to an ecumenical theology are entirely biblical. Always, Koyama speaks of such contributions in reference to Scripture.

Rather, Koyama's concern in constructing a theology which reflects the wider perspectives and experiences of humanity is a natural product of his own experience and faith. Christianity has always incorporated the experiences and values of the cultures it meets into its theology. That is part of its missionary nature and task. Koyama, as an Asian missionary, contributes to that task. Moreover, as Koyama perceives, insofar as all life, culture, and faith is within God's ultimate embrace, it is not only natural but necessary to utilize the various resources of every culture and age as the material of Christian proclamation.

However, Koyama is aware that incorporating such a wide spectrum of new data—such as that found in Asia—into Christian theology today involves a rather revolutionary transition. To illustrate the necessity and legitimacy of this endeavor, Koyama uses the image of the interchange between "center" (or, traditional theology), and "periphery" (new ingredients in theology).

As Koyama puts it, it is a matter of Christianity "going to the periphery" to find itself. The creating and healing power of the periphery—in Buddhism, Marxism, animism, or whatever—must inform the theology of today.

> It is not the center but the periphery that emancipates us from parochialism, from the theology of self-righteousness. It is not the center but the periphery that will bring devotion and ethics together. It is in the precariousness of the periphery that the mutual inspiration between faith and action takes place. It is so because in the periphery Christ affirmed his ecumenical centrality.[33]

To Koyama, the image of center/periphery is an intensely Christological one. Koyama expresses this Christology elsewhere in a variety of similar contrasts which exemplify his understanding of God's presence and activity in the world: Christ affirmed his lordship through self-denial; God heals through brokenness; Jesus, the Messiah, was crucified "outside the city," rejected by those to whom he was sent; in God inefficiency is efficiency; powerlessness is power; Jesus, "when most dethroned is the most enthroned,"[34] and so on.

Underlying these dichotomies, again, is *theologia crucis*, theology of the Cross, and, in a sense, Luther's idea of God hidden in opposites. Perhaps it is Koyama's

Asian intuition that makes this theology of paradox sensible and appealing. At any rate, he utilizes the Christology of paradox as a tool for turning Christian theology towards an ecumenicity that includes a very broad range of human experiences and values.

In so doing, Koyama might be said to be among the theologians of the future. For, no longer can Christian theology be constructed primarily with the materials of the "center," or of the past. From now on any theology that intends to stretch beyond its own regional or cultural framework must go to the "periphery"; it must incorporate the values and experiences of a wide range of humanity. Theology such as Koyama's, in both method and content, illustrates such an ecumenical, future-orientated theology.

Christology and Idolatry

As mentioned earlier, Koyama's Christology serves as a critique of all absolutes. To Koyama all human absolutes are idolatrous and need to be criticized by the Crucified Mind. Indeed, one way to understand Koyama's theology is to see it as a prophetic critique of all attempts to absolutize human institutions, whether cultural, political, religious, or otherwise.

In practical terms, as all human beliefs and experiences become the material of Christian theology, so do they all come under critique by the Crucified Mind. Militarism, especially as embodied in modern nuclear weapons systems; cultural imperialism, be it Asian or European; materialism based on the exploitation of others— these and other such forms of human self-righteousness are basic expressions of idolatry to which the Crucified Mind is opposed.

Koyama's impassioned opposition to idolatry, it might be added, is atypical of Asian religiosity, which is typically tolerant of diverse values and deities. Behind Koyama's theology is a basic monotheism and a firm commitment to biblical values and a biblical view of human being and history. Being a third generation Christian probably accounts for some of this commitment, as does its reinforcement by exposure to largely "monotheistic" environments.

Yet, Koyama's resistance to idolatry may at the same time stem not only from Western Christian values and personal experiences but in fact also from Asia's very inclination to tolerance. For, idolatry—the absolutization of a belief system or object—inevitably breeds intolerance. Koyama, in opposing idolatry, opposes intolerance. Of course, his concern is that people turn their loyalty to Christ, rather than to human absolutes. But, at the same time, he avoids expressing Christ in absolute terms. All in all, Koyama's theology bridges Eastern and Western values in unique and faithfully Christological ways

Summary

Koyama's concept of the Crucified Mind is the most complex and in a sense "slippery" aspect of his theology. Its existential essence is not easily reduced to propositional form. What makes it especially difficult to critique is that it is not only a theological principle but also a personal confession. It reflects the perception of faith. In other words, there can be no purely objective external measure by which to discern the value or validity of such a perspective. In such a case, confession precedes theory; a faith claim constitutes the truth claim.

What can be said about such a claim or principle, however, is that it is a very orthodox one. Koyama may take the concept of self-denial or living with a "crucified mind" farther than do others in its application to specific issues or to theology itself. Indeed, that is in part what makes Koyama unique and constitutes his value as a theological model. However, the concept itself of Christians denying themselves, patterning their lives after Jesus and following the way of the Cross is thoroughly traditional.

Koyama accepts the norms of Christian faith. He does not call the fundamentals into question nor seek to completely rework them as do some of his contemporaries (in regard, for example, to the salvific purpose of Jesus or to the validity and relevance of Israelite experience and faith). For Koyama the Incarnation and Crucifixion of Jesus, as the primary pattern of God's activity among humanity, has a vital and living power. It is reality, not theory.

However, Koyama's theology of the Crucified Mind does raise some wider questions and does include various tensions. The question of how the Crucified Mind relates to the use of power, for example, has been raised earlier. Although the Crucified Mind is intended to reflect the image of God who is unwilling to manipulatively "handle" human life, the fact remains that in ordinary life human beings are regularly faced with choices about the use of power. Often it may be difficult to discern what constitutes a manipulative versus a self-denying or healing usage of power. At times it is conceivable that what is self-denying for one party could be destructive for another, or vice versa. Often, long-term implications of choices are not at all clear.

Consequently, theology of the Crucified Mind needs to allow for a certain amount of ambiguity or failure. Or, such theology may need to further spell out its appropriate applications and limitations. To some extent, Koyama's theology of the Crucified Mind might even be seen as overly optimistic in its estimation of the human capacity to clearly see and carry out the crucified life. Perhaps more attention needs to be given to the concept of sin and human fallibility.

However, none of this diminishes the appropriateness or effectiveness of Koyama's call to Christians to follow the Cross of their Master in their encounter with the modern world. It is a call Koyama articulates with a freshness and conviction that can serve to inspire Christians in a variety of contexts. In his own way Koyama revitalizes one of the most fundamental dimensions of Christian faith and pursues its application on a new and wider scale.

A more abstract question which arises in relation to the concept of self-denial and a crucified life concerns its corollary assertion about the universal salvific implications of self-denial. Koyama's stated assumption is that the kind of self-denial associated with the Crucified Mind and based on God's revealed pattern of involvement in human history will ultimately lead to universal healing or salvation. The "energy" of the Crucified Mind will eschatologically prevail over manipulative, destructive kinds of energy.

A question which might be raised, however, is whether or not there is some kind of contradiction between the claims of self-denial and the corresponding claims of eventual universal harmony based on such self-denial. Crudely put, is self-denial simply another strategy for achieving eventual "victory" or dominance for the Christian view?

Part of the problem here is that Christian claims, as other such religious claims, are by intent and definition universal. Unless religious truth claims are deliberately intended to be of only limited and provisional value (in which case they would most likely cease to be truth claims as commonly understood), then there is no alternative but to presume universal validity.

For Koyama, one of the functions of the Crucified Mind is to counter-balance the human propensity to express or accomplish Christian universality in arrogant, manipulative or other such ways that might prove incompatible with the basic nature of divine revelation. The image of God working through human weakness and even through Jesus' crucifixion to accomplish God's saving purposes may be said to portray the way in which God in effect absorbs into the salvation process itself the contradiction between self-denial and universal ends.

It is a contradiction built into the heart of the Christian understanding of God. On the one hand, God is all-powerful Creator and eschatological Ruler to whom one may pray with the expectation of a concrete response. On the other hand, God becomes incarnate, vulnerable, crucified and either unable or unwilling to exercise divine power in the expected ways. The Crucified Mind epitomizes this contradiction for Christians. To live by the Crucified Mind is to subscribe to a different kind of power than that commonly deemed effective in the world. It is a self-critical, self-qualifying kind of power. It is not self-serving, self-orientated or doctrine-orientated, but other-orientated.

Inevitably, such theological assertions have a power of their own, as do other religious assertions, in that people do base decisions and actions on their religious beliefs. However, all theological assertions will be flawed by the imperfection that pervades all human existence, according to the Christian view. Accordingly, it is the intent of Crucified Mind theology that these assertions themselves be subject to the self-critical criteria of self-denial and crucifixion. In other words, there is built into Crucified Mind theology the possibility for ongoing, internal, existential dialogue and self-qualification.

In the end, however, the Crucified Mind never escapes the contradiction between a power-less or power-yielding and a power-ful or power-using God. It is a tension built into Christianity from the beginning, as in the biblical contrast between God as merciful and God as judge.

There is a direct correspondence between the image of God as both power-yielding and power-using and the image of there being both a "now" and a "not yet" to God's kingdom, as referred to in the introduction to this study. Koyama's concept of the Crucified Mind illustrates one possible way of addressing the tensions between these two perceptions of reality.

Ethics

Twentieth-century theology, Koyama suggests, reflects the idealism of eighteenth and nineteenth century Europe, as evident in its very form—proudly systematic and supposedly comprehensive.[35] But today, Koyama continues, a new world situation—one of dangerous militarism, economic travail, and radical encounter—requires a new kind of theology. Very important to such a new theology, Koyama insists, is an emphasis on Christian ethics.[36] "Ethics is a fundamental concern of theology. Theological thought which does not involve ethical concern is an empty theology."[37]

In general, Koyama defines ethics as the building of positive human relationships, the creation of community well-being. In particular, he mentions a variety of contemporary ethical issues: nuclear weapons (an urgent concern of Koyama's); militarism in general; racism; economic deprivation; the treatment of marginal peoples; and so on.

Earlier it was asked how Koyama derives specific ethical guidelines from his theology of the Crucified Mind. It was pointed out that in fact the Crucified Mind does not provide specific ethical guidelines. Nor does Koyama set about developing a deliberate system of ethics. Rather, the Crucified Mind expresses one's ultimate concern, which then provides a foundation upon which specific ethical decisions can be made within the context of varying cultures and circumstances.

Yet Koyama does believe that there are universal issues which Christian theology ought to address. "Empty stomach is universal," says Koyama by way of illustration.[38] But he believes theology often avoids asking the universal questions which could help develop universal Christian ethics.

Koyama sees his own theology as very much ethics-orientated. The enormity of human need in the world today and the extent of injustice push him to an ever deeper concern for ethics. Because of this growing concern, Koyama describes his theology and his Christology as becoming more "imminental." He increasingly thinks of the Kingdom of God in terms of Jesus' image, "the tree shall be known by its fruit."[39] Where human greed and exploitation prevail, idolatry is close at hand. Where mercy, justice, and ethical responsibility are evident, there Koyama sees the presence of God, the *shalom* of Jesus, even if that *shalom* is outside the Church. Accordingly, Koyama can criticize Christianity where it injures humanity and laud Buddhism where it demonstrates mercy and healing.

This does not mean that Koyama abandons his Christocentrism. It is precisely his belief in Jesus' universal lordship that undergirds Koyama's perspective. Also, as noted earlier, the criteria by which Koyama discerns the fruits of the Kingdom are thoroughly biblical.

However, another question emerges from Koyama's concern for ethics which also relates to other key aspects of his theology, such as "neighbourology" and Koyama's critical appraisals of Christianity. That is, does Koyama's theology run the danger of degenerating into mere anthropology, wherein the primary focus is not actually God, but human beings?[40]

While Koyama's theology does indeed exhibit an emphasis on the human—in contrast, for example, to much of traditional theology's focus on abstract ideas, propositions about God, and so on—Koyama is, nevertheless, clear about what he is doing. At one point, he specifically compares theology and anthropology and points out their different natures. He concludes, "Theology does not and cannot just speak about God apart from man. Theology is then, 'God-man-ology'."[41]

Here, Koyama is in line with other theologians who recognize the essential link between a concentrated emphasis on humanity and faithfulness to God. "A genuine theology speaks always of God and man together."[42] Or, as Karl Barth put it, theology would better be understood as "the-anthropology."[43]

Theology, then, it may be said, must be anthropocentric in practice, while theo-centric in origin, essence, and intent. Inevitably, theology is a kind of anthropology. But theology must be qualified by recognition of the fact that true anthropology begins and ends with the praise of God.[44] It seems quite fair to say that Koyama's theology falls within these bounds.

Koyama's deep commitment to ethics—especially insofar as ethics refers to the whole of Christian life—reinforces his lack of enthusiasm for doctrinal arguments. Koyama is more interested in action than argument; increasingly, he looks for the tangible fruit of Christian faith.

Yet there is some irony in Koyama's theology in that it is itself primarily argument. In the main, Koyama is not known as a social activist. This may reflect an important aspect of Koyama's Japanese heritage. For, in Asia in general and in Japan in particular right attitude is essential to right action. Action is seen to flow naturally from attitude. Koyama's theology, which deals primarily with attitude underscores and reflects this Asian perspective.

In comparison it may be said that the West often has difficulty linking ethical actions with faith propositions, for it tends to conceive of them as separate entities in the first place. This sort of contrast is especially apparent in the approach to form in the presentation of Christian ethics. In the West ethics are traditionally formulated discursively, that is, in terms of systems, arguments, and propositions.

Koyama, on the other hand, approaches ethics via imagery and what he calls "poetic language." "I belong to Old Testament language," says Koyama in relation to ethics, pointing to Jeremiah as an example of one who presented ethics in a poetic medium.[45]

To Koyama, ethics can be approached intuitively and expressed poetically. Poetic language, Koyama notes, is universal, though always culturally communicated.[46] Thus, Koyama believes that the poetic expression of ethics can contribute directly to Christian ethical action on a world scale.

One further observation that may reinforce the Asian character of Koyama's approach to ethics concerns the Asian emphasis on personal and social relationships. The line of connection between belief and action in Asia is not one of mechanically linking the abstract to the concrete, as in the West. In Asia the line of connection between belief and action is intentionally via relationships, not propositions. In its deliberate use of imagery and intuition, and in its direct emphasis on relationship, Koyama's theology reflects this Asian emphasis.

It may be noted that Koyama's approach to ethics, Asian though it may be, differs noticeably from that of some other Japanese Christians. While Koyama may be close to Uchimura, as Koyama himself claims, in his poetic approach to ethics, he is far from Kagawa and others among Japan's early Christians who were extremely active social reformers. Perhaps the fact that Koyama was the product of a later generation of Japanese Christians partially explains this fact. Whereas Japan's early Christians were zealous converts, part of a society open to rapid and radical change, Koyama was the product of an established Church concerned for its institutional self-preservation in a period which permitted little social flexibility. Nevertheless, Koyama's concern for social changes and for Christian ethical action in general seems both sincere and deeply rooted.

Overall, his concern for ethics, his anthropocentric focus, his attention to underlying attitudes, and his specific efforts to inform and encourage Christian ethical action in the modern context provide a valuable contribution to contemporary Christian theology.

CHAPTER NINE

KOYAMA'S THEOLOGY OF RELIGIONS

A theology of other religions must develop in any encounter of Christianity with the non-Christian world. For Christians living in an Asian context, i.e., in an overwhelmingly non-Christian environment, development of such a theology will be particularly necessary and important.

Having grown up in a society where Christians are a tiny minority, and then having been a missionary in another such society, Koyama has had to come to grips with the challenges presented to Christianity by non-Christian religions and cultures. To some degree his whole understanding of the Christian faith has been shaped in the context of Christianity's encounter with the non-Christian world.

The following sub-sections present Koyama's definition of the issues involved in such an endeavor, his perspective on the relationship of other faiths to the Christian faith, and his reflections on the problems of idolatry and syncretism. Grounded on the insights of the crucified mind, Koyama seeks to explore new directions in Christianity's relationship with other faiths.

The Issue

The roots of Koyama's theology of other religions lie in his own personal encounter with the issue, as he himself describes:

> Early in my work in Thailand, my neatly established system of Christianity was challenged. The focus of the issue was "non-Christian spirituality," which virtually no theological textbooks talked about when I was a theological student. My system, which I thought to be an enlightened and broad-minded one, told me that somehow an authentic spirituality can be born and nurtured only by the power of the gospel of Jesus Christ. This scheme made me regard the spirituality of Thai Buddhists as either undernourished or misguided. It was not the subject of the difference of history and doctrine between Christianity and Buddhism that caught my attention. That has not given me

"spiritual" trouble. But I was shaken by the reality of Buddhist spirituality. I came to know the people who call themselves Buddhists "with fragrance of the Buddha." They live a life of piety, humility and dedication to the ideal given by the Buddha. Above all, their poverty and the freedom they enjoy in being poor impressed me. I cannot define spirituality. It is a kind of fragrance that comes from the depth of personality. How is Buddhism capable of producing men of such spiritual beauty? I had thought it was a monopoly of Christians. Yet, I have known people of fragrance (II Cor. 2:14) not only among Christians but also among the Buddhists, Hindus and Moslems. Often I was bothered by a contrast between the security-minded and budget-minded Protestant missionaries and the orange-robed Buddhist monks in Thailand. In their spirituality the monks appeared closer to the image of the stigma of Christ than the Christian missionaries! Is such a thing possible?[1]

Unfortunately, as Koyama sees it, Christian attitudes toward other religions have been largely negative and narrow. "Christian theology and ministry have consistently looked upon the religious life of man only negatively."[2] Koyama notices how even the terms in which we think of the world's great religions have been shaped by non-dialogical European categorizations.[3] The names, for example, by which the great world religions have been described and judged are the product of European investigation. "The most complex reality of religious thoughts and practices were neatly packaged and labelled 'so-and-so-ism'."[4]

While such categorization is natural, necessary and useful for outsiders in their encounter with differing sets of human thoughts and values, it is not sufficient, as Koyama sees it, for comprehending these other thoughts and value systems. "Living religion cannot be contained in these boxes."[5]

In their consideration of other religions Christians need first of all to recognize the presuppositions and limitations of their own initial attitudes toward other faiths. This does not mean that we can escape or avoid limitations. But remembering them can temper our judgments.

This is the case, for example, even in delineating non-Christian faith from Christian faith. Koyama points out the facility with which we distinguish Christian from non-Christian. A non-Christian is basically thought of as one who has not been converted or baptized, who is not a church member. However, this definition does not take into account all that makes up the person who is categorized as a non-Christian.

Whether he is a Muslim, a Buddhist, a Hindu, a Marxist, rich or poor is of no account; what classifies him is his relation to Christianity—he is a non-Christian.[6] Such a classification is too narrow. It "defines a man in terms of what he is not, not what he is."[7]

Koyama argues that this kind of definition is deceptive, and can even be destructive.

> When we label a person as a non-Christian, we are looking at
> him as an object, negatively and arrogantly. No one can appre-
> ciate being viewed in this way—it is certainly not a healing
> action, but opens the wounds of division. It negates the very
> inclusive Christian love we are trying to teach.[8]

Koyama goes on to point out how static definitions can never contain human beings anyway. Because God has created human beings in freedom, there can be no "such static condition as non-Christian or Christian."[9] Faith itself is dynamic.

Koyama, therefore, calls to mind the limits of definitions and concepts in Christian thinking about other religions and the people who follow them. At the same time he recognizes that the problem goes deeper than simply words.

There is for many Christians, for example, a real threat in acknowledging that worth or truth might be found in other religions. To these Christians, admission of value in another religion implies some inadequacy in Christianity. Thus, to defend what they see to be the perfect integrity of Christianity, they must insist upon its uniqueness, completeness and supremacy over other religions.

To Koyama, such defensive Christianity exhibits a lack of trust in and a lack of understanding of the God of the Bible. God, who was crucified and died for the world, the God whose foolishness and weakness overwhelms human strength and wisdom, cannot be bound by a religion or destroyed by a set of human definitions or contradictions. Likewise, Christianity as the faith which follows and proclaims this God does not lose its truth or worth in relation to the content of other religions.[10]

On the other hand, Christian faith does not exist in a vacuum, unrelated to other faiths. Rather, Christian faith finds itself "moving between two points,"[11] namely, between the arena of Christ's universal lordship and the arena of the servanthood in which Christ's lordship expresses itself. This means that Christians can both trust in the sufficiency of "the Lord's Table"[12] and, through the freedom found there, be concerned about the messages of "other tables." "We are called to partici- pate in all situations of life as the Incarnate Lord fully did."[13] This includes entering into and appreciating the worth and beauty of other religions. But this participation finds its limit in remembering that "there is a demonic sacramental depth in all these other great tables which invite us to the feast of worshipping them."[14]

Christian faith therefore moves within the dynamic spectrum of human life as a whole. What is most important is the attitude which motivates and guides this movement. For Koyama, this attitude must be that of the crucified mind. As such it will open us to seriously face the questions put by the other great faiths of humankind, and it will provide the resources for appreciating them and relating to them.

With this in mind Koyama outlines the critical questions which need to be faced in Christianity's encounter with the other great human faiths. Thinking of theological issues facing Asian theologians, Koyama lists four basic sets of questions.

The first set concerns life as it is fostered by each religion. What are the characteristics of the Christian life and how does it relate to life as engendered by Buddhism, Hinduism, Islam and so forth? Given that all human life includes powerful elements of suffering, frustration and despair, is there a common religious basis on which these human experiences can meet and be shared? Is, for example, the suffering Christ such a basis?

A second set of questions of special concern to Koyama has to do with mercy. Christianity proclaims mercy but has in much of its history failed to demonstrate it. Other religions, too, advocate mercy, and often succeed in demonstrating it.

> How is mercy shown by men of other faiths and ideologies related to mercy shown in the name of Jesus Christ? . . . If mercy is found "outside" the name of Jesus Christ, what is the meaning of "no other name" in "and there is salvation in no one else, for there is no other name under heaven given among men by which we must be saved" (Acts 4:12)? What is the *uniqueness* of God's mercy demonstrated in his Son, Jesus Christ?[15]

Similar to the question of the uniqueness of God's mercy is the question of Jesus' uniqueness altogether. That is, there is the classic question of whether or not there is salvation apart from Jesus Christ. Quoting the Vatican II position that those who do not know the gospel of Christ or his church may also attain salvation, Koyama wonders what implications this view has for practical mission endeavors in the world.[16]

Finally, Koyama questions the relationship between proclamation and dialogue. Emphasizing that proclamation must be not merely verbal but existential, Koyama wonders, "how can the gospel be transmitted to another person when our theology and life are divided?"[17] The Christian failure to live the gospel diminishes the meaningfulness of dialogue.

Koyama does not set about providing specific answers to these questions. Rather, he concerns himself with the attitudes with which we approach them. In this process he first considers the great historic religions in terms of their positive contribution to human history.

The Great World Religions and Their *Shemas*

In the religious experience of humankind it is clear that religion contains both "demonic" and "angelic" possibilities. Yet over the centuries the great historic religions have overall insisted upon the building up of the human community through love and respect. They have resolutely resisted the destruction of human community by greed and self-aggrandizement.[18]

Overall, the great historic religions stand against the easy abuse of religion for immediate personal gain. As Koyama puts it, the "great religions are not 'instant' religions promising instant and cheap salvation."[19] The great religions, rather, demand self-discipline, self-sacrifice and even radical self-denial. "Real salvation," as envisioned by the great religions costs something; cheap, easily obtainable salvation would be false salvation.[20]

Koyama describes the great religions with their constructive, costly concern for human salvation as the "time-honored spiritual words" of humankind.[21] Koyama points to the way in which each of them directs humanity outside of itself. Each one, as it were, calls us to self-denial.

Using the Hebrew word *shema* to signify the fundamental commitment to the self-denial intrinsic to each religion, Koyama summarizes the *shemas* of Judaism, Christianity, Islam, Hinduism, Buddhism, and Confucianism.[22] He then goes on to consider how these *shemas*—the creeds of self-denial for the sake of God, neighbor, and salvation (as appropriate to each religion)—play a very crucial role in human experience both past and present.

> The *shemas* originated in the historical experience of human spirituality . . . They point to the refreshing possibility of restoring personal and communal integrity. The rejection of the value that the *shemas* are trying to point out for us must be one of the most fundamental reasons for the tragic world situation today. We can ignore the messages of the *shemas*. But if we do so, somehow we will injure ourselves.[23]

Often in their appeal to the hearts and minds of humankind, the *shemas* use extreme language. They speak of denying one's self, of extreme devotion, and of suffering. But Koyama suggests that,

> this extreme quality in the *shemas* is strangely not destructive but creative, not deceptive but truthful . . . Each *shema* presents self-restraint, self-control, self-denial as a historically more meaningful and hopeful spiritual attitude for mankind that the attitude of greed and self-aggrandizement.[24]

Although the *shemas* may seem out of place to many in the modern world they are nonetheless meaningful. Although they may

> sound like baby-talk in a world of astronomical expenditure on armaments and of nuclear energy, yet they are able to speak the language of ultimate human value, to which even nuclear energy must be made submissive if man is to remain human.[25]

In a world of complexity, struggle and change on an unprecedented scale, these "time-honored spiritual words" are as appropriate as ever.

Altogether, by thinking of the great world religions in these terms, Koyama thus places them in a framework to which his theology of the crucified mind can relate. Next, on the basis of this theology of the crucified mind, Koyama seeks to develop a Christian response to these other great religions.

A Crucified Theological View of Other Religions

In considering where other religions stand in relation to Christianity, that is, in shaping a Christian understanding of other faiths, Koyama addresses himself to several basic issues. One of the first things he points out is that there was no direct scriptural or historical link between Christianity and most of the other great historical religions, Judaism excepted. Jesus did not, for example, encounter or address Hindus or people who were followers of the Buddha. Islam, of course, did not even exist at the time of Jesus.

Jesus and his followers belonged to a particular, limited cultural context. Their message was shaped primarily in relation to this context and not to any other.

Correspondingly, the Buddha worked in a different, particular historical context. The Buddhist *shema* spoke to people who lived far outside the realm of first century Jewish culture.

Aware that the human mind constantly endeavors to measure unfamiliar human experiences by familiar ones, Koyama uses the case of Buddhism to remind Christians of the fundamental gaps between differing religions.

> There is no "straight" relationship between the teaching of the Buddha and faith in the God of Abraham, Isaac and Jacob. There is no such "efficient quick colonial" line between them![26]

This does not necessitate a suspension of encounter between differing religions. Indeed, Koyama notes that there are "many indirectly related spiritual experiences between them."[27] The Christian may even, as Paul did in Athens, "accept the unknown god," that is, appreciate rather than condemn the existing spirituality of a people. For, this spirituality may serve as a basis for communicating Christian commitment.

The important thing is that Christians recognize natural cultural and historical limits in their thinking about other religions. This is especially true in the application of Scripture. Too often Christians have used Scripture in a manner that demonstrates not a "crucified" awareness of contextual limits, but rather a power-oriented, over-simplified understanding of human situations.

Koyama uses Jesus' condemnation of all who came before him (John 10:8) and a passage from Ephesians which excoriates the corruption of Gentiles as examples of Scripture applied in totally inappropriate ways within the Asian context.[28] These abuses demonstrate the need for Scriptural interpretation and application to be informed by both the historical context in which it originated and the historical context in which it is applied.

While Koyama makes the point that, clearly, not every part of Scripture can be simply applied to every human situation, he does believe that Scripture can address itself to humankind as a whole. It is not then a matter of one cultural or religious message being applied to people of another situation. It is rather a matter of recognizing the meaning of the New Testament for all human beings, including those who already subscribe to it.[29]

The question of the meaning of mercy as demonstrated by those not of the Christian faith is a second basic issue which forms Koyama's crucified theology of other religions. Having described the *shemas* of other religions, which also advocate mercy, as words of valuable and necessary spiritual guidance for humankind, Koyama also accepts the fruits of such guidance as being in accordance with God's will.

To know the need to "Be merciful, even as your Father is merciful" (Luke 6:36) is an illumination to the spiritual life of man. But if he is not merciful even though he sees this illumination, then someone who is merciful even without knowing the merciful father will stand closer to the mind and practice of the Father.[30]

Koyama sees this perspective to be quite clear in Scripture, especially in various words of Jesus.

In general, Koyama believes that the primary attitude of Jesus, as demonstrated to those he encountered in his lifetime, and therefore the attitude which Christians should have toward people of other faiths is one of love and acceptance. This is especially believable to Koyama in terms of the faithfulness of people outside the Christian faith to their own *shemas*, their own creeds of self-denial, moral behavior, and service for others.

But this raises the whole issue of where people of other faiths stand in relation to Jesus, and of what that means for Christian judgment of other faiths.

> The people of the *shemas* . . . have their own understanding of mercy and they practice mercy with their spirituality. But they do not say that Jesus is the Lord. Even though they practice mercy . . . since they do not confess the name of Jesus Christ as Lord, are they separated from Jesus Christ?[31]

The difficult response to this question relies not so much on a judgment about people of other faiths as it does on belief in who Jesus is, and on a recognition of the utter imperfection or limitations of all human beings. Realistically, Koyama says, we all come sooner or later to a "limit-line" beyond which we can do nothing to accomplish our own salvation, or to fulfill our responsibility before God. Yet, even if when we come to an awareness of our own limits in relationship to God and at that point find ourselves unable to respond to Jesus as he instructs us (here Koyama uses the illustration of the rich young ruler who went away sorrowful from Jesus' love and command),[32] still, Koyama maintains, God does not therefore reject us. Our relationship with God—which God has created—cannot be so easily broken.[33]

Even more so, those people who have never met this God cannot, as Koyama sees it, automatically be rejected by God. Koyama asserts that even those who have heard of Jesus do not normally curse him. Indeed, by many people in Asia Jesus is highly revered, despite the fact that Christians seldom demonstrate equal reverence for the central figures of other faiths, and despite the noteworthy fact that people from countries with a Christian background themselves actually use Jesus' own name as a curse.[34]

Koyama refuses to accept a human judgment of the relationship of the people of other faiths to Jesus.

> "No one can say, 'Jesus is Lord,' except by the Holy Spirit" (I Cor. 12:3). Do the Buddhists say, "Jesus is Lord"? No. They say, "The Buddha is Lord" instead. But they do not say "Jesus be cursed"! Then do they stand somewhere between "Jesus be cursed" and "Jesus is Lord"? In some nebulous middle-ground? I do not think so. I cannot define where they stand in relation to Jesus Christ. I know they do not say "Jesus be cursed." I know they do not say "Jesus is Lord." I believe Jesus Christ must know where they stand.[35]

The crucified mind yields judgment to him who was crucified for the sake of all humankind.

Yet Koyama goes on to consider the relationship of people of other faiths to Jesus in terms of the relationship of believers in Christ to him. Because Jesus did not reject even those who rejected him, e.g., Peter, Koyama is convinced that the relationship between Jesus and the people of the *shemas*—those who have not known him, and indeed those who have known him and still rejected him—cannot be a superficial and fragile one.[36]

> The people of the other living faiths cannot betray Jesus as Peter did. Betrayal is a possibility that can come only to those who have been "intimately committed."[37]

In the end Koyama holds that the Christian evaluation of other religions must be one which both reflects the style of and trust in the event of the cross. The crucified mind looks at the *shemas* of humankind as concrete, living messages, grounded in the historical experience of humankind, which speak constructively "to the minds of the millions at this critical moment of human spiritual crisis."[38] The crucified mind trusts in the Crucified One who is "drawing the people of the *shemas* to himself in this way, the way of the mystery of self-denial of the Son of God."[39]

This whole perspective weighs against any simplistic comparison of the various faiths of humanity. Sadly, Christian apologists have often argued for the superiority of Christianity over other religions. This is, to Koyama, an arrogant, superficial and unreligious understanding of Christianity.

First of all, the word "superior" here is misplaced. Koyama does not believe that religion can be measured in terms of superiority and inferiority. To try to set religions over against each other in these terms is to indulge in what Koyama calls a sort of "divine beauty contest."[40] This mentality clearly does not reflect or project the crucified mind.

Koyama points out the impossibility of knowing differing religions intimately enough and at the same time being objective enough to compare them. Moreover, while religions incorporate discernible historical facts, religious life itself is deeper and more complex than any aggregate of these facts.

> Religious commitment belongs to the world of "I-Thou-relationship" (I and the Buddha, I and *Allah*) and not "I-It-relationship" (I and desk, I and car), to put it in the language of Martin Buber. ("It" can be comparatively treated. "Thou" cannot be . . . Religious faith cannot be "it-ized." That which refuses to be "it-ized" cannot be objectively compared.[41]

On the other hand, Koyama makes it clear that neither can people's religions be subjectively compared. For, subjective comparison "does not do justice to the concept of comparison."[42] Besides, subjective comparison is usually self-centered, and as such is incongruous with the crucified mind.

No, spiritual commitment such as found in the great historic religions cannot be described and systematized in categories such as superior or inferior. "Those words are . . . not useful for the spiritual life of the church."[43] Christianity itself would lose nothing if Christians gave up thinking of their religion as best or superior, especially in light of the Christian commitment to truth as embodied in the weakness, powerlessness and foolishness of a crucified God. By its own nature, the substance of Christian faith is "not an ordinary truth which can be established by comparative studies."[44]

In further pursuing a perspective in which to better understand Christianity's relationship with other religions, Koyama turns to the concept of the impartiality of God. He sees this impartiality of God first of all in God's universal, eternal sovereignty over the world.

> Often I am reminded that Jesus Christ was present among the peoples of the world even before the arrival of missionaries, Christians and churches.[45]

This hidden presence of Jesus expresses itself in various ways, but is particularly apparent to Koyama in the acts of mercy demonstrated by people of other faiths. That they do what Jesus has commanded is not only a sign of the universal God, but also an admonition to Jesus' own followers on their failures to demonstrate mercy. But, Koyama adds, "This makes our Christian life possible since there is no Christian life apart from humility (Phil. 2:1-11)."[46]

Mercy in particular testifies to the impartiality of the universal God. It is when one encounters impartial, indiscriminate mercy, i.e., mercy which does not choose its object, that one meets God, surrenders, and begins a religious life.[47] "Theology," Koyama insists, "must be acquainted with the indiscriminate dimension of the mercy of God."[48] More often, Christian theology is too preoccupied with elaborate distinctions and demarcations, which in Koyama's perspective, are too "wise" and "strong," too power and judgment-oriented to appreciate and convey the "foolish" and "weak" mercy of God. Only as theology itself is confronted by love which transcends distinctions is the meaning of God's mercy perceived.

> I maintain that mercy which has never reached the depth of
> indiscriminateness is not merciful enough to save sinful man.[49]

Koyama turns to Scripture to express his conviction here: " . . . God has consigned all men to disobedience, that he may have mercy upon all" (Rom. 11:32). More specifically, Koyama quotes Romans 2:9-11 emphasizing the point that "God shows no partiality."

This view has been an unpopular one in the history of Christian mission, says Koyama. It seems to diminish the gospel declaration of God's specific salvific act in Christ. However, Koyama argues that God's impartiality is the fundamental context in which the message of Christ is presented. "It is Good News to know that God is not partial. It would be Bad News to know that God is partial."[50]

Moreover, Koyama argues that a recognition of God's impartiality is critical in today's world where the human community has grown so inter-related and so aware of its diversity.

> In this historic juncture of mankind's life, the message that
> "God is not partial" has become very important. For it is here
> that Christianity finds the basis to remain and develop as a uni-
> versal faith for mankind today.[51]

This remarkable potential in the idea of the impartiality of God finds particular relevance in Asia today. "Asian Christians and perhaps even more the Asians who are not Christians are sensitive to the Christian message of the impartiality of God."[52] Indeed, Koyama sees this awareness of the impartiality of God to be a particular contribution of the churches in Asia to Christianity as a whole.

> This awareness of the impartiality of God has emerged within the church as a result of its being caught within the inter-religious situation in Asia. The people of the other living faiths are demanding that the Asian Christians take the impartiality of the Christian God seriously. *They* are saying that Christian authenticity must be rooted in the sense of the impartiality of God. I believe that they are making a historic contribution to the Christian faith.[53]

While this awareness of the impartiality of God serves Christian mission and undergirds Christianity as a universal faith, at the same time it calls the Christian church, too, to examine itself in the light of God's impartiality. "Has the church not lived in self-confidence and self-admiration forgetting that God, the Father of Jesus Christ, is not partial?"[54]

Koyama draws attention to the "distance between Jesus Christ and Christianity as we know it."[55] Christians fail to be Christ-like. The Church is fraught with divisions that belie the will of the Creator. Christianity itself is a historically developed religion just as Buddhism, Hinduism and Islam. It is not divine, pure or uncontaminated. "As a religion . . . Christianity with other religions must stand under the judgment of the Gospel of Christ."[56] This judgment takes place within the context of the impartiality of God. ("The impartiality of God is the righteousness of God.")[57]

In this context and in the inter-religious situation in which Christianity finds itself in the world today, the impartiality of God is not an abstract theological concept. Christians meet, live and work with those of other faiths every day. In such a situation, as Koyama sees it, the Christian church has a special opportunity to witness according to the truth of the crucified mind.

> The Christian church has an opportunity to demonstrate her rootedness in history by rejecting (self-centered theology) and being confronted by the historical judgment of the impartiality of God.[58]

Failing to do so, the Church will be "irresponsible to history."[59]

All of these issues concerning the relationship of Christianity to other religions relate to the fundamental nature of the crucified mind. It is not a mind of objective proofs, judgmental pronouncements or religious comparisons. It is a mind which expresses Jesus' relationship to people of other faiths in a life "poured out for many."

Theological preoccupation with the absoluteness, finality, and exclusivity of Jesus Christ fails to understand or to witness to the essence of the crucified mind. For the crucified mind is not simply one of propositions. It understands what is meant by Jesus being the "Way" only in the process of following him and participating in his life.

In various ways, Koyama emphasizes that the finality of Jesus, the question of his definitive significance for human salvation, cannot be considered apart from the context of the cross, of a life "poured out for many."

> If Jesus Christ was mocked, spat upon and stripped, then his "finality" is mocked, spat upon and stripped. The "mocked finality" is, then, the Christological finality. But "the mocked finality" and "spat-upon finality" do not come under any ordinary concept of finality or primacy.[60]

Those who would proclaim Christ's "finality" are called to exemplify it through lives involved in similar self-denial.

It is significant to note that Koyama envisions Christ's "mocked finality" being expressed not only through Christian mission, but also in the social and political struggles of the contemporary world. Because Christ as universal Lord is associated with all human situations and struggles and because he stands as the source, redeemer and direction of human life, his power is at work even where it is not recognized. "Jesus Christ is profoundly there since it is impossible to stop the one whose name is spat-upon finality from coming and being there.[61]

The crucified mind accepts that Christ establishes his own finality and accomplishes his purposes in his own manner. The mind that seeks to absolutely and comprehensively define Christ's finality or superiority is one which has not understood or submitted to the truth of the cross.

> The concepts of finality, superiority, and the best presuppose the result of a comprehensive assessment. But theological perception is primarily grace-grasped instead of data-grasped.[62]

Religion itself can be a form of "grasping," and as such a form of unbelief, a form contradicting the "form of Christ."[63] Religion may be a tool by which humans seek to exercise their own authority and power, rather than accepting the saving freedom of self-denial as expressed in Jesus Christ. Over against such religion Koyama proclaims the possibilities for the life of faith initiated by Christ's self-denial.

> We are caught by the power of the living Lord. Our foundation
> of faith is infinitely more secure since we have not laid it . . . In
> his suffering finality (cross) we find the possibility of our life
> renewed and resurrected. It has come to us! We have not
> created it! No handle on the cross![64]

Idolatry

Relevant to the whole question of the relationship between Christianity and other religions is the matter of idolatry. Koyama takes up this matter by examining the nature of idolatry in general and then by redefining it in relation to Christian salvation history.

The Nature of Idolatry

Idolatry is understood in different ways by different religions. To Christians the multiplicity of images associated with Hindu religious practice are clearly idolatrous and the use of them is to be condemned. But, Koyama points out that by a Hindu definition of worship and idols the use of these images is a wholesome religious practice. In contrast, the Christian use of images, in the eyes of Muslims, is thoroughly idolatrous.[65]

Koyama seeks to understand idolatry in terms of what it implies about human attitudes and desires. For this he uses an image from Jeremiah 10:5:

> Any "god" we can carry is, according to Jeremiah, an idol . . .
> That which we can carry is subject to our control. To suggest
> that something that we can carry is carrying us is to have an
> upside-down perspective of life. Such a style of life would be
> confusing and destructive. Idolatry is just such a confusion.[66]

In other words, Koyama roots idolatry in the human desire to control and manipulate the world. But this desire reflects a misunderstanding of the meaning and nature of God.

Koyama also speaks of this tendency in terms of human beings seeking to make God visible.

> The faith of Israel is against making God visible. A visible God is, in truth, not a God. It is an idol. Thus it stands opposed to one of the most fascinating preoccupations of man—making God visible![67]

By "making God visible" human beings suppose to place God within the realm of what they can comprehend and control. They project onto the idols which they create their own glorification and their own needs. Whether born out of loneliness, fear, or out of a hunger for money, power, prestige, influence, and the like, idolatry tends to serve humanity's self-enlargement and self-centeredness.[68] As such, idolatry is a self-deception which inevitably disappoints and injures humanity.

Koyama contrasts the God of Christianity with the human desire for a visible, comprehensive God.

> The "obvious" God is an idol. Idols we can tame, but we cannot domesticate the living God. Jesus Christ crucified is the furthermost point from idols. Why? He at this point becomes most intensely "baffling," "scandalous," "mysterious," "untamed," "not obvious" and "not comprehensive" to us.[69]

The God of Christianity cannot be made visible; this God cannot be domesticated. The fundamental "truth" which Christians need to recall is that God carries them; they do not carry God.[70]

Because of the extraordinary nature of God's penetration into history, it also becomes idolatrous for Christians to contradict God's self-denying salvation by self-assertive tactics of Christian mission. This temptation is depicted by Koyama in terms of the human preoccupation with efficiency. Efficiency describes for Koyama that attitude in Christian mission which thinks in terms of quick, direct, manipulative proclamation of the story of Jesus. For Koyama, "The 'truth' which tends to work efficiently at our command is most likely an untruth (idol)."[71]

For example, Koyama considers the case of Thai Buddhists paying their respects to the image of the Buddha. "They are not engaged in idolatry. If you think they are, then your theology is too efficient."[72]

Idolatry is much more subtle than this centuries-old act of religious obedience. Idolatry arises when the focus of religious commitment turns away from the reality to which worship is directed to the person who is worshipping and to his or her own priorities.[73] One of the examples Koyama gives to illustrate this kind of idolatry is that of the people of Israel setting up a golden calf as the focus of their worship. This event demonstrates the close connection between idolatry and history and between idolatry and the history of salvation that was taking place among the people of Israel.

> In order to be able to give an exalted name to a calf, one must have a historical model of salvation. When the salvation enacted in history is said to have been done by idols, then genuine idols begin to exist. God was the One who "brought you out of the land of Egypt." This historical event is now transferred to the molten calf. Transference of some imagined salvation from one agent of salvation to another agent of salvation does not constitute "strong" idolatry. But when transference has to do with a historical event, it does constitute "strong" idolatry. Here lies a strangely dangerous relationship between history and idolatry. Where there is weak history-awareness there is weak idolatry-consciousness. A stronger history-awareness produces stronger idols.[74]

With this perspective Koyama's redefinition of idolatry in terms of other religions comes into focus. Koyama relates idolatry first of all to the general history-consciousness of human beings and secondly, to the specific salvation-history of Israel.

Koyama makes a distinction between weak-history-consciousness and strong history-consciousness. The former is normally represented by the karmic, circular view of history, the latter by familiarity with the Judaeo-Christian concept of God as ruler and redeemer of human history.

Koyama sees the idolatry of weak-history-awareness to be less destructive than that of strong-history-awareness. The former does not entail the outright rejection of God's saving events in human history as does the latter. Yet Koyama says that weak history-awareness idolatry is still poisonous. "It is poisonous since idol's *raison d'etre* is found usually in its promise of salvation."[75]

Of crucial significance is the fact that idols are indeed intended to save, not damn people. But that they cannot do so, since they are instruments of humanity's own self-deception and self-enlargement, means that they are "poisonous" or injurious to humankind.

In relation to biblical salvation history Koyama even goes so far as to suggest that apart from knowledge of this salvation there is no such thing as idolatry in the Christian sense—at least certainly not in the view of the adherents of other faiths. While nations and people may be living in idolatrous situations in the general sense,[76] *"It takes history of salvation to produce idolatry"*[77] in the biblical sense:

> Scripture first of all warns that idolatry takes place within Israel and the church. Idolatry is possible in the tradition which makes the distinction between God and idols. In the traditions which do not have this distinction, in the view of such adherents, there cannot be idolatry in the Christian sense.[78]

On the other hand, Koyama speaks not of biblical idolatry and general historical idolatry, but of "insider's idolatry" and "outsider's idolatry."

> The conspicuous example of insider's idolatry took place at the foot of the mountain at the un-holy transference of the historical salvation from the holy God to the calf idol . . . This insider's idolatry happens only "inside" Israel and the Church (and Christendom). The second then may be called "outsider's' idolatry." This idolatry takes place "outside" Israel and the Church, among those ignorant of the knowledge of the God of Abraham, Isaac and Jacob, the Father of Jesus Christ.[79]

For those outside Israel and the Church, idolatry still has meaning in the Christian sense in that both insiders and outsiders are related to the crucial human concern for salvation. Those outside the church do not stand untouched by the circumstances of the insider's idolatry (namely the message in the context of which idolatry arises). For, Koyama cautions,

> The distinction between weak idolatry (outside idolatry) and strong idolatry (inside idolatry), however, must not give any theological comfort to those who are engaged in "outside idolatry." If one is aware or expecting theological "comfort" or theological attenuation, then he is already in the "inside" situation. It takes the strong history-awareness to appreciate this distinction.[80]

With this thought Koyama is channeling Christian thinking about idolatry away from judgment of other religions back to Christianity itself. This he finds in keeping with Scripture.

> Scripture does not declare *all* other religions than Christianity to be idolatry . . . Scripture does not mention the word "religion" . . . Scripture is not directing its attentions to religions. It speaks to the living men in all times and all cultures. In the light of Jesus Christ Christianity can be judged as adulterous as any other religion . . . The question of idolatry is not primarily directed to other "religions" but to Christianity first.[81]

The crucified mind does not occupy itself with statements about other religions. It seeks rather to relate to them in a crucified manner—remembering that judgment begins with the household of God (I Peter 4:17).

Syncretism

In the context of his thinking about the relationship between Christianity and other religions, Koyama directs some of his attention to the issue of syncretism. Although he does not go into the subject in great depth, Koyama makes several fundamental observations about Christian attitudes towards syncretism and about the nature of syncretism itself.

He begins by recognizing that Christian faith inevitably faces the challenges of syncretism. This is so simply from the fact that Christianity exists in the midst of various human cultures and religions. Moreover, as Christian faith is intrinsically a mission-faith, i.e., one that by nature comes into contact with other faiths through mission, Christianity will always have to wrestle with the issue of syncretism.

With this recognition, the next question to be faced is what syncretism means. To many Christians syncretism implies the threatening influence of other religions upon Christianity. But too many Christians abhor syncretism, Koyama asserts, with too simple a grasp of the issues involved in it.[82] Koyama points to the 1966 Wheaton Congress view of syncretism[83] as one which exhibits a hard-line condemnation of all other religions as idolatrous and which considers the theological offerings of other religions as syncretistic influences which are to be rejected and condemned. This perspective exhibits a wooden understanding of both other religions and of Christianity.

Opposite this kind of outright hostility in regard to syncretism there is the description of syncretism as a constructive theological endeavor towards creating one universal religion for human kind. This is to be accomplished by the harmonization of various human religious ideas and experiences.[84] Such a definition of syncretism falls on sympathetic ears in Asia, Koyama notes. For the Asian mind is generally less iconoclastic and less history-conscious than that of the West. Accordingly, "the non-monotheistic (non-jealous) Asian religious mind provides fertile soil for syncretism."[85]

In between these two extremes is the simple definition of syncretism as the merging and mixing of differing types of experiences and belief. Koyama is quick to emphasize, however, that the mixing and merging of different religions is no simple or rapid process. As an example of the implausibility of direct, simple syncretism, Koyama combines the Apostle's Creed with the Buddhist Four Noble Truths.

> ... And in Jesus Christ, the Buddha, that is, the Enlightened One, only Son our Lord ... was crucified; thus he completed the Noble Truth of the fading away and extinction of all kinds of cravings: The third day he rose again as the Detached One . . .[86]

This sort of straightforward combination is, says Koyama, "a blasphemous caricature of both Buddhist and Christian faiths."[87] It unrealistically and artificially distorts both religions. To reduce religions, first of all, merely to an arrangement of ideas that can be alternatively arranged is to misunderstand and to dangerously distort each religion. Besides, the great, established religions of humankind could not be so fully syncretized, even over a long period of time.

To better understand what syncretism involves it is necessary to recognize the constant flux of human societies and values as a whole. For, syncretism is a gradual, historical process that "takes place within the wider context of the meeting of cultures, races, and peoples."[88]

> Religious syncretism is a part of the general cultural amalgamation through migration, trade, common settlements, colonization, military campaigns and other contacts.[89]

It is therefore an intrinsic part of human experience.

Indeed, says Koyama, syncretism itself originates in the human mind and spirit. Struggles about syncretism are therefore not merely theoretical or intellectual; they are the existential struggles of human spirituality in historical communities.[90]

Having this broad understanding of the nature of syncretism, Koyama goes on to consider the nature of Christian faith in this context. He does this by discussing the situation wherein a Thai Buddhist converts to Christianity. The person who converts to Christianity will do so within the framework of a complex cultural background of which he or she is a product and a part. Even as a Christian, a Thai convert would be bearer of a culture shaped by Buddhism for thousands of years, a culture embodied in the customs, attitudes and the very language of its members. It would be extremely unrealistic to suppose that as a Christian one would or could lose one's cultural formation. "The mother culture, like the mother tongue, will follow a person throughout life. He wears it as he wears his skin."[91]

The Thai Buddhist convert is no different in this sense from predecessors in the biblical faith. All believers hold their faith in the context of a given culture. Christian faith itself, as presented in the New Testament "speaks with the accent of the mother culture, Judaism."[92] For that matter, God cannot be conceived apart from human culture. There is no such thing as a "chemically pure" God, for God chose to be identified with humanity, first of all through the people of Israel, and ultimately in the first century Jewish carpenter, Jesus.[93]

Syncretism, then, cannot simply be a matter of Christian faith being contaminated by contact with human cultures and religions. For Christianity does not itself exist apart from the context of human cultures and religions. There is no such thing as "pure" Christian faith, independent of cultural embodiment.

Likewise, syncretism cannot be merely the bringing of one's cultural personality into one's Christian existence. For there is no alternative but to express faith in terms of one's cultural experience.

Here it is important to recognize, too, that culture, and therefore faith, is not a monolithic, unchanging reality.

> Culture, like language is a continuous reality . . . culture is a process in which there is much bringing of "gifts" from other cultures and religions. No culture is pure. No history, no religion, no language, no race, no philosophy is "pure." There are only interactions, adaptations, assimilations, integrations and disintegrations. Culture is the process of reception-rejection.[94]

How one's faith and culture inter-relate, however, may vary. Paul, as a Pharisee, both rejected and utilized various aspects of his cultural heritage in the expression of his new faith.[95] Likewise, other converts to Christianity may re-evaluate their previous cultural commitments upon becoming Christian. But they can never completely distance their new faith and even how they came to it from the environment in which they live. Indeed, they may find areas of their cultural heritage that can usefully be "baptized" into the service and expression of their new-found faith. This is a frequent experience in Christian history which has led not to the syncretistic dissolution of Christianity, but to its enrichment.[96]

The inescapable interaction of faith and culture arouses Koyama's concern not so much for syncretism as for the process of "accommodation," i.e. faith's finding expression in a given culture. For while syncretism may be a *danger* in the interaction of faith and culture, accommodation is the key *direction* with which Christianity needs to be concerned.

Koyama defines accommodation as "the dynamic mode through which the gospel is given to us."[97] Its greatest expression is God's incarnation into human life in Jesus Christ. God "accommodated" to human language, culture, and religion.

> He was not "pure" in the sense that he kept himself from involving in a concrete culture and history. The *incarnation—* the Word which "became flesh" was the *in-culturation* for it "dwelt among us" (John 1, 14).[98]

Koyama stresses that God thus incarnated is not "god-syncretized."[99] Rather, God's incarnation, or "in-culturation,"[100] is testimony to the basic way in which God communicates love and salvation to humanity.

Thus the encounter of Christianity with culture, especially as Christian faith relates to non-Christian cultures, is not primarily an event of syncretism but one of accommodation along the pattern of God's own self-expression in human history. Accommodation is thus the proper emphasis for Christian encounter with other cultures and faiths.

Koyama explores what this means in terms of Christianity's encounter with Buddhist culture, for example. Just as Christianity in its early days had to find terms to express itself in a meaningful way to people in a Hellenistic environment, so it must explore meaningful expression within the language and thought-patterns of Buddhist culture. This can definitely be a dangerous situation. For if the "strong religious words" of another culture (e.g. *logos* in Greek culture or *Tamma* in Buddhist culture) overcome the Christian meaning intended by using those words to express Christian belief, then syncretism can ensue. However, appropriate and "successful" accommodation can "control syncretism by dissolving it into elements and making them useful 'baptized servants'."[101]

This view of accommodation and syncretism clearly expresses the missionary intention to draw other faiths and cultures into relationship with and acceptance of the unique Christian claims of a sovereign, loving God. But Koyama adjusts his emphasis here by stating that "accommodation is thus a process of *inviting* the world into the context of the grace of God."[102]

This understanding of accommodation remains faithful to Koyama's fundamental conviction that God authors and initiates human salvation. God's grace creates and motivates the community of faith. Syncretism, on the other hand, acts to paralyse this context of grace.[103]

Koyama thus identifies syncretism in relation to the accommodational, incarnational task of Christian witness. When Christian content is lost in inter-faith encounter (as in the search for words to express Christian meaning),[104] or when the communication of the Christian message is obscured by a blurred understanding of God's unique grace, (e.g. by a search for a lowest-common-denominator universal religion), then syncretism becomes apparent.

But, again, this understanding of syncretism takes shape within the context of a fundamental commitment to Christian faith's seeking to express itself by accommodation to the world's cultures and people. Christian faith, like the God who is its source, is faith "in contact" with the world. It is not an intact, pure truth, apart from human culture. The mark of Christian "purity" is that it is involved with the day to day contexts of human life.[105]

For an example of this Koyama turns to the life of Jesus. Jesus, the Holy One, the ultimate expression of God's relationship with humanity, did not draw back from intimate contact with the most "contaminating" situations. He touched lepers. He ate with sinners. His "purity" was the "purity" of self-giving and involvement with others, which often transcended accepted religious and social boundaries.

Christian faith cannot with integrity establish itself on a different standard than that demonstrated by Jesus. Christian doctrine and practice must reflect the nature of its source, namely, him who was willing to enter into personal relationship with his hearers, to associate with them in their own situations. For Christianity to seek intact, uncontaminated, non-involved purity is for it to betray Jesus' example and command. (Koyama uses the parable of the talents [Matt. 25:14–30] as a relevant injunction here towards involvement as opposed to self-protective isolationism.)[106]

Of course it is in this context of involvement that the questions of syncretism and of compromise necessarily arise. Koyama argues that fear of Christianity's being compromised by its accommodational activity, is however, misplaced. Compromise implies the willingness of different parties to give up some essential elements, positions, or beliefs for the sake of a mutually acceptable agreement. Such negotiation cannot exist in a situation which is founded exclusively on one party's initiative.

That is to say, the world, human being, and the message of God's love do not depend on mutual promise or concession. Creation and Christ's redemption do not originate in negotiation but in God's absolute decision and action. This means that compromising the essence of the Christian proclamation is not a human possibility.

On the other hand, precisely because Christians may be sure that what they proclaim is an event and a message beyond their own abilities to control or compromise, they have the freedom to pursue the accommodation or contextualization of their message without fear that it will be lost or destroyed. This is not to deny the reality of syncretism.

> Is there, then, no such thing as syncretism? There is. When we bring all to bow at the name of Jesus we are not syncretic. But if we place the name of Jesus with any other name and say that there is really no difference between it and the other names we become syncretic.[107]

But Koyama seeks in his conversation about syncretism to keep the fundamental accommodational character of proclamation in focus. His emphasis is on the direction rather than the dangers involved.

For Koyama, this direction is that of invitation into an awareness of God's grace. The invitation allows for such awareness to express itself according to the rich variety of human cultures. With typical respect and appreciation for the richness and worth of varying human experiences, Koyama sees the meeting of faith and culture not in terms of its negative, syncretistic possibilities, but in terms of its natural and positive effects.

> Bringing our religious customs and orientations to his presence is not syncretic. It is an ecumenical movement. Such an ecumenical movement is a spiritually awakened one. It is an exciting spiritual and culturally refreshing experience. One should see his own culture blessed and enriched.[108]

Koyama does not ignore the problem of syncretism. Syncretism does exist, and it is possible that the Christian invitation into an awareness of God's grace can be abused and confused. But in the end Koyama trusts that as God's love was powerful enough to make itself known within and beyond the limits of the incarnation, so can the power of this love guide the Church's work of accommodation. "It is this creative power of love that safeguards the Church from falling into syncretic confusion."[109]

CHAPTER TEN

AN EVALUATION OF KOYAMA'S THEOLOGY OF OTHER RELIGIONS

Unquestionably the issue of Christianity's accelerating encounter with other faiths requires fresh thinking among modern Christians. This encounter raises both personal and theological questions.

> To recognize that another intelligent, ethical, and
> religiously sensitive person may believe something
> different from what one cherishes as a superlative value
> oneself . . . raises a profound question about the validity
> of one's own views.[1]

In this encounter with other faiths Christians are increasingly challenged to rethink traditional attitudes towards other faiths and to reformulate their theologies accordingly. Indeed, as one theologian emphasizes,

> From now on any serious intellecutal statement of the
> Christian faith must include, if it is to serve its purpose
> among men, some sort of doctrine of other religions.[2]

Both the attention Koyama gives to other religions and in particular the unique theology he has developed provide a model for others. To evaluate Koyama's theology of other religions and to examine how it might serve as a model in the formulation of other such theologies will be the concern of this chapter. To that end some general observations will be made and questions raised about the nature of Koyama's theology, followed by a discussion of fundamental issues at stake in formulating theologies of other religions.

General Observations

Given Koyama's intense concern with idolatry, it is intriguing that Koyama does not consider other religions within that framework, as have many other Christians. Instead, as mentioned earlier, Koyama actually defends other religions as not being essentially idolatrous or at least being exempt in many ways from the kind of measurements which are usually applied when identifying idolatry.

Rather, Koyama is concerned to point out the positive value of other religions, especially in reaction to the negative view Christians have so often held towards them. This interest reflects Koyama's personal experience of encounter with other religions, being surrounded by them from youth, as well as the appreciation of them which has grown through his deeper exposure to their tenets and practices.

For Koyama other religions are not remote or abstract entities available to objective, mental evaluation. They represent people who are, so to speak, fellow actors already present on the shared stage of human history, participants along with Christians in the drama of life. Koyama does not approach other religions with a colonial-type mentality. He has not had that experience with them. Instead, he has experienced the ordinary daily life of being Christian in contexts where the majority of one's fellow citizens and workers were adherents of different faiths.

Accordingly, Koyama has sought to encourage a more positive attitude towards other religions based on fundamental tenets within Christianity itself. Besides applying Scripture's admonition to think appreciatively about what is good and beautiful in life to other religions, Koyama has developed a theology of religions based not on doctrines of revelation, on some theory of the unity of all faiths, or on problematic scripture passages—the interpretation of which will always be controversial—but rather on core Christian teaching. Koyama has found within Theology of the Cross the grounds for constructive relationships with people of other faiths. In this theology all human judgments stand under divine judgment.

Furthermore, by focusing on a Christocentric attitude towards other religions, Koyama also keeps the discussion centered on Christians and their following the model of their Master. In accord with Koyama's theology of the Crucified Mind and non-handling spirituality, the encounter between Christians and people of other faiths thus becomes more a matter of relationship than of doctrine.

One side benefit of the relational approach is that it offers something of a middle way between universalism and exclusivism without diminishing the Christian responsibility for mission (an important missiological concern these days). A Christian is still called to witness to members of other faiths, but not to pre-judge them. Rather, the witness itself is to be informed by and conformed to the kenotic perspective of the Crucified Mind.

However, questions remain. Even in such a relational, existential approach, doctrine plays an inevitable part, shaping the assumptions and decisions of those involved in inter-faith encounter. Always, questions will arise, too, as to what constitutes a crucified relationship and what does not. Some may also wonder whether more in fact might be said about other religions in judging their value or validity than the Crucified Mind approach would seem to allow.

Indeed, it may be questioned whether Koyama himself treats other religions too superficially or optimistically. But to ask such questions requires analyzing the criteria which one brings to the discussion. All Christians who seek to draw conclusions about other religions and how to approach them carry along certain assumptions and criteria from outside the milieu they wish to address. So does Koyama. Such biases are unavoidable. There are no neutral, objective terms by which to evaluate another's religion. That is why Koyama's consistent focus on Christian attitudes is so appropriate. The critical question is whether one's assumptions are in harmony with the fundamental tenets of one's own faith.

However, Koyama is still not off the hook regarding his presuppositions. Some might argue, for example, that his use of Scripture is too selective in regard to other religions. But here, fundamental questions of interpretation are at stake which depend again more on initial presuppositions than on subsequent applications.

More realistic, perhaps, is to ask how Koyama's theology actually works. Is it usable or being used by Christians in inter-faith encounter? Does it contribute effectively to inter-faith dialogue?

Obviously, the answers to such questions require the kind of research and information that can only accumulate over a considerable period of time. Koyama's theology is probably not yet well-enough known or discussed to measure its results. However, that Koyama is being recognized as a significant theologian on inter-faith issues is becoming apparent in the solicitations for his opinion that other theologians are increasingly making.[3] That his insights are being sought for practical application is evident in a recent Lutheran manual on Buddhism prepared for missionaries being sent from the United States to serve in predominantly Buddhist cultures.[4]

As to the depth of his treatment of other religions, it can be pointed out that Koyama has continued to pursue ever more sophisticated studies of Buddhism in both published and as yet unpublished work. As a missionary himself, he recognizes the need for more intensive research into Buddhist doctrine and practice to make intelligible the otherwise alien presuppositions and categories of Christian belief. In this pursuit Koyama is undertaking a natural, common, and essential task of Christian mission. For, communication between different cultures and great faiths requires the establishing of some mutually intelligible concepts.

At this point there is still a certain incompleteness to Koyama's theology of religions and how it may be applied. Yet his application of the Theology of the Cross to this area of Christian life may in the long fun be his greatest contribution to wider Christian theology.

As he insistently directs Christians to reexamine the inner nature of their own faith, he presents a fresh way for approaching other religions. His approach resists the reduction of theology of religions and inter-faith encounter to a simplistic, mechanical process. He draws Christians away from pat answers to an existential encounter not only with adherents of other faiths but perhaps also with God. When it comes to inter-faith incounter, Koyama calls Christians away from the idolatrous aspects of pre-judgment and a certitude based on ignorance and the misuse of power. Instead, he calls Christians in the fullest and finest sense to live by faith.

Theories and Objectivity

A common desire in the encounter between faiths is the desire for certitude, for clear, unequivocal standards by which judgments can be made about the validity or value of other religions. But it is a fundamental mistake to assume that Christianity's relationship to other religions can be described by a single, comprehensive theory. Various theologians have stated as much, for multiple reasons. For example, in seeking to move the discussion of other religions out of a purely systematic or dogmatic framework into a broader historical context, Ernst Troeltsch remarked, "The question of the relationship between Christianity and other religions cannot be decided by dogmatic prejudice, by prejudgment."[5]

Gordon Kaufman also argues the need to understand the relationships between religions from an historical point of view. Because, Kaufman reasons, all religions are part of the historical process of human existence, which places them in a state of continual flux,

> It is a mistake to look for any such permanent structural solution to the problem of the relations of the various religions to each other . . . it is surely a mistake in principle to attempt to grasp this encounter theoretically . . . Rather, we must attempt to grasp the dynamic of the historical movement in which these faiths are involved.[6]

Paul Tillich points out that any theory of other religions which tries to argue, for example, the absoluteness or universality of Christianity, which would supposedly become manifest in the historical process, depends on certain unprovable assumptions.

How can you prove today as a Christian, or as a theologian, that the Christian message is universal and valid for all cultures and religions so that Christ must become what he potentially is, the center of history for *all* historical developments? How can you prove this? Obviously the answer is that you cannot prove it at all in terms of a theoretical analysis, for the criteria used in order to prove that Christianity is universal are themselves taken from Christianity. Therefore, they do not prove anything except for those who are within the Christian circle.[7]

It could be argued that the penchant for proof, especially in a theoretical mode, received extra impetus following the Enlightenment. The emphasis in Europe, especially during the late nineteenth century, on surveying religions as relative entities and on evaluating them from a "scientific" or objective point of view was based on the illusion that religious truth could be so judged.

Today, however, it is more widely recognized that no theologian can make a completely objective or fully informed evaluation of Christianity or other religions. Besides being simply too vast and complicated for such evaluations, religions are fundamentally expressions of human faith, which, by nature, is existential. Objective tools may be useful at times for religious discussions, but are ultimately inadequate.[8]

A more realistic approach to take is that modeled by Lesslie Newbigin who recognizes the intrinsic limits of any given theological perspective:

I must repeat the simple truth that no standpoint is available to any man except the point where he stands; that there is no platform from which one can claim to have an "objective" view which supersedes all the "subjective" faith-commitments of the world's faiths; that every man must take his stand on the floor of the arena, on the same level with every other, and there engage in the real encounter of ultimate commitment with those who, like him, have staked their lives on their vision of the truth.[9]

Kosuke Koyama resonates in his theology to this kind of perception. In his concern for contextualization, in his theological style, and in his existential Christology he focuses not on objective, theoretical proofs of Christianity or other religions but on the dynamics of faith itself. For him the discussion of such issues as the meeting of different human histories, human spirituality, or the juxtaposing of key concepts of different religions is a secondary exercise. It is a methodological or functional tool for an existential commitment.

If one accepts that there can be no objective, comprehensive, "final word" on the relationship between Christianity and other religions, then Koyama is correct to keep an existential focus at the center of his theology. While Koyama's existential interpretation of Christ might itself be challenged as simply another form of theory, it at least may be affirmed as self-consistent and self-critical. Koyama's focus is on his own confessional claim and that of other Christians; he does not pretend to offer a judgment of others' religions based on an external, neutral criterion.

A Christian Anthropology for Encounter

Clearly, constructing a Christian theology of other religions is a complex process. It requires a carefully worked out Christology. It involves a deep examination of both religious practice and religious theory. Also, it must include an understanding of the historical context of interfaith encounter, of how religions develop and interact.

Any Christian theology of other religions also inevitably involves a certain "anthropology," or understanding of what human beings are and how they relate. By focusing on this particular aspect of faith and encounter, a useful avenue for dealing with the issue may be identified.

Koyama's theology is one example of a theology of other religions that develops this focus. After formulating his Christology, and along with a practical and doctrinal study of other religions, he emphasizes the need to understand inter-faith encounter in terms of "neighbourology." He puts the focus on people, not theories.

Lesslie Newbigin also identifies the value of keeping this perspective central in the Christian encounter with other faiths. He writes,

> The real point of contact between Christian and non-Christian is not in the *religion* of the non-Christian but in his *humanity* . . . This means, incidentally, that in seeking the point of contact for the gospel (and we certainly cannot preach at all unless there is some point of contact) we shall expect to look for it not in men's religion, but in those simple facts of human experience which are—so to say—pre-religious.[10]

Where one might differ with Newbigin here is in the notion that religion can be separated from life, that there is, in fact, anything "pre-religious" about human beings.

But the point is that there are basic human experiences which form a common ground for encounter. As a result, "anthropology" or "neighbourology" or a practical appreciation of human experience needs to be very near the heart of any Christian theology of other religions.

When this is established, the process of encounter then becomes the relating of one set of human experiences to another. Put another way, the process of encounter becomes the meeting of human histories, or stories. This is very much what Koyama is doing in linking the history of Asian faiths and cultures with the faith and the history of Israel. Out of this process new understanding can be born and the gospel can be better communicated and contextualized.

Such focusing on "anthropology," on relating varying histories as a tool for inter-faith encounter, is to see encounter as fundamentally a relational experience. It emphasizes a dynamic as opposed to a static approach to other faiths.

A problem with this approach is that it might imply too concrete a distinction between theory and practice, between concept and experience. In reality, experiences and reflections about them—namely concepts or theories—are inseparable. Each informs and depends on the other. To determine which exists prior to the other is a virtually insoluble epistemological dilemma.

Altogether, the dynamic, relational approach would, however, seem to be more faithful to Scripture and to the gospel accounts of a Jesus who spent his ministry not in promulgating theories but in personal engagement with different kinds of people. Naturally, this perspective is itself a particular interpretation of the Scriptural texts.

Alternatively, the New Testament accounts of Jesus could be understood as themselves already dogmatic, meaning that Jesus is more or less essentially dogma. However, the fact that the New Testament story does center on a person would seem to allow Jesus to be responded to relationally, as a living being, as well as in other ways.

Broader Issues

No matter how it is constructed, any Christian theology of other religions will intrinsically be exclusivistic and in regard to others, arrogant, insofar as it is based on Christian truth claims. From an outside point of view, Christian truth claims and

Christian claims about other faiths are but one set of views among many. They are not at all self-evident.

Put another way, all Christian claims are essentially confessional. By nature, they can never be objective or neutral. To speak, for example, of salvation history is to speak "a priori" in Christian terms. There are no other, universally accepted terms for such an interpretation of human history.

In other words, the first reality to be recognized in constructing a Christian theology of other religions is that all Christian theologies of other religions are formulated within the bounds of certain Christian presuppositions. All Christian theologies of other religions are exactly that, neither more nor less than confessionally Christian claims. They are not obvious, absolute, claims in any universally demonstrable sense.

The cause for formulating Christian theologies of other faiths is clear, as stated already several times. Such theologies result from the experience of encounter, from the existence of alternatives, which produces both doctrinal and existential crises for Christian faith.

Other faiths clearly do challenge Christian beliefs in ultimate reality. They do continually stimulate reflection on the Christian understanding of God. They do affect Christianity's various understandings of the Church itself, its nature and its purpose. When, for example, Christians claim to have perceived the presence or work of God in peoples of other faiths, prior perspectives about God are often put into question.

Such was the experience of the early Christians. They had a similar challenge in coming to terms with their experience of Christ, who shattered their prior expectations. Likewise, Christians today, argues John V. Taylor, are challenged in this way again through the modern situation of encounter, especially since, "our irreducible loyalties belong to our experiences, and only secondarily to the doctrines that enshrine them."[11] Whether one result of the experience of encounter will be a change in our understanding of God, whether the modern situation of encounter will have a developmental impact on Christology, as some contemporary theologians are encouraging, cannot yet be ascertained. But the profound impact of the experience of encounter on Christian faith and theology today is becoming clearer.

Purpose and Process

The purpose of formulating a Christian theology of other religions in this or any context is to help Christians articulate and establish their own faith identity. In that sense, theologies of other religions are primarily for Christians and only secondarily for others. Such theologies are not primarily tools for converting others or for explaining Christian faith to those outside the Christian community, although they may assist that process. Theologies of other religions serve first of all to help Christians understand their own identity and to help explain Christianity to Christians.

To a large extent, this has to do with identifying who is outside the community as opposed to who is within it. There is a certain security in a group identity based on this process but perhaps also an element of self-divinization in setting up one's own group as distinct from and usually superior to others in its understanding of truth. Still, the primary intent of such a process is not so much to make statements about the salvation or damnation of others but about the identity and beliefs of believers themselves.

At stake, of course, are profound claims about the nature of life, death and reality. For the Christian any discussion of other religions is inevitably a deep discussion about Christian faith itself. In fact, the Christian experience of encounter with other faiths can be seen to symbolize the struggle which goes on within any Christian between faith and unbelief.

The ultimate Other Religion, in a sense, is unbelief, whether expressed via another religion or in atheism or in the internal doubts of an individual Christian. From this point of view a Christian theology of other religions can have the extra value of helping Christians come to terms with their own failures and questioning. In this sense the modern situation of encounter can be seen as an unusual boon to Christians.

Relational Encounter

God has not made the entire world Christian. This is both a cause of inter-faith encounter and a legitimation for it. Encounter becomes the instrumentality by which Christians discover the implications of their own faith and through which they convey it to others. The process of encounter, seen in this way, itself becomes the primary argument for a relational approach to other religions. Nothing so undermines the idea that there is a clear, abstract, absolute, propositional and rationally grasped universal Truth as the fact of religious plurality. If the Christian truth were so obvious, if God were absolute in a propositional sense, people would perceive it, and respond in such a way as to dramatically decrease or even eliminate the plurality of faiths in the human community. But such is not the case.

Instead, the acceptance of Christian truth claims seems to depend more on the relational transmission of faith, grounded in personal encounter.

Given that fact, the formation of a Christian theology of other religions cannot operate on the assumption that it is essentially and only a form of rational apologetic for the Christian faith which will convince others to adopt it. Again, there are no external, neutral common grounds upon which to establish the claims of faith. Rather, Christian theology can only be built from within. It may certainly borrow external terminology, and may and must constantly find contact points with other faith claims. But, as Koyama and Tillich have illustrated in their theological formulations, Christ remains the inner criterion by which Christianity itself must be judged.

The question, then, as far as constructing a theology of other religions is concerned, is not whether a definitive conclusion can be reached in regard to the relationship between Christianity and other religions, or whether the salvation or damnation of people in other faith communities can be determined. The question, rather, is whether or not such theology is consistent with its inner hermeneutic, namely, the incarnate, crucified and risen Christ.

In a sense, most theologies are consistent. The radically exclusivist position is faithful to its interpretation of the judgmental implications of Christ; the radically open positions are faithful to understandings of Christ that either separate Jesus from soteriology or disregard traditional Christology at critical points.

But it can be argued that Koyama's theology of other religions, based on the crucified Christ, presents a position which is both faithful to traditional Christology and open to other faiths. Koyama's hermeneutical principle offers a way to appreciate other religions, seeing them, for example, as instruments of grace or participants in salvation history, without compromising the "absoluteness" of Christ. This perspective recognizes the absolute reality claims of Jesus while respecting and affirming the integrity of people of other faiths.

Within such a perspective the meaning of Jesus is understood more in relational terms than in propositional, judgmental terms. Accordingly, as Jesus is seen as respecting the faith and integrity of others, commonly meeting people on their own ground—and often at the far borders of acceptable religious behavior in his day— so are Christians called to relate in such a way to others, going to the borders of faith and unbelief.

As Tillich and others have noted, such borders are often the place of greatest growth and discovery.[12] Repeatedly the Christian may find that God's Spirit has already crossed such perceived frontiers, and created experiences of salvation.[13]

Certainly, it is clear that Scripture pictures a God who is not only Creator, Redeemer, and loving Judge of all humanity, but, as the Incarnation epitomizes, a

God who comes seeking a personal, intimate relationship with creation. This scenario is far from the kind of metaphysical exclusivism which turns human destiny into a kind of unloving game in which only select people have been given the rules.

Ends and Attitudes

Practically speaking, Christian theologies of other religions are not much good for anyone other than Christians. Any Christian comments on other religions, again, are primarily comments about Christianity. That is why Koyama is on the mark in focusing his primary attention not on judgments about other religions but on Christianity itself and on Christians developing a "crucified," "apostolic" attitude towards other faiths.

Where Koyama does engage in discussion of other faiths it is not so much on their salvific character as on their practical, ethical contribution to human existence. Where Koyama does take up deeper doctrinal issues between religions, it is primarily with the intent of opening dialogue and increasing understanding of the depths and challenges of other faith traditions.

Koyama, more than most, illustrates the observation made by John V. Taylor that Christian theologies of other religions are basically "conversations within the family," Christian to Christian, so to speak, which are overheard by others.[14] Always, these conversations are based on presuppositions intrinsic to the family. They are not, as has been noted, subject to objective external verification.

The whole attempt to establish provable truth claims reflects not only recent Western predilections for rationalistic, scientific analysis, but also the human propensity towards mechanical religion, which Scripture itself resists. In both Old Testament and New there is a repeated emphasis on the existential, experiential response to God described as faith. Whether voiced in the decisional words of a Joshua calling people to "choose this day whom you will serve" (Joshua 24:15) or in the New Testament admonition to "repent and believe in the gospel" (Mark 1:15), the emphasis is not on proof but on free human choice.

As argued previously, there is no neutral ground from which anyone can make a purely objective assessment of religious truth claims for the purposes of such choosing. Nor is there a single, comprehensive, definitive theoretical framework from which Christians can fully evaluate other religions or unequivocally convince others of the validity of Christian claims. Within the Christian tradition, rather, there are the resources for a variety of approaches to other faiths. A plurality of theologies of other religions, rather than just one, will continue to develop in the historical Church.

But the wider options are inevitably limited. A person is either already within the Christian framework in general—or some hybrid of it, as various inter-faith theologians are trying to create—or one belongs within the framework of some other religion or belief system. The range of choices is not infinite.

Although some adherents of other faiths may be converted or attracted to the Christian framework by the force of argument or rational appeal, for most people the real issue is the personal and relational value of the religion, the way it affects them and their relationship with their neighbors. Consequently, no matter how emphatically Christ may be proclaimed by Christians, it is at least as important that Christ be "lived" by Christians in their relationship with their neighbors. For, as Koyama seeks to assert, that is the true nature of the Christian religion. To follow Christ, to trust God without a present or provable outcome is the fundamental process of faith.

In the end, the existential option is the only legitimate option for Christians, especially given that even theoretical claims are fundamentally confessional claims anyway. Ultimately, Christians cannot make objectively verifiable religious truth statements about either themselves or people of other faiths. They can only make faith claims, which may prove to be true, partially true, or even false.

Koyama's Contribution

In regard to the modern situation of encounter Kosuke Koyama's "truth statement," as embodied in his theology of other religions, is a good faith statement in that it stands at the central locus of Christianity—namely, Jesus' Cross and Resurrection—and at the same time deals with the modern pluralistic religious context. Koyama's theology is self-consistent, consistent with his understanding of Scripture and tradition, and consistent with its larger context.

In one sense, the contribution Koyama has made is to develop the kind of "theology of the cross" first articulated by Martin Luther and made it a vehicle for the Christian encounter with other religions. Koyama does not develop Luther's idea of the hiddenness of God as a way of talking about other religions, but does succeed in keeping the Cross as the focus for Christian spirituality and life, whether in regard to people of other faiths or to other Christians. As such the Cross stands not as an instrument of damnation; its judgement is of human sin, not human destiny. The Cross, rather, stands as an instrument of salvation in the freedom it brings and in the way of life it engenders for individual Christians and for the whole Church, who are called to incarnate the same sacrificial, redemptive presence in the world at large.

In Koyama's hands theology of the Cross becomes the key to the Christian encounter with people of other faiths. It focuses on the people for whom Christ died rather than on abstract religious judgments about them. It constantly centers the Christian on Christ, not on any external reality or rationalistic measuring stick. Insofar as it is both Christocentric and universally inclusive, Koyama succeeds in directly linking the meaning and experience of Jesus and the Cross to the meaning and experience of life today.

What Koyama demonstrates in the process is that Christians are called to live in an existential, day by day awareness that the Cross is not there for us to manipulate or handle. It is not an instrument upon which to hang other people. It is, rather, a bridge, a tool, and a model for Christians in reaching out to others. This perspective is no small contribution to make towards a Christian theology of other religions in the modern context of encounter.

PART THREE

KOYAMA'S STYLISTIC CONTRIBUTION

INTRODUCTION—AN ENCOUNTER OF THEOLOGIES

The modern situation of encounter precipitates a crisis for Christianity in general and for Christian theology in particular. A sense of crisis, especially in relation to the meaningfulness of Christian theology and the faith it expresses has been voiced by many theologians. On the one hand, this crisis is external in the sense that Christian claims are measured against changing circumstances. The modern situation of encounter, for example, makes clear the relativity of all theological claims as well as the forms in which they are conveyed, if only on the basis of their being products of particular cultural frameworks. Moreover, the competitive environment in which Christianity exists—an environment of secularism, powerful ideologies, and various religions—is one in which the claims of Christian theology are obviously not accepted by the majority of humankind. In the West, from which so much of the world's theology has come, science and philosophy, the previous bed-partners of theology, have seriously undermined the authority of Western Christian theology. In these and other ways, the crisis is external.

On the other hand, the crisis for Christianity and Christian theology has an internal dimension. It relates to the structure of Christian theology, or, to the framework in which Christian theology is formed. Walter J. Hollenweger has pointed out a significant aspect of the relationship between culture and theology: within a culture the dominant theology is that of the dominant class.[1] By extension it can be proposed that in an intercultural milieu the dominant theology will be that of the dominant culture.

Such has been precisely the case in a world permeated by the influence of Europe through the processes of colonialization and the spread of Europe's technology, its religion, its political and economic structures, its ideologies, and other aspects of European values and culture. Thus, the dominant theology of Christianity in its global dimensions has been theology formulated predominantly against a European background.

This is not to ignore the theological traditions of Eastern Orthodoxy or of such churches as the African Coptic church or the Mar Thoma church of South India. Yet it seems clear that Christianity as it has developed in most of Africa, Asia and other parts of the globe in the last two centuries is a Christianity heavily influenced by the theological perspectives of Western Europe.[2]

In the contemporary situation of encounter Christian theology, as developed and practiced in the European tradition and as exported to other parts of the world, increasingly comes into question through the development of other theological perspectives and styles by Christians in different cultures in other parts of the globe. With the waning of Western European cultural dominance new frameworks for Christian theology are free to develop. No longer can the theological structures, nor indeed the theological issues, that organized European theology be considered normative for all Christians at all times and in all places.

Previously, for example, it was assumed that Christians outside of Europe should adopt the theological structures and content of European theology, and that these provided an adequate expression of Christian faith in all circumstances. Until recent times, for example, the Roman Catholic Church, not unlike Islam, maintained the necessity for all its followers—in whatever cultural context—to adhere to one particular European language as well as to one particular ecclesiastical and liturgical form for the expression of their faith. Protestantism, perhaps more through accident than intent, allowed more flexibility and diversity in the expression of faith in other cultures, while nevertheless exporting a particular—that is, European—heritage of theological interpretation and practice, especially in relation to doctrine, morality, and denominational ecclesiologies and liturgies. Of course, the Europeans, as any people of a given historical context, could probably not have done otherwise.

The modern situation of encounter—within the church itself—is now altering the inherited patterns in the dissemination of Christian faith, as is becoming evident in the recognized development of indigenous church structures, liturgies and theologies in non-European contexts.[3] Indeed, the very identification of something like a dominant theology associated with European cultural dominance owes its occurrence in large measure to the modern situation of encounter in which the intercultural diversity of Christianity is both revealed and fostered. Of course, it must be recognized that there is in fact a wide diversity of cultures and theologies within Europe itself. However, enough of a European culture-theology may be identified to raise certain questions.

For instance, can the terms and patterns that were appropriate and necessary to European Christianity suffice to express the faith and experience of Christians in very different cultural contexts? Will not Christian theology, as it crosses into the cultures of Africa and Asia, for example, need to be reformulated within the frameworks of those cultures just as it was formulated in the frameworks of Europe?

Today as Christianity becomes established in a diversity of the world's cultures, it is reasonable to suppose that theology framed within the European context is neither the only nor necessarily the best option for Christianity in the world today.

There is, in other words, an intercultural dimension to the formulation of Christian theology. To a large degree, the current internal crisis in theology stems from the predominance of one cultural-theological framework over others. In part, this crisis can be described in regional terms, that is, the predominance of the European framework over other cultural frameworks. However, such a description can be misleading. For, as mentioned above, Europe itself is a region of significant diversity. Its various cultures and traditions cannot justly be lumped together in facile, monolithic terms. Europe has its own multiplicity of theological frameworks that vary with its different cultures. Moreover, Europe, too, is a milieu of constant change; its theological frameworks are not altogether static.

An alternative way in which to consider this internal theological crisis is to speak of it as a matter of language, or, of theological genre. Indeed, one benefit of the modern situation of encounter is that it enables the clearer identification of a plurality of theological languages, or, of theological genres. It reveals the complex variety of Christian theology as Christianity expresses itself theologically not only via the language of systematic tomes, but also in such "languages" as liturgy, dance, and drama. So doing, the intercultural character of contemporary Christianity makes clear that there is no universally accepted formula to which all Christian theology must conform. Rather, there is a plurality of theologies. In short, within the modern situation of encounter there is an encounter of theologies.

This encounter becomes apparent in a figure like Kosuke Koyama. He represents a strain or genre of theology that provides a stimulating contrast to the Europe-centered genre of theology that has been so prevalent. To consider just how Koyama exemplifies and contributes to the contemporary encounter of theologies two general streams or genres of theology will be posited and placed in contrast with each other. Neither exists as a unified, easily identifiable entity. Yet, by speaking of theology in terms of two genres, it will be possible to more clearly picture the contemporary encounter of theologies and Koyama's place in it.

The first genre of theology to be identified is what might be called the theoretical, propositional, abstract genre of theology. Inevitably, whatever terms are chosen to describe this genre will be inadequate, for the category itself is broad and unwieldy. Yet such words help to describe its general nature.

In contrast to the theoretical, propositional genre of theology stands the more existential, narrative genre which may be characterized by its propensity towards intuition, imagery, story, symbol, and paradox. As this category, too, is broad in scope and to some degree artificial, the terms that describe it must be seen more as descriptive than as precisely definitive.

The nature and significance of these two theological genres, especially in relation to the contemporary encounter of theologies and Koyama's role in it, will be more fully developed in succeeding chapters. For now it is enough to say that Koyama's theology belongs more to the second, narrative genre of theology.

The importance of contrasting these two theological genres or languages relates directly to the modern situation of encounter. For, the theology that spread with Western European culture over the last two centuries, becoming the predominant measure of Christian theology world-wide, or, at least heavily influencing the understanding and formulation of Christian theology in other cultures was, by and large, of the theoretical genre. While this genre certainly has universal dimensions, as will be noted later, it can also be argued that its particular, powerful expression via European culture can be criticized from an intercultural perspective as provincial. That is, the theology which issued from Europe, shaped as it was by the Reformation, the Enlightenment, and the rise of Western science, was the product of a cultural framework different from frameworks in other parts of the world. Thus, while the theoretical genre of theology, which was developed to a highly sophisticated level in Europe, was appropriate to the European situation, it is not necessarily therefore the definitive norm for theology in all contexts. Yet, so entrenched did the theoretical genre become in Europe itself and beyond Europe via the pervasive influence of Western European culture that only with the recent waning of Western power have other genres of theology—including those latent within the European context itself—come to be more fully recognized and accepted.

Today the modern situation of encounter virtually demands the rediscovery of alternative theological languages. For, a plurality of cultural frameworks requires a plurality of theological languages. An important step towards the recognizing and developing of such a plurality of languages is coming to terms with the dominance of the theoretical genre of theology and encouraging the development of other genres.

That a shift away from the predominant theoretical genre is desirable in the modern situation of encounter is evident to an increasing number of theologians. As one theologian notes, there is widespread "dissatisfaction with abstractions, with ideas and doctrines"[4]—the typical focus of the theoretical genre of theology. Another theologian adds that people today distrust abstract truth; they listen more to the experience of others than to ideas.[5]

At the same time, it is increasingly recognized that the traditional categories and questions of theology no longer suffice to meet the problems of the modern context even in the West.[6] In particular, the intellectual approach typical of the theoretical genre of theology is seen as valid only for a limited segment of society.[7] In harmony with this drift away from a theology of abstractions and traditional categories, there is in the modern context an increased concern that theology become more flexible and dialogical. "The confrontation of modern man with Christian faith cannot take the form of a dogmatic and non-dialectical formulation of a final truth to the world."[8] Altogether, the need for a shift away from the dominant patterns of theology as represented by the theoretical genre of theology is best indicated by the observation that because there has been "something counterfeit about the old words for so long, something exhausted about reason, a new language will have to grow."[9]

Kosuke Koyama is representative of those who endeavor to develop such a new language for Christianity in the modern situation of encounter. On the one hand, he provides a contrast to the predominant theoretical language of theology, thereby calling that language into question. On the other hand, he models another genre of theology that may speak more adequately to the greatly expanded intercultural framework within which Christianity now exists.

The following chapters clarify the nature of both the theoretical and narrative genres of theology, discuss them in the context of the modern situation of encounter, and examine Koyama's role in this encounter of theologies. Due to the nature of the subject, these chapters will invariably contain some overlaps. The necessary terminology is itself somewhat repetitive and ambiguous. But in the end, the need for and the avenue towards a theological language appropriate to the modern situation of encounter and how Koyama's theological style might play a role in that process should become apparent.

CHAPTER ELEVEN

ELEMENTS OF THE THEORETICAL GENRE

The word "theology" carries a multitude of meanings. In Greek philosophy it was the speech of poets about divine things.[1] It referred to various accounts of the gods and their involvement in daily life. However, in Christian usage, theology came to mean different things at different times. Referring in the early Christian centuries to the Christian Scriptures themselves and to their account of God's dealing with humanity through Christ, theology was in the Middle Ages expanded to include philosophical treatment of Christian doctrines and academic study of Scripture and tradition.[2] After Aquinas, theology was increasingly seen as the climax of all human knowledge, the "Queen of the Sciences," even up until the Enlightenment when it was described as "the comprehension of all other knowledge, directed to its true end."[3]

In the sense that Christian believers today hold that their faith contains the essential explanation of ultimate reality, theology still serves as the vehicle for comprehending and expressing the origin, essence, and end of all human life and knowledge. However, in practical, prosaic usage theology is perhaps more generally understood as a particular type of human thinking within a particular arena of human experience. It has become an academic, abstract discipline among other such disciplines. "Theology" is now a generic term applied to various branches of religious study (and not only Christian religious studies) such as biblical theology, moral theology, and dogmatic theology.[4]

Emil Brunner argues that this generic usage of theology as an all-inclusive term emerged only with the division of Christian thinking into various specialized categories, for example, church history, biblical theology, and practical theology.[5] In that sense, Brunner stresses, the use of theology "as a comprehensive term covering various intellectual studies connected with the Bible, and in the service of the Church, is a modern idea."[6]

"Theology," therefore, is an inconstant term. Whereas once seen as the consummation of all human knowledge, theology is now seen as a sub-category of general knowledge, and one which, even for many Christians, is of little practical significance. This particular shift reflects a change of frameworks within European Christianity itself, namely, a change from the perspective of medieval Christendom to the perspective of a post-Enlightenment, scientific era in a Europe gradually returning to paganism.[7]

At the same time, the changing understanding of theology can also be connected to the association of theology with dominant cultural patterns. As theology accommodated itself (necessarily) to the presuppositions and methodologies of its European environment, it inevitably yielded to the peculiar limitations of those same presuppositions and methodologies.

For example, with the application of empirical methods to biblical research, theology became more specialized and therefore less available to ordinary Christians as a tool for expressing their faith. Of course, while it must be recognized that theology had long been an enterprise mainly of the elite, that is, those who could read and those who belonged to the clerical establishment, it was also inevitable that as theology endeavored to maintain or to re-establish itself in the highly cognitive, philosophical, science-orientated milieu of eighteenth, nineteenth, and twentieth century Europe, it increasingly lost the ability to express Christian faith on an ordinary, experiential level.

It is exactly this "intellectualization" of Christian theology which helps to describe the theoretical genre being considered. Further evidence that this genre emerged as dominant in the cultural milieu of Europe surfaces in various definitions of theology and its main categories: systematics and dogmatics.

First of all, Thomas Aquinas is the man accredited with defining theology as a "science." By this he was referring to the speculative or theoretical character of theology[8] and its compatibility with human reason. This concept of theology as a science persisted into the modern era. Early in this century, for example, theology was described as that "branch of science" aiming to give systematic expression to the Christian faith.[9] Similarly, since the end of the nineteenth century there have been continued efforts to evaluate and express Christian faith, particularly in the area of biblical studies, in "scientific" terms.

However, several problems with this understanding of theology become immediately apparent. One is that what "science" has come to mean to people of the twentieth century can hardly be what Aquinas had in mind seven hundred years ago. But more critical to the notion that theology is a science, either in Aquinas' terms or in modern-day terminology, is that it implies a particular methodological framework in which theology must operate, namely, a deliberately propositional, systematic framework.

That such a framework has indeed prevailed is nowhere more evident than in the areas of systematic and dogmatic theology. The very esteem accorded this kind of theology reflects the predilection in recent times for theology expressed in scholarly, propositional terms.

For example, Emil Brunner, in a discussion of dogmatics, can refer to theology as "a comprehensive term covering various intellectual studies connected with the

Bible."[10] Paul Tillich describes all theology as the "methodical explanation of the contents of the Christian faith."[11] John Macquarrie, in turn, describes systematic theology as the attempt to articulate with what he calls "architectonic reason" the whole of Christian faith and all its component parts "in the clearest and most coherent language available."[12]

Behind Brunner's comment that theology refers to "intellectual" studies connected with the Bible, behind Tillich's view of theology as "methodical explanation," and behind Macquarrie's vision of theology as ordered by "architectonic reason" is an apparent assumption that intellectual reasoning and a systematic framework in some way supply an especially desirable or superior framework for Christian theology. In fact, each of the individuals cited realize the limits of reason and religious language. Nevertheless, the power of a scientific or empirically orientated environment, one which places high value on analytic, propositional expression, draws them, too, into seeking to express Christian faith in language appropriate to the environment.

While more attention will shortly be given to dogmatic and systematic theology and to the nature and influence of a "science-orientated" environment, it should already be clear that dogmatic and systematic theology epitomize theology of the theoretical genre. The general dominance of this genre derives largely from the fact that this type of theological language was compatible with those aspects of European culture which became dominant globally, for example, European technology, European political structures, and European education systems—all of which put a premium on analysis, systematic organization and intellectual apprehension.

Two points can be made. First, theology itself is an ambiguous enterprise, taking different content and form at different times in response to changing cultural frameworks. Secondly, it can be said that theology in the European cultural framework—that which became dominant world-wide—tended to become that of the first of the two theological genres or languages under consideration, that is, the theoretical genre.

In fact, as noted once earlier, the theoretical language of theology has universal aspects. It is not merely regional or culturally conditioned. For, everywhere, theology is formed in relation to some sort of rational, organized framework, if only on a linguistic level. Nevertheless, there are important questions about the theoretical genre of theology which the modern situation of encounter poses: a) Is it the only viable mode for expressing Christian theology? b) Is it a sufficient mode for expressing the fullness of Christian faith? c) Is it a universal mode, one which can hold for all Christians in all situations and times? d) Can the particular framework which suited European Christianity, particularly in recent centuries, function adequately for Christians—European or otherwise—in the present global context? e) In short, what are the limits and potentialities, the advantages and disadvantages of this particular genre? Before pursuing these questions, and to further delineate the contours of the theoretical genre of theology, more attention will be given to systematic and dogmatic theology in particular.

Dogmatics

A problem already referred to and especially apparent at this point is that of overlapping terminology. For, dogmatics, systematics, and doctrine are terms often used interchangeably. Indeed, one theological dictionary states that the terms dogmatics and systematics are interchangeable, yet goes on to offer differing definitions for each.[13] Some theologians consider dogmatics as a category of systematics.[14] Others equate the two.[15] In general, a picture of "dogmatic theology" emerges that relates to the history and function of theology in church history, while "systematics" refers to the organization and presentation of the theological products of that history, especially in a sophisticated frame of logical argument.

To better distinguish the nature and characteristics of dogmatic theology, several viewpoints can be utilized. John Macquarrie, for example, considers Christian dogma to be distinguished by three marks: 1) that it is based in revelation; 2) that it is proposed by the church, expressing the mind of the community; and 3) that it has a propositional form, usually in philosophical terminology.[16] This latter mark clearly identifies dogmatics as belonging in form to the theoretical genre of theology.

Historically, Macquarrie observes, dogma is formulated in response to external threats to Christian belief and therefore focuses on only some subjects at particular times and in particular circumstances, which means that dogmas must be reinterpreted by other Christians in other situations and times.[17] Today, the modern situation of encounter requires precisely such a reinterpretation of dogma itself along with a re-evaluation of the dominant forms in which dogma is presented.

Emil Brunner, too, points out that Christian dogmatics are rooted in the polemical labors of the church, particularly in response to threatening situations. But Brunner adds to the concept of dogma that it is a summary of biblical doctrine and that it is an instrument of Christian catechesis.[18]

Whatever the understanding of Christian dogmatics, a theoretical, abstract dimension inevitably emerges. For, any expression of faith depends upon a coherent set of conceptual and linguistic reference points.

Scripture itself is, of course, hardly dogmatic in the modern sense. While certain segments of Scripture, for example, the letter to the Romans, might be described as a dogmatic dialogue with Greek philosophy,[19] there is, overall, little actual dogma in Scripture.[20] Moreover, the apostles did not set out to produce dogmatic or systematic theology; neither did the church fathers for most of Christianity's first two centuries.[21] Apologetic and catechetical requirements naturally gave rise to an expanding volume of Christian literature. But it was in large measure Christianity's encounter with Greco-Roman culture that produced dogmatic theology. For, "Rome with her practical bent and love of organization helped to institutionalize the religion."[22] In architecture, liturgy, church polity and theological formulation Christianity adapted itself to the framework of Greco-Roman culture. Thus began what has been termed "the Latin captivity of the church" which lasted well into the Reformation era.[23]

Part of this institutionalizing captivity included a natural and necessary propensity to create and to codify church dogma. This gave rise to attempts at systematizing the whole of Christian dogma, the first major attempt being seen by some scholars to be that of Origen.[24] Others credit Peter Lombard with having created classical Western dogmatics, his work becoming a standard reference for Reformation and post-Reformation theology.[25]

Becoming ever more methodical in medieval schools of theology,[26] dogmatics came to be considered the infallible, central, authoritative teaching of the church, the center of belief.[27] But the German, Luther, though he too was schooled in Latin theology,[28] challenged the authority of Latin dogmatics on the principle that Scripture alone was infallible.[29] The view that faith was not relationship to a doctrine but to Jesus Christ, with the implication that doctrine was relative and not absolute, dealt a significant blow to the authority of dogma.[30]

Thus, on the one hand, through the development of dogmatic theology the theoretical genre of theology gained power and prestige in the European context. On the other hand, the final authority of this form of Christian theology was continually being called into question.

Germanic Protestantism soon lost sight of Luther's existential critique of dogmatics and reverted to a strict emphasis on creeds, confessions, and doctrines.[31] Nordic pietism, at the other extreme, eschewed dogmatics for an emphasis on practical concerns, personal piety, and biblical exegesis.[32] But with the Enlightenment came a still more radical shift in the entire framework of Christian theology, one which began to undermine dogmatics altogether. For, philosophy of religion displaced Christian faith as the framework for theological thinking. To reground Christian dogmatics in the secularized, philosophical framework of post-

Enlightenment Europe, Christian theology was required to adapt itself to completely new terms.

The modern scientific and philosophical framework affected dogmatics in other ways as well. With the rise of the historical-critical method of biblical research, for instance, a gap arose between the dogmaticians and the biblical scholars. The latter were considered to be working on scientific grounds while the dogmaticians were dealing with unfounded theories.[33]

Altogether, the historical development of dogmatics in the European context illustrates at least the provisional nature of theological patterns. Originally non-dogmatic, Christian theology became increasingly defined by dogmatic forms. At the same time, the "scientific" authority of Christian dogmatics was being undermined by the analytic methodology which, to some degree, it had both spawned and later mimicked.

What has become apparent in the modern context is that European Christian dogmatics cannot suffice as a definitive norm for Christian theology in a widely intercultural context. Rather, such dogmatic theology, typified by its analytic, philosophical form, particularly as derived from the European context—despite the fact that this form achieved a certain authoritative influence world-wide—can be seen as but one genre of Christian theology. Indeed, the modern context clarifies the true nature of dogmatics as well as its advantages and disadvantages. For, dogmatics is not in the end neutral, scientific language; nor is it the science of the Christian religion.[34] It is, rather, as Emil Brunner puts it, "believing thinking," which presupposes faith and the Christian church with its apologetic and teaching functions.[35]

To maintain certain dogmatic structures and formulations as universal absolutes for Christian theology is to misunderstand the nature of theology. For, at the most basic level all dogmatics will be relative and problematic in at least epistemological and philosophical terms. The very diversity of existing dogmatic formulations demonstrates that dogmatics can never be monolithic. Besides, to offer dogmas based on Scripture as norms for Christian faith and life is to miss a central point of Scripture, namely, that Scripture recounts the story of human failure to live by rules and dogmas.[36]

Obviously, dogmas and dogmatic theology are necessary to the life of the church. Doctrinal formulations preserve faith, guide the community, and provide a balance to individualistic tendencies.[37] Such theology clarifies Christian proclamation and teaches Christians what they must believe and do.[38] However, highly structural theology is not a sufficient tool for Christian conversation with a predominantly non-Christian world. Instead, the modern situation of encounter requires more flexible forms in which Christianity can communicate itself. The theoretical language of dogmatic theology does not adequately meet current needs.

To be sure, it is probably providential that theology as it developed in Europe, with its dogmatic, theoretical form, achieved universal dominance. For, this dominant theology constitutes a foundation upon which Christian theology on a global scale may be built—both in reaction to it and in continuation of it. Later theologians may consider whether or not specific doctrines formulated in the European situation need reformulation in other contexts, for example, Hindu or Chinese, or whether they may stand as inherited. For now, it is enough to recognize the need for more freedom in theological form, and to pursue the development of alternative forms or languages for Christian theology which may be more appropriate to the modern context of encounter.

Systematics

Mention has already been made of the ambiguity and overlap of such terms as dogmatic and systematic. Yet, by treating them separately perhaps some subtle distinctions will surface which will further clarify the nature of the theoretical genre of theology and the reason for its dominance.

Systematic theology generally receives rather broad definition. It is what provides the "norms" which are necessary for Christian faith and life.[39] It is, precisely, an ordering of the mass of biblical and other material in the Christian heritage into a coherent, consistent system.[40] At its grandest it is the total theological enterprise unified by, as John Macquarrie has put it, "archtectonic reason."[41] Altogether, systematic theology attempts to articulate all the constituent elements of theology as a whole as well as to relate the whole itself to the totality of human knowledge.[42]

This ambitious picture of systematic theology inherently implies that the reason-orientated, analytic form of theology is superior to other kinds of theological language. It is not surprising that systematic theology has thus been set in the center of the theological curriculum as the highest "philosophy of the Christian life."[43]

Underlying such a view is the idea that Christian Scripture and tradition present a collection of truths which need to be systematized.[44] One of the most obvious characteristics of systematic theology, of course, is its sequential, thematic structure. Traditional systematics are organized around such themes as the nature and existence of God, creation, redemption, humanity, sin, the church, ministry, sacraments, and so on. Karl Barth's *Church Dogmatics* exemplifies such a structure, filling several volumes with sixteen thematic chapters utilizing seventy-three subcategories.[45] Paul Tillich's three volume *Systematic Theology* consists of five general parts, divided into thirteen topical sections with forty-four sub-divisions, not counting introductory materials.[46] Even a cursory glance at Kosuke Koyama, on the other hand, reveals that he does not develop or utilize any such system.

The roots of systematic theology lie in Christian Scripture, church history, and the history of religions and culture.[47] All of these relate to experience. Yet systematic theology, while expressing convictions drawn from experience,[48] intends to speak in theoretical terms about something which transcends both human experience and human terminology. At this point, the systematic, theoretical language of theology breaks down. Systematic theology, like dogmatics, cannot suffice as a theological language, for it, too, is relative, provisional, and by nature problematic.

It is not surprising, however, that systematic theology became a dominant, authoritative theological language in and beyond the European context. In a cultural framework that put a premium on analytical form, logical argument, and philosophical expression, theology which spoke in those terms easily came to the fore. Systematic theology—at least on the surface—was theology allied with reason and science in an age that emphasized both. That under the surface systematic theology was not in fact scientific increasingly became apparent not only through the struggle to construct systematic theology in a secular, scientific environment, but also as the presuppositions of that environment changed.

The idea that any system of theological truth was infallible evaporated with the recognition that Scripture itself was hardly infallible.[49] At the same time, philosophical epistemology threw into question the meaning of all religious terms, heightening the contrast between scientific and theological language. In the end,

> attempts to elaborate a theology as an empirical-inductive or a
> metaphysical deductive "science," or as a combination of both,
> have given ample evidence that no such attempt can succeed.[50]

Moreover, the changing presuppositions of the secular environment have affected systematic theology. Undermined by the recognized uncertainty of science itself as well as by increased understanding of the complexity of the world and its cultures,[51] systematic theology is necessarily fading as a universal, primary language for Christian theology. Objectivism is called into question by science itself; relativity enters human awareness as an almost axiomatic reality.[52] Thus, the framework for Christian theology has once again changed. That framework in which systematic theology provided a definitive guide for Christian theology has been superseded by a framework whose hallmark is relativity, plurality and diversity.

Systematic theology does still have a place, however; the type of theological overview it intends to provide is useful and necessary.[53] Also, systematic theology encourages theological consistency.[54] In introducing the final volume of his systematic theology Tillich considers the criticism that producing a theological system is itself the decisive error of his theology.[55] He argues that while there are certainly dangers in a theological system, above all the dangers of rationalizing revelatory experiences, of diminishing divine revelation with human reason, there are nevertheless practical advantages to systems.[56] Theological systems, Tillich points out, provide important "points of crystallization" that are helpful to Christian thinking.[57]

However, all systems are provisional and relative. In the modern situation of encounter it is clear that the systematic modes of Europe can no longer be deemed universal. Indeed, the modern situation of encounter reveals not only that Christian theology needs to be developed in different cultural systems, but also that in many contexts, systematic theology can in fact be detrimental to Christian witness.

R. H. S. Boyd, for example, points out that in the Indian context, dogmatic or systematic theology is disdained as incompatible with the mysterious character of religious truth.[58] Of course, Indian culture has certainly produced very sophisticated religious systems of her own. But M. M. Thomas, in a setting where Christianity has yet almost infinite possibilities for development, argues that

> today we have realized the deadening effect of total systems of thought on human creativity in any field of life; and we are justly suspicious of premature systematization.[59]

It is right, Thomas goes on, to refuse to "confuse the reality of theological existence with the development of theological systems."[60] For, Christian theology may speak in other languages. It may speak with the mysticism preserved in Eastern Christianity,[61] or through the narrative genre now developing in Asia, Africa, and elsewhere.

Faith and Reason

A key aspect of the theoretical genre of theology is the relationship between faith and reason, particularly as developed in the European framework. Again, the terms and issues involved are highly complex, but the point is to further clarify the nature of the theoretical genre of theology against a European background and in relation to the requirements of the modern situation of encounter. To that end, a brief sketch of the general development of the faith-reason dialectic in the European framework can be instructive.

An Asian theologian has observed that it was unfortunate that the author of the Gospel of John chose the word "logos" in speaking of God. For, consequently, there was an inordinate association of reason, word, order, and so on with God.[62]

In line with Anselm's dictum that Christian theology consists of faith in search of rational articulation, it has always been the aim of theology to give rational expression in terms of the philosophical ideas of the day to belief in Jesus as the supreme revelation of God.[63]

This orientation of Christian theology stems from its earliest days. Conceived and carried in the conceptual framework of the Judaic tradition, Christian faith was already with the New Testament writings being born into the philosophical categories of its surrounding culture. This was true to the intention of Christian faith as an event and an experience to be communicated to others. For, Christianity was not faith in something unknowable; it was not a mystery religion like many others at the time.[64] It was a religion confident in expressing its understanding of God's truth. Christianity was a religion which believed in its own intelligibility and communicability.[65]

From its inception, then, Christian theology was the attempt to communicate truth, to make the credible intelligible.[66] Theology became, as it remains, the means by which the Christian message was organized, interpreted, and presented to both Christians and non-Christians.[67]

There was, therefore, from the beginning a dialectic between faith and reason in Christian theology. Christian belief and experience sought (and found) expression through the philosophical categories of Greek culture.

This, however, was a peculiarly Christian enterprise. For, within the Greek tradition itself there was no distinct dichotomy between philosophy and theology. Some say that it was Christianity, particularly under Pauline influence, which formulated an either-or distinction between philosophy, the "wisdom of the world," and Christian faith, the true wisdom.[68] Subsequently, it was Christianity's task to harmonize the two.

Thus, the adaptation of Christian belief to a philosophical framework, especially to one of exceptional sophistication in terms of human reasoning, began with the entry of Christianity into Greek culture. There, some would argue, began the abstraction of Christian beliefs.[69]

Naturally, the Greek categories and terms which Christianity adopted had a decisive impact on Christian theology. That this Greek philosophical framework presented certain problems for Christian theology not only centuries ago but also today is apparent in both early credal controversies, and in more recent doctrinal discussions, for example, on the nature of God.[70]

As early as the fourth century Augustine had ardently opposed the idea that human reason, corrupted by the Fall, could attain the knowledge of faith. Yet it was his extensive familiarity with Greek philosophy that at the same time enabled him to argue the "reasonableness" of faith.[71]

Subsequently, Anselm, while echoing Augustine's concern for the priority of faith, advocated reason as a necessary servant of faith in order that Christians might try to understand what they believed.[72]

But it was with Aquinas that the great synthesis between Christian faith and natural reason was initiated[73] with the rediscovery of Aristotle via Islam. Aquinas, as opposed to Anselm, argued that natural reason was complementary to revelation as a source for human knowledge of the divine.[74] By the time Erasmus came on the scene in the late fifteenth century, the Thomistic view was firmly established. Erasmus, for example, viewing Scripture as a collection of truths accessible to the moral intellect of all people and all times, advocated an anthropocentric "Christian philosophy."[75]

Against this view Martin Luther, out of the Augustinian tradition, argued the utter inadequacy of human reason for grasping the truth of faith. Against the Christian rationalism of Erasmus, Luther emphasized the finitude of man and advocated the separation of theology from philosophy.[76] In contrast to both the mysticism of his time and the tendency to deduce God from his works via natural reason, Luther held to a theological epistemology that tied faith to experience, knowledge of God to practice.[77]

With the advent of the Enlightenment human reason emerged ascendant over faith as the measure of human knowledge. Descartes' "methodological doubt," which established truth through subjective certainty,[78] augured a shift toward the general absolutization of human reason as the avenue to all truth.[79] Truth as perceived from the perspective of Christian faith, that "powerful, great certitude" which, according to Luther, the Holy Spirit writes on human hearts,[80] was no longer recognized as an acceptable, normative, or, for that matter, valid type of human knowledge.

The conversation that had begun, then, between Christian faith and Greek philosophy in the beginning of the Christian era has, in a sense, come around one hundred and eighty degrees. Christianity, which set out to utilize human reason for its own self-expression has found itself domesticated by and under attack by modern reason. The wrestling with the relationship of faith to reason which attracted the attention of such luminaries as Augustine, Aquinas, and Luther seems, for the time being at least, to have yielded a victory for reason.

In this process Christian theology has increasingly been pressed into a defensive or apologetic position. Evidence of the fact that Christian theology has had to operate on reason's terms is abundant not only in the direct dialogues between philosophy and theology, but also in a variety of attempts to reground Christian theology within or over against the framework of a reason-orientated environment, for example, via the philosophical subjectivism of Schleiermacher,[81] or the revelation emphasis of Barth,[82] by various existential or linguistic theological endeavors,[83] or through varieties of specifically secular theologies.[84] A mountain of books testify in their structure, content, language, and intent to the fact that the agenda for European theology over the last one hundred years or so has been set by a secular, reason-orientated environment.[85]

Some recent Protestant theologians have insisted that because faith is based on divinely given revelation, faith is not to be rationally argued.[86] For, to do so is to measure God by human standards, which is blasphemy.[87] Theology is thus cut off absolutely from philosophy in essence, though not necessarily in form. Another recent approach seeks to resolve the faith-reason dialectic by grounding theological questions in a wider framework than that of philosophical discussion, namely, that of general human experience.[88] Koyama may be said to belong to this camp. For, not only does he advocate using the philosophical tools of local cultures for constructing theology, he also trusts basic human experience as a medium for comprehending and communicating the essential truths of Christian Scripture.[89] This does not mean that Koyama distills a clear set of abstract questions to be utilized in the formation of a universal Christian theology. Nor does Koyama suggest that God can be deduced from human experience. Rather, Koyama sees in the conversation between Scripture and human experience—mediated by whatever the prevailing philosophy—the materials for expressing Christian faith.

In the modern situation of encounter, this approach has considerable merit. For, it allows for a dynamic interplay of philosophy and theology in a context of multiple and diverse philosophies which undeniably affect the formulation and expression of faith. Certainly, a fresh approach to the faith-reason dialectic is both necessary and inevitable. Previously, the issue has been the relationship between "faith" as understood by the West and "reason" as understood by the West. In that dialectic there have been multiple currents and counter-currents as to the compatibility of faith and reason.[90]

Now a situation has arisen in which there are distinctly new ingredients in the faith-reason dialectic. For, now Christian faith takes shape in and must relate to a multiplicity of philosophical frameworks and not just those of the West.

Some of the frameworks are exceedingly different from those in which Christianity has previously found itself. Parts of Buddhist Asia, for example, operate with a methodology or philosophical model that proceeds from different presuppositions than those of the West. Whereas Western metaphysics operates in terms of "either-or" distinctions, for instance, some Buddhist philosophy begins with the assumption that ultimate reality is beyond human comprehension and therefore must be conceived in "neither-nor" terms.[91] Or, as in Chinese "yin-yang" philosophy, and in traditional Japanese metaphysics, there is deliberate blurring of distinctions between subjective and objective knowledge. Instead there is a "both-and" understanding of reality.[92]

At the extreme is Zen Buddhism which forcefully insists that reason—the foundation of Western philosophy—can in fact be an obstacle to human understanding. According to Zen, enlightenment comes through instantaneous insights that may in fact utilize irrational statements. Ironically, this sort of insight may compare more closely with the insight of faith than the insights achieved by philosophical reasoning.

At any rate, Christian faith now stands in a dialectic with a variety of attitudes towards reason itself. These new frameworks will at least add new tones to the faith-reason dialectic, if they do not alter it completely.

Inescapably, reason is involved in the expression of Christian faith. For reason relates to language and language is a prerequisite for communicating faith. Naturally, people describe their experiences, religious ones included, in the terms and concepts familiar to them, which take an ordered form in correspondence to the structure of their language.

However, problems arise when the products of one language system—in both its basic forms and in its wider philosophical developments—are perceived and treated as universal. Such has been the case to a large degree as Christian theology in European terms—particularly in its theoretical genre—has been considered normative in other cultural contexts, even though the European philosophical framework out of which it comes is not itself universal.

The basic problem, then, is not that faith must find expression in the rational forms of any given framework. Indeed, that human beings should seek rational expression for faith, or that human beings seek to establish religious certitude by rational frameworks, testifies to the basic affinity between ultimate reality and the human capacity to reflect on and to express it.[93] As one theologian puts it, "the moving plight of man" is that we are created to quest for religious certainty but cannot achieve it by our own efforts (namely, reason).[94]

Reason is indeed a tool of faith, one which Barth and other theologians who reject reason as a source for faith themselves profoundly utilize. It is impossible to convey the Christian message without the reference points of language, reason, and philosophy. In this sense, as Barth ingeniously pointed out, God must confer upon human language (and reason) the capacity to speak meaningfully about God.[95]

To be sure, Scripture's authors utilized propositions and arguments. They inherit the ordered traditions of their predecessors. But those pieces of Scripture which can be said to be systematic or theoretical in form—even as credal or liturgical statements—are clearly used in conjunction with other theological forms, for example, stories, poems, myths, and so on.

In the end, a diversity of theological languages is necessary. For, reason and systematic, theoretical language are inadequate for expressing the whole of faith. Normal language itself is inadequate for expressing the totality of human experience. Hence, other mediums are developed and utilized, for example, music, art, dance, and the metaphorical use of language, as in story, poetry and drama.

In theology, too, this diversity is required. On the one hand, a dominant theological form can provide some unity to Christian theology, a degree of balance to the theological enterprise as a whole, and a point of contrast for alternative theological forms. But, on the other hand, without recognized diversity, certain forms can dominate theology to the point of obscuring or suffocating the Christian message.[96]

What is needed in the modern situation of encounter is to recognize and develop alternative theological forms or languages. For, as with Christianity in the apologetic context of its early centuries, so today the most urgent need for Christian theology is to communicate the Christian message—to its adherents as well as to others. Such communication requires a flexibility of form, an ability for Christian theology to adjust to changing frameworks as it has done in the past.

CHAPTER TWELVE

LIMITS AND ALTERNATIVES IN THEOLOGICAL LANGUAGE

A presupposition of the theoretical genre of theology is that God can be known or described in intellectual, systematic terms. Such a presupposition is clearly open to question. For, the means by which human beings perceive, understand and convey religious experience are immensely diverse and complex. Even such basic issues as the meaning of terms used, the origin and function of concepts, and the relationship between experience and expression are highly complex. It should be obvious that in fact no theological language can be entirely adequate for conveying the whole of religious insight and experience.

That the theoretical genre of theological language achieved preeminence as an authoritative form for Christian theology is, again, not simply a matter of intrinsic superiority of form, but rather the result of a complex confluence of historical and cultural trends. But as has been argued, this language alone can not suffice for conveying Christian faith in all its complexity. In this chapter the complicated nature of theological language will be briefly considered in terms of 1) the limits of intellect in theological language, 2) the paradoxical character of theological language, and 3) the necessary relationship between theology and experience. Subsequently, the value of symbolic, narrative, or story-theology as alternative forms of theological language will be explored.

The Limits of Intellect

The limits to an intellectual, theoretical approach to theology are apparent from several different angles. By definition, God is beyond human comprehension, beyond all languages and concepts. Cognitive discussion of God, therefore, is self-contradictory.[1] It is intrinsically impossible to identify divine truth with a human set of dogmatic propositions. God's Word, because of its living, dynamic, transcendent character, cannot be equated with written theology.[2]

It is absurd therefore to think of dogma as defining God.[3] Theology is only that understanding or speech about God which God may inaugurate and enable.[4] In that sense, human knowledge of God expressed theologically is not a human achievement, not a static truth that can be defined and possessed but a dynamic gift.[5]

Strictly speaking, theology can say nothing of God directly. Rather, knowledge of God is always mediated via human experience and human thought and language.[6]

As a form of human discourse, theology aims at intelligibility and consistency. But theology intrinsically deals with something beyond itself, beyond human standards of intelligibility.[7] This is all the more apparent when those standards are narrowed to such a degree that reason, intellect, philosophical analysis and the like are considered the authoritative criteria for Christian theology.

That such standards are unequal to the task of the theological enterprise has been recognized by theologians both past and present. As C. S. Song puts it,

> Rational theology, that is, theology intent on exploiting human reason to let the mystery of Being yield to human understanding, does not conform to the ways in which God relates himself to the world.[8]

Instead, Song argues, what is needed is the understanding of the heart.

Luther, too, argued the inadequacy of the intellect alone for Christian theology. The "problem of God, according to Luther, could not be mastered by analytic intellect."[9] Rather, it extends beyond the limits of human thinking, defying any systematic statement.[10] To Luther, faith, the foundation of theology, could not be derived from the intellect. For, "it contains in itself a contrary element against all substantive experience. It stands in permanent conflict with perception."[11]

Theology thus must deal with an intrinsic dilemma. For it seeks always to relate and interpret religious experience, but at the same time to point beyond that experience.

> What is wrong with dogmatic language is that words are taken to be descriptions of the unknowable, which prevents man's proper function. Man functions properly so long as he recognizes the words . . . are to do with neither the unknowable itself nor simply his own attempted description of it but something of both, in which the connection between his understanding and reality is faith—and experience.[12]

Here a clue to the resolution of the dilemma is found. Theology stands on faith; faith relates to experience. Theology that does not reflect faith and connect with experience is deficient.

This means that theology must relate not just to human being, but also to human doing. As an expression of religious knowledge theology is not understandable in merely intellectual terms. Rather, the meaning of the religious claims that theology presents must be discovered in practice.[13] The trueness of what is expressed by theology or religious language can be measured by its effects.[14] It is an existential enterprise. Koyama's repeated quotation of Luther illustrates this existential dimension: "Not reading books or speculating, but living, dying and being damned make a theologian."[15]

The experience of God which theology seeks to convey involves something more than merely intellectual knowing. It involves a passion, an involvement, an effect on the whole person.[16] Statements of belief are thus more statements about a person's commitment than about ultimate reality.[17]

One of the most important ramifications of theology's existential character has to do with the relational quality of theology. For, fundamental to knowledge of God, which is what theology seeks to express, is that such knowledge is mediated via relationship. God is not accessible independently as an object of conceptual apprehension. Rather, God is known through a relational encounter, and as mediated by others.[18] Because religious truth involves something greater than the human mind, relationship is both possible and necessary. Correspondingly, relational knowledge of God is greater than conceptual knowledge of God, and theology which fails to go beyond conceptual language about God fails.

Part of the strength of Koyama's theology rests in his recognition of this fact. Through his emphasis on "neighbourology" Koyama firmly builds the relational dimension into his theology. Christian faith and witness, including theology, Koyama asserts, are critically dependent on an active, kenotic relationship with one's neighbors as well as with the God who is made known historically in the life of Israel and particularly through Jesus and those who follow him.

In general, therefore, theology cannot be confined to a theoretical mode. For, religious truth cannot be easily located in the realm of empirical or factual discourse.[19] Christian theology does not present "a body of timeless truths of reason."[20] Theological language is not neutrally descriptive, but involves those who use it and is thus existential.

Deliberately, theological language goes beyond ordinary discourse. It includes prayer and confession;[21] it claims an indissoluble connection with the transcendent, living reality it seeks to represent.[22] To convey the transcendent, sacramental character of this reality, theology requires not only conceptual language, but symbolic language as well. Though related to the language of science, it must also be metaphysical.[23] It thus maintains within itself the dialectic of subjective knowledge and objective abstraction.[24]

All in all, because of its complex character and requirements, theology must seek a diversity of forms and not succumb to permitting one particular, culturally biased form of theological language to prevail as universally authoritative. For, religious truth transcends any single form.

The Paradoxical Character of Theological Language

A fundamental paradox qualifies all theological assertions. Namely, the center of all theology is not any doctrine but a person. Jesus of Nazareth is the "truth" of Christianity.

Jesus the person is the "absolute antithesis of all abstractions."[25] He is a truth that is, acts, and communicates. He is personal, not abstract.[26] Theology that loses touch with the living, dynamic character of its author and subject becomes defunct. Yet theology itself cannot embody a living person. This is the paradox of theology.

In the New Testament God is present as a person, not a doctrine.[27] There God communicates know-ableness in the paradox of the Incarnation.[28] Accordingly, theology must bear this paradox, attempting to communicate something intrinsically beyond itself.

Christianity thus relates first of all to a particular historic event.[29] Jesus who is the center of that event both comes before and goes beyond all propositions related to him.[30] He becomes the criterion by which the truthfulness of Christian doctrine is evaluated.[31] Nevertheless, while truth is never available as doctrine, but as a person, doctrine is necessarily and instrumentally related to God's Word as ultimate truth.[32] The closer doctrine points to the living Christ, the more accurate and faithful it is.[33]

Koyama has insightfully captured this necessity in his theology of the crucified mind. Christian theology and witness, Koyama maintains, must manifest the Christ-like dynamic of the apostolic life, that is, it must in a living way continually pour itself out for others. In this way theology remains faithful to its purpose.

Perhaps because of his Japanese background, Koyama can better accept the paradoxical nature of religious truth. Coming from a culture that blurs distinctions between objective and subjective, between animate and inanimate, which does not depend upon a base of philosophical rationalism, and which can even posit reason as an obstacle to enlightenment, Koyama cannot only tolerate contradiction but can embrace paradox as a necessary vehicle for religious expression.

At any rate, theology exhibits paradox as it seeks to convey ultimate truth in finite language. It reflects the paradoxical unity of Word and flesh, of transcendent and human. In the end, theology must depend upon God to make the finite capable of carrying the infinite.

Thus, paradox is necessary to theology. That theoretical, systematic theology has difficulty with paradox is inevitable, for such theology seeks definitive, non-contradictory, either-or statements. Paradox, on the other hand, may involve contradiction, ambiguity, illogicality, and "both-and" assertions.

A language perhaps better able to convey the paradoxical truths of Christian faith is the language of image, story, and symbol. That language will be taken up in the next section, after first giving some consideration to the relationship between theology and experience in general.

The Relationship Between Experience and Theology

One problem with the theoretical genre of theology is that it tends to become too far removed from the realm of ordinary experience. In the modern situation of encounter there is a fresh awareness that theology needs to more closely reflect and relate to personal experience. This is true not only for Christians in Asia, Africa, and Latin America who seek to construct theology relevant to their own experiential context, but also for Europeans who feel that the theology they have inherited is too entrenched in the experiences and ideas of the past.[34]

Theology formulated predominantly in the European framework, of course, reflects only the experiences of Europeans. Moreover, it reflects the dominant European attitudes toward experience, which may be different from attitudes of people elsewhere. Consequently, in the modern global framework, there is a need to reconsider the role and value of experience in relation to Christian theology. There is a need "to connect the meaning of theological ideas with human experience and to show their bearing on the life of each individual."[35]

Of course, Scripture itself is the product of experience. It is the story both of particular human experiences and of human interpretations of those experiences. The stories of Genesis, the records of Israel's national history, the historical dating and content of prophetic writings, the accounts of Jesus' life and ministry—all of these are built around particular human experiences. Overwhelmingly, the Bible is an experiential story book, not an abstract philosophical treatise. Likewise, Christian doctrine, church history, and even systematic theology are the products of experience—not only of those experiences presented by Scripture, but also of the experiences of later believers.[36]

In the ebb and flow of church history there have, however, been varying understandings of the relationship between theology and experience. With the Reformers, for example, this issue received special attention. In a sense, they "discovered the role of experience as the key to understanding in religion."[37] Luther, for one, saw an essential connection between the experience of the individual and the basic meaning of Christian doctrine. Indeed, for Luther and Calvin personal experience played a formative role in initiating as well as in formulating their theology.[38]

Unfortunately, later Protestantism lost much of their experiential insight.[39] On the one hand, their appreciation of personal experience was turned into a preoccupation with private piety disconnected from the balancing influence of inherited Christian doctrine and wider Christian community. On the other hand, much of Protestantism rejected personal experience as "insubstantial, unstable, evanescent, subjective,"[40] and otherwise to be held in low esteem.

More recently, experience has again become a focal point for Christian theology, particularly as some Third World theologians endeavor to construct theology expressive of and appropriate to their own socio-political experience, or, to their own cultural context. But, as mentioned earlier, a dissatisfaction with abstract doctrines is turning some European Christians, too, towards a more consciously experience-orientated theology, as apparent in the view that "only through an experiential medium can we hope to recover a sense of the reality expressed through Christian ideas."[41]

However, connecting theology and experience is problematic for several reasons. For one thing, there is the danger of theology being circumscribed by subjective experience. This happens, for example, when a given set of personal experiences become the authoritative criteria of faith and critical evaluation is disallowed. Theology in this circumstance is stillborn.

It was partially the criticism that the Lutheran faith was merely built upon the private, questionable experience of one man that pushed many Protestants into a rigid emphasis on doctrines, creeds and confessions.[42] Yet, many other Protestants continued to pursue an unbalanced emphasis on personal experience, piety and morality.

Luther himself realized that experience could not be equated with faith, however. While faith is experiential—faith "is" not experience, but it "is experienced"—and while the experience that itself flows from faith is indeed a criterion for faith, faith nevertheless refers to something more than just experience.[43]

> Faith is oriented toward Christ, hence not to something that belongs to objective experience . . . Being oriented to Christ means removal from all objective experience.[44]

Theology, which seeks to articulate faith, thus faces the recurring paradox of having to express something beyond experience. It cannot be circumscribed by a given set of personal experiences, but must convey reality which transcends all experience. This is a primary problem in connecting theology and experience.

Related to the theological problem of making personal experience normative is the theological problem of making social experience normative, as evident in much of recent liberation theology. There again, one experiential perspective is tendered as a faith criterion for all Christians.

Gerhard Sauter offers a thoughtful critique of this development.[45] Sauter questions the degree to which particular, contextual, experience-centered theologies can be universal, or, relevant to the whole church. More pointedly, Sauter asks, can they be critically evaluated by Scripture and tradition when they often deliberately marginalize Scripture and tradition? "How grievously we falsify the witness of the Bible by making a theology of our own area of experience."[46]

Sauter goes on to argue that it is an impoverishment of theology and of ecumenical dialogue when certain biblical situations, turned into stereotypes, dominate Christian theology. That happens when present concerns and contexts are read into Scripture in a way which ignores centuries of experience and misses much of the biblical message.[47]

Scripture, Sauter says, does not provide an authoritative set of experiences by which to measure theological truth in all times. Thus, Sauter suggests, "the less we attach profound interpretation to our experiences, the more likely these experiences are to advance our theological understanding."[48]

In contrast, Koyama might argue that attaching profound interpretations to personal experiences may greatly enhance faith—as Koyama has done with his own experiences and as he advocates others doing. But Koyama would certainly agree with Sauter's main thrust—that the absolutization of one set of experiences as authoritative or normative for all other Christians is grievously mistaken, if not, as Koyama does not hesitate to say, actually idolatrous. Of course, Koyama is an ardent advocate of experience-based theology. But for Koyama experience is always a tool of theology, not its essence or end. Consistently Koyama places experience in the light of Scripture, finally subjecting all experience and theology to the pattern of the Crucified Mind.

Although speaking from the milieu of Asian experience, a milieu which dominates his concern, Koyama nevertheless does not absolutize Asian experience. Of course, the vastness and diversity of Asian experience would prevent the facile simplification necessary to any absolutization. But Koyama resists taking even one stream of Asian experience as theologically normative.

Yet the way in which Koyama's theology is composed, at least in its autobiographical sections, makes another of Sauter's observations worth noting. Sauter points out that one of the dangers of formulating theology too much in experiential terms is that of theology becoming biography, with theologians being their own subject.[49] Koyama might indeed run this risk were it not for the fact that the experiences to which his theology refer are so wide-ranging, often not his, and always subject to a standard greater than himself, that is, Scripture and the Crucified Mind. The diversity, Christocentricity, and missionary nature of Koyama's theology so far keep it from being simply self-centered autobiography.

Inevitably, Christian theology must continually reflect and come to terms with human experience. "Theology always moves in a dialectical tension between the pole of identifying what is specifically Christian and the pole of integrating the common world of human experience into the Christian reality."[50] Certainly, theology that is not rooted in experience is out of touch with the basis of religious knowledge.[51] Revelation itself depends on human experience for its intelligibility; that is, its meaningfulness to some extent depends on existing frameworks of human experience and reflection.[52]

In the modern situation of encounter there is a renewed sense of the need for theology to express experience. To create a language appropriate to the modern situation of encounter, theology must rid itself of the "ingrained tendency to seek exclusively for eternally valid theological ideas."[53] Rather, Christian theology in the modern situation of encounter needs to abandon abstracts and absolutes to seek "middle distances."[54] Essential to this task are the development of alternative theological languages and recognition of their legitimacy and value. In the following sections, some dimensions of an alternative theological language are considered.

Symbolic Language in Theology

Language is by nature symbolic. Words, whether vocal or visual, signify something beyond themselves, for example, objects, experiences and ideas. At a more explicit level language functions symbolically via myth, metaphor, simile, parable, image, and the like. Because ordinary objective language is inadequate for expressing the totality of human experience, such symbolic forms are necessary. Symbols point human consciousness beyond the limits of familiar categories and experiences. Symbols carry consciousness past the paradoxical impossibility of expressing the extraordinary in ordinary terms.

Theological language is symbolic by nature. In origin and intention it refers to something beyond the limits of ordinary human categories and concepts. To speak about God, symbolic language is essential.[55] In the sense that all talk of God must by definition be indirect, it may thus be more appropriate to always speak of theology as symbolic rather than as definitive or dogmatic.[56] Likewise, it is intrinsically a mistake to define theology primarily in systematic terms when its essence is beyond categorization or systematization. But most important is that symbolic language does communicate reality. It is not empty, illusory language, but sheds light on actual experiences and situations.[57]

Christian Scripture, of course, is deeply dependent upon symbolic language. Scripture abounds with myth, metaphor, simile, parable, image, and allegory.[58] Throughout Christian history Christian liturgy, art and literature have made extensive use not only of the symbols of Scripture, but also of the symbols of Christian tradition. More recent theology has turned away somewhat from the richness of symbolic language, adapting instead to an environment obsessed with rationalism and scientific language. While this shift is most obvious in the general emphasis on sophisticated systematic theology, it is also apparent in specific topical discussions, for example, on the meaning and function of myth in Christian faith.

In an age predisposed towards "scientific" criteria of truth, much of Scripture is regarded as myth which cannot be considered as true or relevant today except in analogous, existential terms.[59] "We ourselves live in a post-mythical age . . . modern man finds that myth does not communicate to him."[60]

That myth, however, remains an integral part of human communication and understanding—even within the world of modern technology—has been convincingly argued by Walter J. Hollenweger.[61] Myth, Hollenweger argues, is fundamental to human being and indispensable for every kind of communication.[62]

In general, theology must rediscover the necessity and validity not only of myth, but of symbolic language in all its dimensions. For, symbolic language speaks with an authority of which scientific language is incapable. It shows meaning in a way that argument cannot.[63]

Koyama has understood the necessity and capability of symbolic language in theology. His images carry the reader beyond the pale of scientific, systematic understanding. His "koan-like jabs"[64] stimulate the reader to both prayerful meditation and moving personal insight. As one review has put it, Koyama provides kaleidoscopic reflections that both challenge and comfort his readers.

> There is a unique flex in the hand that turns this kaleidoscope, a twist of the wrist that leaves the reader in a curious melange of disturbance and delight.[65]

Koyama's image-rich theology thus illustrates the potential of symbolism for affecting people at a deeper level than that associated with systematic, theoretical theology. Indeed, images can work on a number of levels, triggering different responses at different times and in different contexts.

That in fact images may provoke different responses from different people, or that different people may have different relationships to or interpretations of the same set of images Koyama sees as part of the potential of image-theology. For, imagery—a basic and familiar form of communication for all human beings—can serve as a tool for dialogue amidst the limitless diversity of the modern framework.

Indeed, one of the obvious advantages of symbolism in theology is its cross-cultural potential. Myths and symbols are more readily transferable or communicable from one framework to another, one experience to another[66] than is, for example, theoretical theology, which requires a transference of a mass of educational and cultural data to provide the context and methodology of even the terms being employed.

Finally, symbolism is open-ended. It does not seek a deliberate narrowness of meaning as does systematic theology. It can therefore achieve a more personal and lasting dialogue with its recipient. The comment of one reviewer of a Koyama book illustrates this possibility.

> The 119 pages of this volume may require another 500 pages or so of your own as you carry through his study and apply his metaphors to your own life.[67]

The theological metaphors which Koyama creates may be uniquely a product of and a contribution to Christianity in an Asian environment. Yet, Koyama's metaphors themselves have already reached and affected the West. Thus, Koyama's particular work in an Asian context illustrates the value and potential of pursuing such an alternative genre of theology for Christianity as a whole. In the modern situation of encounter this rediscovering and development of symbolic language in theology can enhance and revitalize much of Christian theology

Story in Theology

Story-telling is a central feature of human communication. It is far more ancient and basic than written, theoretical communication. Naturally, the form and function of stories may vary. Myth, history, autobiography, and fiction—each of these is, in its own way, story. The important point is that stories are an enduring, viable and necessary method of human thinking and communication.

Stories give coherent shape to human experience.[68] They interpret life and convey meaning. Through symbolism stories can make the abstract understandable, the unknown familiar, and the difficult digestible.[69] Even fictional stories may convey truth, for example, moral truth. Above all, stories by design perpetuate tradition, and in so doing create, organize, and preserve human communities.[70]

Christianity itself is founded upon stories. Genesis, Exodus, the historical accounts of Israel, the Gospels, the Acts—these are but the more explicit examples of the Scriptural stories upon which Christianity is based. Behind the stories sophisticated reflection may often be found. But overwhelmingly, story is the primary medium by which the biblical message is communicated. Accordingly, Christianity remains radically dependent upon this narrative mode of communication.[71]

The institutional church, however, has often had to struggle with this fact. On the one hand, the early church depended upon its inherited stories too much to ignore or deny them.[72] But to establish and preserve itself as an institution, the church needed to codify, organize and "doctrinize" these stories. In the process Scripture came to be treated as a collection of facts or moral truths rather than stories—a perspective which continued long afterwards.[73] The Church as an institution, uncomfortable with poems and stories, presented the Bible as a set of literal truths or moral guidelines, often taking it in bits rather than as a whole.[74]

To be sure, Scripture itself presents a diversity of forms besides stories and poems.[75] Also within Scripture are creeds, legal codes and propositional statements. Understandably, the church was caught between its institutional needs, the ambiguity and diversity of Scripture, and the apologetic demands of its surrounding context. But in adapting to the complexities of its changing environment, the church often became unfaithful to its own tradition and message, becoming in a sense, the denier of Christ[76] (see Koyama's criticisms of the crusading church, for example, *No Handle on the Cross*, pp. 98–109). Yet the church has at the same time remained that framework which preserves "the truth of the story, the history, the art, the secret."[77]

In the modern context of encounter the story again emerges as a crucial medium for Christian theology. Like the myths and symbols which it includes, story-theology holds a cross-cultural potential lacking in abstract theoretical theology. At the same time, story-theology allows for directly integrating experience into theology—a critical requirement for any living theology, but especially for the modern context with its enormous diversity of experiences.

Another advantage of the use of story in theology is its universal familiarity as a tool for thinking and communicating. Nearly all people, whether Christian or not, can interact with a story. Many cultures outside the European philosophical-technological milieu seem particularly able to appreciate and utilize the story form. However, Europeans, too, incorporate it into their daily life, whether through the arts (including television), politics, religion, or social rituals.

Stories in theology, as W. J. Hollenweger points out in a discussion of narrative exegesis, have a variety of advantages and disadvantages. The multi-dimensional character of narrative theology can communicate to different people on different levels at the same time. Different points of view can be brought into interplay simultaneously.[78] However, a certain degree of ambiguity and a possible lack of definitive resolution to the dialogue are inevitably part of such narrative theology.

Another advantage of story-theology is its sustainability. Theoretical theology, or theology based on a chain of inter-dependent arguments, is only as strong as its weakest link. If a portion of it is not grasped, the whole of it may be misunderstood. In contrast, a story can generally communicate and be understood even where particular details are unfamiliar, lost, or changed.[79] In a similar manner, stories can communicate more freely over significant periods of time, whereas propositions are often circumscribed by particular historical and philosophical frameworks.

Closely related to the whole matter of story in theology is the question of authority of form. By nature, stories carry their own sort of authority. It is a rather recent and deceptive development that authority is seen as resting primarily in scientifically framed propositions. Particularly, it is ironic and misleading that Christian theology, derived originally from a set of stories, should be seduced by the notion that systematic, theoretical language carries greater authority than the language of story.

As previously noted, Scripture itself is not a set of arguments, but more a collection of stories, poems and visions, having the kind of authority that accrues to experience, art and image. "The Bible's authority depends on something intrinsic."[80] In the modern situation of encounter, it is one of the challenges to Christian theology that it should dare to trust the authority of stories in its composition.

Next, the dialogical potential of story-theology should be pointed out. For, in the modern situation of encounter one of the most urgent needs for Christian theology is a dialogical orientation. The proclamatory approach for expressing Christian faith—that of simply stating personal or institutional positions, often without a spirit of humility or love—tends to alienate the majority of humanity with whom the Christian minority is now so fully in contact. What is needed today, rather, is a dialogical expression of faith. Theology needs more to "converse with" people— both Christians and non-Christians—as Jesus conversed with his hearers.[81] Put another way, "We must begin to understand evangelism dialogically."[82]

To do so requires a theology that "starts from the spiritual situation of the hearer and is addressed to it,"[83] a theology that enters into a conversation between Christian and non-Christian, listening to the non-believer's questions and structuring itself in the terms of the non-believer's world.[84]

Christian theology finds a ready resource for this task in the medium of the story. New Testament evangelism, after all, was not embodied in propositional statements.[85] Rather, the New Testament conveys the origin and expansion of Christian faith in terms of stories, especially in the Book of Acts. The records of the early Christian community contain stories in which the listener was involved, stories which grew out of specific questions and concrete circumstances.[86] Just as the evangelistic experiences of the early church were themselves dialogical and relational, so was the form in which these experiences were related and preserved, namely, the story form.

Theology today can benefit from recovering this biblical pattern. The story form is intrinsically participatory—far more so than the systematic, theoretical genre of theology. Stories readily provide a medium in which the experiences of different cultures and contexts can meet. Stories can be built around specific questions and circumstances while at the same time exposing those questions and circumstances to discussion from several different points of view. Also, within stories are contact points for discovering common experiences.

Koyama has adroitly understood and developed the story as a tool for theology. Indeed, as has been mentioned, he sees theology at its best to be an invitation to people to create a story of their own,[87] a story emerging from the dialogue between their own experience and the stories of Scripture.

Certainly, Koyama's Asian instincts and the demands of work in an Asian context have spawned and shaped his propensity towards story-theology. Yet it needs also to be re-stated that he had alternatives. He could have employed Western systematic theological forms and topics as have some of his Asian colleagues.

Yet, Koyama's dedication to contextual theology and to neighbourological theology, with its deliberate emphasis on dialogue and relationship, found its most natural expression in the vehicle of story or narrative theology.

Such theology, it should be noted, in no way involves a sacrifice in quality or scholarship. As Koyama's own work attests, extensive "homework"[88] is a necessary part of such theology. W. J. Hollenweger emphasizes this point as well. It is his ambition to

> develop a method of theology which does not give up its commitment to critical exegesis while using the mode of narration.

If such exegesis . . . is to be of any value, it cannot be any less scholarly than other forms of exegesis. The critical element of exegesis and theology must not be sacrificed.[89]

Through their development of story-theology Koyama and Hollenweger both expertly illustrate that scholarship—applied to both the original and the contemporary context—"is only the threshold of interpretation."[90]

The need for story-theology is increasingly discernable. Its complementary role alongside theoretical theology will be further considered in a subsequent portion of this chapter. Before that, some of Koyama's specific observations about story and systematic theology will be presented, along with a few more remarks from Koyama's critics.

Koyama and Systematics

"I have a certain amount of distrust of doctrine,"[91] says Koyama. To this remark Koyama quickly adds that he is not therefore actually hostile towards theological doctrine. Rather, his concern is "to make doctrine exciting."[92] Koyama pursues this by seeking to "critically expand" doctrine via imagery. Concrete images, which bring out the action behind the idea, he proposes, are the key to understanding and appreciating Christian doctrine.[93]

Koyama supports this perspective by appealing to the teachings of Jesus. Jesus' sayings, Koyama points out, were not doctrinally structured. Rather, they were dialogical, situational, or, as it were, "ad hoc."[94] While recognizing that doctrine is a useful way of arranging certain experiences, Koyama nevertheless notes that formulating doctrine is not a "front-line" exercise. Doctrine is the product of reflection from a distance. Jesus, on the other hand, was engaged in "front-line" situations that necessitated utilizing the images, materials, and circumstances immediately at hand to present his message.[95]

Likewise, in the Old Testament—the form and language of which Koyama feels a strong affinity towards[96]—Koyama points out that even the doctrines embodied there, such as the doctrine of the covenant, were communicated in the form of story and image. The shaping of doctrine in conceptual terms is, Koyama states, a secondary activity, useful and necessary, but secondary to experience.[97] Unfortunately, reflections on experience can easily become abstract and unrelated to experience. Images, as a theological tool, can provide a fresher, closer association with the original experience.

However, images, too, Koyama adds, must be critically evaluated. To ensure that they are faithful and to prevent them from taking on demonic dimensions it is necessary to check them with one's own experience, with the Christian community past and present, and above all with Scripture.[98]

This qualification in the use of imagery makes it clear that Koyama is not an entirely unsystematic thinker but one who does in fact understand the importance of organized, critical thinking. Indeed, Koyama asserts that no one is born into a conceptual vacuum; nor does anyone create a completely original theological system. Rather, we all "jump in" to already existing systems in which we then proceed to formulate our own particular story.[99] What is unique and opportune about today's world—for Koyama as well as for others—is that there are a wider variety of frameworks from which to draw in formulating theology. Koyama has himself "jumped into" systems from both East and West and utilizes both in his theology.

Yet Koyama adds that what is known of the Holy Spirit indicates that the Holy Spirit acts regardless of human theological systems. Therefore following the Holy Spirit requires a readiness to "jump in unprepared" without a one hundred percent perfect system.[100] Koyama speaks of the need for Christians to have a "pneumatic system," or one which enables openness, flexibility, and a variety of mediums.[101]

At the same time, Koyama emphasizes that the biblical picture is of a God who acts through what is imperfect and broken—through what is weak and foolish by human standards. Western Christianity's preoccupation with systems, its "obsession with analysis,"[102] Koyama finds disturbing. He understands that, faced with the powerful efficiency of the secular, non-believing world, or what he describes as the efficiency of Baal, there is a natural desire to seek equally powerful, efficient systems. But he contrasts this desire with the insight of Paul who maintained that God does not need the strength of human systems to accomplish divine purposes.[103]

An emphasis on theological systems and programs has intrinsic drawbacks and limitations. First of all, can theological analysis ever be objective or comprehensive? Koyama doubts it. Secondly, an emphasis on systematic theology tends to suffocate those Christians, for example in Asia, whose theology develops in stories and sermons, or which is done more by groups than by individuals. Third, the cognitive, systematic approach to theology exhibits an element of "handle-mindedness" which conflicts with the kenotic, self-denying mode of God's self-presentation. Fourthly, there is a practical frustration with the bureaucratic effects of a church which emphasizes efficient organization and programs. Koyama laments the energy that goes into institutional "subsections, subsections, subsections . . . position papers, position papers, position papers" in a world that challenges Christianity not only to dramatic action in the face of human suffering but also to a deeper encounter with the overwhelming numbers of people who do not subscribe to the Christian faith.[104]

This is not to say that Koyama would disband the institutional church. But Koyama's attitude towards the institutional church may in part reflect the influence of Uchimura Kanzo, who did in fact seek to chart a course away from the traditional church institution. Certainly, Koyama's overall impatience with systematic, deductive reasoning derives partially from Japanese culture where theoretical reasoning never has been as important as intuition.[105]

Yet Koyama's view of systems also reflects a wider grasp of theological necessity in the modern situation of encounter. For, all systems come into question in such a context. Also, broader understandings of theological systems arise. Koyama, for example, argues that when one is committed to something, some kind of system will naturally emerge. It may not be systematic. Images, for instance, can constitute a system, too. But whether a system is one of images or of theoretical discourse, it will reflect certain commitments and underlying understandings of reality.[106]

Not surprisingly, Koyama draws frequent criticism for not adapting his theology to the dominant understanding of systematic theology. One Asian colleague, frustrated by Koyama's style and scope, remarks,

I wish that Koyama would take time, however, to bring bits of his insights together and present a unified, systematic treatise on a specific topic in depth.[107]

A European of similar persuasion says,

Someone is bound to ask, however, whether the time has come for the author to attempt a more in-depth analysis of a particular theological issue, or a more detailed examination of some of the ongoing problems of Asian societies today . . . one also hopes that Koyama will bring to the fore his other skills for sustained and careful analysis.[108]

Koyama himself has said that someday he may set about more traditional, systematic work.[109] But so far, his choice of style has been deliberate, as several observers recognize. Koyama's intense concern for contextual theology and his "bias against the abstract means that he could not choose a systematic [and in the ordinary sense of the word] a coherent approach for his theology."[110] "A student of Luther and influenced by Uchimura, the Japanese Kierkegaard, Koyama steadfastly evades the systematic."[111]

In a sense, Koyama is a missionary for alternative approaches to theology. His Asian background and broad missionary exposure in Asia inspire and equip him for this undertaking. On the one hand he is perhaps a forerunner to future Asian theology. "His books are prolegomena to an Asian theology rather than mature pieces of such a theology (Justin Martyr rather than Athanasius . . .)."[112] He is a reminder that indigenous theology develops slowly as it addresses an environment as complex as that of Asia. Yet, Koyama also provides a challenge to the West. His theology raises questions as to how theology in pluralistic societies—in both East and West—should be formulated. He provokes the question: is theology in the West as arrogant, superficial and crucifying as it was in parts of Asia?[113]

In the modern context Koyama believes that theology must be expansive and adventurous. There are other ways to do theology than as it has been done in the West. There are other standards of excellence in Christian theology and human communication than those represented by footnotes and academic position papers.[114]

Above all, Koyama is concerned that theology embody the spirituality described in Scripture. Just as the Gospel is not a proposition but an event, as it is a story of God's dialogical, relational, kenotic encounter with humanity, so should theology seek to incarnate in both form and content a spirit of dialogue, openness and humility. Dogmatic, theoretical theology abstracted from personal relationship and human experience cannot accomplish this. Story-theology, on the other hand, both incorporates experience and invites participation. As a readily understandable, widely accepted medium of communication, the story form of theology thus constitutes a promising theological language for the modern situation of encounter.

The Interface of Story and Theory

Having set out to contrast the systematic, theoretical genre of theology with the narrative, symbolic, genre of theology, and having argued the value and need for the latter in the modern situation of encounter, it should also be stated that these two theological languages or genres are in the end complementary and interdependent.

Scripture, as has been mentioned, actually contains both story and proposition. Within Scripture's predominantly narrative framework are doctrines, codes, and creeds—developed in the Hebrew tradition and also in a preliminary form by the early Christian community. Scripture's composition illustrates that story and proposition are interdependent. Stories carry propositions. Propositions grow out of stories.

In a wider sense doctrinal proposition are themselves stories. For, to be fully understood they must be considered within the context of how they were shaped, by whom, in what cultural context, and for what purpose. Christian dogmas represent the story of the Christian church—how its thought developed in particular periods and contexts.

Both stories and propositions therefore are necessary to theology. As mentioned already, theology needs a multiplicity of forms or languages. Especially in the modern context of encounter a balance of forms is particularly important. Bishop Lesslie Newbigin points out the need for dialogue between the two kinds of theology so evident in the Third World, namely, that which exists in the books and languages of the European heritage and that which is embodied in song, story, preaching, catechesis, and drama.[115] There is a great need for the two to meet—not only in the Third World, but everywhere. For if they do not come together in dialogue, all theological debate will become increasingly empty and one-sided.[116] The Church today, as Harold Ditmanson puts it,

> requires both testimony and theology. We will have to live with two rather different modes of thought—the pictorial and the abstract, the dramatic and the analytical—and seek ways to cope with their incompatibility for the sake of a witness that is authentic, intelligible, and capable of communicating with the culture of our times . . . Reality is so rich and human experience so complex that we must tell at least two "stories" if we are to avoid reducing our grasp of things to a false simplicity.[117]

Today there is a nascent awareness that Western theology, having defined theology in its own philosophical and cultural terms, is too narrow, myopic, and even ethnocentric.

> The entire church should let itself be enriched by the theologies of the Third World, even though at this point, Westerners may not recognize them as theologies. Such a step would, of course, require admitting that we are not "Number One."[118]

Koyama frames this discussion in even wider terms. He speaks of the psycho-cultural milieu that shapes human thinking. Western theology he argues, arose out of a perspective that is alien to most of the world. While valid and significant in its own way, this perspective, he asserts, needs to be informed by the differing per-spectives of the great majority of humanity. In Koyama's unique terminology, "theology built upon the primary fascination of the mystery of discontinuity" needs to enter dialogue with "theology built upon the primary fascination of the mystery of continuity."[119] The "eschatological Moses" and the "cosmological Aaron" need each other.

Put in other terms, Koyama, too, is speaking of the need for theology to include the wider wealth of human understanding and experience: inductive as well as deductive thinking; story as well as proposition; concrete experience as well as abstract idea, and so on.

Traditional, dogmatic theology as shaped in the European mold will continue to be necessary and useful both historically and as a guide to future theology. System-atic theology will not be entirely displaced by the development of alternative theo-logical languages. But, as one Asian theologian notes, the church in the future might not give the same weight to systematic theology as in the past. Systematic theology may be a necessary theological language, but one of secondary importance.[120]

On a wider scale, systematic theology in a universal sense is obviously impossi-ble. There is no universal framework, no absolute set of concepts or experiences by which Christianity can be defined. There is, rather, relativity—in Scripture itself, in Christian history, and in the diverse contexts in which Christianity finds itself today.

At best there are multiple systems in which Christianity can be framed. Previ-ously, Christian theology was framed in the philosophical heritage of Europe. In the future Christian theology might equally find systematic expression in Hindu or Chinese philosophical frameworks. Instead of describing God in Greek terms such as "logos" or "homo-ousias," Christian theology as a whole might turn to speaking of God as "atma" or in "yin-yang" terminology as some Christians already do.[121]

To be sure, Christianity will always be expressed in some sort of systematic terms, for all languages and cultures employ some form of systematic organization of thought. Except perhaps in mysticism, human experience will always depend on theoretical language for expression to some degree. Doctrinal structures will con-tinue to provide the framework for the living words of experience and faith. But a balanced framework is one which includes stories, images, symbols, and the like as an integral part of it. At times it may be difficult and always it will be somewhat artificial to differentiate between story and system. For each includes the other. Certainly, to be faithful, stories need to be informed by doctrine. Doctrine, for its part, needs to be kept alive by story.

Even Koyama's theology is a mixture of story and proposition. His theology of the Crucified Mind, of the apostolic life, of non-handling spirituality, of cosmological thinking—all of these ideas can be thought of and expressed as specific propositions. But it is their living form, shaped by story, intricately informed by Scripture, and in dialogue with a multiplicity of images and situations, that makes them so effective. Thus they provide a model for intercultural theology in the modern context.

CONCLUSION

The Koyama mixture provides a disturbing new flavour of
Christian thought for Western readers. This is partly due to the
difficulty Koyama poses when we try to fit him into our usual
ways of doing theology . . . the problem (for Westerners, at least)
is finding a point of entry into this baffling Koyama world.[1]

The preceding chapters have sought to provide various points of entry into the
"baffling Koyama world." Koyama's personal background has been outlined,
along with the Japanese and Asian context from which he comes. Key themes of
his theology have been presented, along with evaluations of his Crucified Mind
theology and his theology of other religions. Finally, the value of his theological
style has been explored in the context of narrative and theoretical theological
languages.

To round out this presentation of Kosuke Koyama and his theology two tasks
remain. First, some general questions about Koyama's overall contribution can be
raised. Secondly, it is helpful to finally consider Koyama's contribution from the
point of view of missionary theology in the modern intercultural milieu referred to
at the beginning of this undertaking.

General Questions

A variety of questions remain regarding Koyama's own theology and his value
as a model for intercultural theology. Many of these questions have as yet no con-
clusive answer.

To what degree Koyama is simply a product of his time and culture and to what
degree he transcends them are open questions, as is the case with any theologian.
That some of Koyama's emphasis on self-denial, on Theology of the Cross, and
openness to other religions is partially a product of his Japanese cultural background and of the minority status of Christianity in Asia has already been mentioned. The more one reads Koyama, the clearer it becomes that he does indeed
give the most attention to concerns that dominate general Asian theology, such as
the meaning of suffering, the encounter with other religions, contextualization, militarism, and the impact of Western culture and technology.

One might wonder how Koyama's theology has affected the Japanese or Asian
church and whether because of his ecclesiastical roots there he may be taken to

represent a Third World theologian. Again, some comments in this regard have been made earlier, both in reference to Koyama's practical labors in the Southeast Asian theological education system and as to his lack of recognition in Japan, where he has not actually lived for many years.

Despite his Asian background, Koyama does not neatly fit into the Third World Theologian category, especially since for the last twenty years he has lived and taught in Western contexts, and since Japan itself, for that matter, is no longer considered a Third World country.

As far as Thailand is concerned, it is difficult to judge the impact of Koyama's work there. Individuals he knew and taught could certainly evaluate his personal influence, and his involvement in Buddhist-Christian dialogue can be documented in articles that grew out of such encounters. However, Koyama's time and efforts in Thailand were, after all, limited. He did not become a life-long missionary there. His main works on Buddhism and on a Christian approach to other religions appeared after he left Thailand.

Koyama's work and intentions transcend that local situation, valuable though it might be after twenty years now to return to Thailand to search out clues to his contribution there. But again, it must be noted that this period of his life constituted the first phase of his career; it was very much a time for personal growth and development, preceding the bulk of his published work.

A more useful question to pursue, perhaps, is how Koyama's experiences and conclusions, including those gained in Thailand, serve as an example for others. How transferable is Koyama's theology in style and content? Can others utilize the same methods? Or, is Koyama's style too idiosyncratic to reproduce?

Realistically, Koyama's style is unique. The Japanese linguistic and cultural base from which he operates, combined with Koyama's own creative gifts, would be nearly impossible to duplicate. However, there are two dimensions of his method from which others might benefit. One, as described at length already, lies in the application of a narrative style in theology. The other, which enables such narrative theology to take shape, includes a thorough study of one's own culture and the culture to which one hopes to speak.

Koyama's emphasis on and examination of local culture and religion—Japan's, Thailand's or that elsewhere—is fundamental preparation for relevant theology. Recent Western theology has perhaps paid too little attention to the cultures which surround it. Western theologians, among others, might learn from Koyama's example how to re-evaluate primary values and suppositions in their surrounding cultures. This will require a certain sense for theological adventure, a willingness to break new ground as Koyama attempts to do.

What this requires at some point is a certain detachment from the surrounding culture(s). Since this is often not easy to accomplish, the value of listening to an outsider, e.g., a missionary, becomes clear. This indeed illustrates one of the primary advantages and values of having cross-cultural missionaries. To some extent all theologians are called to be "outsiders" in their surrounding cultures. They naturally need an intimate knowledge of the culture(s) they wish to address, but also a prophetic distance. For achieving this an open dialogue with other theologians and "missionaries" is essential.

For Koyama this is sometimes an easier process than it might be for Western theologians. For, Koyama has worked in and addressed cultures that were overtly non-Christian. As any missionary must do in such a context, Koyama has sought to develop conceptual and linguistic tools for conveying Christian faith. Asia as a whole does not know of Jesus Christ. Traditional Christian theological presuppositions cannot be readily presumed. The fundamental missionary task in such a context is to translate the necessary terms and concepts of Christian belief into relevant terms for one's audience.

In Western society where traditional Christian presuppositions have also been eroded, it may be time to pursue a similar process. Koyama's missionary example may illustrate for others an experimental process by which the Christian message may be tested, communicated, and contextualized. This would constitute useful modeling on Koyama's part.

In that sense, Koyama is not so much simply a representative of Asian theology but a bridge between East and West. He is something of a "hybrid," a product of both worlds. While the price paid for that is a degree of homelessness in each and sometimes outright rejection, he nevertheless is widely admired by members of both households. Thus, in both his person and his theology he can represent one to the other while calling them both to a larger perspective. The fact that he does not absolutize any one situation or get caught up in single issue theologies or common theological fads adds to his value as a bridge person between East and West.

A few other questions remain as to Koyama's theology. One of the difficult ones is whether or not his assumption of such universal values as love, self-denial or greed can be confirmed. By what criteria it could be decided that such universal values or experiences exist as common reference points is uncertain. Any such evaluation would involve a certain subjective or confessional perspective not entirely available to objective analysis. Once again the proof can only be in the pudding; the validity of Koyama's theology resides in its existential reception.

Another set of questions that can be raised concern Koyama's use of Scripture. What exegetical methods does he use? Does he not use Scripture too loosely at times, fitting it to the points he wants to make without revealing his guiding interpretive principles?

To be sure, Koyama uses Scripture extensively in his writing. At times he seems to take Scripture at face value, using it in a somewhat literal fashion. At other times, he applies common Western exegetical techniques. To Western minds more clarification and consistency might be desirable.

But the question might be raised as to the primacy of Western methods and attitudes. Are there not other valid ways of utilizing or interpreting Scripture than those deemed best by many Westerners? The Bible is not, after all, an intrinsically Western book. Its stories may resonate to the Asian mind in ways different from those in the West. This is not to denigrate the value of sound exegesis. Nor does Koyama underestimate the contributions of Western academics to Christian theology. But he may represent the capacity for a multi-faceted approach to Scripture as modeled by an Asian mind.

Another question that needs mention in passing is whether or not Koyama's theology is simplistic. Does his appealing, narrative style merely cloak a superficial approach to issues that are actually quite complex? Or, is his theology better understood as "poetic theology" in the sense that while good poetry may on the surface appear simple and merely clever, in reality it is the product of great effort and discipline? Music offers a similar parallel. A beautiful melody or appealing arrangement may seem simple enough at first hearing, but usually builds on a complex structure and sensitivity underneath, honed by years of practice on the part of the performer(s).

Whether Koyama's theology is taken as simple or complex will depend to some extent on the perspective and knowledge of the perceiver. Those more familiar with the Asian scene and those who take time to read Koyama more thoroughly and more than once may well find an unexpected depth to him.

To be sure, Koyama writes for the times in which he lives. It is part of his missionary commitment to produce a theology in which people from diverse backgrounds can see themselves and their concerns reflected. Sometimes he succeeds at this task; sometimes he does not. But part of that commitment means writing in a simple, sometimes almost "journalistic" style, although Koyama has also put considerable effort in more recent years into more specialized theology for use by his academic peers.

There may in fact be advantages in the modern context to more deliberately moving towards overtly simplified and provisional theology, shedding the illusion that any given theological formulation is an unchangeable statement of eternal truth. After all, all theology is to some extent a commentary on the times in which it is written and its value is often more short-term than permanent. It may often be a false assumption that traditional systematic theology is as objectively neutral and timeless as some might assume. In the long-run a blend of both simple and sophisticated theological styles may be most appropriate for the overall task of intercultural theology.

Finally, it must be remembered that Koyama's theology is still "in process." The final sum of his work may be greater than particular parts. In the meantime, Koyama's theology can be taken as the offering of one man, unique in both style and perspective.

Accordingly, Koyama's theology faces all the problems that any theology does, especially as a theology based on and emphasizing experience. It is by nature limited, partial, and in need of being informed by theologies derived from the experiences of others. Insofar as Koyama's theology already comes from and incorporates into itself an unusually wide spectrum of experience, it can inform other theologies of a more limited base. At the very least, Koyama represents an "over-against-which," an alternative that others in the global context may consider in the development of their own theological style and content. In that sense, he can prove to be an interesting and perhaps most challenging model.

Missionary Theology

This study began with an emphasis on the current context of encounter. It is fitting as part of the conclusion to focus again on that context.

Cross-cultural and inter-faith encounter is an existential reality for most Christians today. It is part of their concrete daily existence, whether that is always consciously recognized or not. Koyama is therefore correct in focusing on the experiential dimension of encounter through his focus on "neighbourology" and in developing a usable pattern for Christians to refer to (the Crucified Mind) in their encounter with fellow members of the global human family.

Theology in this encounter context must be attuned to the apologetic challenges which that context presents. The kinds of theology that best suit this global context will need much further exploration. The deep diversity of the regions and cultures in which the church itself now exists may mean that there will indeed need to be a plurality of theologies informing the church of the future. This in turn carries ramifications for both the form and the content of theology.

For example, Christianity in the twentieth century again includes a large number of illiterate persons, just as it did during the European Middle Ages. They, and a great number of others, may have a special appreciation for narrative, symbolic, or other such modes of theology. Likewise, theology today is again becoming an enterprise not only for individual specialists but also for conferences, councils, and ecumenical gatherings as it was in its earliest centuries. Lay people, too, are increasingly participants in shaping contemporary theology, whereas previously theology was more exclusively the purview of the clergy. Altogether, the theology of the contemporary context is exceptionally multi-dimensional: global as well as regional, diverse in modality; and broad in base.

Theology in this context will benefit from an awareness of its own limitations, recognizing that all theological claims and concepts are relative, conditioned by culture, context, and era: "The cultural factor is present not only in God's self-revelation in scripture, but also in our interpretation of it... [therefore] no theological statement is culture-free."[2] This revolutionary awareness—one of the most important theological insights of the modern era—substantiates the essentially intercultural character of theology and the critical need for theology to be even more deliberately intercultural in the modern context. Henceforth, all theology must manifest a recognition of its intrinsic relativity.

Perhaps the best way to think of such theology, as suggested in the introduction, is as missionary theology. For the Church "is now, in a sense which has not been true for many centuries, in a missionary situation everywhere."[3] What is thus required of Christian theology is that it come to terms with the modern context by becoming first and foremost missionary theology. "The original matrix of Christian theology is the missionary church."[4] As mission was the "mother of theology"[5] in the first place, so today will the missionary encounter of the modern context be the critical source of theology for the future. Here, Arend van Leuwen's observation bears repeating:

> It is time the missionary encounter were set firmly at the center
> of our theological concern. That... offers the real way of escape
> from the narrow limitations of a one-sided "Western" theologi-
> cal tradition. A shift of that sort, which for the theology of the
> twentieth century will be tantamount to another Reformation, is
> urgently needed.[6]

In practice, "the modern missionary movement has for the last century-and-a-half been one of the most powerful forces shaping world civilization."[7] But theology, by and large, has been stifled by a Eurocentrism in that the dominant methods, materials, and dogmas of Christianity have been shaped primarily within the

Western framework. Consequently, there has been a damaging divorce between theology and mission, between theory and the actual life of the church in the world.

Westerners themselves have felt this divorce in their own context, for example, in the gap between experience and doctrine or between the faith of the lay person and the theology of the specialists. Now, the development of fresh theologies outside the Western context makes possible a clearer understanding of the prevailing dilemma in theology.

Modern missionary theology requires careful attention to both the internal dimensions of theology as well as to the external context. Of course, missionary theology is always apologetic, that is, concerned with presenting the Christian message to a non-Christian world.[8] But part of that apologetic task today is a concern for the nature, purpose and composition of Christian theology itself.

At its best, missionary theology is the product of a dialectic involving such ingredients as inductive and deductive perspective, propositional and narrative theology, Western and Asian values, oral and written theology, existential experience and rational reflection, and so on. This is not to advocate a theological dualism, for example, between existential and philosophical theology, between East and West, or between narrative and theoretical theology, for that would be hollow and simplistic.[9] Instead, some degree of paradox is more likely as differing perspectives meet and engage. In the end, flexibility, balance, and dialogue are the keys to a successful missionary theology.

Koyama's Mission Theology

More than most, Koyama is keenly aware of the missionary context in which the Christianity of this era finds itself. Concerned lest Christianity be merely a "tribal religion,"[10] today Koyama explores means by which Christianity can meaningfully address the modern context. He clearly recognizes that theology must be deeply intercultural.[11] Accordingly, Koyama brings those Asian experiences and insights which he can convey into dialogue with the Christianity promulgated by the West. The results are generally informative, provocative, and even entertaining. Yet they can also be complex and difficult.[12]

Undoubtedly, the language Koyama employs is one of his major contributions to Christian theology in the current era. He models an alternative to the dominant, increasingly obsolete language of traditional Western theology. "He communicates in a way to enchant the young, intrigue the mature, and upset the theologians."[13] It is indeed one of Koyama's main desires that he can contribute to making Christianity and Christian theology more meaningful to lay people as well as to trained theologians. That he succeeds is apparent, for example, in the albeit somewhat jaundiced perspective of some of his lay readers: "Koyama writes for human beings, not for other theologians."[14] Or, as one laywoman put it, borrowing a term from computer slang, "Koyama's theology is 'user-friendly.'"[15]

Yet Koyama's contributions to contemporary theology are as important as they are popular. For example, his advocacy for and efforts towards transposing Christian theology into Asian frameworks place him in an historic movement. Koyama supplements the work done by other theologians in setting the stage for an Asian theology of the future. H. D. Beeby, for example, frames the issue as follows in a consideration of how Old Testament theology can inform contemporary Asian theology:

> If Israel was in fact a great debtor to the Gentiles, and all evidence suggests she was, what does this mean for Churches surrounded by neo-Confucianism, resurgent Buddhism, reviving Taoism, militant Islam, etc. and touched with nationalism and racial pride? If it can be shown that Israel borrowed extensively to good purpose and with no loss to her own distinctive faith, does this not mean that such borrowing is not only possible but incumbent upon the younger churches?[16]

In other words, as Israel, in constructing her theology borrowed from the epics and customs of surrounding pagan cultures, as New Testament Christianity borrowed terms, concepts, and even institutional structures from the pagan Greco-Roman culture, and as later Christianity borrowed theological methods and church festivals from such diverse pagan sources as Greek philosophy and indigenous European religions, so is it reasonable and necessary for Christianity in the modern context to utilize elements in its surrounding environment—whether from modern science or from other religions—to express Christian faith and life. Scripture, tradition, and ecumenical discussion can ensure that such borrowing is essentially Christian. An illustration is Koyama's own theology which is already to some degree an incarnation of Christian theology in an Asian frame.

In developing a theology which is Asian, existential, relational and understandable, Koyama is doing for his time and context what others have done before. In broad terms, Koyama stands in a recognizable historical stream. His concern for connecting theology with experience follows the example of someone like Luther.

Like a Kierkegaard, Koyama is a reminder of the necessity of the existential dimensions in theology.

In more contemporary terms Koyama belongs to a growing number of theologians whose style is clearly more narrative than systematic. Among them in the West are such figures as Dietrich Bonhoeffer, C. S. Lewis, and Helmut Thielicke. An illustration of this point is the remark of one reviewer of Koyama's *Fifty Meditations:* "these theological *haiku* constitute an Asian *Screwtape Letters.*"[17]

To be sure, many theologians, including such luminaries as Karl Barth whose interest in practical, personal theology was strong,[18] do in fact turn to narrative theology for more personal expressions of faith and for such practical theological tasks as preaching (homiletic theology in particular being more closely associated with the narrative mode in language, audience and intent). Increasingly, it would seem, theologians can benefit from being bilingual—that is, fluent in both the narrative and systematic languages of theology in the diversity of the modern context.

Such a development, heralded particularly by Christians in Asia and elsewhere, signals theological progress for the church in the modern era. It does not necessarily imply a consequent dichotomy in theology based on cultural preferences. For, in the end, narrative and systematic theology, deduction and intuition, experience and reflection are complementary aspects of all cultures and people. As one Asian has suggested,

> There are no fundamental distinctions between the East and the West. Each one of us is both Eastern and Western . . . [East and West] are two possibilities which every man in every age carries within himself, two movements of the human spirit.[19]

If East and West are here taken to refer to such features as deduction and intuition, narrative and propositional thinking, or humanity's religious and scientific impulses,[20] East and West may indeed be thought of as two movements of the human spirit. Yet it cannot be denied that strong tensions often exist between these complementary aspects of the human soul.

For Koyama this tension manifests itself in a theological encounter between two mountains: Mt. Fuji, the symbolic mountain of Asian culture, history, and experience; and Mt. Sinai, the symbolic mountain of biblical history and culture, as brought to Asia by the West. In his theology Koyama wrestles with the tensions between these two mountains. He intertwines their stories. In the end, Koyama believes, they are both part of one larger story, part of an organic whole, created and held together within the crucified embrace of a loving God.

ENDNOTES

INTRODUCTION

1. Kosuke Koyama, Interview, New York, August 4, 1980.
2. Ibid.
3. Koyama himself says that he is not now interested in being systematic, though he foresees a time some years away when he may set about systematic work. Intriguingly he comments that in his opinion it is not yet time for systematic Asian theology. That will come, he says, when Asians write commentaries on Scripture.
4. John V. Taylor, "The Theological Basis of Interfaith Dialogue," in *Christianity and Other Religions*, ed. John Hick and Brian Hebblethwaite, vol. 3 (Glasgow: Fount Publications, 1980), p. 213.

CHAPTER ONE

1. Koyama Interview, New York, August 4, 1980.
2. Ibid.
3. Ibid.
4. Ibid.
5. Kosuke Koyama, *Three Mile an Hour God* (London: SCM Press, Ltd., 1979), p. 108.
6. Koyama Interview, August 4, 1980.
7. Ibid.
8. Ibid.
9. Donald L. Larson, *Guidelines for Barefoot Language Learning* (St. Paul: CMS Publications, Inc., 1984). Dr. Larson, an admirer of Koyama, acknowledges that his essay title and approach were inspired by Koyama's style.
10. Kosuke Koyama, *Fifty Meditations* (Belfast: Christian Journals Ltd., 1975), pp. 187-191.
11. Kosuke Koyama, *Waterbuffalo Theology* (Maryknoll: Orbis Books, 1976), p. 211.
12. Ibid., p. 212.
13. Koyama, *Three Mile an Hour God* , p. 13.
14. Inazo Nitobe, *Bushido: The Soul of Japan* (Tokyo: Charles E. Tuttle Co., 1974), p. 163. See also Raymond Hammer, *Japan's Religious Ferment* (London: SCM Press Ltd., 1961), p. 75.

278

15. For example, see Nitobe's book in general, or see Ruth Benedict, *The Chrysanthemum and the Sword: Patterns of Japanese Culture* (London: Secker and Warburg, 1947), pp. 228ff.
16. Kosuke Koyama, "Ritual of Limping Dance—A Botanical Observation," *Union Seminary Quarterly Review*, vol. XXXVI, Supplementary (1981), p. 91.
17. For example, see Alan W. Watts, *The Way of Zen* (USA:Thames and Hudson, 1957), p. 157.
18. See Hammer, *Japan's Religious Ferment*, pp. 75-80, or Benedict, *The Chrysanthemum and the Sword*, chapter eight especially.
19. Hammer, pp. 75–6, p. 106.
20. Koyama, *Fifty Meditations*, pp. 56–58.
21. Hammer, pp. 38–39.
22. Ibid., pp. 25,43.
23. Ibid., p. 82.
24. Interview with Dr. Yoshiro Ishida, Geneva, June, 1980.
25. Koyama, "1945 and ICU," Address to the Board of Directors of the Japan International Christian University Foundation, May 21, 1980, p.3.
26. Hammer, p. 27.
27. Edwin O. Reischauer, *Japan: Past and Present* (Tokyo: Charles E. Tuttle Co., Inc., 1964), pp. 59-60.
28 Hammer, p. 84.
29. Koyama refers to this disillusionment via his own experience in his address "1945 and ICU," pp. 2–3.
30. Hammer, p. 123.
31. Ibid., p. 125.
32. Koyama Interview, August 4, 1980.
33. Ibid.
34. For example, Koyama, *Waterbuffalo Theology*, pp. 95–105.
35. Masaharu Anesaki, *History of Japanese Religion* (London: Kegan Paul, Trench, Trubner and Co. Ltd., 1930), pp. 122–123.
36. Hammer, pp. 29–30.
37. Charles H. Germany, *Protestant Theologies in Modern Japan* (Tokyo: IISR Press, 1965), pp. 50–65.
38. Ibid., pp. 211–212.
39. For example, see *Waterbuffalo Theology*, pp. 14–15.
40. Ibid., pp. 25–26.
41. Benedict, p. 191.

42. Koyama, *Three Mile an Hour God*, pp. 83–87; see also Koyama, *Mount Fuji and Mount Sinai* (London: SCM Press, Ltd., 1984), pp. 59–68.
43. Ibid., *Three Mile an Hour God*, p. 87.
44. Ibid.
45. Germany, p. 38.
46. Ibid., pp. 20–21.
47. For example, see Ibid., chapter III.
48. Personal correspondence with Koyama, March, 1982.
49. Koyama, *Waterbuffalo Theology*, pp. 73–74.
50. Koyama Interview, August 4, 1980.
51. Koyama, *Ritual of a Limping Dance*, pp. 101–104; developed further in Koyama, *Mount Fuji and Mount Sinai*, pp. 53–56.
52. Ibid.
53. Ibid., pp. 33–34; see also Koyama, *Mount Fuji and Mount Sinai*, pp. 59ff.
54. Germany, pp. 22–23.
55. Ibid., pp. 24–25.
56. Ibid., pp. 69–70.
57. For example, see Germany, p. 214.
58. Benedict, pp. 222–223.
59. Germany, for example, p. 102.
60. Koyama, *Ritual of a Limping Dance*, pp. 99–104.
61. Germany, pp. 3–4.
62. Hammer, pp. 85–86.
63. Germany, pp. 25–26.
64. Ibid.
65. Ishida Interview, June, 1980.
66. Anesaki, p. 210.
67. Watts, pp. 134–135.
68. Ibid. p. 115.
69. Koyama, *Fifty Meditations*, p. 188.
70. Ibid.
71. Hammer, p. 28.
72. Ibid.
73. Koyama Interview, August 4, 1980.
74. For example, *Three Mile an Hour God*, pp. 113–144 and *Fifty Meditations*, pp. 95–98, 102–103, 75–77, etc.
75. Koyama, *Mount Fuji and Mount Sinai*, pp. 96, 112ff.
76. Anesaki, p. 309.

77. For example, Benedict, p. 191.
78. Edward Norbeck, *Changing Japan* (New York: Holt, Rinehart and Winston, 1965), p. 9.
79. For example, Germany, p. 49.
80. Ibid., p. 183.
81. Ibid., p. 188.
82. Ibid., p. 142.
83. Ibid., p. 15.
84. Ibid., p. 143.
85. Norbeck, pp. 4–6,10.
86. Germany, p. 14.
87. Hammer, p. 107.
88. Ichiro Hori, Editorial Chairman, *Japanese Religion: A Survey by the Agency for Cultural Affairs* (Tokyo: Kodansha International Ltd., 1972), p. 25.
89. Hammer, p. 141.
90. Germany, p. 188.
91. Anesaki, p. 209.
92. Ibid., pp. 375–384.
93. Carl Michalson, *Japanische Theologie der Gegenwart* (Gütersloh: Gütersloher Verlagshaus Gerd Mohn, 1962), pp. 83ff.
94. Germany, pp. 34,73–74.
95. For example, see Koyama, *Fifty Meditations*, pp. 166ff.
96. For example, see *Waterbuffalo Theology*, p. 211 and 418ff. respectively.

CHAPTER TWO

1. See Junichi Natori, *Historical Stories of Christianity in Japan* (Tokyo: Hokuseido Press, 1957), pp. 62–73; Edwin O. Reischauer and John K. Fairbank, *East Asia the Great Tradition* (Boston: Houghton Mifflin Co., 1960), pp. 588–598; pp. 596–598. See also Hammer, *Japan's Religious Ferment*, pp. 96–103.
2. Hammer, pp. 96–103.
3. Chitoshi Yanaga, *Japan Since Perry* (New York: McGraw-Hill Book Co. Inc., 1949); Natori; and Richard Storry, *A History of Modern Japan* (Baltimore: Penguin Books, 1960).
4. Ichiro Hori, Editorial Chairman, *Japanese Religion: A Survey by the Agency for Cultural Affairs*, trans. Abe Yoshiya and David Reid (Tokyo: Kodansha International, Ltd., 1972), p. 74.

5. Ibid. Also, see Masaharu Anesaki, *History of Japanese Religion* (London: Kegan Paul, Trench Trubner and Co., Ltd., 1930), p. 338.
6. Hori, pp. 80–81.
7. Akio Dohi, "Christianity in Japan," in *Christianity in Asia*, ed. T.K. Thomas (Singapore: CCA Press, 1979), pp. 41–42.
8. Hammer, p. 106.
9. Anesaki, pp. 339ff.
10. Hori, pp. 80–81.
11. Ibid.
12. Hammer, p. 106.
13. Germany, pp. 3–4. See footnote number four on p. 4.
14. Ernest E. Best, *Christian Faith and Cultural Crisis: The Japanese Case* (Leiden: E.J. Brill, 1966), pp. 87–88.
15. Hori, p. 24.
16. Ibid.
17. Richard H. Drummond, *A History of Christianity in Japan* (Grand Rapids: Eerdmans Publishing Co., 1971), p. 171.
18. Inazo Nitobe, *Bushido the Soul of Japan*, p. 180.
19. Ibid., p. 173.
20. Ibid., p. 191.
21. Ibid., p. 174.
22. Hori, p. 75.
23. Drummond, p. 168.
24. Edwin O. Reischauer, *Japan Past and Present* (New York: Alfred A. Knopf, 1951), p. 128.
25. Ibid., pp. 135–140.
26. Germany, pp. 21–22.
27. Ibid., p. 14.
28. Dohi, "Christianity in Japan," p. 44.
29. Hori, p. 85.
30. Ibid.
31. Hammer, p. 96; Hori, p. 84.
32. Dohi, "Christianity in Japan," p. 45.
33. Hammer, p. 105.
34. Ibid., pp. 105–106.
35. Anesaki, pp. 360ff.
36. Drummond, p. 191.
37. Germany, p. 16.

38. Ibid., p. 17.
39. Hori, pp. 83–84.
40. Anesaki, pp. 368–369.
41. Hammer, p. 44.
42. Masatoshi Doi, "The Nature of Encounter Between Christianity and Other Religions as Witnessed on the Japanese Scene," in *The Theology of the Christian Mission*, ed., Gerald Anderson (London: SCM Press Ltd., 1961), p. 171.
43. Ibid. pp. 170–171.
44. Ibid; see also Carl Michalson, *Japanische Theologie der Gegenwart* pp. 127–128.
45. Doi, "The Nature of Encounter," p. 171.
46. Hammer, pp. 75–76.
47. Doi, "The Nature of Encounter," p. 171.
48. Hammer, pp. 66–67.
49. Dohi, "Christianity in Japan," p. 42.
50. Doi, "The Nature of Encounter," p. 172.
51. Anesaki, p. 346.
52. Ibid., pp. 307ff; 334.
53. Germany, p. 3.
54. Nitobe, p. 106.
55. Anesaki, p. 375.
56. Germany, pp. 6–7.
57. Ibid.
58. Ibid., pp. 5–6.
59. Ibid., pp. 3,8–9.
60. Ibid., pp. 9–10.
61. Ibid., p. 15.
62. See Anesaki, pp. 373–374.
63. For example, see Dohi, p. 43.
64. Germany, p. 22.
65. Hori, p. 82.
66. Drummond, pp. 206–207.
67. Best, p. 93.
68. Drummond, pp. 160–162; See also Best, pp. 88ff.
69. Best, p. 94.
70. Koyama Interviews, August 4, 1980; August 9, 1981.
71. Anesaki, p. 373.
72. Cyril J. Davey, *Kagawa of Japan* (New York: Abingdon Press, 1960).

73. Hori, p. 81,
74. Dohi, "Christianity in Japan," pp. 48ff; See also Koyama, *Three Mile an Hour God*, p. 104.
75. Hammer, p. 112.
76. Germany, p. 18; Hammer, p. 87.
77. Germany, pp. 50–80.
78. Ibid., p. 81.
79. Ibid., p. 86.
80. Ibid., pp. 47–48.
81. Ibid.
82. Ibid., p. 49.
83. Ibid.
84. Ibid., p. 18.
85. Ibid., pp. 120ff.
86. Ibid., pp. 132–133.
87. Ibid., pp. 142-143.
88. Ibid., pp. 144–145.
89. Ibid., pp. 157ff.
90. For example, Michalson, pp. 36ff., 58ff., 83ff.
91. Ibid., p. 9.
92. Hammer, p. 106.
93. Germany, pp. 160–163.
94. Ibid.
95. Cecil Hargreaves, *Asian Christian Thinking* (Delhi: Indian Society for Promoting Christian Knowledge, CLS, and Lucknow Publishing House, 1972), p. 24.
96. Germany, pp. 172–173.
97. Ibid., p. 86.
98. Robert Fukuda, commenting in a book review in *The Northeast Asia Journal of Theology*, vol. 16 (March, 1976), pp. 52–57.
99. Hammer, p. 58.
100. Koyama, *Three Mile an Hour God*, p. 98.
101. Fukuda review p. 53.
102. Germany, pp. 175–176.
103. Fukuda review, p. 53.
104. Dohi, "Christianity in Japan," pp. 56–58.
105. Kosuke Koyama, "Openness-in-Pain," in *National Christian Council Review*, vol. XCIV (April, 1974), p. 205.

106. Koyama, *Three Mile an Hour God*, pp. 97–99.
107. Koyama, *Fifty Meditations*, pp. 184–186.
108. Germany, pp. 185–186.
109. Ibid., pp. 178–180, 199.
110. Ibid.
111. Ibid., pp. 183–184, 200.
112. Ibid., p. 183.
113. One example is Masayoshi Ohira, Prime Minister, who died in office in 1979.
114. Germany, pp. 188, 204.
115. Ibid., p. 152.
116. For example, Paul Tillich's book, *Christianity and the Encounter of the World Religions* (New York: Columbia University Press, 1964), written after a visit to Japan.
117. Kazoh Kitamori, *Theology of the Pain of God* (Richmond: John Knox Press, 1958).
118. Germany, pp. 73–74.
119. Simon Baynes, "The Japanese and the Cross," in *Japan Christian Quarterly*, vol. XLVI (Summer, 1980), p. 148.
120. Ibid.
121. Michalson, p. 83.
122. Drummond, pp. 297–298.
123. Michalson, pp. 196ff.
124. Ibid., p. 9.
125. Kazoh Kitamori, "Is 'Japanese Theology' Possible?" in *The Northeast Asia Journal of Theology*, (September, 1969), p. 78.
126. Germany, p. 220.
127. Michalson, p. 60.
128. Kitamori, "Is 'Japanese Theology' Possible?" p. 87.
129. Ibid., p. 77.
130. Ernest D. Piryns, "Contemporary Theology: The Japanese Case" in *Philippiniana Sacra*, vol. XIV, No. 40 (Jan.—April, 1979), p. 151.
131. H. Waldenfels, "A Japanese Theology for Japan," in *The Japan Missionary Bulletin*, vol. XXVIII (Sept., 1974), p. 3.
132. Yoshinobu Kumazawa, "Non-Christian Context as Post-Christian Context: The Hermeneutical Task in Ministerial Formation as Seen in the Japanese Context," in *The Northeast Asia Journal of Theology*, (March/Sept., 1980), pp. 76–77.
133. Piryns, "Contextual Theology," p. 153.

134. Germany, p. 216.
135. Michalson, pp. 135–136; See also Germany, p. 210.
136. Interview with Koyama's wife, New York, August 2, 1981 (New York).
137. Koyama, *Three Mile an Hour God*, p. 23; See also Ibid..
138. Koyama, "Christ at the Periphery," n.p. 1981, p. 5.
139. Koyama, *Three Mile an Hour God*, pp. 83–88, for example.
140. Koyama Interview, August 9, 1981.
141. Germany, pp. 216–217.
142. Ibid., pp. 218–220.
143. Koyama Interview, August 9, 1981.

CHAPTER THREE

1. Drummond, *History of Christianity in Japan*, p. 241.
2. Ibid., p. 240.
3. Ibid., p. 241.
4. Germany, *Protestant Theologies in Modern Japan*, pp. 32–33.
5. Ibid., p. 35.
6. Ibid., pp. 36–37.
7. The basically positive view of human nature that both Koyama and Kagawa have undoubtedly reflects their common Japanese heritage with its emphasis on the optimistic possibilities of life.
8. Germany, pp. 32–33.
9. Koyama Interviews, August 4, 1980 and August 9, 1981.
10. Koyama, *Three Mile an Hour God*, p. 105.
11. Dohi, "Christianity in Japan," p. 50.
12. Ryusaku Tsunoda et al, eds., *Sources of Japanese Tradition*, vol. II (New York: Columbia University Press, 1965), p. 350.
13. Ibid., p. 349.
14. Michalson, *Japanische Theologie der Gegenwart*, p. 9.
15. Tsunoda, p. 350.
16. Raymond P. Jennings, *Jesus, Japan, and Kanzo Uchimura*, (Tokyo: Christian Literature Society, 1958), pp. 27–28.
17. Ibid., pp. 22, 30ff.
18. Ibid., pp. 54ff.
19. Drummond, pp. 296–297.
20. Choan Seng Song, *Third-Eye Theology*, (London: Lutterworth Press, 1980), p. 26.

286

2

21. Michalson, pp. 60ff.
22. Koyama, *Waterbuffalo Theology*, p. 116.
23. Hargreaves, *Asian Christian Thinking*, p. 25.
24. Ibid.
25. Choan Seng Song, *Doing Theology Today*, (Madras: Christian Literature Society, 1976), p. 56.
26. Drummond, p. 297.
27. Michalson, p. 60.
28. Koyama, *Waterbuffalo Theology*, pp. 115–125.
29. For example, Koyama, "Ultimacy and Universality," pp. 7ff. (n.p.) where Koyama reverses the meaning of the terms "vulnerability" in a paper written during discussions by the Reagan administration of America's "window of vulnerability" in a nuclear confrontation with Russia.
30. Michalson, p. 60; see also J. Verkuyl, *Contemporary Missiology*, trans. Dale Cooper (Grand Rapids: Wm. B. Eerdmans Publishing Co., 1978), p. 274.
31. Koyama Interview, August 9, 1981.
32. Hargreaves, pp. 23–24.
33. Ibid., p. 24.
34. Koyama, "Openness-in-Pain," p. 204.
35. Michalson, p. 61.
36. Koyama, *Waterbuffalo Theology*, p. 115.
37. Ibid.
38. Germany, p. 221.
39. Kitamori, p. 90.
40. Ibid., pp. 8,16,150; Koyama, *Waterbuffalo Theology*, pp. 125,174.
41. Koyama, "Ritual of a Limping Dance," pp. 101–102.
42. Compare Kitamori, p. 58.
43. Koyama, "The 'Wrath of God' and the Thai *Theologia Gloriae*," in *Christ and the Younger Churches*, George F. Vicedom, ed. (London: SPCK, 1972), pp. 42–50.
44. Ibid.
45. Ibid.
46. Ibid.; Koyama, *Waterbuffalo Theology*, pp. 95–105, and Koyama, "The Wrath of God," pp. 42–50.
47. Kitamori, p. 71.
48. Ibid., pp. 54ff.
49. Hargreaves, p. 26.
50. Koyama, *Waterbuffalo Theology*, p. 117.

51. Germany, pp. 220–221.
52. Michalson, p. 63.
53. Kitamori, p. 95.
54. Michalson, p. 137.
55. Koyama Interview, August 9, 1981.
56. Song, *Third-Eye Theology*, p. 62.
57. Song, *Doing Theology Today*, p. 58.
58. Song, *Third-Eye Theology*, p. 62.
59. For example, Hargreaves, p. 25.
60. Koyama Interview, August 9, 1981.
61. Kitamori, p. 47.

CHAPTER FOUR

1. Hendrik Kraemer, *The Christian Message in a Non-Christian World* (London: Edinburgh House Press, 1938), pp. 2–3.
2. Ibid., p. 18.
3. Edwin O. Reischauer and John K. Fairbanks, *East Asia the Great Tradition* (Boston: Houghton Mifflin Co., 1960), p. 109.
4. Benjamin Rowland, *The Art and Architecture of India: Buddhist, Hindu, Jain* (Harmondsworth: Penguin Books, 1953), pp. 69–77, especially pp. 73-74.
5. Aloysius Pieris, "Western Christianity and Asian Buddhism," in *Dialogue*, vol. VII (May-Aug., 1980), pp. 61–62. The Buddha's life was transmitted to medieval Europe in the figure of St. Joasaph or Josaphat. Besides Francis of Assisi, no other saint was considered so great a model of moral life and worldly renunciation. Through St. Joasaph the story of the Buddha even filtered into Shakespeare's "Merchant of Venice" and various Jesuit morality plays.
6. Reischauer and Fairbanks, pp. 280–285.
7. Ibid., pp. 265–271.
8. Kraemer, p. 21.
9. Ibid.
10. Kor L. Cheng, "The Church and Missions," in *Readings in Third World Missions: A Collection of Essential Documents*, ed. Marlin L. Nelson, (South Pasadena: Wm. Carey Library, 1976), p. 151.
11. See, for example, Aloysius Pieris, "Contemporary Ecumenism and Asia's Search for Christ," in *Teaching All Nations*, vol. XII (January, 1976).

288

12. Cheng, "The Church and Missions," p. 151.
13. George Mark Moraes, *A History of Christianity in India* (Bombay: Manaktalas, 1964), pp. 25–45.
14. Stephen Neill, *A History of Christian Missions* (Harmondsworth: Penguin Books Ltd., 1975), pp. 95–96. Or, see Dennis Hickley, *The First Christians of China* (London: China Study Project, 1980), pp. 1ff.
15. M. Abel, "Social and Political Challenges to the Churches in Asia," in *Third All Asia Lutheran Conference* (Singapore: Lutheran World Federation, 1976), p. 95.
16. Ibid., pp. 95–96.
17. Ibid., p. 97.
18. Ibid., p. 90.
19. Gerald H. Anderson, ed., *Christ and Crisis in Southeast Asia,* (New York: Friendship Press, 1968), p. 10.
20. Abel, "Social and Political Challenges," p. 100.
21. Ibid., p. 103.
22. Emerito Nacpil, "Mission in Today's World," in *Asia Focus*, vol. IV (1969), p. 54.
23. Anderson, p. 10.
24. T.K. Thomas, ed. *Testimony Amid Asian Suffering* (Singapore: Christian Conference of Asia, 1977), pp. 19–20, including reflections on the theme—"Jesus Christ in Asian Suffering and Hope."
25. Ibid., p. 20.
26. Ibid., p. 9.
27. Ibid., p. 14.
28. Ibid., p. 22.
29. Pieris, "Western Christianity and Asian Buddhism," p. 76.
30. H. Parkin, "Challenges of Ancient Faiths and Modern Technology to Christianity in Asia," in *Third All Asia Lutheran Conference*, pp. 80–81.
31. Ibid.
32. Ibid., p. 84.
33. Ibid., p. 83.
34. Carl J. Hellberg, "Director's Greetings," in *Third All Asia Lutheran Conference*, pp. 3–4.
35. Parkin, "Challenges of Ancient Faiths," pp. 78–79.
36. Charles W. Forman, ed., *Christianity in the Non-Western World* (Englewood Cliffs: Prentice-Hall, Inc., 1967), p. 141.

37. Paul Tillich, *Theology of Culture*, ed., Robert C. Kimball (New York: Oxford Univeristy Press, 1959), pp. 204–205.

38. Anderson, p. 11.

39. P. Sormin, "Lutheranism in the Context of Ecumenism in Asia," in *Third All Asia Lutheran Conference*, p. 141.

40. Chaeok Chun, "An Asian Missionary Commenting on Asia Mission," in *Readings in Third World Missions*, p. 125.

41. See, for example, James Scherer (Section B), "Response From the Churches," in *Third All Asia Lutheran Conference*, p. 195 and Pieris, "Contemporary Ecumenism," pp. 11–13.

42. Chun, "An Asian Missionary Commenting," p. 123.

43. Parkin, "Challenges," p. 84.

44. Kunchala Rajaratnam, "Self-Reliance for Mission," in *Third All Asia Lutheran Conference*, p. 162.

45. Vinay Samuel and Christ Sugden, "Mission in the 1980's in Asia," in *Occasional Bulletin of Missionary Research*, vol. 4 (April, 1980), pp. 50–52.

46. Kenneth Scott Latourette, "The Christian Mission in Asia," in *East and West: Conflict or Cooperation?*, ed. Basil Matthew (London: SCM Press, 1936), p. 111.

47. Douglas Elwood, ed., *Asian Christian Theology: Emerging Themes* (Philadelphia: The Westminster Press, 1980), p. 4. In a "Foreword by an Asian theologian," Koyama remarks, "Asian Christians ... live in a world of great religious traditions, modernization impacts, ideologies of left and right, international conflicts, hunger, poverty, militarism, and racism."

48. T.K. Thomas, "Waterbuffalo Communication," in *Christian Conference of Asia News*, vol. 16 (April, 1981).

49. William Cadwallader in a review of *Waterbuffalo Theology*, in *Asia Focus*, vol. VI (1971), pp. 1–3.

50. Kosuke Koyama, "Three Theological Perspectives to 'Jesus Christ Frees and Unites'," in *The Northeast Asia Journal of Theology*, vol. 16 (March, 1976), p. 34.

51. Douglas J. Elwood, ed., *What Asian Christians are Thinking* (Quezon City: New Day Publishers, 1976), p. xxiv.

52. This personal anecdote was related by an educator from Sydney, Australia; Selly Oak, March, 1980.

CHAPTER FIVE

1. Raymond Fung, "On Doing Theology in Asia: An Industrial Missioner's Reflections on the Manila Theological Consultation," in *Ching Feng*, vol. XX (1977), p. 150. This may actually have been said by Koyama in the conference to which Fung refers.
2. Douglas Elwood, ed., *What Asian Christians are Thinking* (Quezon City: New Day Publishers, 1976), p. xix.
3. Ibid., p. xx.
4. Ibid.
5. Choan-Seng Song, ed., *Doing Theology Today* (Madras: The Christian Literature Society, 1976), p. iii.
6. Cyril B. Papali, "Developing An Asian Theology," in *Teaching All Nations*, vol. IX (1972), p. 201.
7. Arend Th. Van Leeuwen, tr. H. H. Hoskins, *Christianity in World History* (New York: Charles Scribner's Sons, 1964), p. 426.
8. Ibid.
9. Elwood, *What Asian Christians are Thinking*, p. xx.
10. Ibid., pp. xx–xxi.
11. Ibid., p. xx, quoting G. V. Job from *Rethinking Christianity in India* (Madras: CLS, 1938), p. 15.
12. Van Leeuwen, pp. 424–425.
13. Elwood, *What Asian Christians are Thinking*, p. xx.
14. Pieris, "Western Christianity and Asia Buddhism," p. 81.
15. See J. A. Veitch, "Is an Asian Theology Possible?" in *South East Asia Journal of Theology*, vol. 17 (1976), p. 3.
16. Choan-Seng Song, *Third-Eye Theology*, p. 5.
17. Yong Bock Kim, "Doing Theology in Asia Today: A Korean Perspective," in *Asian Christian Theology: Emerging Themes*, pp. 315ff.
18. Ibid., p. 315.
19. Ibid.
20. Kosuke Koyama, "Foreword by an Asian Theologian," in *Asian Christian Theology*, p. 13.
21. Ibid.
22. See, for example, Kim, "Doing Theology in Asia Today," pp. 316ff. Song, too, tends to fall into this category.
23. Elwood, *Asian Christian Theology*, p. 35.

24. "Towards a Theology of People: I," (Tokyo: Urban Rural Mission, Christian Conference of Asia, 1977), p. i. A good sample of the artistic dimension of Asian theology can be found in *The Northeast Asia Journal of Theology*, which regularly displays Asian Christian art work.

25. H. D. Beeby, "Thoughts on Indigenizing Theology," in *The South East Asia Journal of Theology*, vol. 14 (1973), p. 34.

26. Ibid., p. 35.

27. Ibid., pp. 35, 38.

28. Ibid., pp. 36–37.

29. Pieris, "Western Christianity and Asian Buddhism," p. 77.

30. Ibid., pp. 27–28.

31. Ibid.

32. Elwood, *What Asian Christians are Thinking*, p. xxxi.

33. Van Leeuwen, p. 415.

34. Ibid.

35. Ibid.

36. Elwood, *Asian Christian Theology*, p. 29.

37. Ibid.

38. Ching-Fen Hsiao, "Asian Theology in Retrospect and Prospect," in *The South East Asia Journal of Theology*, vol. 19 (1978), p. 1.

39. D. S. Amalorpavadass, "New Theological Approaches in Asia," in *Verbum SVB*, vol. 21 (1980), pp. 290ff.

40. Ibid., p. 287.

41. Fung, p. 150.

42. Veitch, pp. 9–11.

43. Song, "Love of God-and-Man in Action," in *Doing Theology Today*, pp. 49–50.

44. Song, *Third-Eye Theology*, pp. xiff.

45. Song, *Doing Theology Today*, p. 55.

46. Ibid., p. 56.

47. Hargreaves, *Asian Christian Thinking*, p. 3.

48. Ibid.

49. Ibid., especially Chapter Two and pp. 178–179.

50. Luis Gutheinz, "Asian Theology Today: Where is it; What is it About?" in *East Asian Pastoral Review*, vol. XVI (1979), p. 203.

51. Ibid.

52. Song, *Third-Eye Theology*, p. 200.

53. Ibid.

54. Elwood, *What Asian Christians are Thinking*, p. xxviii.

55. Ibid.
56. Ibid., p. xxix.
57. Koyama, "Foreword by an Asian Theologian," in *Asian Christian Theology*,.p. 15.
58. Charles West, "Foreword by a Western Theologian," in *Asian Christian Theology*, p. xii.
59. Paul Tillich, ed. Robert C. Kimball, *Theology of Culture*, (New York: Oxford University Press, 1959), p. 159.
60. Ibid., p. 160.
61. Veitch, p. 3.
62. Elwood, *What Asian Christians are Thinking*, p. xxi.
63. Ibid., pp. xxi–xxii.
64. Alan Geyer, "Toward a Convivial Theology," in *The Christian Century* (April 23, 1969), p. 542.
65. Koyama, "Foreword by an Asian Theologian," where he says, "Our commitment to the ecumenical movement gives us the inspiration to study the following pages." p. 15.
66. Elwood, *What Asian Christians are Thinking*, p. xxviii.
67. Ibid.
68. Koyama, "Foreword by an Asian Theologian," p. 15.
69. Geyer, p. 543.
70. L. Harold DeWolf, "International Dimensions of the Seminary," in *The Christian Century* (April 23, 1969), p. 547.
71. Van Leeuwen, p. 432.
72. Ibid., pp. 426–427.
73. Ibid., p. 427.
74. Hendrik Kraemer, "The Quest for a Christian World Outlook," in *East and West: Conflict or Cooperation?* (London: SCM Press, 1936), ed., Basil Matthews, p. 135.
75. Ibid., p. 137.
76. Veitch, p. 3, and Basil Matthews, "There is Confusion," in *East and West: Conflict and Cooperation*, pp. 137–138.
77. See Pieris, *Contemporary Ecumenism*, pp. 6–8 for a thought-provoking depiction of the relationship between Asia and the Christianity of the West as well as Pieris, "Western Christianity," pp. 59 and 67, for a special note on Asian religions coming to the West. Note, too, Charles West's attitude towards what he calls the "pseudo-salvations from the East" in his "Foreword by a Western Theologian," p. xii. Harvey Cox's book, *Turning East: The*

Promise and Peril of the New Orientalism (New York: Simon and Schuster, 1977) also illustrates the Western concern over Eastern religions entering the Western sphere.

78. Kraemer, "The Quest for a Christian World Outlook," pp. 137–138.
79. Kosuke Koyama, "Three Theological Perspectives to 'Jesus Christ Frees and Unites'," in *The Northeast Asia Journal of Theology* (March, 1976), p. 43.
80. Ibid.
81. Karl Barth, "No Boring Theology: A Letter from Karl Barth," in *The South East Asia Journal of Theology*, vol. 11 (Autumn, 1969), pp. 3–5. This open letter to Asian Christians was written in Basel in November, 1968, three weeks before Barth's death.
82. Forman, *Christianity in the Non-Western World*, p. 140.
83. Ibid., p. 141.
84. Ibid.
85. Virginia Fabella, ed., *Asia's Struggle for Full Humanity* (Maryknoll: Orbis Books, 1980), pp. 152–160.
86. There is irony, of course, in the fact that most theologians who pronounce judgments do not themselves belong to the poor and powerless classes; moreover, very very few of Asia's poor are either Christian or, if Christian, inclined to formulate any kind of Asian theology whatsoever.
87. Song, *Third-Eye Theology*, pp. 1–20, pp. 210ff.
88. Pieris, "Western Christianity and Asian Buddhism," p. 78.
89. J. D. Kraan, "Towards a Relevant Theology," in *Al-Mushir*, vol. XXI (Summer, 1979), p. 62.
90. *Towards a Theology of People: I* (Tokyo: Urban Rural Mission—Christian Conference of Asia, 1977), pp. iff.
91. M. M. Thomas, "An Overview: Christian Action in the Asian Struggle," in *Towards a Theology of People: I*, pp. 12–15.
92. Koyama Interview, August 9, 1981.
93. Taped response to a letter to Koyama, March, 1979.
94. Koyama Interview, August 4, 1980.
95. Taped response to a letter to Koyama, March, 1979.
96. Ibid.
97. Koyama, *Three Mile an Hour God*, pp. 119–120.
98. See, for example, Kenneth Latourette, "The Christian Mission in Asia," in *East and West*, pp. 108–109.
99. Yoshiro Ishida, "Lutheran Contribution in Asia in the Ecumenical Context," in *Third All Asia Lutheran Conference*, p. 179.

100. Andrew Hsiao, "Effective Proclamation of the Gospel in Asia," in *Third All Asia Lutheran Conference*, p. 72.
101. Elwood, *What Asian Christians are Thinking*, p. xxvii.
102. Elwood, *Asian Christian Theology*, p. 28.
103. "The Willowbank Report: Gospel and Culture in *Lausanne Occasional Papers*, no. 2 (Wheaton: Lausanne Committee for World Evangelization, 1978), p. 32.
104. Elwood, *Asian Christian Theology*, p. 28.
105. Ibid.
106. Ibid.
107. Van Leeuwen, p. 423
108. Ibid.
109. Ibid., p. 424.
110. Ibid., p. 423.
111. DeWolf, "International Dimensions of the Seminary," p. 545.
112. Koyama, "We Had Rice With Jesus!" in *Towards a Theology of People: I*, pp. 117ff.
113. Elwood, *What Asian Christians are Thinking*, p. xxix.
114. Beeby, "Thoughts on Indigenizing Theology," p. 34.
115. Elwood, *What Asian Christians are Thinking*, p. xxix.
116. Cf. Beeby, who, noting that it took one thousand years for Denmark to produce a systematic theologian, adds that at any rate, Asian churches have more important things to do. (Beeby, "Thoughts on Indigenizing Theology," p. 34). Elwood, too, uses the reminder that "The Church Fathers came *after* the Apologists!" to support the notion that the time is not appropriate for systematic theology in Asia, *What Asian Christians are Thinking*, p. xxix.
117. Quoted in Elwood, *What Asian Christians are Thinking*, p. xxix.
118. Ibid., p. xxx.
119. Cf. Elwood, *What Asian Christians are Thinking*, quoting Kierkegaard, p. xxix.
120. Geyer, "Toward a Convivial Theology," p. 542.
121. Elwood, *What Asian Christians are Thinking*, p. xxiv.
122. Hsiao, "Asian Theology in Retrospect and Prospect," p. 2.
123. Veitch, "Is Asian Theology Possible?" p.12.
124. See, for example, Geyer, "Toward a Convivial Theology," and Elwood, *Asian Christian Theology*, p. 35.
125. For example, see Van Leeuwen, p. 419.
126. T. K. Thomas, "The World in Which We Preach Christ," in *Witness in Six Continents*, ed. Ronald K. Orchard (London: Edinburgh House Press, 1964), pp. 17–19.

127. Veitch, "Is an Asian Theology Possible?" p. 12.
128. Pieris, "Western Christianity and Asian Buddhism," p. 84.
129. Ibid.
130. Koyama Interview, August 9, 1981.
131. Ibid,
132. Ibid.

CHAPTER SIX

1. Koyama, *Waterbuffalo Theology*, p. 228.
2. Ibid., p. 229.
3. Ibid.
4. Koyama, *No Handle on the Cross*, p. 57.
5. Ibid., p. 58.
6. Ibid.
7. Ibid., p. 60.
8. Kosuke Koyama, *Theology in Contact* (Madras: CLS, 1975), pp. 36–37.
9. Koyama, *Waterbuffalo Theology*, p. 9.
10. Ibid.
11. Koyama, *Three Mile an Hour God*, p. 62.
12. Ibid. p. 63.
13. Ibid.
14. Ibid. pp. 63–64.
15. Koyama, *Waterbuffalo Theology*, p. 9.
16. Ibid., p. 120.
17. Koyama, *Waterbuffalo Theology*, pp. 107–108.
18. Koyama, *Three Mile an Hour God*, p. 45.
19. Ibid., p. 46.
20. Koyama, *Fifty Meditations*, p. 142.
21. Koyama, *Three Mile an Hour God*, p. 47.
22. Koyama, *Fifty Meditations*, pp. 141–142.
23. Ibid., pp. 140–141.
24. Koyama, *Waterbuffalo Theology*, pp. 11–12.
25. Kosuke Koyama, "The Place of Australia in South East Asia—Theologically Speaking," in *South East Asia Journal of Theology,* vol. 15 (1973), p. 54.
26. Koyama, *Waterbuffalo Theology*, p. 12.
27. Kosuke Koyama, "Theology in the Time of Acute Complexity in History," in *South East Asia Journal of Theology*, vol. 12 (Spring 1971), p. 6.

28. Koyama, "The Place of Australia," p. 51.
29. Ibid.
30. Ibid.
31. Koyama, *No Handle on the Cross*, p. 19.
32. Ibid., pp. 19–20.
33. Ibid., p. 20.
34. Ibid., p. 21.
35. Koyama, "The Place of Australia," p. 53.
36. Koyama, *Waterbuffalo Theology*, p. 111.
37. Kosuke Koyama, "The Lord's Controversy with Thailand," in *International Review of Mission*, LXI (July 1972), pp. 230–231.
38. Koyama, *Waterbuffalo Theology*, p. 48.
39. Ibid., p. 49.
40. Ibid.
41. Koyama, *Waterbuffalo Theology*, p. 50.
42. Koyama, *No Handle on the Cross*, pp. 38–39.
43. See Koyama, *Waterbuffalo Theology*, pp. 201–203.
44. Koyama, *No Handle on the Cross*, p. 77.
45. Ibid., pp. 5–6.
46. Ibid., p. 100.
47. Ibid.
48. Ibid., pp. 100–101.
49. Ibid., p. 102.
50. Ibid.
51. Ibid., p. 93.
52. Ibid., p. 107.
53. Quoted in Koyama, *No Handle on the Cross*, p. 108.
54. Ibid.
55. Ibid., p. 109.
56. Ibid.
57. For example, see Koyama, *Waterbuffalo Theology*, p. 57, and *No Handle on the Cross*, p. 100.
58. Ibid., p. 109.
59. Ibid.
60. Ibid.
61. Koyama, *Waterbuffalo Theology*, p. 183.
62. Ibid., p. 185.
63. Ibid., p. 232.

64. Koyama, *No Handle on the Cross*, p. 104.
65. Koyama, *Three Mile an Hour God*, p. 46.
66. Ibid., p. 47.
67. Koyama, *Fifty Meditations*, p. 176.
68. Ibid., p. 52.
69. Ibid., p. 55.
70. Ibid., p. 52.
71. Ibid.
72. Ibid.
73. Koyama, *Waterbuffalo Theology*, p. 182; see also *Fifty Meditations*, pp. 15–17, 54–55.
74. Koyama, *Waterbuffalo Theology*, pp. 182–183.
75. Koyama, *No Handle on the Cross*, pp. 13–14.
76. Ibid., p. 14.
77. Ibid., pp. 69–71.
78. Ibid., p. 71.
79. Ibid.
80. Ibid.
81. Ibid., p. 24.
82. Ibid., p. 26.
83. Ibid., pp. 2–3.
84. Ibid., p. 76.
85. Ibid., pp. 73–76.
86. Koyama, *Fifty Meditations*, p. 170.
87. Ibid., p. 170.
88. Ibid.
89. Koyama, *Waterbuffalo Theology*, p. 106.
90. Ibid., p. 107.
91. Ibid., p. 120.
92. Koyama, *No Handle on the Cross*, p. 34.
93. Koyama, *Fifty Meditations*, p. 53.
94. Koyama, "The Place of Australia," p. 50.
95. Koyama, *No Handle on the Cross*, p. 3.
96. Koyama, *Theology in Contact*, p. 63.
97. Koyama, *Waterbuffalo Theology*, p. 183.
98. Koyama, "Theology in the Time of Acute Complexity," p. 9.
99. Koyama, *No Handle on the Cross*, p. 37.
100. Koyama, "Theology in the Time of Acute Complexity," p. 9.

101. Koyama, *Fifty Meditations*, p. 32.
102. Koyama, *Waterbuffalo Theology*, p. 20.
103. Ibid., p. 136.
104. See Ibid., pp. 134–137.
105. Ibid., p. 122.
106. Ibid., p. viii.
107. Koyama, "Theology in the Time of Acute Complexity," p. 6.
108. Koyama, *Theology in Contact*, p. 63.
109. Koyama, *Waterbuffalo Theology*, p. viii.
110. Ibid., p. 115.
111. Ibid., p. 121.
112. Koyama, *Theology in Contact*, p. 83.
113. Koyama, "Theology in the Time of Acute Complexity," p. 6.
114. Koyama, *Waterbuffalo Theology*, pp. 73–77.
115. Ibid., p. 120.
116. Ibid., pp. 125, 123.
117. Ibid., p. 75.
118. Koyama, "Theology in the Time of Acute Complexity," p. 7.
119. Ibid.
120. Koyama, *Fifty Meditations*, p. 83.
121. Koyama, *Waterbuffalo Theology*, pp. 44–45.
122. Ibid., p. 82.
123. Koyama, "Theology in the Time of Acute Complexity," p. 7.
124. Koyama, *Waterbuffalo Theology*, pp. 21–22.
125. Koyama, "Theology in the Time of Acute Complexity," p. 7.
126. Koyama, *No Handle on the Cross*, p. 99.
127. Koyama, *Fifty Meditations*, p. 104.
128. Ibid.
129. Koyama, "The Place of Australia," p.54.
130. Ibid., pp. 54–55.
131. Ibid., pp. 48–49.
132. Ibid., p. 48.
133. Koyama, *Waterbuffalo Theology*, p. 51.
134. Ibid., p. 52.
135. Koyama, *Theology in Contact*, pp. 49–50.
136. Koyama, *Fifty Meditations*, p. 105.
137. Ibid.
138. Ibid., p. 106.

139. Ibid., p. 140.
140. Koyama, "Theology in the Time of Acute Complexity," p. 6.
141. Koyama, *Waterbuffalo Theology*, p. 44.
142. Ibid., p. 213.
143. Ibid., p. 212.
144. Koyama, *No Handle on the Cross*, p. 99.
145. Koyama, "Theology in the Time of Acute Complexity," p. 6.
146. Koyama, *Waterbuffalo Theology*, p. 52.
147. Ibid., pp. 103–104.
148. Ibid., p. 212.
149. Ibid., p. 148.
150. Ibid., p. 152.
151. Ibid., p. 214.
152. Ibid., p. 43.
153. Koyama, *Theology in Contact*, p. 50.
154. Koyama, *No Handle on the Cross*, p. 13.
155. Ibid.
156. Ibid., p. 71.
157. Ibid., p. 69.
158. Ibid., pp. 69–70.
159. Koyama, *Waterbuffalo Theology*, p. 23.
160. Koyama, *No Handle on the Cross*, pp. 98–99.
161. Ibid., pp. 105–106.
162. Koyama, *Waterbuffalo Theology*, p. 23.
163. Ibid., p. 23.
164. Koyama, *No Handle on the Cross*, p. 109.
165. Ibid., p. 101.
166. Koyama, *Three Mile an Hour God*, pp. 6–7.
167. Ibid., p. 7.
168. Koyama, *Waterbuffalo Theology*, p. 106.
169. Ibid., pp. 97ff.
170. Ibid., p. 101.
171. Ibid., p. 102.

300

1. Koyama, *Waterbuffalo Theology*, pp. 175–178.
2. Koyama, *Three Mile an Hour God*, p. 26.
3. Koyama, *Waterbuffalo Theology*, p. 180.
4. Koyama, *Three Mile an Hour God*, pp. 24–25.
5. Ibid., p. 4.
6. Ibid., p. 7.
7. Koyama, *Waterbuffalo Theology*, p. 181.
8. Ibid., p. 182.
9. Ibid., p. 231.
10. Ibid.
11. Ibid.
12. Ibid., p. 238.
13. Ibid.
14. Koyama, *No Handle on the Cross*, p. 11.
15. Ibid., p. 12.
16. Koyama, *Three Mile an Hour God*, p. 42.
17. Ibid., pp. 34–35.
18. Koyama, *No Handle on the Cross*, p. 46.
19. Koyama, *Three Mile an Hour God*, p. 35.
20. Ibid., pp. 25–62.
21. Koyama, *Theology in Contact*, p. 73.
22. Ibid., p. 6.
23. Koyama, *No Handle on the Cross*, p. 30.
24. Ibid., p. 32.
25. Ibid., p. 33.
26. Ibid., pp. 33–38.
27. Ibid., p. 41.
28. Ibid., p. 34.
29. Ibid., p. 105.
30. Ibid., p. 33.
31. Ibid., p. 83.
32. Ibid.
33. Ibid., p. 93.
34. Ibid.
35. Ibid.
36. Koyama, *Waterbuffalo Theology*, p. 199.

37. Ibid., pp. 220–221.
38. Koyama, *No Handle on the Cross*, p. 86.
39. For example, Ibid., p. 12.
40. Koyama, *Waterbuffalo Theology*, p. 24.
41. Koyama, *No Handle on the Cross*, p. 12.
42. Ibid., p. 9.
43. Ibid., p. 10.
44. Ibid.
45. Koyama, *Fifty Meditations*, p. 34.
46. Ibid., p. 182.
47. Ibid.
48. Koyama, *Three Mile an Hour God*, p. 54.
49. Koyama, *No Handle on the Cross*, p. 12.
50. Koyama, *Three Mile an Hour God*, p. 54.
51. Ibid.
52. Koyama, *Fifty Meditations*, p. 182.
53. Koyama, *No Handle on the Cross*, pp. 112–113.
54. Ibid., pp. 113–115.
55. Ibid., pp. 39, 119.
56. Ibid., p. 112.
57. Koyama, *Waterbuffalo Theology*, p. 224.
58. Koyama, *No Handle on the Cross*, pp. 113–115.
59. Koyama, *Three Mile an Hour God*, pp. 130–132.
60. Koyama, *Waterbuffalo Theology*, p. 224.
61. Ibid., p. 24.
62. Koyama, *Fifty Meditations*, p. 43.
63. Ibid., p. 44.
64. Ibid.
65. Ibid., p. 45.
66. Ibid.
67. Koyama, *Waterbuffalo Theology*, p. 210.
68. Ibid., pp. 210–211.
69. Ibid., pp. 67–68.
70. Ibid., p. 129.
71. Ibid.
72. Ibid., p. 131.
73. Ibid., pp. 131–132.
74. Ibid., p. 132.

75. Ibid., p. 131.
76. Koyama, *Fifty Meditations*, p. 41.
77. Ibid.
78. Ibid., p. 61.
79. Ibid.
80. Ibid., p. 62.
81. Koyama, *Three Mile an Hour God*, p. 123.
82. Ibid.
83. Ibid., p. 134.
84. Ibid., p. 138.
85. Ibid., pp. 138–139.
86. Ibid., p. 127.
87. Ibid., p. 128.
88. Ibid., pp. 128–129.
89. Koyama, *Fifty Meditations*, p. 182.
90. Koyama, *Waterbuffalo Theology*, pp. 206–208.
91. Ibid., pp. 206–207.
92. Ibid., p. 207.
93. Ibid.
94. Koyama, *Fifty Meditations*, p. 183.
95. Koyama, *Waterbuffalo Theology*, p. 208.
96. Koyama, *Theology in Contact*, p. 79.
97. Ibid., p. 80.
98. Ibid.
99. Ibid., p. 83.
100. Koyama, *Waterbuffalo Theology*, pp. 112–113.
101. Ibid., p. 113.
102. Koyama, *Theology in Contact*, p. 84.
103. Koyama, *Waterbuffalo Theology*, p. 91.
104. For example, Ibid., pp. 216–269.
105. Ibid., p. 91.
106. Ibid.
107. Ibid., pp. 91–92.
108. Ibid., p. 92.
109. Ibid., p. 93.
110. Ibid., p. 233.
111. Ibid.
112. Ibid.

113. For example, see Ibid., pp. 107, 91.
114. Koyama, *Fifty Meditations*, p. 53.
115. Ibid.

CHAPTER EIGHT

1. Jürgen Moltmann, trans. R. A. Wilson and John Bowden, *The Crucified God* (London: SCM Press Ltd., 1974), pp. 207–208.
2. Ibid., pp. 208–212; and Walther von Loewenich, trans. Herbert J. A. Bouman, *Luther's Theology of the Cross* (Belfast: Christian Journals Ltd., 1976), pp. 113, 118ff.
3. Moltmann, p. 208.
4. Koyama Interview, August 9, 1981.
5. Koyama Interview, August 5, 1980.
6. Loewenich, pp. 20, 29ff.
7. Koyama Interview, August 5, 1980.
8. See, for example, Hajime Nakamura, trans. and ed. Philip P. Wiener, *Ways of Thinking of Eastern Peoples* (Honolulu: East-West Center Press, revised 1964), pp. 531-534.
9. Ibid., p. 545.
10. Yoshiro Ishida (fellow seminarian of Koyama's in Tokyo), Interview, Geneva, June 1980.
11. Song, *Third-Eye Theology*, p. 62.
12. Ibid.
13. Koyama Interview, August 5, 1980.
14. Ibid.
15. Ibid.
16. Ibid.
17. Moltmann, p. 72.
18. Ibid., p. 204.
19. Ibid.
20. Ibid.
21. Ibid., pp. 201ff.
22. Loewenich, p. 113.
23. Ibid., p. 27.
24. Ibid., p. 113.
25. Koyama Interview, August 9, 1981.

26. Ibid.
27. Koyama Interview, August 9, 1981.
28. Paul Tillich, *Christianity and the Encounter of World Religions* (New York: Columbia University Press, 1964), p. 79.
29. Ibid., p. 80.
30. Kosuke Koyama, "Christ at the Periphery," (taken from an unpublished article, p. 2.; but compare with "Christ at the Periphery," in *The Ecumenical Review*, 34 (January 1982), pp. 67–75.
31. Ibid., p. 5.
32. Ibid., pp. 5–6.
33. Ibid., p. 6.
34. Ibid., p. 11.
35. Koyama Interview, August 9, 1981.
36. Ibid.
37. Koyama, *Mount Fuji and Mount Sinai*, p. 96.
38. Koyama Interview, August 9, 1981.
39. Ibid.
40. I am grateful to H. Dan Beeby for observations in this regard in an interview at Selly Oak, October, 1980.
41. Koyama, *Fifty Meditations*, p. 55.
42. John Macquarrie, *Thinking About God* (London: SCM Press Ltd., 1974), p. 10.
43. Ibid., quoting Barth, p. 10.
44. Beeby Interview, October, 1980.
45. Koyama Interview, August 9, 1981.
46. Ibid.

CHAPTER NINE

1. Koyama, *No Handle on the Cross*, p. 40.
2. Ibid., p. 43.
3. Koyama, *Three Mile an Hour God*, p. 69.
4. Ibid.
5. Ibid.
6. Koyama, *Fifty Meditations*, p. 124.
7. Ibid., p. 125.
8. Ibid.
9. Ibid.

10. Koyama, *Three Mile an Hour God*, p. 73.
11. Koyama, *Waterbuffalo Theology*, p. 236.
12. Ibid., p. 237.
13. Ibid.
14. Ibid.
15. Ibid., pp. 109–110, 7.
16. Ibid., p. 110.
17. Ibid.
18. Koyama, *No Handle on the Cross*, p. 42.
19. Koyama, *Fifty Meditations*, p. 86.
20. Ibid.
21. Koyama, *No Handle on the Cross*, p. 44.
22. Ibid., pp. 44–56.
23. Ibid., p. 60.
24. Ibid., p. 61.
25. Ibid.
26. Ibid., pp. 78–79.
27. Ibid., p. 79.
28. Ibid., pp. 90–92.
29. See Ibid., pp. 82–83.
30. Ibid., p. 64.
31. Ibid., p. 65.
32. Ibid., pp. 61, 65.
33. Ibid., pp. 65–66.
34. Ibid., p. 66.
35. Ibid.
36. Ibid., p. 67.
37. Ibid.
38. Ibid., p. 68.
39. Ibid., p. 67.
40. Ibid., p. 84.
41. Ibid., pp. 88–89.
42. Ibid., p. 89.
43. Ibid.
44. Ibid., p. 92.
45. Koyama, *Fifty Meditations*, p. 72.
46. Ibid.
47. Koyama, *No Handle on the Cross*, p. 24.

48. Ibid.
49. Ibid.
50. Koyama, *Three Mile an Hour God*, p. 50.
51. Ibid.
52. Ibid.
53. Koyama, *Three Mile an Hour God*, p. 50.
55. Koyama, *No Handle on the Cross*, p. 103.
56. Ibid.
57. Ibid., p. 104.
58. Ibid.
59. Ibid., p. 105.
60. Ibid., p. 92.
61. Ibid., p. 96.
62. Ibid., p. 94.
63. Ibid., p. 42.
64. Ibid., p. 97.
65. Koyama, *No Handle on the Cross*, p. 90.
66. Koyama, *Three Mile an Hour God*, p. 34.
67. Ibid., p. 93.
68. Ibid., pp. 94–95; Koyama, *Theology in Contact*, pp. 45–47.
69. Koyama, *No Handle on the Cross*, p. 71.
70. Koyama, *Three Mile an Hour God*, p. 74.
71. Koyama, *No Handle on the Cross*, p. 101.
72. Ibid.
73. Ibid.
74. Koyama, *Theology in Contact*, p. 48.
75. Ibid., p. 51.
76. For example, see Koyama's comments on Taiwan in *Waterbuffalo Theology*, pp. 17–19, and on Japan in *Three Mile an Hour God*, p. 73.
77. Koyama, *Waterbuffalo Theology*, p. 18.
78. Koyama, *Three Mile an Hour God*, p. 73.
79. Koyama, *Theology in Contact*, p. 52.
80. Ibid., pp. 52–53.
81. Koyama, *Three Mile an Hour God*, p. 73.
82. Ibid., p. 64.
83. Ibid., pp. 68–69.
84. Koyama, *Theology in Contact*, p. 57.
85. Ibid., p. 58.

86. Ibid., p. 55.
87. Ibid., p. 56.
88. Ibid.
89. Ibid.
90. Ibid., p. 69.
91. Koyama, *Three Mile an Hour God*, p. 65.
92. Ibid.
93. Ibid.
94. Ibid., pp. 65–66.
95. Ibid., p. 67.
96. Ibid., pp. 66–67.
97. Koyama, *Theology in Contact*, p. 58.
98. Koyama, *Three Mile an Hour God*, p. 65.
99. Koyama, *Theology in Contact*, p. 60.
100. Ibid.
101. Ibid., p. 61.
102. Ibid., p. 62.
103. Ibid.
104. See Ibid., pp. 62–63.
105. Ibid., pp. 63–64.
106. Ibid., pp. 64–65.
107. Koyama, *Three Mile an Hour God*, pp. 67–68.
108. Ibid., p. 68.
109. Koyama, *Theology in Contact*, p. 62.

CHAPTER TEN

1. Frederick J. Streng, "Selfhood Without Selfishness: Buddhist and Christian Approaches to Authentic Living," in *Buddhist-Christian Dialogue*, ed. Paul O. Ingram and Frederick Streng (Honolulu: University of Hawaii Press, 1986), p. 178.
2. Wilfred Cantwell Smith, *The Faith of Other Men* (New York: New American Library, 1963), p. 133.
3. Paul Varo Martinson, for example, submitted the manuscript for his book on interfaith encounter to Koyama for review and comment: Paul Varo Martinson, *A Theology of World Religions* (Minneapolis: Augsburg Publishing House, 1987).

308

4. See Mark W. Thomsen, ed., *Suffering and Redemption: Exploring Christian Witness Within a Buddhist Context* (Chicago: Evangelical Lutheran Church of America, 1988). Koyama served as a consultant on this project.
5. Quoted in Carl Braaten, *The Flaming Center* (Philadelphia: Fortress Press, 1977), p. 104.
6. Gordon Kaufman, "Christian Theology and the Modernization of the Religions," in *Bangalore Theological Forum*, vol. VIII (July–December 1976), p. 85.
7. Paul Tillich, "Missions and World History," in *The Theology of the Christian Mission*, ed. Gerald Anderson (London: SCM Press Ltd., 1961), p. 286.
8. Masatoshi Doi, "The Nature of Encounter Between Christianity and Other Religions as Witnessed on the Japanese Scene," in *Theology of the Christian Mission*, pp. 173–174.
9. Lesslie Newbigin, *The Open Secret* (London: SPCK, 1978), p. 190.
10. Lesslie Newbigin, *A Faith for This One World?* (London: SCM Press, Ltd., 1961), p. 74.
11. John V. Taylor, "The Theological Basis of Interfaith Dialogue," in *International Review of Mission*, vol. LXVIII (October 1979), p. 382.
12. Quoted in Doi, "The Nature of Encounter," pp. 168, 174.
13. Braaten, p. 113.
14. Taylor, "The Theological Basis of Interfaith Dialogue," p. 229.

PART THREE—INTRODUCTION

1. Walter J. Hollenweger, "Intercultural Theology," in *Theological Renewal* (October 1978), pp. 2–14.
2. While the same general conditions hold true for both Roman Catholic and Protestant Christianity, the concern of this study is for Protestant theology in particular.
3. Walter J. Hollenweger, "The Religion of the Poor is Not a Poor Religion," in *The Expository Times*, vol. LXXXVI (May 1978), pp. 228–232.
4. John E. Smith, *The Analogy of Experience* (New York: Harper and Row Publishers, Inc., 1973.), p. xiv.
5. Nicholas Mosley, *Experience and Religion* (London: Hodder and Stoughton, 1965), p. 151.
6. Gerhard Sauter, "How Can Theology Derive from Experiences?" in *Doing Theology Today*, ed. C. S. Song (Madras: The Christian Literature Society, 1976), pp. 70–72.

7. Ibid., p. 71.
8. Smith, p. xviii.
9. Mosley, pp. 153–154.

CHAPTER ELEVEN

1. Emil Brunner, *The Christian Doctrine of God*, vol. I, trans. Olive Wyon (London: Lutterworth Press, 1949), p. 89.
2. Alan Richardson, ed., *A Dictionary of Christian Theology* (London: SCM Press, Ltd., 1969), p. 335.
3. Ibid.
4. Ibid.
5. Brunner, pp. 89–90.
6. Ibid.
7. Lesslie Newbigin, "Mission in the 1980's," in *Occasional Bulletin,*. vol. 4 (October 1980), p. 155.
8. E. L. Mascall, *Theology and the Gospel of Christ* (London: SPCK, 1977), p. 31.
9. William Adams Brown, *Christian Theology in Outline* (Edinburgh: T and T Clark, 1907), p. 3.
10. Brunner, p. 89.
11. Paul Tillich, *Systematic Theology*, vol. 1 (Chicago: University of Chicago Press, 1975), pp. 15, 28.
12. John Macquarrie, *Principles of Christian Theology* (London: SCM Press, Ltd., 1966), pp. 1, 35.
13. *A Dictionary of Christian Theology*, pp. 98, 331.
14. Macquarrie, *Principles of Christian Theology*, p. 35.
15. Brown, p. 3.
16. Macquarrie, *Principles of Christian Theology*, pp. 164–165.
17. Ibid.
18. Brunner, p. 95.
19. Ibid., p. 91.
20. Macquarrie, *Principles of Christian Theology*, p. 164.
21. Brunner, p. 4.
22. S. Radhakrishnan, *East and West* (New York: Harper and Brothers, 1956), p. 80.
23. Robin H. S. Boyd, *India and the Latin Captivity of the Church* (London: Cambridge University Press, 1974), pp. xiii, 60, 64–65, 67ff.
24. Brunner, p. 91.

25. Ibid.
26. Bernard J. F. Lonergan, *Method in Theology* (London: Darton, Longman and Todd, 1975), p. 296.
27. Brunner, pp. 103ff.
28. Boyd, pp. 60, 64.
29. Brunner, pp. 103ff.
30. Ibid.
31. Smith, *The Analogy of Experience*, p. 29.
32. Brunner, p. 92.
33. *A Dictionary of Christian Theology*, p. 98.
34. Brunner, p. 97.
35. Ibid., pp. 3–5.
36. Mosley, *Experience and Religion*, pp. 52–53.
37. Macquarrie, *Principles of Christian Theology*, p. 11.
38. Compare Emil Brunner, *Truth as Encounter* (London: SCM Press, Ltd., 1964), p. 66.
39. Tillich, *Systematic Theology*, vol. 1, pp. 47ff.
40. Lonergan, p. 297; Walter Marshall Horton, *Christian Theology* (London: Lutterworth Press, 1956), p. 34; and *A Dictionary of Christian Theology*, p. 331.
41. Macquarrie, *Principles of Christian Theology*, p. 35.
42. Ibid.
43. Brown, p. 5.
44. *A Dictionary of Christian Theology*, p. 331.
45. Karl Barth, *Church Dogmatics*, Index vol., ed. G. W. Bromiley and T. F. Torrance (Edinburgh: T and T Clark Ltd., 1977).
46. Paul Tillich, *Systematic Theology* (Chicago: University of Chicago Press, 1951, 1957, 1963). 3 Volumes.
47. Tillich, *Systematic Theology*, vol. 1, pp. 34–40.
48. Brown, pp. 1–2.
49. *A Dictionary of Christian Theology*, p. 331.
50. Tillich, *Systematic Theology*, vol. 1, p. 8.
51. Nikos A. Nissiotis, "Ecclesial Theology in Context," in *Doing Theology Today*, pp. 101–102.
52. Brunner, *Truth as Encounter*, p. 15.
53. *A Dictionary of Christian Theology*, p. 331.
54. Tillich, *Systematic Theology*, vol. 3, p. 3.
55. Ibid.
56. Ibid.

57. Ibid., p. 4.
58. Robin H. S. Boyd, *An Introduction to Indian Christian Theology* (Madras: Christian Literature Society, 1975), p. 3.
59. M. M. Thomas in Ibid., p. vi.
60. Ibid.
61. Radhakrishnan, p. 80.
62. C. S. Song, "Love of God-and-Man in Action," in *Doing Theology Today*, p. 48.
63. *A Dictionary of Christian Theology*, p. 258.
64. Smith, p. 2.
65. Ibid.
66. Macquarrie, *Thinking About God*, p. 8.
67. Compare *A Dictionary of Christian Theology*, p. 155.
68. Karl Loewith, "Knowledge and Faith: From the Pre-Socratics to Heidegger," trans. Harold O. J. Brown in *Religion and Culture: Essays in Honor of Paul Tillich*, ed. Walter Leibrecht, (London: SCM Press Ltd., 1959), pp. 197ff.
69. Macquarrie, *Principles of Christian Theology*, p. 169.
70. See, for example, Jung Young Lee, "Can God Be Change Itself?" in *What Asian Christians are Thinking*, pp. 173–193.
71. Loewith, "Knowledge and Faith," p. 200; *A Dictionary of Christian Theology*, pp. 25–27.
72. *A Dictionary of Christian Theology* (article by Alberic Stacpoole), p. 10.
73. J. Calvin Keene, et al. eds. *The Western Heritage of Faith and Reason* (New York: Harper and Row, 1963), pp. 464–465.
74. *A Dictionary of Christian Theology* (article by Gordon Leff), pp. 336–337.
75. Heinrich Bornkamm, "Faith and Reason in the Thought of Erasmus and Luther," trans. Anne Liard Jennings in *Religion and Culture: Essays in Honor of Paul Tillich*, p. 134.
76. Ibid., pp. 137–138.
77. Moltmann, *The Crucified God*, pp. 207–208.
78. Loewith, "Knowledge and Faith," p. 204.
79. Keene, pp. 556ff.
80. Loewith, "Knowledge and Faith," p. 204.
81. Compare Brunner, *The Christian Doctrine of God*, p. 92.
82. Compare *A Dictionary of Christian Theology*, p. 258.
83. Compare Macquarrie, *Principles of Christian Theology*, pp. 121–122; Brunner, *Truth as Encounter*, p. 15; Horton, *Christian Theology*, p. 7; Stuart C. Brown, *Do Religious Claims Make Sense?* (London: SCM Press Ltd., 1969), pp. xiii–xx.

84. For example, Harvey Cox's *Secular City* or various "Death of God" theologies.
85. M. J. Charlesworth, *Philosophy of Religion: The Historic Approaches* (London: Macmillan, 1972), p. 62; John A. Howard, ed. *Belief, Faith and Reason* (Belfast: Christian Journals Ltd., 1981), p. 11; Mosley, *Experience and Religion*, pp. 48ff.; Keene—these are a few current examples.
86. Horton, *Christian Theology*, p. 5.
87. Ibid.
88. Ibid., p. 7.
89. See Koyama, *Waterbuffalo Theology*, p. 75, for example, where Koyama illustrates this conviction in relationship to the experience of love.
90. Macquarrie, *Principles of Christian Theology*, p. 12.
91. Yoshinori Takeuchi, "Buddhism and Existentialism: The Dialogue Between Oriental and Occidental Thought," in *Religion and Culture*, pp. 301–302.
92. See, for example, Wilfred Cantwell Smith, *The Faith of Other Men* (New York: New American Library, 1963), pp. 70ff.; and Nakamura, *Ways of Thinking of Eastern Peoples*, pp. 574ff.
93. Kraemer, *The Christian Message in a Non-Christian World*, p. 11.
94. Ibid.
95. *A Dictionary of Christian Theology*, p. 189.
96. Macquarrie, *Principles of Christian Theology*, p. 12.

CHAPTER TWELVE

1. Brian Wicker, *The Story-Shaped World* (London: The Althone Press, 1975), p. 71.
2. *A Dictionary of Christian Theology* (article by James Richmond), p. 95.
3. Mosley, *Experience and Religion*, p. 66.
4. Ibid., pp. 53ff.; *A Dictionary of Christian Theology*, p. 189.
5. Ibid.; Brunner, *Truth as Encounter*, p. 28.
6. See Mosley, pp. 53ff. and Koyama, *Fifty Meditations*, p. 176.
7. Macquarrie, *Principles of Christian Theology*, p. 3.
8. Song, "Love of God-and-Man in Action," in *Doing Theology Today*, p. 50.
9. Bornkamm, "Faith and Reason," in *Religion and Culture: Essays in Honor of Paul Tillich*, p. 136.
10. Ibid.
11. Walter von Loewenich, *Luther's Theology of the Cross*, pp. 91–92.

12. Mosley, p. 141.
13. Ibid., pp. 141ff.
14. Ibid., p. 67.
15. For example, Koyama, *Waterbuffalo Theology*, p. 182.
16. Mosley, p. 64; Loewenich, pp. 93–94.
17. Mosley, p. 64.
18. Wicker, p. 103.
19. Macquarrie, *Thinking About God*, p. 8.
20. Ibid., p. 12.
21. Ibid., p. 7.
22. Brunner, *Truth as Encounter*, p. 133.
23. Macquarrie, *Thinking About God*, p. 8; Wicker, p. 85.
24. Macquarrie, *Thinking About God*, p. 13.
25. Brunner, *Truth as Encounter*, p. 26.
26. Ibid.
27. Wicker, p. 104.
28. Mosley, p. 140.
29. Macquarrie, *Thinking About God*, p. 12.
30. Ibid., p. 22.
31. Ibid., p. 25.
32. Brunner, *Truth as Encounter*, pp. 76, 133.
33. Ibid., pp. 136–137.
34. Smith, *The Analogy of Experience*, p. xiv.
35. Ibid.
36. Compare Tillich, *Systematic Theology*, vol. 1, pp. 34–40.
37. Smith, p. 25.
38. Ibid., pp. 26–27.
39. Ibid., pp. 28–29.
40. Ibid., p. 33.
41. Ibid., p. xiv.
42. Ibid., p. 29.
43. Loewenich, pp. 94, 97.
44. Ibid., p. 106.
45. Gerhard Sauter, "How Can Theology Derive From Experiences?" in *Doing Theology Today*, pp. 72ff.
46. Ibid., p. 80.
47. Ibid.
48. Ibid., p. 78.

49. Ibid., p. 73.
50. Carl E. Braaten, *The Flaming Center*, p. 13.
51. Compare Mosley, p. 141 and Macquarrie, *Principles of Christian Theology*, pp. 5–6.
52. Ibid., p. 7.
53. Sauter, "How Can Theology Derive From Experiences?" p. 81.
54. Ibid.
55. Macquarrie, *Thinking About God*, p. 13.
56. Macquarrie, *Principles of Christian Theology*, p. 162.
57. Ibid., pp. 162–163.
58. Ibid., p. 164; See also Harold Ditmanson, *Grace in Experience and Theology* (Minneapolis: Augsburg Publishing House, 1977), pp. 30–31. Ditmanson presents an excellent discussion of experience, theology, and symbol.
59. Macquarrie, pp. 121–122.
60. Ibid., p. 120.
61. Walter J. Hollenweger and Theodor Ahrens, "Volkschristentum und Volksreligion im Pazifik. Wiederentdeckung des Mythos für den christlichen Glauben," in *Perspektiven der Weltmission; Scriftenreihe der Missionsakademie an der Universität Hamburg*, vol. 4 (Franfurt/Main: Verlag Otto Lembeck, 1977), pp. 83–105.
62. Ibid., pp. 84–86.
63. Mosley, p. 51.
64. Robert Faricy reviewing *Fifty Meditations* in *Missiology*, vol. VII (October 1979), p. 521.
65. Eileen Storey, reviewing *Three Mile an Hour God* in *Biblical Theological Bulletin*, vol. X (July 1980), p. 29.
66. Macquarrie, *Principles of Christian Theology*, p. 119.
67. Diane G. Ogasawara reviewing *No Handle on the Cross* in *Sojourners*, (November 1978), p. 36.
68. Wicker, pp. 85–86.
69. Interview with David Grey, Woodbrooke College, Selly Oak, May 6, 1981.
70. Wicker, p. 102.
71. Ibid., pp. 102, 106, 214.
72. Mosley, p. 52.
73. Compare Bornkamm, "Faith and Reason,", p. 134 and *A Dictionary of Christian Theology*, p. 331. Erasmus saw Scripture as a collection of rational truths. Systematic theology often treats Scripture as a collection of facts to be systematized.

315

74. Mosley, p. 52.
75. Brunner, *The Christian Doctrine of God*, p. 91.
76. Mosley, p. 60.
77. Ibid.
78. Hollenweger, "Intercultural Theology," in *Theological Renewal*, p. 11.
79. Ibid.
80. Mosley, p. 51.
81. Smith, *The Analogy of Experience*, p. xviii.
82. Walter J. Hollenweger, *Evangelism Today* (Belfast: Christian Journals Ltd., 1976), p. 41.
83. Brunner, *The Christian Doctrine of God*, p. 102.
84. Ibid., pp. 102–103.
85. Hollenweger, *Evangelism Today*, p. 81.
86. Ibid.
87. Koyama Interview, August 5, 1980.
88. Ibid.
89. Hollenweger, "Intercultural Theology," p. 12.
90. *A Dictionary of Christian Theology*, p. 155.
91. Koyama Interview, August 5, 1980.
92. Ibid.
93. Ibid.
94. Ibid.
95. Ibid.
96. Koyama Interview, August 9, 1981.
97. Ibid.
98. Ibid.
99. Koyama Interview, August 5, 1980.
100. Ibid.
101. Koyama Interview, August 9, 1981.
102. Ibid.
103. Koyama Interview, August 5, 1980.
104. Ibid.; Koyama Interview, August 9, 1981.
105. Nakamura, *Ways of Thinking of Eastern Peoples*, p. 575.
106. Koyama Interview, August 9, 1981.
107. Jung Young Lee reviewing *Three Mile an Hour God* in *International Bulletin*, vol. 5 (April 1981), p. 88.
108. James M. Phillips reviewing *No Handle on the Cross* in *Occasional Bulletin*, vol. 1 (October 1977), p. 42.

109. Koyama Interview, August 5, 1980.
110. Walter J. Hollenweger reviewing *Waterbuffalo Theology* in *The Expository Times*, vol. LXXXVI (January 1975), p. 123.
111. Alan Thomson reviewing *Fifty Meditations* in *Occasional Bulletin*, vol. 3 (July 1979), p. 116.
112. David Paton reviewing *No Handle on the Cross* in *Theology*, vol. LXXX (November 1977), p. 465.
113. Ibid.
114. Koyama Interview, August 5, 1980.
115. Lesslie Newbigin, "Mission in the 1980's," in *The Occasional Bulletin of Misionary Research*, 4 (October 1980), p. 154.
116. Ibid.
117. Ditmanson, *Grace in Experience and Theology*, p. 32.
118. Ronald Nelson, "Reflections on a Study Leave," in *World Mission Newsletter*, (American Lutheran Church, January 1982), p. 6.
119. Koyama, "Ritual of a Limping Dance," in *Union Seminary Quarterly Review*, pp. 103–104.
120. M. M. Thomas, "Foreword" to *An Introduction to Indian Christian Theology*, p. vi.
121. Compare Lee, "Can God Be Change Itself?" in *What Asian Christians Are Thinking*, pp. 173–193.

CONCLUSION

1. John Bluck, "The Cross Has No Handle—the Faith No Explanation," in *One World* (July–August 1977), p. 7.
2. "The Willowbank Report—Gospel and Culture: Lausanne Committee for World Evangelization," in *Lausanne Occasional Papers*, No. 2 (Wheaton 1978), pp. 10–13.
3. Lesslie Newbigin in "Foreword" to *The Theology of the Christian Mission*, ed. Gerald Anderson (London: SCM Press, 1961), p. xi.
4. Braaten, *The Flaming Center*, p. 13.
5. M. Kahler, quoted in Braaten.
6. Arend Van Leeuwen, *Christianity in World History*, p. 426.
7. Braaten, p. 14.
8. Compare *A Dictionary of Christian Theology*, p. 12, and Brunner, *The Christian Doctrine of God*, p. 98.

9. Macquarrie, *Principles of Christian Theology*, p. 169.
10. Koyama Interview, August 5, 1980.
11. Taped letter exchange with Koyama, March, 1982.
12. For example, see "Ritual of a Limping Dance," in *Union Seminary Quarterly Review*, pp. 91–104.
13. Alan Thomson review of *Fifty Meditations* in *Occasional Bulletin*, p. 116.
14. Discussion on Koyama in a class on Third World Theologians at Luther-Northwestern Theological Seminary, St. Paul, USA, February 23, 1982.
15. Comment made by Eileen Piehl, laywoman, in a discussion on Koyama at the Institute for Ecumenical and Cultural Research, St. John's University, Collegeville, Minnesota, USA, March, 1987.
16. H. D. Beeby, "The Old Testament and the Redemption of Culture," in *The South East Asia Journal of Theology* 8 (April 1967), p. 18.
17. Thomson review, p. 116.
18. D. T. Niles, "Karl Barth—A Personal Memory," in *The South East Asia Journal of Theology* (Autumn 1969), pp. 9–13.
19. Radhakrishnan, *East and West*, p. 120.
20. Ibid.

STUDIEN ZUR INTERKULTURELLEN GESCHICHTE DES CHRISTENTUMS
ETUDES D'HISTOIRE INTERCULTURELLE DU CHRISTIANISME
STUDIES IN THE INTERCULTURAL HISTORY OF CHRISTIANITY

Begründet von/fondé par/founded by
Hans Jochen Margull †, Hamburg

Herausgegeben von/edité par/edited by

Richard Friedli	Walter J. Hollenweger	Theo Sundermeier
Université de Fribourg	University of Birmingham	Universität Heidelberg

Jan A.B. Jongeneel
Rijksuniversiteit Utrecht

Band   1   Wolfram Weiße: Südafrika und das Antirassismusprogramm. Kirchen im Spannungsfeld einer Rassengesellschaft.

Band   2   Ingo Lembke: Christentum unter den Bedingungen Lateinamerikas. Die katholische Kirche vor den Problemen der Abhängigkeit und Unterentwicklung.

Band   3   Gerd Uwe Kliewer: Das neue Volk der Pfingstler. Religion, Unterentwicklung und sozialer Wandel in Lateinamerika.

Band   4   Joachim Wietzke: Theologie im modernen Indien - Paul David Devanandan.

Band   5   Werner Ustorf: Afrikanische Initiative. Das aktive Leiden des Propheten Simon Kimbangu.

Band   6   Erhard Kamphausen: Anfänge der kirchlichen Unabhängigkeitsbewegung in Südafrika. Geschichte und Theologie der äthiopischen Bewegung. 1880-1910.

Band   7   Lothar Engel: Kolonialismus und Nationalismus im deutschen Protestantismus in Namibia 1907-1945. Beiträge zur Geschichte der deutschen evangelischen Mission und Kirche im ehemaligen Kolonial- und Mandatsgebiet Südwestafrika.

Band   8   Pamela M. Binyon: The Concepts of "Spirit" and "Demon". A Study in the use of different languages describing the same phenomena.

Band   9   Neville Richardson: The World Council of Churches and Race Relations. 1960 to 1969.

Band   10   Jörg Müller: Uppsala II. Erneuerung in der Mission. Eine redaktionsgeschichtliche Studie und Dokumentation zu Sektion II der 4. Vollversammlung des Ökumenischen Rates der Kirchen, Uppsala 1968.

Band   11   Hans Schöpfer: Theologie und Gesellschaft. Interdisziplinäre Grundlagenbibliographie zur Einführung in die befreiungs- und polittheologische Problematik: 1960-1975.

Band   12   Werner Hoerschelmann: Christliche Gurus. Darstellung von Selbstverständnis und Funktion indigenen Christseins durch unabhängige charismatisch geführte Gruppen in Südindien.

Band   13   Claude Schaller: L'Eglise en quête de dialogue. Vergriffen.

Band   14   Theo Tschuy: Hundert Jahre kubanischer Protestantismus (1868-1961). Versuch einer kirchengeschichtlichen Darstellung.

Band   15   Werner Korte: Wir sind die Kirchen der unteren Klassen. Entstehung, Organisation und gesellschaftliche Funktionen unabhängiger Kirchen in Afrika.

Band   16   Arnold Bittlinger: Pabst und Pfingstler. Der römisch katholisch-pfingstliche Dialog und seine ökumenische Relevanz.

Band   17   Ingemar Lindén: The Last Trump. An historico-genetical study of some important chapters in the making and development of the Seventh-day Adventist Church.

Band   18   Zwinglio Dias: Krisen und Aufgaben im brasilianischen Protestantismus. Eine Studie zu den sozialgeschichtlichen Bedingungen und volkspädagogischen Möglichkeiten der Evangelisation.

Band   19   Mary Hall: A quest for the liberated Christian, Examined on the basis of a mission, a man and a movement as agents of liberation.

Peter Schüttke-Scherle

From Contextual to Ecumenical Theology?
A Dialogue between Minjung Theology
and "Theology after Auschwitz"

Frankfurt/M., Bern, New York, Paris, 1989. XI, 232 pp.
Studies in the Intercultural History of Christianity. Vol. 60
Edited by Richard Friedli and others
ISBN 3-631-41890-6   DM 61.--/sFr. 51.--

The emergence of "contextual" Third World theologies, the specific
reflections within Christian-Jewish-dialogue and efforts towards an
ecumenical theology form the framework for this study. It creates an
ecumenical dialogue between South-Korean Minjung theology and
West-German "theology after Auschwitz", both of which are analyzed
and confronted in terms of context, peculiarities and theological topics
(methodology/hermeneutics, exegesis, christology, ecclesiology, political theology). This dialogue is a contribution to an ecumenical
hermeneutics and shows substantial challenges for an ecumenical
theology.

Contents: In analyzing and confronting South-Korean Minjung
theology and West-German "theology after Auschwitz" in terms of
context, peculiarities and theological topics a dialogue is created,
which contributes to an ecumenical hermeneutics and challenges
ecumenical theology.

Verlag Peter Lang Frankfurt a.M. · Bern · New York · Paris
Auslieferung: Verlag Peter Lang AG, Jupiterstr. 15, CH-3000 Bern 15
Telefon (004131) 321122, Telex pela ch 912 651, Telefax (004131) 321131
– Preisänderungen vorbehalten –